Home Theater

FOR

DUMMIES®

2ND EDITION

Home Theater

FOR

DUMMIES®

2ND EDITION

by Danny Briere and Pat Hurley

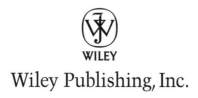

WILEY

Wiley Publishing, Inc.

Home Theater For Dummies® 2nd Edition

Published by
Wiley Publishing, Inc.
111 River Street
Hoboken, NJ 07030-5774
www.wiley.com

Copyright © 2006 by Wiley Publishing, Inc., Indianapolis, Indiana

Published by Wiley Publishing, Inc., Indianapolis, Indiana

Published simultaneously in Canada

For general information on our other products and services, please contact our Customer Care Department within the U.S. at 800-762-2974, outside the U.S. at 317-572-3993, or fax 317-572-4002.

For technical support, please visit www.wiley.com/techsupport.

Wiley also publishes its books in a variety of electronic formats. Some content that appears in print may not be available in electronic books.

Library of Congress Control Number: 2006924029

ISBN-13: 978-0-471-78325-1

ISBN-10: 0-471-78325-0

Manufactured in the United States of America

10 9 8 7 6 5 4 3 2

2O/RW/QW/QW/IN

WILEY

About the Authors

Danny Briere founded TeleChoice, Inc., a telecommunications consulting company, in 1985 and now serves as CEO of the company. Widely known throughout the telecommunications and networking industry, Danny has written more than 1,000 articles about telecommunications topics and has authored or edited 12 books, including *HDTV For Dummies, Wireless Home Networking For Dummies,* and *Smart Homes For Dummies.* He is frequently quoted by leading telecommunications and technology publications and can often be seen on major TV networks providing analysis on the latest communications news and breakthroughs. Danny lives in Mansfield Center, Connecticut, with his wife, four children, and two dogs.

Pat Hurley is head of research at TeleChoice, Inc., specializing in emerging telecommunications technologies. Pat currently concentrates on the field of consumer electronics and their impact on home and wireless networking. Pat is also TeleChoice's IPTV industry analyst. Pat is the coauthor of seven books, including *HDTV For Dummies, Wireless Home Networking For Dummies,* and *Smart Homes For Dummies.* He lives in San Diego, California, with his wife, daughter and two dogs.

Authors' Acknowledgments

Danny wants to thank his wife Holly and his kids, who, for the past four years, had to "wait for next year when the neat new stuff is out" before upgrading the house's home theater arrangement. Holly holds the record for patience endured; Danny is always testing new home theater gear in the house — in his defense, Danny is able to say that he at least has gotten rid of the 11 remote controls in the living room! Danny also thanks his Mom and Dad, whose unfailing support has been special throughout the years. And especially to his Mom who made him take those typing lessons as a kid with all those yucky girls at the all-girls school — it has really come in handy.

Pat, as always, thanks his wife, Christine, for her infinite patience. (Is it patience when one refrains from bonking his or her spouse over the head with a cast iron skillet?) He also thanks her for gamely smiling and nodding when he introduced, over and over again, pictures of the newest future member of the Hurley family home theater, only to change his mind when he discovered the next silicon (not silicone!) -laden object of his desire. Pat also thanks his parents for letting him spend entirely too much time during his Christmas visit hunched over his Powerbook. Pops — hope you get that universal remote control figured out! Finally, he thanks his beautiful little girl, Annabel, who provided ample distractions and smiles throughout this process — and Daddy *always* lets her hog the plasma for the near-daily screening of *The Lion King*.

Danny and Pat want to thank the following people and organizations for their support in writing this book: Joel Silver at Imaging Science Foundation, Jeff Denenholz at X10 Ltd., Larry Becker at Crutchfield, Nick Carter and the rest of the crew at AudioRequest, Kaleo Willess and Roger Dressler at Dolby Laboratories, Shawn Gusz at G-NET Canada, John Dahl and Amy Brighouse from THX, Ltd., and all those people manning the booths at CES '06 in Las Vegas who let us stare and gape at their rear-projection, plasma, and LCD screens for hours on end. We'd thank them personally, but none of them gave us one.

Also to our Acquisitions Editor, Steve Hayes, whom we kept on his toes as usual, and to our Project Editor, Paul Levesque, who had the unenviable task of Danny and Pat wrangling. Paul's patience was the stuff of legends, and his editing let us say what we wanted to say — only in proper English. Thanks Paul!

Publisher's Acknowledgments

We're proud of this book; please send us your comments through our online registration form located at www.dummies.com/register/.

Some of the people who helped bring this book to market include the following:

Acquisitions, Editorial, and Media Development

Project Editor: Paul Levesque

Acquisitions Editor: Steve Hayes

Copy Editor: Andy Hollandbeck

Technical Editor: Dennis Cohen

Editorial Manager: Leah Cameron

Media Development Manager: Laura VanWinkle

Editorial Assistant: Amanda Foxworth

Sr. Editorial Assistant: Cherie Case

Cartoons: Rich Tennant (www.the5thwave.com)

Composition Services

Project Coordinator: Tera Knapp

Layout and Graphics: Carl Byers, Andrea Dahl, Joyce Haughey, Stephanie D. Jumper, Barry Offringa, Alicia B. South, Julie Trippetti

Proofreaders: Leeann Harney, Jessica Kramer, Dwight Ramsey, Techbooks

Indexer: Techbooks

Publishing and Editorial for Technology Dummies

Richard Swadley, Vice President and Executive Group Publisher

Andy Cummings, Vice President and Publisher

Mary Bednarek, Executive Acquisitions Director

Mary C. Corder, Editorial Director

Publishing for Consumer Dummies

Diane Graves Steele, Vice President and Publisher

Joyce Pepple, Acquisitions Director

Composition Services

Gerry Fahey, Vice President of Production Services

Debbie Stailey, Director of Composition Services

Contents at a Glance

Table of Contents

Introduction

The on-screen image looks crisp and sharp, like a huge moving photo-graph. You feel entranced. More to the point, you feel the immediate urge to own this video projector, provided it works with the DVD player and the rest of your fledgling home theater gear.

An enthusiastic salesperson sees your look and enters the demonstration room. "It's really beautiful," the salesperson proclaims. "That's the first DLP unit that works in true 1080p at 16:9. Yup, she's a dream."

Moments like that make you wish that people came with a pause button — or at least an instant replay and color commentary.

For all the fun they bring and the good times they facilitate, home theaters (and their sundry technologies) come with a bewildering blizzard of terms and acronyms. Worse yet, it seems like everybody involved with the industry either knows what the terms mean but can't explain them or has no clue about the true meanings but spouts the terms anyway. And neither of those cases helps *you* make any sense of the whole thing.

That's where the new and greatly improved 2nd edition of *Home Theater For Dummies* makes its heroic entrance. (We'd cue up a low fog, some dramatic lighting, and that mysterious "something cool might happen anytime now" music to enhance the moment, but there's only so much you can do in a book.) Even without the special effects, this book still rescues you from all kinds of home theater perils. Read on to find out how.

About This Book

The book takes you through the world of home theater from the bottom to the top. Starting with a broad look at the basics of home theater concepts and technology, *Home Theater For Dummies* presses onward with more detailed information about source devices, surround sound gear, video dis-play equipment, and PCs. The book even advises you about the theater room itself, giving guidance about everything from furniture to popcorn machines.

Best of all, this book delivers the information in the friendly, patient, and easy-to-understand manner that you know and expect from a title in the *For Dummies* line.

Get ready for one of the most enjoyable trips of your life. With this book at your side, you're ready for anything and everything that the industry (and those questionable salespeople at the local equipment store) can throw at you.

Conventions Used in This Book

Unlike its famous and prolific computer-oriented brethren, *Home Theater For Dummies* keeps things pretty simple in the "conventions" department. We use just a single bit of textual oddness that relates to Web sites. Any time we talk about a World Wide Web address, you see the site address formatted in a special font, like this: www.dummies.com.

Why? For one thing, the font makes the text stand out so that you know exactly what to type into your browser. (Besides, we think the production department got a special deal on that font, so they just like seeing it in the books as much as possible.)

Just the (Techie) Facts, Ma'am

Although everything in the book meets rigorous standards for comprehension, usability, and lack of pointless geekiness, a few technical tidbits slipped in accidentally. Well, they didn't slip in accidentally; we wrote them that way.

At some point in the home theater process, you come face to face with technical tripe whether you want to or not. It's better that you hear this stuff from us than from some name-tagged know-it-all on a sales floor.

Foolish Assumptions

To write this book, we had to spend a lot of time in malls, video stores, and movie theaters (that's the hard part) doing "research." While doing so, we pondered all kinds of questions concerning you, the reader. Who are you? Where are you? What did you eat for lunch? Which movies pique your interest? How do your home theater desires line up with your budget? Queries like that fill our minds constantly, much to the consternation of our spouses, who prefer more useful thoughts like, "Shouldn't you take the trash out?"

Because we never get to meet you in person, we end up making a few assumptions about you and what you want from this book. Here's a peek at our thoughts about you:

✔ You love movies, television shows, or video games — or perhaps all three.

✔ You've experienced wide screens and surround sound at the theater, and you liked it.

✔ For one reason or another, a 19-inch TV set with a single built-in speaker doesn't adequately meet your audio or video entertainment desires.

✔ You probably own a computer or will soon.

✔ You don't shy away from high-tech products, but you also aren't the first person on the block with the latest electronic goodie.

✔ The weird technicalities of home theater circle around you like planes buzzing King Kong.

✔ You know something about the Internet and the Web and probably have high-speed access to the Internet or will soon.

✔ You (or someone in your family) enjoy watching movies, listening to MP3 audio, playing games, and possibly making movies on your computer.

If that describes you in detail or at least catches some of your shadow in passing, then this book is for you.

How This Book Is Organized

Rather than haphazardly fling information at you and hope that some of it sticks, we clump related topics together into six parts. Here's a peek at what they cover.

Part 1: Welcome to the World of Home Theater

With home theater, the trek begins here, in Part I, which covers the basics of the basics, starting with a look at what home theater really means, includes, requires, and offers. From there, it looks at what it takes to get into a home theater, in terms of space, timing, budget, and equipment. In Chapter 4, we get a little techie, but necessarily so, by giving you some solid insight into the terms and technologies that you will encounter. More and more, terms like DLP, 3LCD, and HDMI are on the shelf description tags when you go to Best Buy. You need this baseline knowledge for the rest of the book, so read Chapter 4 closely. In fact, read it twice. (It's even better the second time around.)

Part II: What Are You Going to Watch?: Source Devices

Home theater installations really contain two parts: source and presentation. Part II covers all kinds of sources, ranging from the prerecorded offerings of DVD players and VCRs to the over-the-air-and-through-the-sky action of broadcast TV and satellite dishes. As an added bonus, this part even takes you on a tour of the personal video recorder (PVR), possibly the most groundbreaking entertainment device since the VCR itself, as well as state-of-the-art gaming platforms. (Pat performed that excruciating gaming research.) We also talk about your PC and the growing role it plays in sourcing audio, video, gaming, and other content for your system. To top that, we then tell you all you need to know about accessing the Internet for cool things like finding that episode of *Lost* that you missed.

Part III: Watching and Listening: Display and Control Devices

Part III focuses on the control and presentation aspects of your system, with in-depth looks at your receivers, controllers, speakers, and video displays. We look at all-in-one receivers and separates, such as controllers and power amps. On the video side, this part explores the strange world of television sets (which looked pretty simple until a few years ago when HDTV arrived on the scene) and video projection systems, which are home theater's answer to the movie house's silver screen, and which are becoming so affordable we think you'll get one just so you can watch the Super Bowl on a 12-foot screen! Then, all eyes — er, ears — turn to audio for details about surround sound systems, speakers, and more. Finally, we talk about remote controls — an often overlooked area that deserves more attention. A remote control is your single biggest interface to the system, so we give you some options here.

Part IV: Putting It All Together

With your location selected, your gear picked out, and your walls trembling in fear, it's time to install your theater, and Part IV guides you through the process. In fact, hooking up your home theater is one of the harder parts of the experience. We start with the basics — the different types of cabling — and work our way up to connecting all the different components into a working system. Toward the end of Part IV, we give you advice on how to link your home entertainment system to other TVs and systems in the house. After all, you paid a lot of money for your theater — why not get the most use from it that you can?

Part V: Letting Your Home Theater Be All It Can Be

You might think that your home theater equipment is out-of-the-box ready to be plugged together and to start playing movies, but it's not that simple. Almost every part of your system needs to be tuned like a nice grand piano. Although we use big words and phrases such as *calibration* and *bass management* in this part, these merely relate to fine-tuning your system to itself and its environs. We also give you ideas for sprucing up your home theater with fancy lights and soundproofing (the latter of which is great for those late-night sleepovers the kids have). We tell you how to access your home theater content from your car as well as from your cellphone (very cool) and laptop when out and about. We end the part with a cool look at the higher end of home theater — the things you can dream about during those long trips to Grandma's.

Part VI: The Part of Tens

Like all other *For Dummies* books, *Home Theater For Dummies* closes with a look at life from the humorous side with perky Part VI, the Part of Tens. Each chapter counts off a bunch of goodies that help you show off, troubleshoot, and generally accessorize your theater.

Icons Used in This Book

There's a lot of stuff in here, and amidst all that material, the really important details can sometimes be overlooked. To point out the important stuff (and highlight the technicalities you might want to avoid), the book relies on several helpful icons. Each icon identifies a particular type of information. Here's a quick field guide to what each of these little billboards means:

Whenever you see the Remember icon, grab a handy mental highlighter (and maybe a real one, too) and mark the section because this information might come in handy at any moment, either now or in the future.

Everybody looks for tips (particularly in the stock market, at the race track, and at your favorite restaurant). When a Tip icon shows up in *Home Theater For Dummies,* it points out information destined to simplify your life. You can't go wrong with a Tip!

When a topic includes technology, technical tripe always finds its way into the book. At some point or another in the home theater experience, you need to know the geek-speak. Don't fear paragraphs with these icons, but don't rush to them, either. Just brace yourself for the technical onslaught, secure in the knowledge that this book protects you from the worst of the techno-drivel.

Nothing in your home theater really threatens personal peril — at least no more peril than you get from plugging in a toaster or accidentally watching a bad movie at your local theater. In those rare moments when inserting the right plug in the wrong socket could spell doom for your gear, the Warning icon hops into action. When you see one of these, stop for a moment, read the text, and double-check your progress before continuing.

Where to Go from Here

Apart from the pleasing shade of yellow on the cover, the best part of a *For Dummies* book is its open and available layout — you can start anywhere you want. If you already know the stuff in Chapter 1, dive in somewhere else instead. Where you start and what you read depends entirely on what you need to know right now.

Read over the Table of Contents to see whether any topics really jump out at you. If nothing does, try finding a starting point in one of these:

- ✔ If you just jumped into the front row of home theater enthusiasts, start in Chapter 1. It gives you a good overview of how a home theater works, what it takes, and what to do next.

- ✔ Curious about the content — the movies and shows — appearing in your theater? Part II delves into DVD and VHS, plus satellite, broadcast, and cable TV. It even peers into the promising realm of personal video recorders (the TiVo is good example here) , and PC-driven content.

- ✔ For an in-depth look at the sound and video presentation side of your entertainment empire, visit the chapters of Part III.

- ✔ For help getting your system connected and tweaked for the finest audio and video quality, skip on over to Part IV.

With that, leap into the world of home theater. Lights, camera, action — welcome to your adventure!

Part I

Welcome to the World of Home Theater

"I don't care how good it will look on the 60" plasma display."

In this part . . .

1t's important to start your adventure with some solid basics — what's a home theater, why do you want one, what do all the various terms mean?

Part I lays a solid foundation for talking about home theater. An understanding of all your options not only helps you on the showroom floor but also helps you when the time comes to install your gear and tune it so that it does what it was intended to do. Indeed, a lot of home theater is about making sure that your system is configured correctly for your environment, and to do that, you need to know what it's supposed to be doing in the first place. (We're sure there's some pithy phrase, like "cart before the horse," to throw in here now, but we never use those correctly. So think of a phrase of your choice here.)

We then follow up with some high-level basics about your home theater and its environment. We discuss things like where to put a home theater in your house and how to control it. We also delve into that hot topic — price.

Then we walk you through all the things that make up the home theater at a high level — sources, outputs, PCs, cables, broadband, and so on.

And finally, we go a little deeper into the key terms, standards, and technologies that we use throughout the book. Here's where we talk about a lot of the things that probably got you to buy this book in the first place — the alphabet soup of home theater.

After you finish this part, you'll know enough to be dangerous in your local electronics store. (So be sure to read the rest of the book, too, so that you know how to control your now dangerous mind.)

Chapter 1

The Zen of Home Theater

*W*hen you hear the term *home theater,* you probably think of big screens, cool sound, DVDs, CDs, and lots of remote controls sitting around your living room. We're sure that football games, beer, and other fun images sneak into that image as well.

Home theater is truly for everyone — regardless of the size of your house or apartment, your economic wealth, or your taste in movies. And home theater is bound to mean something different to everyone. It's not just about the gear — the boxes, the cables, the remotes, the DVDs, the CDs, the iPods, the whatever. It's really about embarking on what can be a great adventure.

Appreciating the Art of the Home Theater

Before you start on your home theater adventure, it's critical to understand what the makers of the equipment, movies, standards, audio CDs, and so on mean when they say that they support home theater.

To the companies that produce the equipment and media, home theater is all about trying to re-create — in your home — the experience of watching a film in a movie theater, hearing the cheers of the crowd in a football stadium, or feeling the reverberations of music at an open-air concert. Many of the people who devote themselves to creating atmosphere and mood using this medium consider what they do to be an art form. These are usually the people who are listed in the credits at the end of a movie.

When you take all the sensations of a movie theater and insert them in your living room, you're on your way to successfully re-creating that "immersive" feeling you get at the movies. All the improvements in sound compression, surround sound, digital screen imaging, and so on, have been done not to sell more equipment at Circuit City or Wal-Mart, but to try to perfect the ability to draw you into another world where you can experience a truly creative piece of work.

So a lot of this book is about explaining the technologies and ideas behind the home theater that you are going to put together, because it's not just about seven speakers hooked into your stereo or a big honking TV screen. It's about how to make sure everything is put in its proper place to maximize your home theater out-of-body experience — the way the media creators intended.

Fitting Home Theater's Many Faces into All Kinds of Spaces

You've probably watched enough TV shows and movies about Hollywood and the rich and famous to know that, for some people, home theaters are as common as a kitchen or a bedroom. Indeed, home theaters were spawned from the necessity of filmmakers to preview footage, screen tests, and full movies. They gradually grew to be a status symbol among actors, too, and spread out from there.

In those early days, a home theater was pretty much literally that: a small theater with Peerless Magnarc carbon-arc lamphouses and theater seating. They were often extensive and elaborate affairs — to match the surrounding house.

Today, you too can get into the act, and you're lucky enough to have a broad range of projectors, screens, displays, seating, and equipment — heck, even popcorn machines — available to create your own home theater.

Probably the first big decision you have to make is where you want to put your home theater. It was one thing to figure out where to put your 19-inch TV set; it's another thing to think about where to put a big-screen TV with six speakers and associated A/V gear. Few people are prepared for how overpowering a full home theater setup can be in a small home, so it's especially important to plan ahead if you have limited space.

Defining your home theater space is a necessary first step. If the only place to put a TV is on the mantle above the fireplace, then you're looking at a plasma screen TV and not much else. If you have to fit the whole system into the corner of the living room, then that narrows the search as well. Remember, you don't want to buy a home theater that just won't fit into your home and your lifestyle. A home theater is all about creating a surround atmosphere, so pick your spaces and work from there.

You can most certainly put a home theater in your present living room, in your bedroom, or in a room devoted to your theater. In the end, what matters is not so much the size, but the way you establish its ability to coax you into its sound field and video experience.

Budgeting for Home Theater

We believe in setting expectations. We don't want to get you salivating over a 37-inch LCD and a nice Harmon Kardon system and then smack you over the head with an unrealistic price. Unfortunately, a quick stroll through any consumer electronics store could lead you to believe that you can get an entry-level whole-home theater in a box (without the video display, of course) for just $199. However, that $199 system will be right for some people and not for others.

Exploring equipment and prices

So what does it cost to get into a home theater system? Table 1-1 gives you an idea of what you can spend. We've broken this table down by the roles that each group of audio/video (A/V) components plays in your home theater. (*Audio* sources are devices that provide audio-only playback in your system, whereas *video* sources provide movies or TV content.) The A/V system provides the control for your home theater (meaning it lets you select what you want to watch or listen to) and does all the heavy lifting in terms of sending surround sound signals to your speaker system. The video display, of course, is what you watch (think TV). We've also included some optional components — gaming systems and home theater PCs (which let you use a PC as a high-quality audio and/or video source device).

 Over time, components have been doing the integrating thing better and better. You can find really good DVD/VCR combos, for instance. Receivers can now control your video signals as well as audio ones. Personal video recorders are coming as part of many digital cable and satellite set-top boxes. We talk about the advantages of individual components versus more integrated units in Chapter 11.

Also note that these prices are a snapshot in time — they are continually dropping, so don't be surprised to find everything on this list available for even less money when you go shopping.

Table 1-1	Home Theater Budget Guide	
Role	**Device**	**Price Expectations**
Audio sources	Audio cassette player*	$100 to $250
	CD player/recorder*	$60 to $600+
	Turntable*	$100 to $5,000+ (really!)
	AM/FM tuner*	$200 to $1,000
	Satellite radio tuner	$75 to $300
Video sources	DVD player	$50 to $1,200+
	High-def DVD player (Blu-ray or HD-DVD)	$500+
	VCR*	$50 to $500
	Personal video recorder*	$50 to $700
	Satellite TV system*	$100 to $800
Computer/gaming	Gaming console*	$100 to $400
	Home theater PC*	$1,000+
A/V system**	All-in-one systems	$200 to $3,000+
	A/V receiver	$200 to $4,000
	Controller/decoder	$800 to $5,000+
	Power amplifier	$500+
Speakers	Center, left, right, and surround speakers	$150 to $10,000+
	Additional surround sound speakers*	$100 to $5,000+
	Subwoofer speakers	$150 to $5,000+
Video display***	27- to 34-inch direct-view tube TV	$200 to $2,000
	Up to 65-inch rear-projection TV	$1,000 to $6,000
	Up to 120-inch front-projection TV	$1,000 to $15,000+
	32- to 60-inch plasma or LCD flat-panel TV	$1,000 to $15,000+

Role	Device	Price Expectations
Portables	Portable MP3 player*	$50 to $350
	Portable video player*	$100 to $500
Car system	Car PC*	$800 to $2,000
Accessories	Speaker and A/V interconnection cables	$50 to $1,000+
	Surge suppressor/Power conditioner	$20 to $1,500
	Home media server*	$1,000+
	Internet media access devices*	$150+

* *Optional.*
** *You don't need all of these parts, just an all-in-one system, an A/V receiver, or a controller/decoder and power amplifier combo.*
*** *You only need one of these displays.*

Certainly, you don't need all the gear in Table 1-1. You can buy a nice all-in-one home theater system and a relatively big-screen, direct-view (picture tube) TV for not much more than $500. Of course, you can spend a lot more money, too. One thing is for sure: Pricing is competitive and is changing all the time. Two years ago, a lot of the gear listed in Table 1-1 cost twice as much as it does now. As we go to print, the first 42-inch plasma screen TVs for under $2,000 are hitting the market.

To get a quick grasp on pricing, go to a few Web sites, such as www. circuitcity.com and www.plasmatvbuyingguide.com to get a sense of the going rate for different items. Compare that with Table 1-1 to get a sense of how much pricing has dropped just in the time that it took for this book to hit the shelves.

Buying on a budget

Given that you are probably working within a budget, here are some ideas about what you can expect to buy and install for different total budget ranges:

- ✔ **$0 to $500:** Definitely the entry-level package for home theater, a system in the under-$500 range basically uses your existing TV (or includes an inexpensive TV in the 27-inch range) and an entry-level all-in-one home theater system package (which comes with all the speakers you need for surround sound and a receiver/DVD player combo). You can probably throw in a $50 VCR if you don't already have one, but even the lowest level all-in-one home theater sets include DVD players. (Gotta have DVD!)

✔ **$500 to $2,000:** By spending a little more, you can go up a range in a number of the components and get HDTV into your home theater (which we highly recommend — especially as all TVs convert to digital in 2009!). You can spend some of this money on an entry-level tube HDTV (you can get a 30-inch widescreen HDTV-ready TV for under $800). You could even move up to a rear-projection TV; they start around $1,200 for a 40- to 52-inch screen. There are a range of options for better surround sound systems in this price range, with packaged options available for your five surround sound speakers plus your subwoofer. And you can buy a fairly good A/V receiver to drive the system. Top this all off with a portable MP3 player and a DVD player for the car, and your kids will love you (more).

✔ **$2,000 to $5,000:** At this level, you start to create serious options for a very decent home theater system. The lowest-cost plasma and LCD screens are under $1,000, or for a bigger picture, you can go with a digital (LCD or DLP) rear-projection unit with a great high-def picture (starting at around $1,500). You might budget $500 or more for a high-definition-capable DVD player in this price range as well. On the audio side, you can spend $1,000 or so on a relatively fancy all-in-one system, but at this price level, you can also start to get serious with separate components, getting a very good A/V receiver, DVD/CD player/recorder, personal video recorder, gaming system, surround sound speakers, and potentially even more. At this price range, the average person can get a mighty fine system.

✔ **$5,000 to $10,000:** When you top $5,000 as your budget, you can start expanding in some wonderful ways by adding more throughout the house through multizone capabilities, whole-home audio, and universal remote control capability, or you can continue to go up the ladder in terms of higher-quality separates. We swear by audio servers that store all your music in one box. Get one for the car, too, and have them sync up when you drive in the driveway. Front-projection TVs become a viable option in this price range; good projectors start around $2,000. No matter what you choose — flat-panel, rear-projection, or front-projection — in this price range, you should expect a big (50-inch or more) high-definition display. Or, you can get fancy with furniture. Good home theater seats start around $350 each. A high-quality universal remote control costs about $500.

✔ **$10,000+:** Above $10,000, the sky is truly the limit. For $10,000 to $20,000, you get to enjoy a lot of the next generation of home theater. Your TV should be big and capable of playing 1080p (1920 x 1080 pixels — the highest resolution of HDTV) signals. Your DVD player should be top of the line, supporting Blu-ray or HD-DVD. You probably want some extra amplifier equipment in the system, and you may also want to boost your controls, perhaps with a nice Crestron wireless touch screen control. If you get above $20,000, you are into high-end audiophile-type stuff all the way. Whole-home audio and video, integration with home automation systems, consultants — the works. Believe it or not, it is not unusual for people to spend $1 million or more on a home theater. At that point, we think a lot of money is being paid for custom interior design, top-of-the-line projectors, and so on. Nothing is held back. To us, given more modest expectations, a $25,000 system is stunning in almost all senses of the word.

Getting Your Money's Worth

In deciding how much to spend overall, we can give you only this advice: Your home entertainment system is probably one of the most-used parts of your home. It helps define your family, social life, business relationships, and so on. It's important, but spend within your means. You also want to save something for the future. Building and growing a home theater is fun, too.

One of the great things about home theater is that it is modular, so you don't have to buy the whole thing all at once. If you really want a great TV display, get it, and go cheaper on the other components. And when you are ready to trade up, figure out what you want next. The better stereo stores have a trade-up policy that gives you credit toward getting something better. And then there's always eBay (www.ebay.com) or similar auction sites, where you can get all sorts of gear in great condition — everyone is always trading in stuff to move to higher levels, so don't feel pressured to do it all at once.

Realize that, even if you are installing home theater wiring and speakers into the walls and such, you're not likely to 'get that money back' when you sell the house. People are leery of other people's home-grown solutions — even the professional ones — and equipment becomes outdated quickly in this industry. So if you are going to do some remodeling and spend some money, recognize that you are doing it for yourself first, everyone else second, and by all means not for the money.

Indeed, a lot of this book is about getting your money's worth out of whatever you buy. If you get an all-in-one home theater system for $199 from Radio Shack, or a high-end system with, say, a $37,000 Faroudja projector, $18,000 worth of MartinLogan Prodigy speakers, a $4,000 B&K Receiver, and other similarly priced (but well worth it) components, you're still going to need to figure out how to get the most out of the system. So stay tuned to find out how to get more per kHz, or disc, or channel, or whatever you track your home theater fun by.

Chapter 2

Defining Your Home-Theatered Home

Consumer electronics have played a major role throughout the years in defining not just how we live in our own homes, but also how we live as a society. The radio, then black-and-white TV, then color TV, and then all the various adjuncts to the TV and radio — VCRs, gaming consoles, tape decks, and so on — have all helped define who we are and how we interact with each other. The "edgier" radio and TV shows over the years have had a profound social impact by acting out for us the crossing of various social barriers — for instance, the first on-screen interracial kiss, the first portrayal of a woman president, and the first portrayal of a black president.

The home has grown around these devices, so when it comes time to put these together on a pedestal and proclaim them a "home theater," this act seems to acknowledge the role that home electronics have come to play in our lifestyles.

The Basic Home Theater

So what's in a home theater then? Well, a home theater is largely what you make of it, but we think that at least three major elements constitute the core of a home theater:

  ✔ **A large-screen display:** Note that we do not say *television*. More and more, the receiver aspect of a television is being divorced from the display aspect, in the form of set-top boxes, external TV tuners, computers, and other source devices. Appropriately, the display is being optimized for its main purpose — displaying the wide range of video output from a home theater system. These displays can be huge. We're talking greater than 120 inches diagonally, which is 10 feet for those of you who didn't do the math!

✔ **A digital video source:** At a minimum, this means a DVD player, and for most folks, it will also mean a TV source (like digital cable or a digital satellite TV service). We think that DVD is a bottom-line must-have when you're building a home theater because that's the way most of us access the movies we want to watch.

For most people, this includes a source (or sources) of *high-definition* video, from TV broadcasts or the next generation of DVDs.

✔ **A surround sound capability:** You find out about the details of surround sound in a few pages, but you need to have surround sound to take full advantage of all the audio power stored in your DVD content. With surround sound, you truly start mimicking the theater experience.

If you're lacking any of these, you really don't have a home theater. Without the display and surround sound, you lose the impact of the visual and audio experience, and without a digital video source, you just have a loud and big TV system. You really need all three. Figure 2-1 shows these elements in their native environment — your home.

Figure 2-1:
A home theater with a surround sound system, a video display, and a digital video source.

DVD player, DTV tuner, satellite/cable box, etc.

Multichannel audio electronics

Left

Right

Center

Left Surround

LFE (sub)

Right Surround

But you need not stop there. There are all sorts of other great ways — besides a DVD player — to get digital video up on your big screen display for you, as well as great devices you can add to enhance your overall experience. The rest of this chapter is devoted to really fleshing out the boundaries of your home theater realm.

The Complete Home Theater

In our discussion of budgets in Chapter 1, we give you a peek at what a really fleshed-out home theater might contain. Here's a fairly comprehensive list of what you typically put in your home theater (we leave out the all-in-one units because they merely integrate various combinations of these devices into one unit):

✔ **Sources:** These provide the content you watch or listen to.

- Audio cassette player/recorder

- CD player/recorder/MP3 player

- Turntable

- AM/FM tuner

- DVD player/recorder

- VCR

- Personal video recorder (PVR, also called a digital video recorder [DVR] by some folks)

- Camcorder

- Satellite or cable set-top box

- Video/audio server

- Gaming console

- Home theater PC or Windows XP Media Center PC (a specific Microsoft software product; see Chapter 8)

✔ **Receivers/controllers:** The heart of the system, these feed content to your displays and speakers.

- A/V receiver

- Controller/decoder

- Power amplifier

✔ **Displays:** This is what you watch.

- Direct-view, rear-projection, or flat-panel TV display
- Front-projection system with separate display screen

✔ **Speakers:** These are what you listen to.

- Two front speakers
- One front center speaker
- Two side speakers
- Two or four rear speakers
- Subwoofer

✔ **Connections:** These are connections to content inside and outside your home.

- Over-the-air antenna
- Satellite or cable video feed
- Internet connectivity — preferably broadband, such as DSL or cable modem
- Home network — preferably both wired and wireless to make the connection between your Internet service and your home theater and your home theater and your PC (with Media Center Edition) or Mac (with Apple's Front Row)

✔ **Accessories:** These are devices that make your home-stored content accessible from elsewhere.

- Universal remote controls and touchpads
- Internet access devices
- Home media servers and digital media adapters

Naturally, as you extend your home theater to other points in your home, you can add to the quantities mentioned here, but most of the components are the same. You also might choose different qualities and (in the case of displays) sizes of these things, but the basic formula remains the same.

Using Your Existing Gear

A question that comes across most people's minds when they look to upgrade to a home theater is whether any of their existing A/V gear can be used in their new home theater.

The answer usually is, "Well you probably can, but you lose a lot by doing so (unless the gear is less than two years old, and in some cases, even that is old)." If you are thinking about using existing equipment, consider the following:

✔ **TVs:** If it's smaller than a 27-inch display, why bother? Home theater needs a big-screen display for maximum effect. The most important thing to consider when reviewing the capabilities of your old TV is this: Can it display HD (high-definition) pictures? If not, you'll probably want to consider an upgrade. Also check for features like picture-in-picture, and make sure your TV has the right kinds of inputs to accept the latest and greatest source devices (look for HDMI or DVI, discussed in Chapter 13).

TV size requirements are actually a mix of three things: the size of the display, the display's *resolution* (or number of individual picture elements that make up the picture on your screen), and your viewing distance from the screen. In Chapter 13 we provide some concrete guidance about the best size display for your particular home theater. For most home theaters, a bigger display *is* better, but if you're planning on viewing from a relatively short distance (a few feet, for example), you might be better off with a relatively small screen.

✔ **Receivers:** Chances are your receiver is an audio (stereo) receiver, which probably doesn't have surround sound processing capability, inputs for video gear, or built-in amplifiers for your surround sound speakers. You can use an audio-only receiver as an amplifier to drive some speakers, but if you want to listen to the latest surround sound capabilities, which are encoded on most DVDs, then you're going to need a new audio/video receiver, period. What's more, if you have a lot of video sources, you are going to want to switch among them — and for that you'll need a receiver with sophisticated video switching.

✔ **VCRs:** As long as your VCR is a VHS HiFi VCR, it's just fine. But it won't replace a DVD player, which has about four times the picture resolution of a VCR (meaning the picture is about twice as sharp and detailed).

✔ **CD players:** Your CD player will probably work fine. Depending on your space constraints, however, you might just use your DVD player to play your CDs because the two are compatible. Over time, CD players will disappear from your system in favor of a combined disc playing/recording unit.

✔ **DVD players:** Your DVD player will probably play fine, but if it cannot record, you'll miss out. With the latest personal video recorders, you will want to archive and offload all sorts of content to DVDs, and for that, you'll want a DVD player/recorder to burn the DVDs. Keep in mind that you can often use a PC (with the right software onboard) for the DVD recording functionality — we talk about PCs in the home theater in Chapter 8.

- ✔ **Speakers:** Chances are these are not going to be very useful because you really want a *set* of speakers, not ones that are pieced together. Speakers work in tandem and therefore should have a similar foundation of performance. If you have a pair of stereo speakers that you can match into a complete set of surround sound speakers from the same manufacturer, you might be able to use what you have (we recommend that you choose additional speakers that are *timbre matched* with your existing speakers).

- ✔ **Other stuff:** Most other stuff can work with your system. Turntables, cassette decks, laser disc players, and so on can plug in and play their part without any problems.

- ✔ **Internet connection:** Okay, your connection isn't gear in the traditional sense, but still, if you're using a dialup connection, you should seriously consider upgrading to broadband if you want your home theater to take advantage of the Internet. As present and future consumer devices become increasingly reliant on the Internet for accessing information and content, you'll need a broadband connection to download this content.

Choosing a Room

As you build your home theater, all roads lead back to optimizing that illusion of participation, and where you put your system plays a big part. Here's a list of things to think about when determining the right place for your home theater — and there are definitely *wrong* places to put your home theater:

- ✔ **Think about lighting:** The amount of ambient light in a room, day or night, can substantially affect the experience. A nice, dark room actually makes the room itself disappear when watching a film, enabling that suspension of disbelief we keep aspiring to. Think about how lights from other rooms or street lighting might affect the experience.

- ✔ **Think about dimensions:** You tend to get more awkward sound patterns in perfectly square rooms. The best place to put the centerpiece of your system — the TV display — is along the short wall of a rectangular room, preferably a wall without windows or doors on it. Fully enclosed rooms are best for sound. You can pull heavy curtains across an open wall when you are watching films in your home theater.

- ✔ **Think about sound:** Although people typically place a couch up against a wall, with a home theater, you want enough space behind you so that the sound can get in back of you and truly surround you. So the ideal position for the seating is more central to the room.

✔ **Think about the picture:** Sit close enough to your display to maximize the perceived size of the picture, but not so close that you see a somewhat grainy picture because you can see the lines on the TV set (that's too close). The bigger your display, the farther back you need to be to not see the lines. Also think about angle of viewing — all displays have a preferred angle of viewing.

✔ **Think about walls:** A rather muted color or wall covering — book cases are ideal — absorbs stray light. A dark gray or black room is best, or one with heavy, colored drapes. (Now you know why you see all those drapes and carpeted walls in theaters!) The *last* thing you want is a brightly colored high-gloss paint that reflects light, creating light ghosts to the sides of the screen! Think also about removing or covering mirrors and picture frames; they do the same thing.

Take note of the front and rear wall surfaces because, in general, you want to control the way your sound reflects off these surfaces. Typically, you want the back wall to be a little reflective to help build a more general sound field behind your seating area.

✔ **Think about floors:** Yup, the floors, too. Bare tile or wood causes acoustical reflections that mess up your sound field. A good rug can absorb stray sounds that can affect the crispness of your signal.

✔ **Think about stray noise:** Listen closely to your room for regular interfering sounds, such as a clock ticking or a fish tank pump. Consider moving these devices if you can. And if the sound is coming externally, like from the dryer or washer, consider some cheap absorptive wall coverings to muffle it.

We talk about creating a home theater environment in more detail in Chapter 20.

Organizing Your Gear

The most obvious and easy place for all your home theater gear is where you historically have placed it — right next to the TV. And indeed, there's nothing inherently wrong with this approach. However, we ask you to look ahead for a moment and think about the investment you'll make in your home theater and how you'd like to take advantage of that throughout your home. To do this, you need to think of ways your home theater's components can be used in a whole-home network. This whole-home planning can make your home theater itself better, too, because it facilitates connections between the home theater and other networks that might feed into it, such as your cable connection or your Internet connection.

Setting up a central wiring panel

Think about designating a space in your house as a *central wiring panel* where you can centrally house a lot of your whole-home infrastructure equipment (devices that let you connect the home theater to the rest of the house).

Remember that most of your commonly used, ultra-sensitive electronics gear will probably go right next to your home theater. You are better off relegating the gear that you just "plug and forget" (like video distribution panels that send your cable TV throughout the home) to a panel in an out-of-the-way place. Some of the devices that you might connect on a wiring panel include the following:

✔ Home cable interconnections with your cable company

✔ Home phone interconnections with your telephone company

✔ A centralized distribution point for your satellite dish wiring, if you have one

✔ Cable, DSL, satellite, or ISDN modems and routers, if you have them

✔ Ethernet hubs or switches for your Internet connection

You can also put items such as home servers and some of your central media equipment on the wiring panel if you don't need to get to it regularly and you need the extra space. Multizone amplifiers or MP3 servers are examples of such equipment.

Appreciating the advantages of a central wiring panel

By designating a central wiring panel, you gain some huge benefits:

✔ **Hiding wires:** Your home theater gear has a lot of cables and can have a lot of gear you rarely touch. A well-integrated home theater setup has a lot of cables hidden in the walls or running out of sight. We're not just talking component wiring (such as the wires between your DVD player and your A/V receiver), but also connections to your phone network (required by a satellite dish), to your Internet connection (could be wireless, but wireline is better long term), to your IR (infrared) remote control network (more on this in Chapter 15), and other connections. Think of your wiring panel as a place where everything can connect to everything else in the easiest fashion.

✔ **Hiding hardware:** Much of the hardware that facilitates home theater and whole-home networking (things such as power amps, video modulators, distribution panels, punchdown blocks, and the like) is designed with function in mind rather than form. A central wiring panel can put this hardware out of view. And that means less clutter for where you have the stuff that you get at the most, like your VCR or your DVD player.

> ✔ **Connecting at a single point:** Having a central connection point makes it easier to get networks like cable or your Internet-connected computer LAN (Local Area Network) into the home theater. It also makes it easier for you to get movies and music *out* of your home theater and share them throughout the home or access them when traveling.

> ✔ **Providing easy access:** When you want to change the capabilities of your networks or troubleshoot a problem, having everything neatly arranged and easily accessible can eliminate a source of frustration.

The wiring panel should be in a place that is out of sight but is also easily accessible. It needs to have plenty of space and adequate power to run a great deal of equipment. Then, whatever you need to bring up to the media hub in the home theater, you can, through a range of easily connected wiring plates that make it look neat and more accessible at the same time.

Locating your wiring panel's home

In the best-case scenario (like when you've struck it rich and are building a custom-designed home), you can create a dedicated room for your home theater and associated equipment — a central wiring panel just like modern offices and other commercial buildings have.

If we were starting a home from scratch this way, we'd try to design the wiring panel

> ✔ On the main floor of the house

> ✔ Near an outside wall for easy interconnection to incoming service feeds

> ✔ Above an accessible part of the basement (if you have a basement)

> ✔ With adequate lighting, ventilation, and climate protection (not in the garage, in other words)

> ✔ With adequate AC power line receptacles to power devices, such as video amplifiers, Ethernet hubs, and phone systems

Such a panel needn't be too large. Most home theater equipment takes up one rack at the most.

Of course, the vast majority of homeowners or remodelers simply don't have the luxury of adding a dedicated space for a wiring panel. In these cases, you have to try to make some part of the house do double duty as your wiring panel. A first stop is the place where your cable, telephone, and electrical connections currently come into the house. You can mount some plywood on the wall on which to mount your gear. Here are some other places to consider locating your wiring panel:

✔ **The utility or laundry room:** The biggest disadvantage of this location is the potential for high humidity, so make sure your clothes dryer is well ventilated to the outdoors. Good ventilation also keeps all the dust and lint from your dryer out of your sensitive electronics.

✔ **A protected garage:** The potential for dust and extreme temperatures may make this location less than optimal for some homes, but the garage can be a useful location.

✔ **The basement:** Many people choose the basement for a central wiring node because it's easy to run wires through a drop ceiling. The basement can be a very good location, but keep in mind that basements can be both dusty and damp.

✔ **A weather-protected outdoor panel:** We recommend this location only as a last resort, but it could be acceptable in a place with a mild climate. We wouldn't recommend putting any active electronics, such as Ethernet hubs or phone systems, out here.

An important thing to keep in mind is that the natural enemies of electrical and electronic equipment are moisture, dust, and temperature extremes. So locations that may work for someone in Florida or California may not make as much sense for your house in Maine.

Setting up a hub

Your home's wiring panel provides a centralized place for all sorts of whole-home networks that connect into your home theater (and elsewhere). Within your home theater, wherever you happen to locate it, you also need a similar centralized connection point for all that A/V gear we discuss in Chapter 1.

For most people, central to this area is the A/V receiver. An important thing to consider up front is the capability of this receiver to act as the hub of your home theater. An A/V receiver should be capable of accepting the connections from just about every single piece of A/V gear in your home theater (with the exception, perhaps, of an HDTV tuner/set-top box) and providing a central connection and control point.

With the right pieces and parts and the right approach to making connections, your A/V receiver (or surround sound decoder/controller, if you go with separate components) should be the primary connection point in a home theater. With a small number of exceptions (mainly related to HDTV), you shouldn't connect components directly to the TV or display unit. All your audio and video should be routed through the A/V receiver, which then *switches* — or distributes — these signals to your speakers and display. We discuss receivers in more detail in Chapter 11.

Switching is a cool concept that we want to make sure you understand. If you think of your receiver as a generic box with lots of cables coming into and going out of it, the switching capability of the device merely cross connects these lines. So let's say you have a Sony PlayStation 2, an AudioReQuest audio CD server (with video output to the TV screen to select your CDs), a DVD player, a VCR, and a TiVo personal video recorder all connected to your A/V receiver, which in turn is connected to your display. In the past, you would have to link these in a daisy chain and press TV/Video buttons and L1/L2 channel selectors and the link in order to see what you want on the TV. With an A/V receiver with video switching onboard, you can switch among these different video sources by merely turning a knob on the receiver or pressing a button on the remote. Simple as that. No more fudging, cursing, and screaming by your spouse that *Desperate Housewives* has already started and you'd better get the TV working *now!* (Not that that ever happened to Pat.)

Some folks feel that sending *any* video through the receiver's video switching circuitry slightly degrades the quality of this video. We think that, unless you're talking about a really high-end HDTV system, you probably won't see the difference. If you're worried about your receiver degrading your video quality, try it both ways (with the source device connected through the receiver and connected directly to your display) and see which looks better to your eyes.

Discreetly installing all this whole-home wiring (and "local" cables within your home theater) for your home theater can be a bit problematic and messy. Your home theater room, unlike your wiring panel, is meant to be a public space in your house, not a place where you can hide away unsightly bundles of wire and racks of equipment. So your aesthetic requirements will be a bit higher.

The best solution to this problem is to design the room so that you have an enclosed equipment-and-connection area where you can put the equipment that you don't need to physically access to watch a program or listen to something — such as special equipment needed for whole-home audio and video systems. Your equipment and connection area could be a well-ventilated closet, if one is available. We've even seen really sophisticated setups with a false wall behind the TV and equipment racks to allow access to the backs of all of the gear (or that have pull-out shelves that give you easy access to the back, as well). If you have space for a rack, you can probably store a lot of your active components there, too.

If you can't find a separate space for your gear, you can at least make your environment neater and more professional-looking by hiding some of the wiring in the walls or in fake molding and by making the local connections available via wall outlets. You can use short cables to connect these outlets to the equipment itself. In this fashion, you don't have lumpy wires traveling under the rugs and cables that little children (or the dog) can easily grab.

Zoning inside your home

When most people think about a home theater, they think within a pretty confined box — the place where the home theater is going to be. And certainly, that's the predominant focus of this book.

However, a major theme that we'll hammer at (until you agree with us) is that you should spend a little extra money and be a little smarter in your planning so that you can access this great asset elsewhere around the house and from the Internet as well.

Creating *zones* around your house is a great way to extend your audio asset. When you buy your receiver or amplifier, the concept of *multizone* is going to come up. A multizone system allows you to access different sources and send them to independent outputs simultaneously. For example, your kids could be watching *Rugrats* in the living room, and you could be listening to Dunne Roman (www.dunneroman.com) in the kitchen. How cool is that!

We don't go into a lot of detail on this here; we cover it extensively in Chapter 18. But we want to mention it up front for the following reasons:

✔ This is a good reason why you are going to need to think outside just your home theater (and another reason why a wiring panel is a good idea).

✔ This is something you need to plan and budget for. Multizone means extra wiring and cables, extra speakers, possibly an extra amplifier, possibly extra controls, and some extra cost. (But it's well worth it.)

Doing It Yourself versus Hiring the Pros

A lot of home theater you can do yourself. However, if you want it done right, you may want to bring in some experts to complement your work. If you don't have the right electrical outlets at your desired electronics station, for instance, you might call in an electrical contractor to put in dedicated home-run electrical cables (so you're not on the same circuit as the dishwasher and don't have electrical current spikes hitting your system all the time). Also, setting up front projection is an art and better left to professionals. And there's nothing like having your system fine-tuned by a professional who really can tell if your video and sound are just right. Still, you can do all of this yourself, with some patience (and respect for the live conductors in your electrical system).

If you want a professional to set up your entire system, you probably need to shop in the high-end price range. We rarely see anyone brought in to help on systems less than $10,000, and it almost always takes a $25,000+ system to get most contractors excited. So if you are on the low end of the equation, you'll probably do a lot yourself or rely heavily on the local installation services of the store from which you buy your equipment. Even if your dealer doesn't want to do the entire installation for you, we suggest you see if they can do a system calibration for you. If you buy on-line, expect to do most of the work yourself.

Home Theater For Dummies does not presume you are going to hire anyone. You should be able to plan, design, and install a very professional sounding (and looking) home theater system after reading this book. We just want you to know your alternatives in case you get halfway through and need some help. Check out the sidebar, "Who can help if you need it?" for some ideas.

Which people get involved in your project depends on the size of your project and whether you are building a new home, renovating an old one, or simply making do with that spare room in the basement. In the end, it will vary according to what you're trying to accomplish. If you plan to put a major home theater in your home — complete with theater seats, a popcorn and candy stand, and screen curtains — you may want to bring a home-theater consultant into the process. However, we've seen some very imaginative do-it-yourself (DIY) home theaters that trade love and patience for consultants and big bills, and the results are truly amazing.

Want some confidence that you can do this (and get some neat ideas for your own installation)? Check out all the DIY home theater projects at www. hometheatertalk.com and www.hometheaterforum.com.

If you do bring in some help, make sure that you choose advisors who share your vision of an ideal home theater. The people you choose should have experience with a broad range of home theaters, not just expensive or cheap ones. Find your home theater personality and match it with your contractor's, and you'll have a winning combination.

You might have a hard time finding some of these contractors. For the more traditional groups of professionals (such as architects), we tend to rely on word of mouth, recommendations from in-the-know friends, and a thorough review of the contractor's references. For contractors who will be installing your home's electronics and wiring infrastructure, we do these same things, as well as check their credentials. The Custom Electronics Design & Installation Association, or CEDIA, has a rigorous training and qualification program for people who do nothing but build and install home theater systems for a living. There is a CEDIA Finder Service at www.cedia.net/homeowners/finder.php. Many home theater magazine Web sites also have directories of contractors — for instance, you can find a listing of installers at *Electronic House*'s Installers Guide: www.electronichouse.com/installer.

Who can help if you need it?

All sorts of people can help you if you need advice:

- **Architect:** If you're building or renovating, an architect is probably involved. Home theater design usually isn't an architect's strong suit, but he or she can help you lay out the initial plans for your home and coordinate with other designers to get their respective visions on paper.

- **Audio/video consultant:** Your audio/video (A/V) consultant helps you select the right mix of components for your sight and sound systems and then integrates all those components. Your A/V consultant makes sure that the appropriate wiring is run to support your installations and then installs the gear when you're ready. If you're installing a dedicated home theater, expect your A/V consultant to get involved with the architect early on, too, making recommendations for room sizes, building materials, and so on. The A/V consultant may also hand you off to a specialized home theater consultant if the job is too complex for his or her comfort. (Home theater consultants get into additional details, such as soundproofing, seating, lighting, and the room's shape and construction.)

- **Contractor/builder:** The general contractor/builder's role is to direct the other specialty contractors and make sure that they carry out the intent of the designers. Passing correct information from one contractor (such as the home theater consultant) to the people doing the work (such as the cabinetmaker who builds the home theater cabinetry) is crucial. The details are what count here, such as cutting out the right size cubbyhole for the kitchen media center.

- **Computer systems contractor:** If you work at home or have complex computer-networking needs, bringing in a computer systems contractor to network your computer hardware and interface it to the appropriate systems can be a great timesaver.

- **Electrical contractor:** Your home theater may require additional or different electrical wiring (for example, running dedicated electrical wiring to your media center).

- **Home networking consultant:** Your home networking consultant will help you create a wired and/or wireless computer network that can carry voice, data, and video all over your home. Many alarm companies, electricians, and others are expanding their services to include home networking. We're big believers in home networking and think it should be a core part of your home theater, too. These folks can also help with a whole-home automation system that can control your home theater and automate things like lighting, drapes, and even movie screens.

- **Interior designer:** This person is responsible for making sure that your home theater technology doesn't stick out like a sore thumb. Installing a state-of-the-art home-entertainment center in the living room is one thing; making it fit with the overall scheme of your home is another.

- **Lighting consultant:** Often an overlooked task on a to-do list, lighting design has an important effect on the ambiance of your home theater, so consider specialized lighting in key accent areas.

Whew! Did we leave anyone out? Depending on the amount of money you want to spend, you may indeed have this many people making your home theater a reality. A more modest project has a more modest number of people stomping around your house. Also, many of the previously mentioned professionals — A/V designers, for example — include their services when you purchase their equipment.

Chapter 3

The ABCs of Home Theater Audio

*I*n the early days of corporate video conferencing, system designers struggled to balance the audio and video needs for a video conference with the cost for the transmission to carry the signals (which was really expensive). Necessity being the mother of invention, a lot of the focus was on compressing the audio and video to low sizes and figuring out the right mix between the two.

One trend became clear rather quickly: When test subjects were presented with all the different variants and permutations possible for different transmission speeds, they always preferred to have better audio at the price of video rather than the opposite. In other words, they preferred to accept crappy video rather than deal with bad audio.

Although you'd like to have the best of all possible worlds in all aspects of your home theater, we think you'll probably focus on audio first (at least we'd recommend it) for three reasons:

- ✔ The video conferencing effect we just noted.
- ✔ The fact that your home theater also doubles as a home concert hall, so you want your audio CDs, MP3s, and other audio sources to sound perfect, too.
- ✔ Video display prices are dropping faster than any other device in home theater, so if you are going to put off one purchase, putting off the video display makes a lot of sense.

For these reasons, we start our discussion of home theater technologies with audio first.

Surrounding Yourself with Sound

Unless you plan on installing a 360-degree Cinema-in-the-Round screen in your home, just like you'd see at Disney World, video plays a rather confined (but still big) role in creating the home theater illusion of being "in the movie." The real job of surrounding yourself in the scene falls to your multichannel surround sound audio system.

Imagine that you see on the screen in front of you the soon-to-be victims of a firing squad, and that — from behind you — you hear the clicks of the rifles as they chamber a round. That sensation is brought to you by your rear-channel-driven surround sound system. Now, if you had heard that sound coming from in front of you — the traditional TV experience — it simply would not have the same impact because, in the "real" world, that click of the rifle would *have* to come from behind you. Which all goes to show that if you really want the dickens scared out of you, you need surround sound.

Two-channel sound versus multichannel surround sound

Most of us are used to age-old *two-channel* sound — that is, the stereo sound that gives us a left and a right speaker effect. *Multichannel surround sound* builds on this by adding a front center speaker between the front left and right speakers and adding two surround speakers. More recent versions of surround sound add even more rear speakers and side surround speakers to really enhance your surround sound field (the latest version of Dolby Lab's surround sound — Dolby TrueHD — can support up to 14 channels!). A subwoofer is part of almost all home theater setups, but as we discuss later in this chapter, a subwoofer is actually more a part of the bass management of the collective speakers than part of the surround sound system itself. Nonetheless, something needs to shake the room when the dinosaur's feet stomp the jeep in *Jurassic Park!*

To understand the impact of the concept of surround sound on your home theater, you need to understand a bit about *encoding* and *decoding* sound. When the master mixers at the movie studios create the audio track to go with the movie, they encode the music in some very specific ways. They designate which *channel* (you can read *speaker* into that if you like) the specific sound goes through. In addition, each different channel is designed to provide *spatial* sound effects — meaning that the channels can work together to make sounds come from different locations relative to you, the listener. The goal is to decode those signals onto the correct channels to replicate the studio's intent.

So, let's say that a squadron of jets in a scene from *Top Gun* is doing a fly-by of the carrier command bridge. If we were in the command bridge, we would hear the jets come in from the left, sweep across in front of us, and then disappear to the right and the rear as they turn off to the starboard side of the ship. If you are sitting in a well-tuned home theater, you should hear no differently. And in fact, as the bridge shakes, your subwoofers (and bass shakers, which we talk about in Chapter 22) provide you with the vibrations to make you feel like you are actually there. Now we're talking surround sound!

To get you to this point, the encoders have to designate on the movie or TV program soundtrack the specific sounds that, at specific times, are to be sent to specific channels in your system. The speakers connected to those channels are given those signals by your surround sound–equipped A/V receiver (see Chapter 11), which properly decodes those tracks from the DVD or other video source. A home theater audio system needs to have it all correct from beginning to end.

In a two-channel system, you might hear some of that effect, in that it might get the left and right part right. A two-channel system can't help with the front to back movement, however, and that's the critical part of a surround sound system — it surrounds you!

Understanding surround sound lingo

For the most part, the entertainment industry boils down a lot of the surround sound terminology into numbers like 2.0, 5.1, and 7.1. Sometimes these numbers refer to the playback system's speaker configuration, and sometimes they refer to the audio signal format being delivered. The lingo can be confusing, especially when the number of speakers in your particular system doesn't match the number of channels in your source — like when you play back a 5.1 channel recording on your 7.1 channel system — but it's all perfectly normal for that to occur. In these numbers, the first number represents the number of speakers or main audio channels involved, and the 1 or 0 after the decimal point indicates whether the system has a subwoofer or supports a low-frequency effects channel. Systems that end in 1 have a subwoofer or an effects channel.

Here's a rundown of the different numbers you'll probably encounter and what they mean:

- ✓ **2.0:** Normal stereo — the kind with a left and a right channel — is 2.0 in surround sound speak.

- ✓ **5.1:** This is the primary format for creating and delivering surround sound. It is in wide use in movie theaters, digital television, DVD-Video and Audio, and even the latest game consoles. Source signals have the five main channels and one LFE (low frequency effects) bass channel. Playback systems usually have five main speakers and one subwoofer.

- ✔ **5.1-channel-ready:** Such an audio system has six discrete inputs to accept a 5.1 signal from a signal source such as a 5.1-channel DVD player. It does not necessarily mean these products can actually decode signals to a 5.1-channel output. The best way to ferret out true 5.1 systems is by reading reviews of the devices before you buy. (We recommend many places to find these reviews in Chapter 23.)

- ✔ **6.1:** 6.1-channel systems have an additional surround channel called the *back surround channel.* This drives a speaker (or preferably two) situated right behind the viewers, in essence providing the same smooth flow in the back sound field that the center speaker enables in the front speaker group. Dozens of DVDs are encoded with extra back surround information for this back surround speaker, and these DVDs also play perfectly well on regular 5.1 systems.

- ✔ **7.1:** Not to be outdone, some have taken the 5.1 or 6.1 channel encoding on a DVD and used some computer horsepower to create two independent back surround speakers for even more surround sound, making it 7.1. Note that 7.1 is not a true discrete surround sound format (there are no DVDs on the market with 7.1 channels of sound), but instead, it refers to manufacturers' own systems used to derive two back surround channels from existing stereo, 5.1, or even the 6.1-channel sources just mentioned.

- ✔ **8.1 and beyond:** You'll probably hear about even higher designations, 8.1, 9.1, 10.2, and so on. These are truly in the realm of the home theaterphile, and if you're evaluating such gear, a home theater consultant is probably standing next to you, so just follow his or her recommendations. The newest systems (like Dolby Digital Plus, discussed later in the chapter) can theoretically support systems up to 13.1. Wow!

Bass management

Bass management is how your home theater manages low-frequency sounds. Better A/V receivers and other controller devices have several options for how to handle the bass sounds in your system. If you have nice, big main speakers that have a very effective bass range of their own (often called *full-range speakers*), you might pass all bass frequencies to them. If you want smaller speakers that can sit on a shelf or hang on the wall alongside your plasma TV, then the bass frequencies might fall to the subwoofer, which is a speaker designed to play low-frequency sounds.

One area that causes a lot of confusion is the difference between the *Low Frequency Effect channel* (LFE), which is part of your movie/game/TV show soundtrack and the physical subwoofer channel on your receiver or amplifier. The LFE channel is encoded in the soundtrack of a DVD or other surround sound source; the subwoofer channel is the connection on the back of your A/V receiver that provides amplified low-frequency sound signals to your subwoofer. The LFE channel is encoded in surround sound material — it's the ".l" in 5.1 and other surround sound formats. This low frequency sound, along with the bass from any channels that cannot be reproduced by the "small" main speakers, is often sent to the subwoofer channel in your surround sound system, but it doesn't necessarily have to be sent exclusively to your subwoofer. For example, some people send these low frequency sounds to both the subwoofer and to the front left and right speakers if said speakers are "large." The bass management system within your A/V receiver (or A/V controller) lets you customize these settings to best fit your A/V system. (We discuss how to set this all up in Chapters 19 and 20.)

 You don't have to have a subwoofer to take advantage of the LFE channel because many normal left/right speakers can take these cues from your receiver and play the sound accordingly. But having a subwoofer gives you that stomach-rattling, vibrating-room effect at just the right times — an effect we're sure you'll want to take advantage of.

Dolby Galore

Here's where surround sound gets complicated, unfortunately. A host of different terms and brand names are applied to everything we just described, and these terms can get downright confusing.

When you start to optimize your home theater, however, you need to understand these terms. Because you probably have some older gear in your home audio and video system already, and because some older movies use older encoding schemes, we mention older terms, too, so that you can have the big picture.

We start with Dolby Laboratories (www.dolby.com). You've probably seen Dolby on your cassette tape deck for years and seen advertisements for Dolby Digital at the beginning of movies. But you've probably never known exactly what Dolby does. Well, stand by, because we're going to make you look smart on your next date at the movies.

Dolby surround sound

You have to go back a few years to get to where we are today. Although Dolby has been enhancing sound for decades, the true mother of all surround sound encoding schemes is Dolby Surround (introduced in 1982), which encodes four analog audio channels into two channels for storage and/or transmission. If you play Dolby Surround on a normal stereo, you get two channels. If you play it on a Dolby Surround–enabled decoder device, the device separates the full four channels for playback. Over 40 million consumer products have been shipped with Dolby Surround Pro Logic (the current version of this system) decoding onboard. That's a lot.

With Dolby Surround, the four channels encode front left, front center, front right, and monophonic surround as their channels. The left, center, and right channels are *full-range* channels, meaning that they carry the full range (20 Hz to 20 kHz) of audio frequencies. The fourth (rear) surround sound channel is a *limited bandwidth channel,* meaning it carries only a subset of the frequency range (not the real low-frequency or high-frequency stuff).

At first, consumer audio/video receivers with Dolby Surround decoders could separate only the left, right, and monophonic surround speaker channels. However, with the advent of Dolby Pro Logic in 1987, receivers could decode the center channel as well. The consumer devices just took awhile to develop the same processing power that the more expensive movie theaters had onboard.

Dolby Pro Logic is what's called a *matrixed* multichannel system, meaning that output channels are electronically derived from input channels. None of the four outputs are identical to the two inputs that are used to transport the encoded signals, but all the signals being output from the decoder are indeed present in the two-channel source — nothing new, such as reverb, is being added.

So with Dolby Pro Logic, you have four channels and five speakers, with the two surround speakers playing essentially the same monophonic sound. You often see a subwoofer channel on Pro Logic receivers as well; note that this is not a separate channel, but is derived from the low-frequency information from the front channels.

One problem with the dual monophonic surround sound channels is that, in some ways, they defeat the purpose of having surround sound. You can't send information specifically to one speaker, as is done with a left or right front speaker. And because they have the same signal, they tend to create a localized sound field between the speakers — and that goes against surround sound's goal of creating a large, diffuse background sound field. Proper placement of the surround speakers on the side walls aiming across the listening area helps achieve the optimal results. (In Chapter 12, we discuss dipole speakers and how they can help with this.)

A newer version of Pro Logic, Dolby Pro Logic II, came out in 2001. The biggest new feature that Pro Logic II offers is a fuller sound experience for two-channel stereo or Dolby Surround–encoded sources that were being played over 5.1 channel systems. Pro Logic II does extra processing and extends the Pro Logic work substantially. Importantly, Pro Logic II decodes the surround sound speakers in full bandwidth stereo, and therefore provides a more complete rear sound field.

Just about all surround sound decoders sold since 2002 or so support Dolby Pro Logic II. Many now support an even newer and more advanced version of Pro Logic — Pro Logic IIx, discussed below.

Dolby Pro Logic turns 7 (point 1!)

As more and more folks build 7.1-channel home theaters to support Dolby Digital EX (discussed in the next section), they find that they have two channels that aren't being used when they view material that's not multichannel encoded (for example, many DVDs of older material have a simple 2.0 channel Dolby Digital soundtrack), or even when playing regular stereo content.

In order to fill all seven speakers with sound, Dolby's engineers came to the rescue with a new version of Dolby Pro Logic II called *Pro Logic IIx*. This system provides a full 6.1- or 7.1-channel output — meaning you can take any incoming stereo (2.0) or 5.1-channel signal and turn it into a 6.1- or 7.1-channel output that uses *all* of the speakers in your home theater system. So don't be afraid to go 7.1! Pro Logic IIx has come to your rescue!

Dolby Digital arrives on the scene

The advent of Dolby Digital in 1997 really started to make things interesting. As you would surmise, Dolby Digital is an all-digital surround format that handles audio compression, so it's available only for digital content. DVDs and HDTV use Dolby Digital (DVDs may also contain some other system, such as DTS). To give you an idea of Dolby Digital's reach into the market, by the beginning of 2006, more than one billion consumer devices had shipped with Dolby Digital onboard, and more than 7,600 films had been encoded in Dolby Digital. It should come as no surprise, then, that it's the scheme we think your equipment should support.

Dolby Digital 5.1 represents the current minimum level of performance that you should require from your system. Also keep in mind that any receiver with Dolby Digital decoding can also decode Dolby Surround Pro Logic.

While Dolby Digital is the more widely known consumer moniker, it also goes by the more techie name of AC-3, which is actually the name used within the official part of the DVD video standard (for "regular" non-HD-DVDs), as well as the ATSC standard for DTV and HDTV. (See Chapter 4 for more on this.) AC-3 is also part of the standards for HD-DVD and Blu-ray discs. As you can see, Dolby Digital is *everywhere,* and you definitely want your home theater gear to support it. Luckily, just about every home theater receiver built since the late '90s supports Dolby Digital.

What's so great about Dolby Digital is that it encodes six discrete audio channels. (*Discrete* means that the sound signal contained in each of the six available channels is distinct and independent from each of the others.) Remember that the older Dolby Surround encoded four channels onto two-channel soundtracks, and that often resulted in all sorts of bleed-overs between channels and less than clear demarcations in the sound details.

Because Dolby Digital has six clean channels, your receivers and controllers can precisely control the different elements of your sound mix. More importantly, the rear surround speakers are each fed by their own independent channels, enabling true spatial separation for that rear sound field. With this setup, when you hear that bullet whiz by or that starship warp overhead, the sound moving across your entire speaker system is smooth and controlled — and digital. This is the home theater your momma always warned you about!

Dolby's ability to encode and decode information is only as strong as its source data. If it is working with a two-channel stereo movie, then you may see something like "Dolby Digital 2.0" on the package, designating that it is a stereo signal being encoded and decoded using Dolby Digital. All fine and dandy, but it's still a stereo signal. However, if your receiver includes Dolby Pro Logic, Dolby Pro Logic II, or even Dolby Pro Logic IIx, the stereo signal on the disc can still be listened to as a multichannel surround signal, thereby allowing you to achieve full playback on your system.

We talk more about how your DVD, HDTV, and other gear supports Dolby Digital, and how to make sure it is all set correctly, in later chapters, notably Chapter 6. For now, know that this is the baseline upon which you grow.

Dolby Digital Surround EX

Rear surround speakers are a relatively new development made possible by an additional surround channel that drives the center rear surround speaker. This is 6.1 in industry parlance. Dolby avoids 6.1 and calls it Dolby Digital Surround EX.

The rear Surround EX channel does not have its own discrete channel. Instead, its signal is *matrixed* in (intermixed) with the left and right surround channels, just like Dolby Pro Logic has the center speaker information encoded in the left and right front channels. When a Dolby Digital EX program is decoded, the three surround outputs are all derived from a 3-channel Pro Logic process — none of them are strictly discrete anymore. It is also the case that many conventional 5.1 movies decode nicely with Dolby Digital EX processing, thus keeping the added back speakers active. Newer processors offer Pro Logic IIx technology, thereby deriving four separate surround outputs instead of three, making much more effective use of 7.1-speaker systems for all movie and music programs, whether Surround EX encoded or not.

The first consumer devices with Surround EX were based on licenses from Lucasfilm THX (www.thx.com), so you'll also see it called THX Surround EX in stores and on-line when you're doing some shopping.

THX isn't a surround sound format itself, but rather a *certification and testing* program for home (and movie) theater equipment and movies. So equipment like A/V receivers and speakers may be THX-certified, as may DVDs themselves. THX's main mission in life is to create a set of standards for surround sound playback and to then certify that equipment or DVDs meet those standards. A big part of these standards revolves around THX's criteria for the levels and equalization of the sound sent to the surround speakers.

Many newer DVDs are encoded for Dolby Digital EX and have that extra channel of surround information onboard. Also, if you're playing a regular Dolby Digital 5.1-channel DVD, a THX Ultra 2 decoder can simulate 6.1- or 7.1-channel surround by processing the audio information in the regular surround channels and sending the information to your rear surround speaker.

If you're playing a movie (say on a DVD) that has been encoded using Dolby Digital EX, and you have only a regular Dolby Digital decoder in your A/V receiver, you won't have any problems. You still get the full 5.1 surround sound you expect, with nothing missing. You just won't get certain sounds re-routed to the extra surround speakers behind you.

DTS: Bring It On!

Dolby is not the only game in town, although it clearly has the lead in the marketplace. Digital Theater Systems (DTS) has invented a competing lineup of surround sound encoding schemes. The first movie to use DTS was *Jurassic Park*.

As with Dolby Digital, DTS Digital Surround provides 5.1 channels of digital audio. However, DTS uses less compression (higher data rate) than Dolby Digital. Where Dolby Digital encodes six channels with 384,000 or 448,000 bits per second, DTS, in its higher quality mode, encodes 1,536,000 bits per second, which many audiophiles believe delivers a better sound quality. Of course, that means that the DTS encoding takes up more space on a DVD, so the DVD doesn't have as much room for extra features, such as foreign languages, commentaries, and multiple versions of the movie.

It's an open question among experts as to which technology (Dolby Digital or DTS) sounds better or is a better choice. On the one hand, people point to DTS's higher bit rate and say, "Aha! Better sound!" Others say, "Well, Dolby is just more efficient at encoding sound, so it can have just as good a sound quality with fewer bits." You know what? It's really a moot point. Both can sound good. You'll most likely use whatever's encoded on the DVD or other programming you watch. Dolby is the most prevalent system, but DTS is also widespread. We suggest you choose receivers and other equipment that support both standards.

The DVD powers that be require all NTSC (the North American standard) DVDs to carry either a Dolby Digital or a PCM (Pulse Code Modulation — a common digital audio format) soundtrack to ensure compatibility with all DVD players. Because DTS is an optional feature of DVDs, DTS has an uphill battle getting studios onboard because the space on DVDs is limited. (For these space reasons, most DVDs containing a DTS soundtrack are encoded at half the 1.536 Mbps rate mentioned above in order to retain sufficient bit rate for high-quality video and other content.) Today, a few hundred DVDs are issued with the higher-quality (1.536 Mbps rate) DTS Digital Surround.

You might hear of some other DTS innovations:

- **DTS-ES:** DTS-ES Discrete uses existing digital multichannel technology to deliver the 5.1 channels of regular DTS. It also adds a *discrete* full-bandwidth back surround channel — meaning that each channel is individually encoded rather than being matrix decoded from the others. That additional channel may be played through one or two speakers, allowing for the ES — Extended Surround — that gives DTS-ES its name. More prevalent is the DTS-ES Matrix system, which is electrically identical to Dolby Digital EX but uses Neo:6 matrix decoding to derive the three surround outputs.

- **DTS Neo:6:** DTS Neo:6 Music and Neo:6 Cinema are decoding techniques for stereo or Dolby Surround–encoded, two-channel sources. Neo:6 Music keeps the front left and right channels intact while synthesizing the center and surround channels from the two-channel source. Neo:6 Cinema can create a 6.1-channel signal from two-channel movie sources.

The bottom line on DTS is that the DTS folks have some innovative algorithms, but the sheer prevalence of the Dolby solutions clearly makes Dolby Digital the most common choice for studios and home theater enthusiasts. Most A/V receivers offer both DTS and Dolby Digital options, so you can try them both and set your receiver (or choose your DVDs) to your preference.

Understanding the Next Generation of Surround Sound

The Dolby Digital EX and DTS-ES surround sound formats that bring 6.1- (or 7.1-) channel sound to your home theater are really great. But time marches on, technology improves, and surround sound keeps getting better. So it should come as no surprise that both companies have something new up their sleeves.

The advent of improved digital connections between disc players or set-top boxes and the receiver (connections like HDMI) and the enhanced data capacities of entirely new formats of recorded high-definition content (HD-DVD and Blu-ray) have made it possible for Dolby and DTS to launch new and improved surround sound formats that promise more channels, purer sound, and an improved surround sound experience.

None of the three new surround sound formats we discuss below are widely available yet — mainly because the high-definition DVD formats that will support them are not on the market as we write. (That's our way of breaking the bad news that, while all the formats are pretty much ready to go — so much so that we've managed to be blown away by them in demos and in labs — they're not really available to normal consumers yet.) Good things do come to those who wait, however.

Dolby Digital Plus

The folks at Dolby Laboratories have improved their super-popular Dolby Digital/Dolby Digital EX system and have created *Dolby Digital Plus*. Dolby Digital Plus improves upon Dolby Digital and EX by

- ✔ **Increasing the *bit rate*:** Dolby Digital Plus can be encoded with up to 6144 Kbps (kilobits per second) of data, where Dolby Digital tops out at 640 Kbps. (448 Kbps is the maximum from current formats, however.) In Chapter 5, we point out that higher bit rates, all else being equal, mean better sound quality because the audio signals need to be *compressed* less.

- ✔ **Improving the *encoding*:** Not only does Dolby Digital Plus provide a much higher bit rate, it also does a better job of encoding (or digitizing and compressing) sound. This means that, at a given bit rate, you get better sound quality. Combine this with the vastly increased bit rate of Dolby Digital Plus, and you get great sound!

- ✔ **Adding more channels:** Dolby Digital Plus can provide up to 13.1 discrete channels of sound (14 total speakers, including the subwoofer). You can really envelop yourself in the action with 14 speakers!

- ✔ **Providing backward compatibility:** Dolby Digital Plus decoders can automatically *downconvert* your sound to the older Dolby Digital formats. So you can play Dolby Digital Plus programs on your older system without having to buy any new hardware. And when you do upgrade, you gain all of the advantages mentioned above. Because the conversion process from Dolby Digital Plus to Dolby Digital outputs a 640 Kbps Dolby Digital stream, your existing system, which normally tops out at 448 Kbps, can actually sound better than ever before.

One drawback of Dolby Digital Plus is that the very high bit rates it supports overwhelm the digital audio connections that are traditionally used to connect DVD players or set-top boxes to your receiver. If all you have on your receiver is coaxial or optical digital connections, you'll still be able to listen to Dolby Digital Plus, but you'll have to get by with using analog audio connections or by letting your DVD player downconvert to 640 Kbps Dolby Digital. In the future, receivers with HDMI or FireWire (IEEE 1394) connections won't have this restriction, and you'll get the full Dolby Digital Plus experience because the decoded signals can be carried as multichannel PCM over these high-bandwidth interfaces without sonic compromise.

As we write, no receivers have the right HDMI or FireWire connections to handle Dolby Digital Plus digital bitstream connections from a disc player to the receiver. Luckily, new HD-DVD or Blu-ray players should have the appropriate circuitry to handle Dolby Digital Plus internally and send the decoded signal to your receiver via analog outputs, as a high-quality Dolby Digital output your receiver can handle, or as high-resolution PCM via HDMI.

Dolby Digital Plus is a *mandatory* format for HD-DVD and is optional for Blu-ray, so any player you buy for one of these formats should support Dolby Digital Plus. Dolby Digital Plus may also be used for other HDTV content — and may end up being encoded in a lot of the HDTV shows you get from your cable, satellite, or other TV service provider.

HD-DVD and Blu-ray discs and players are currently being produced with a limitation of 7.1-channel audio as a maximum, so you won't have that 13.1-channel sound we teased you with for a while. But the format can *eventually* grow into this many channels.

Dolby TrueHD

Dolby's other new format — one that gets us really excited! — is *Dolby TrueHD.*
Like Dolby Digital Plus, this format can support up to 13.1 channels of surround
sound goodness.

The big difference is that Dolby TrueHD is a *lossless* format. That means that
the sound being encoded into the Dolby TrueHD data stream will come out the
far end (at the decoder in your home theater) *exactly the same as it went in.* For
the first time ever, the home consumer will be able to experience multichannel
movie soundtracks exactly as they were heard in the mixing studio during content production. Most of the other surround sound formats we've discussed
(all of them, in fact, except for DTS-HD Master Audio, which we discuss in
the next section) are *lossy* — some data is discarded in the compression/
decompression process. With Dolby TrueHD, the audio track is bit-for-bit
identical to the studio master.

Dolby TrueHD uses the same MLP (Meridian Lossless Packing) encoding as
DVD-Audio (which we discuss in Chapter 5), but with an even higher bit rate,
which allows for more channels of high-resolution audio.

A lossy encoding system throws away bits of the audio (using sophisticated
acoustic modeling that determines what your ears actually do and don't
hear) in order to achieve greater compression of the audio. Greater compression is a good thing if you have a limited amount of storage space on a disc or
a limited amount of *bandwidth* (or data throughput) on your video transmission system (like cable or satellite). But if you have the space (or the bandwidth) — like Blu-ray and HD-DVD do — then you can compress your audio
less and get better sound quality.

You probably won't hear Dolby TrueHD on any broadcast HDTV programming any time soon because of the bandwidth issues we just mentioned, but
Dolby TrueHD support is mandatory for HD-DVD systems and is optional for
Blu-ray. So you'll be able to enjoy some really awesome lossless surround
sound when you watch a movie on one of these new disc formats.

Like Dolby Digital Plus, to listen to Dolby TrueHD, you'll either need to use an
HDMI or a FireWire connector to your receiver (these are still pretty rare as
we write) or have a Dolby TrueHD decoder inside your DVD player and use
analog connections to your receiver.

DTS-HD

The folks at DTS have developed their own lossless surround sound format
known as *DTS-HD Master Audio.* DTS-HD is an optional format on both Blu-ray

and HD-DVD and can provide (to begin with) up to 7.1 channels of lossless surround sound when it's used with one of these discs.

DTS-HD has the great feature of being backward compatible with the older variants of DTS. So while you will need a DTS-HD decoder to gain the full benefits of the lossless encoding that DTS-HD provides, you can still get great sound with your existing gear.

In fact, a DTS-HD-encoded HD-DVD or Blu-ray disc — when connected to an existing DTS-capable receiver — will be able to send a relatively high bit rate (1536 Kbps) surround signal to *any* existing DTS receiver. And while this same bit rate has been used on hundreds of conventional DVDs, this is about twice the bit rate of the average DVDs using DTS encoding, providing a good boost in sound quality.

Of course, when you have a DTS-HD decoder in the loop (we expect that DTS-HD-capable receivers will be shipping in the middle of 2006), you'll get that great lossless decoding and superb sound quality.

Other Key Audio Standards

In the realm of "music only" (and yes, we play a lot of music in our systems, in addition to movies and college basketball games and other video content), you might hear about a few other audio standards. We don't spend a ton of time beating these into your head — mainly because you don't need to do a lot to your system to accommodate them. With the exception of MP3s (which might take some special gear), these are things that you just plug in and they work.

1 want my MP3

MP3 is great for on-line music trading and downloading because it uses a compression scheme to make the files small enough to be easily downloaded. You don't find any MP3 music encoded in movies on DVD, nor will you (typically) find MP3-encoded music in stores. MP3 comes into play when you start getting involved in on-line music downloading or when you want to move your CD collection to a computer hard drive. We talk about these activities in more detail in Chapter 5.

MP3 is designed to be an efficient encoding system for taking big fat PCM music files and moving them into download-friendly computer files. MP3 trades a little sound quality for a lot of room. (It's another of those *lossy* compression systems, which means that the system removes some information.) So MP3 files are typically ten times smaller than the corresponding PCM files on a compact disc.

In Chapter 5, we discuss computer audio files in greater detail, including an in-depth discussion of the MP3 and other encoding systems used for these types of music files — like the AAC files used by Apple's iTunes and the WMA files used by Windows Media Player.

PCM is perfect

PCM (or Pulse Code Modulation) is not really perfect — nothing is. But it's pretty darn close. PCM is an older (but still vital) system for encoding analog music into a digital format that can be saved on a computer or "burned" onto a CD.

We say that PCM is nearly perfect because it's a *lossless* coding system, which means that what goes in comes out exactly the same, bit for bit. In a PCM world, none of the sound is thrown away. The only limitations to PCM are the accuracy, sample rate, and word length (the number of bits used to digitally capture a sound) of the analog-to-digital conversion process, all of which define the quality of the signal carried in the PCM format. If you have sharp ears and a good system, PCM-based files sound better than MP3s, for example. Traditional CDs are based on PCM, as are the sound files on many computers, such as .wav files on a Windows computer.

PCM isn't the only lossless system out there. Another one is MLP, or Meridian Lossless Packing, which is used by the new DVD-Audio format we discuss in Chapter 5. Another new audio format is the SACD, which we also discuss in Chapter 5. It uses its own coding format called DSD (or Direct Stream Digital).

You can also find some lossless codecs in the digital music file realm — both Apple's Apple Lossless compression system and Microsoft's Windows Media Audio Lossless compression system, for example, are lossless formats.

The bottom line here is that for the utmost in digital audio reproduction, lossless is the way to go.

Chapter 4

Getting the Big (Video) Picture

· ·

· ·

*W*e call the video portion of a home theater a *display.* Your display can be a direct-view television, a rear-projected television, a front-projected screen, a plasma or LCD screen, or even a properly painted wall (as long as you combine it with a projector).

Whatever its form factor, the video aspect of your home theater tends to be the main focus for many people. Let's face it — a big-screen display simply overpowers mere A/V source equipment and controllers. Big screens are just plain cool!

There's a lot to know about video formats, though, and in this chapter, we lay the groundwork for a more detailed discussion of specific video options in Part III.

Learning to Talk Videoese

Before we talk about the different kinds of analog and digital video, it's worthwhile to find out how to talk about video. Like any other technology, video has its own set of arcane terms and other jargon that makes casual listeners just want to give up. We promise not to lay too much on you here, but a few key concepts are essential:

✓ **Resolution:** Speaking in (very) general terms, resolution is basically the level of detail that your eyes (or a good pair of eyes, if yours have gotten a little blurry from too much time in front of the computer like ours have) can *resolve* (or see) on the screen. In the PC world, this is measured according to the number of *pixels* (the individual points of light and color) on your monitor. For example, older home-PC displays are set to show 800 x 600 pixels. Video systems are typically measured by the vertical number (the smaller of the two) — usually by measuring the *scan lines* that move across your screen (from left to right) and by adding up the number of these lines stacked on top of each other. Video systems typically display 480, 720, or 1,080 of these lines (though some displays — many plasma TVs, for example — have a nonstandard number of lines, like 768).

When you look at specs for a particular display, you might see resolution discussed in two related but different ways:

- **Display resolution:** Also called a display's *native resolution,* this is simply the number of pixels or lines of resolution that the display has on its screen. Most new TVs (with the exception of traditional CRT "tube" TVs, discussed in Chapter 13) have a *fixed* display resolution — meaning that they are physically built with a certain number of pixels and anything they display on the screen will consist of that number of pixels, regardless of the resolution of the video signal going into the display. Display resolution is what it says it is — the measure of your display's resolution.

- **Input resolutions:** Different video sources (like analog TV, DVDs, and high-definition TV [HDTV] signals) have their own resolution. For example, HDTV signals have 720 or 1,080 lines of resolution, while analog TV signals have 480 lines. A display's input resolutions are simply the resolutions of the video signals that the TV can accept and display. As an example, a specific high-definition display may have a display resolution of 720 lines but be able to accept inputs of 480, 720, and 1,080 lines of resolution — but will display the 1,080 signal at the lower 720 resolution. We talk more about display and input resolutions in Chapters 13 and 14.

- ✔ **Fields and frames:** This is a holdover from the film world, where each individual picture on a reel of film is called a *frame* (and 24 of them flash by the projector bulb each second). When TV was first developed, the technology of the day wouldn't allow full frames to be displayed at the rate at which TV signals worked, so each frame was divided into two *fields,* each of which contained half the scan lines we discuss in the preceding bullet (all the odd lines in one field, and all the evens in the other). Traditional TV systems display 60 fields every second — 30 frames per second — but the newest systems, discussed in the next bullet, can be capable of up to 60 *frames* per second.

- ✔ **Scanning method:** Up until very recently, just about all video systems (all the common ones, at least) used something called *interlaced* scanning, which we actually describe in the preceding bullet. In an interlaced system, half the lines are drawn on the screen in one cycle of the video system, and in the next cycle, the other half are drawn (not the top and the bottom, but weaving — or interlacing — every other line). Because this happens really fast (each set of lines is drawn 30 times per second), your eye can't really tell that things are being drawn this way — unless you stop to think about the flickering you see and the way some vertical and diagonal lines on your TV screen appear jagged. *Progressive scan* systems (see Figure 4-1) draw all the lines (a whole frame) at the same time and can help reduce these characteristics. The effect is a picture that is more like film, which is what we're shooting for in a home theater.

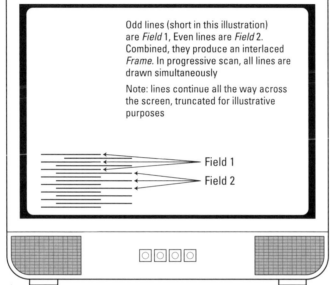

Odd lines (short in this illustration) are *Field* 1, Even lines are *Field* 2. Combined, they produce an interlaced *Frame*. In progressive scan, all lines are drawn simultaneously

Note: lines continue all the way across the screen, truncated for illustrative purposes

Field 1
Field 2

Figure 4-1:
Comparing interlaced video and progressive-scan video.

Making film into video

As if resolution and scan methods were not complex enough, you may run into something called *3:2 pulldown removal or correction,* or simply *3:2 pulldown.* This is a process that deals with the fact that an extra field (screen) image appears when the 24-frames-per-second films are transferred to 30 frames per second for TV (or 60 fields). See, when you take 24 frames and make them fill a 60-field space, your system copies each field two or three times, in alternating sequence, to fill the 60 fields required. This creates *motion artifacts* that appear like jerky movements on the screen when you look closely.

What 3:2 pulldown does is remove that extra third field, so the original balance between frames is restored. You want a progressive-scan DVD player with great 3:2 pulldown removal. You can tell how good it is by looking at sharp lines on the screen, such as telephone wires or porch railings. Many high-definition TVs have their own 3:2 pulldown systems built in as well, in case your DVD player can't do this for you.

Switching from Analog to Digital

Television is undergoing some radical changes — and we're not talking about programming. Like most other devices before it, the television is beginning to make the leap from the analog to the digital world. Unlike many of those devices, however, TV has been making the leap in a series of agonizingly slow steps. In this section, we discuss how this transition might affect your choices in the video world. We talk also about the various kinds of TVs you can buy.

The conversion from analog to digital and old-style TV to next-generation TV comes into play in many places:

- ✔ The encoding of the programming signal itself — whether it goes onto a DVD or over a cable to get to your home theater
- ✔ The transmission (or production) path that the signal takes in getting to your house
- ✔ The receiver — internal or external — that receives and decodes the signal for display

In the progression of standards and technical development, change is taking place along all three of these paths.

Understanding the old standard: The analog signal

The majority of television signals coming into homes are still analog. Analog TV signals reach homes through over-the-air broadcast TV, by traditional cable TV systems, and by satellite.

In North America, an analog system known as NTSC (National Television Standards Committee) has been in place for decades. (The standard is over 60 years old, having been first developed in the 1940s!) In fact, it hasn't been changed or updated since the advent of color television in the 1960s. Although this system is capable of producing a surprisingly good picture under ideal circumstances, its analog nature makes it susceptible to various kinds of interference and signal degradation. Consequently, the picture can be down-right awful by the time it actually gets to your television, which is why the TV world is slowly turning digital.

Analog television displays a maximum of 480 scan lines (525 total, but you can't see them all because some are used for things such as closed captioning), displays 30 frames (60 fields) per second, and is an interlaced system. See "Learning to Talk Videoese," earlier in this chapter, for explanations of these specs.

Just as the NTSC standard is common in North America (and Japan), a couple of other standards — known as PAL and SECAM — are common in other parts of the world. Unless you have a special TV designed for the purpose, you can't tune into PAL broadcasts with an NTSC TV or NTSC with a PAL TV. This is one reason why you can't buy videotapes in many parts of the world and use them in the United States.

Anticipating the rise of digital TV

The move from analog to digital is well afoot. Millions of homes have some form of digital TV, but the conversion from analog to digital is still an evolving process. The key concept behind any kind of digital TV is that the audio and video programming is converted from an analog signal into a series of digital bits (a whole lot of ones and zeros). The primary technology behind any kind of digital TV (at least in the United States and Canada — other countries have their own variant of digital TV) is something called *MPEG* (Motion Picture Experts Group).

Several video and audio compression and digitization standards are based on MPEG. Most are named by adding a number to the end of *MPEG*. The MPEG-2 standard is by far the most common in the video world, with MPEG-4 coming on strong. (Another, older, standard, MPEG-1 is also supported by DVDs and is used for the VideoCD, which is more common outside of the U.S.)

The digital television (cable or satellite) signal and DVDs that most people receive today use MPEG-2 as their encoding to digitally transport or store standard, analog NTSC signals. This is an important fact to repeat: Typically, when you use a digital TV system (such as a DSS satellite system) or a prerecorded digital source (such as a DVD), you get an analog signal that has been transmitted or stored digitally. The signal itself — the program that goes into your TV — is still analog. Digital over digital is our nirvana and is here now, but only for some programming, as we discuss shortly.

As you might have suspected, high-definition TV — which is becoming much more widely available, but which still makes up only a small fraction of the total TV landscape — is digital all the way.

Even though the video signal coming out of a DVD player is NTSC (an interlaced format, as we mentioned above), some DVD players can convert this into a progressive-scan version of NTSC, which you can use if you have a progressive-scan TV.

When this digitized signal gets to your house (over a digital cable system, a DBS satellite system, or on a DVD), a set-top box, satellite receiver, or DVD player converts the signal back to analog NTSC TV, which your TV understands and can display. This digital transmission signal coming into your house usually looks and sounds better than an analog one because the digital transmission path is cleaner and isn't susceptible to the interference that usually messes up analog signals. The same is true of DVD versus analog sources, such as laser discs and VCR tapes. Digital is always better.

You can get better-quality analog content on DVD, and higher-quality DVDs are available. For instance, you might run across Superbit DVD, which is a Sony system for superencoding (using more digital bits and bytes to store) DVD content. Superbit DVD follows the existing DVD format, so you don't need a special player to play a Superbit DVD. These discs simply use storage space that's normally taken up by fancy on-screen menus and extra features (such as movie trailers and outtakes) to store more encoding (about double the bits) for the movie signal itself. The result is a much more stunning picture.

Better DVDs — ones that can display a full high-definition picture (with a much greater resolution than NTSC) — are on their way soon. By the time you read this, the first Blu-ray and HD-DVD discs and players will be on the market, providing the first disc-based true high-definition sources for your home theater. We talk about these new disc formats in Chapter 6.

The real takeaway we want you to understand here is that many things that are called "digital" — like most (but not all) digital cable, digital satellite TV services, and "regular" DVDs (that is, DVDs that aren't using the new Blu-ray or HD-DVD formats) — provide you with a nice digital picture that is not high-definition TV. These digital video signals are (usually) just the same resolution as the older analog TV signal — they're simply stored and/or transmitted by digital systems. There's nothing wrong with these digital systems (they're great, in fact!), but we mention this because we have run into many people who think that digital cable or digital satellite or DVD is the same thing as HDTV, and that's just not true.

Looking toward the next generation of digital TV

Most of today's digital television isn't all it can be. Several years ago, the FCC (the Federal Communications Commission, the controlling regulatory authority for broadcasters, cable companies, and telephone companies in the United States) brought together a big bunch of television industry folks. After a long, painful, and contentious process, the group came up with a new generation of digital TV. This new system goes by the catchy name ATSC (Advanced Television Standards Committee) and follows a bunch of new, higher-definition television standards.

Introducing ATSC

Specifically, ATSC uses digital-video signals (not analog ones) that are transmitted using digital technologies and are played on TVs set up to display these digital signals. Even the connection to the TV itself is digital. "It's digital all the way, baby," as sportscaster Dick Vitale would say. (Did we mention we're Duke Blue Devils fans, too? Nothing better than watching Duke basketball in high definition on the big screen!)

Many people call ATSC *digital TV* or *DTV.* We do, too, sometimes, but we're going to stick with the name ATSC in this discussion to help keep the difference between ATSC and other digital television services (like digital cable or digital satellite TV) distinct. Aren't we user-friendly?

Even though ATSC is all digital, all the time, TVs that are designed for ATSC can also connect to good old analog NTSC systems. And some of the stuff coming in over an ATSC system *is* NTSC. For example, most commercials will probably continue to be taped using NTSC systems for quite some time, and the vast majority of reruns will be NTSC as well (although these NTSC signals will be carried digitally over the ATSC system).

ATSC television standards are different from the digital cable or satellite TV we discuss in the preceding section. To view them in all their glory (and we've seen enough of high-definition television to tell you that it is indeed glorious), you need to buy the newer, fancier, better, more expensive TV — an HDTV.

Exploring HDTV

When we talk about new ATSC-capable televisions, we're talking a whole new ballgame (or at least a whole new way to watch a ballgame). It takes only a glance to see the striking difference between older NTSC displays and the new ATSC ones.

ATSC signals can be divided into different groups, depending on the signal's resolution and the scanning method (which we discuss in the beginning of this chapter). They are further divided into

- ✔ **SDTV (standard-definition television):** These signals are about the same or a little bit better than NTSC.

  Note: A related category here is *EDTV,* or enhanced-definition television, which is essentially a widescreen version of NTSC.

- ✔ **HDTV (high-definition television):** HDTV has truly spectacular — dare we say filmlike? — picture quality.

Within the ATSC standard are 18 SDTV, EDTV, and HDTV variations, but you're most likely to see just six, as shown in Table 4-1.

Table 4-1	Common Digital-TV Variants		
Name	**Resolution**	**Scanning Method**	**Quality**
480i	640 x 480	Interlaced	Standard definition (same as NTSC)
480p	640 x 480 (normal)	Progressive	Standard definition
480p	720 x 480 (widescreen)	Progressive	Enhanced definition (EDTV)

(continued)

Table 4-1 *(continued)*

Name	Resolution	Scanning Method	Quality
720p	1280 x 720	Progressive	High definition
1080i	1920 x 1080	Interlaced	High definition
1080p	1920 x 1080	Progressive	High definition

You sharp readers will probably note that we threw an extra format in here that's not currently available in any digital TV broadcast (or cable system or satellite system) but which may become available some day in the future. That's the final one — 1080p — which has become something of a holy grail amongst TV manufacturers even though there are no 1080p signals available to display on such a set. 1080p is simply a progressive-scan variant of 1080i. The forthcoming Blu-ray and HD-DVD disc formats may support it, and certain video games on the new Microsoft Xbox 360 and forthcoming Sony PlayStation 3 may support it as well, but there are no, we repeat, *no* TV signals today or in the near future that will be 1080p. We mention it for completeness's sake and because you'll hear it all the time when you go shopping. We'll get into 1080p in more detail in the chapters in which we talk about TVs and displays (Chapters 13 and 14, to be precise).

Theoretically, a progressive-scan system has a better picture than an interlaced one, but in our minds, resolution is more important (not everyone agrees). We'd rather have 1080i than 720p if given the choice. But we'd take either kind of HDTV over anything else. It's just awesome to see HDTV in action.

To take advantage of *all* the benefits of digital TV, you need to have a high-definition-capable television and some sort of TV *tuner* that can decode the ATSC signal. That tuner can be inside the display (just as most TVs have analog NTSC tuners), it can be in a separate tuner component, or it can even come inside a satellite TV receiver or cable set-top box.

Traditional televisions don't have the internal circuitry to decode digital TV signals, and they generally don't have screens that can display high-definition ATSC pictures in all their glory. (And HDTV is the big deal in this story — we focus our discussion on HDTV rather than SDTV.)

Traditional TVs aren't even the "right" shape. The *aspect ratio* (the ratio of screen width to height) of HDTV signals is wider than that of NTSC signals. NTSC is 4:3; HDTV is 16:9. Figure 4-2 shows the difference in aspect ratios. The HDTV screen has an aspect ratio like the elongated screens in movie theaters. (You may have already been exposed to this aspect ratio because many movie DVDs today allow for this sort of viewing as an option. See the sidebar, "Wide, wider, widest: Aspect ratios," later in this chapter.)

A lot of people see 4:3 and 16:9, do the math quickly in their heads, and think they are the same thing. It's confusing because 4 and 3 are the square roots of 16 and 9. The actual math used to determine the ratio of screen width to screen height is 16 *divided* by 9 (which rounds out to 1.78) and 4 *divided* by 3 (which is 1.33). So for a given display height, a 16:9 screen is about 34 percent wider than a 4:3 screen.

Figure 4-2:
An HDTV screen is much wider than today's NTSC screen.

4:3 / 1.33:1 Standard TV and older movies	16:9 / 1.78:1 US Digital TV (HDTV)	1.85:1 Standard Widescreen	2.35:1 Anamorphic Widescreen (Panavision or Cinemascope)

HDTV-capable TV sets, which became available at the end of 1998, are more expensive than traditional sets. However, prices have come down significantly. Just three or four years ago, HDTVs often cost more than $6,000, but now you can get one for $1,000 or less. In fact, you can buy a small (27-inch or less) "tube" HDTV for under $500.

Wide, wider, widest: Aspect ratios

Aspect ratios are one of the more confusing parts of video, although they used to be simple. That's because television and movie content was all about the same size, 4:3 (also known as 1.33:1, meaning that the picture is 1.33 times as long as it is high). The Academy (as in, "I'd like to thank the Academy") Standard before 1952 was 1.37:1, so there was virtually no problem showing movies on TV.

However, as TV began to cut into Hollywood's take at the theater, the quest was on to differentiate theater offerings in ways that could not be seen on TV. Thus, innovations such as widescreen film, Technicolor, and even 3-D were born.

Widescreen film was one of the innovations that survived and has since dominated the cinema.

Today, you tend to find films in one of two widescreen aspect ratios:

✔ Academy Standard (or "Flat"), which has an aspect ratio of 1.85:1.

✔ Anamorphic Scope (or "Scope"), which has an aspect ratio of 2.35:1. Scope is also called Panavision or CinemaScope.

HDTV is specified at a 16:9, or 1.78:1, aspect ratio.

If your television isn't widescreen and you want to watch a widescreen film, you have a problem. And the industry powers that be have come up with two solutions (other than "go out and buy a widescreen display").

The most common approach in the past has been what's called *Pan and Scan*. For each frame of a

(continued)

(continued)

film, a decision is made as to what constitutes the action area. That part of the film frame is retained, and the rest is lost. What's left is usually a fraction of the main frame, sometimes as little as 65 percent of it, and this can often leave out the best parts of a picture. Imagine some of the scenes from *Gunfight at OK Corral* with the two gunslingers at each end of the picture. One of the gunfighters would have to go off the screen in Pan and Scan.

The second (and growing more popular) approach is to display the original full image on the TV set without filling the whole screen. When watching content formatted for a widescreen TV (1.85:1, 2.35:1, and so on), you see black bars at the top and bottom of the image. This technique is known as *letterboxing* (after the effect of seeing an image through an open mail slot in a door). Conversely, when watching content formatted for TV (4:3) on a widescreen TV, you see black bars on the left and right of the images. This is known as *windowboxing*.

An obvious problem with viewing widescreen images on a normal 4:3 TV is that the image does not use all 480 scanning lines of the screen. Some of those 480 lines get used just to draw black bars instead of drawing video you actually watch. (Some 4:3 TVs use a technique called *anamorphic squeeze* to eliminate this issue.) This yields lower resolution, something that anamorphic formats attempt to resolve. Also known as *16:9 Enhanced, Widescreen Enhanced,* or *Enhanced for 16:9 Televisions,* anamorphic presentation squeezes the image horizontally until the full 4:3 frame is filled. If you look at an anamorphic picture on a 4:3 screen, the picture appears somewhat distorted because everything is compressed, but the full 480 lines of content are retained. Luckily, when you tell your DVD player you have a 4:3 screen, it puts the anamorphic image back into a letterbox. When played through a 16:9 player, the original width is presented, while maintaining the full 480 vertical lines of resolution.

Most DVDs have both a Pan and Scan and a widescreen format (either letterboxed or anamorphic) on a DVD. Because including both versions creates an added expense to the studios, some DVDs ship with just one format onboard, and some titles actually have different formats on different discs. Be sure to check before you buy a disc if this is important to you.

As an interesting note, there are a few examples (Pixar's *Finding Nemo* being the most famous) where movie producers have specially modified their content to have different widescreen and 4:3 versions — so the folks with 4:3 displays aren't robbed of part of the image while still filling their screens.

We talk a lot more about HDTVs in Chapters 13 and 14.

After the switch to digital TV is complete, you don't have to pitch your old TVs. Special, separate digital TV tuners (much like set-top boxes used for older TVs on cable networks) enable you to watch DTV programming on older TVs. Of course, the picture quality and resolution won't be as high as it would be with a new digital set, and you might not have a widescreen (16:9) aspect ratio, but you'll see (at today's resolutions and quality) the programming coming in over tomorrow's digital networks.

Part II
What Are You Going to Watch?: Source Devices

In this part . . .

Part II builds on the basics with more detailed coverage of all the things that you might want to drive your home theater — the *source devices* that feed audio and video into your system.

We start at the, er, source of 21st-century entertainment — audio sources. These range from the venerable AM/FM tuners up to the fanciest MP3 players. After that, it's on to the video realm, where we talk about things like DVDs, VCRs, and PVRs (personal video recorders) — and even how you can bore your neighbors with home movies on your home theater. Yawn!

Then we discuss sources from outside your home — cable, broadcast TV, satellite, and even new services that offer you video on demand and other network-based content.

Then comes the really fun stuff — the gaming systems. Whether your heart is in Xbox, Nintendo, or Sony, you'll want to know how to set these up — even if you don't have kids. (Since Pat's little Annabel is just two years old, he had to use this book as the main argument to his wife for buying a new Xbox 360.)

PCs are on tap next, and we help you understand how to really take advantage of all the audio and video sources that the Internet has to offer and how to get them into your home theater system. We help you understand how to download movies (legally) off the Internet to watch whenever you want to and how to record those episodes of *The Sopranos* that you keep missing.

We close this part with the really cool component in your home theater — content accessed over the Internet. Whether it's watching Google videos or TV shows you downloaded — either via iTunes or with the help of some more specialized device such as Akimbo — we'll help you make your home theater Internet savvy.

Chapter 5

Treating Your Ears to Music

A home theater is about more than just movies and TV. Most people spend as much money on the audio side of their home theaters as they do on their video equipment.

In this chapter, we discuss the components you might add to a home theater system for listening to prerecorded music and audio broadcasts (what we used to call *radio* back in the old days — but it's more than just AM/FM now).

Checking Out Your CD Player Options

Since the CD format debuted in the 1980s, tens of billions of CDs have been pressed. So it goes without saying that you need a CD player in your home theater, right? Well, actually, that was a trick question.

Although you *definitely* want your home theater to have a device that can play CDs, you may not need (or want) a traditional CD player in your system. Your DVD player, which we think you absolutely must have in your home theater, can do double duty as your system's CD player. You can also play CDs on the game consoles we talk about in Chapter 9, or you can use a home theater–ready PC, which we discuss in Chapter 8.

Despite this, you might want a standalone CD player (instead of using another device to play your CDs) for the following reasons:

- ✔ **You are shooting for the highest-quality CD reproduction:** If you're a real audiophile, you might want to spend a considerable chunk of cash on a fancy, no-holds-barred, top-of-the-line CD player that can eke that last little bit of musical fidelity out of a disc. If so, check out companies like Arcam, Naim, and Rega, which make fancy and expensive ($1,000 and up) CD players.

- ✔ **You want special CD features:** Some people buy jukebox CD players that can hold hundreds of CDs (so they never need to load a new disc after the hours-long initial setup). Others want a CD player that can also burn (create) CDs. Keep in mind that these features are percolating over into the DVD world as well, but for now, the CD versions of these devices are much cheaper.

- ✔ **You are creating a multizone system:** In a multizone system (which we discuss in Chapter 10), you can listen to different source components in different rooms. For example, you can watch a movie on the DVD player in the home theater while the kids listen to a CD in the kitchen. You can't do that if the DVD player is your only CD player.

These three reasons are all perfectly valid — for some people. Don't let them scare you into buying a CD player. Today's DVD players do a great job of playing back CDs, so skipping over the standalone CD player is a good way to save a few bucks.

Choosing a CD Player

So you know you want a standalone CD player, but which one? If you already have a CD player, go ahead and use it. The following list highlights some things you might want to look for if you choose to buy a CD player (or aren't sure about the one you have):

- ✔ **Digital outputs:** You can often get better sound out of a CD player if you connect it to your receiver via a digital connection instead of an analog one. On the back of most CD players, you can find one (or both) of two kinds of digital outputs — optical and coaxial — which are equal in quality. (We discuss these in Chapter 16.) The key thing to consider, however, is finding out what kind of inputs you have on your receiver and buying your CD player accordingly.

- ✔ **The ability to play CD-Rs, CD-RWs, WMAs, and MP3s:** If you're into burning your own CDs or like to listen to others' homemade CDs, make sure the player you buy has these buzzwords on the box. Otherwise, you won't be able to listen to those homemade discs.

✔ **Multidisc capability:** If you like to load up the CD player with a bunch of CDs, consider a CD changer, which usually holds five to ten discs, or a CD jukebox that can hold hundreds.

✔ **Remote control:** Many manufacturers have special connectors that can go between their components (like a CD player and a receiver) to facilitate controlling everything from a single remote control. For example, with Sony's S-Link, a Sony receiver and remote can control a whole bunch of different Sony devices. As you shop for a CD player, keep your receiver in mind, but if you're set on, say, a Sony CD player and a Pioneer receiver, don't let the remote options hold you back. It's very easy to get a universal remote control that can operate gear from different vendors.

In addition, always look for some basic quality measures when you're choosing gear. For example, does the CD tray open and close smoothly? Can you read the display from across the room? Before you buy, always try to test drive gear in the showroom or your home (if you're shopping at the high end).

The New Kids on the Block — SACD and DVD-A

The CD is overwhelmingly the most common source of prerecorded music in a disc format, but around the turn of the millennium, two new formats hit the streets — SACD (Super Audio Compact Disc) and the DVD-Audio disc.

Both formats are designed to sound better than a CD while maintaining that familiar, 12cm (quick — grab that metric converter) disc format. Although you may remember the marketing tag line, "Perfect sound, forever," from when CDs debuted, SACD and DVD-A have managed to improve upon the now old-fashioned CD:

✔ **Sampling:** SACD uses very small sample sizes but records them 64 times more often than regular CDs. The DVD-Audio system uses a lower sampling rate (still two or more times faster than CD), but a much larger sample (20 bits or more, compared with 16 for CDs). Either way, you get higher audio frequencies with less noise and thus greater *dynamic range* (the difference between the quietest and loudest musical passages on the disc).

✔ **Multichannel format:** Because the discs can hold more data than the older CD format, record companies can release DVD-Audio and SACD discs in both traditional 2-channel (stereo) and home-theater-friendly 5.1-channel formats (with five channels of surround sound and a sub-woofer channel). Some folks don't particularly like the surround sound for music; they say it makes sense only for movies, where things are happening all around you. But lots of others, us included, like surround sound for at least some of the music we listen to.

Some of the early SACD players didn't support the multichannel format, though all the current models we know of do. Also, not all SACD or DVD-Audio discs are recorded in surround sound format.

Both the SACD and the DVD-A have been tested by the experts, measured by the measurers, and reviewed by the reviewers, and the consensus is that both sound better than CD. How much better is a matter of great debate, but in a high-quality system, with a good recording, you'll probably be happy to have one of these systems. Before you buy, though, keep three things in mind:

✔ **You can't find much material in either of these formats . . . yet.** Chances are, you can't buy all your favorites on these formats. A lot of classic recordings have been reissued in one or the other format, but the number is still small compared to all of the music out there.

✔ **Not all players can play both formats.** Unless you are committed to only one or the other format (SACD or DVD-A), make sure you choose a "universal" player that can play CD, DVD, SACD, and DVD-A. Pay attention because some manufacturers (notably Sony, who was the primary technical supporter of SACD) don't make many (or even any) universal players.

Most SACD players and DVD-Audio players *do* play regular CDs and regular DVDs, which is nice. Look for ones that can play MP3s, CD-Rs, and CD-RWs, as well, so that you can play homemade CDs, too.

✔ **Because of copy-protection concerns, you might not be able to connect your DVD-Audio or SACD player to your receiver *digitally*.** This means that all that high-resolution audio must travel to your receiver in the analog domain, making the audio more susceptible to picking up noises or generally degrading during its trip to your ears. To make matters worse, multichannel systems require six of these analog cables. Ugh. Luckily, as we write, a few manufacturers have begun to come out with matched A/V receivers and DVD-Audio players that let you use a single digital connector (usually a FireWire cable — see Chapter 16) to connect these devices — but only if you buy both from that manufacturer.

Many home theater receivers have only a single set of multichannel audio inputs. So if you use them to connect an SACD/DVD-A player, they won't be available for other multichannel audio inputs (like an external surround sound decoder or a DVD player with a built-in surround sound decoder). Keep that in mind as you're shopping around.

Neither SACD nor DVD-Audio have really taken off in the marketplace. Both formats sound great, but many folks have begun to move toward on-line music (like Apple's iTunes Music Store) and computer-based audio and away from these higher–quality, disc-based, audio formats. We think that you can't go wrong with a nice universal disc player that handles both formats, but unless you're really an audiophile and have (or plan to buy) a bunch of discs in these formats, you really don't have to spend too much time worrying about SACD or DVD-Audio. The bottom line: Get a universal player if the DVD player you're shopping for includes this functionality, but don't go out of your way for one of these formats unless you're really sure you're going to be using it.

Many SACD discs, like ABKO Records's newly remastered editions of the classic 1960s Rolling Stones CDs, are *dual layer*. This means that there is a layer of CD data *and* a layer of SACD data on the same disc, so you can play the same disc in your car and in your home theater SACD player. You can't do that with a DVD-Audio disc today — at least not until someone comes up with dual-layer DVD-A discs. There are, however, discs known as *DualDiscs* (www.dualdisc.com) that include a CD on one side and a DVD on the other. Note that this isn't DVD-Audio, but rather a regular DVD, which can include video and even a surround sound mix of the record, but which isn't in the higher resolution DVD-Audio format.

Moving Computer Audio into Your Home Theater

The really big trend in audio these days (for the past several years, in fact) is computer-based audio files. At the simplest level, these files are just like any other file on your computer, except that they contain digitally encoded music files that you can play back on your computer, on a portable device, or in your home theater.

MP3 is the most common format for digitally storing music and other audio files on a computer or computer-like device, but it's not the only format out there. A few others, such as Microsoft's Windows Media (WMA) and Advanced

Audio Codec (or AAC, used by Apple's iTunes Music Store), are also incredibly common — and are the formats most often used for music *purchased* on the Internet.

We use the term MP3 to refer to on-line music here, because it's still the most common music format, but on-line music files may be encoded using other file formats (as we discuss throughout the chapter).

MP3-mania has exploded worldwide over the past couple of years, initially because on-line services such as Napster (now dead as a file-sharing program but reborn as an on-line music store — www.napster.com) and KaZaa (www.kazaa.com) have enabled people to share and download songs converted from CDs to the MP3 format. MP3 has retained its popularity because its small file size has made it a very attractive system for carrying music around on computer-like portable audio players, such as our (and everybody's!) current favorite, Apple's iPod (www.apple.com/ipod), or Creative Lab's ZENMICRO (www.creative.com).

Lots of people are moving their MP3 files beyond the PC and the portable player these days and are beginning to find ways to incorporate MP3 music into the home theater. This makes a lot of sense to us — why not listen to all your MP3s on the highest-quality audio system in the house?

Learning about digital audio file types

As we mention in the previous section, MP3 is not the only game in town when it comes to digital audio file formats — other formats, like AAC and WMA, are becoming increasingly popular due to their use in on-line music stores.

There are two main categories of these audio formats (often called *codecs* — from their function, which is to *compress* and *decompress* music into digital files). The first category includes *lossless* codecs. This means that all of the musical information that forms the basis of the audio file is preserved when the file is compressed and stored on the computer. Lossless codecs provide the highest audio fidelity, but the files they create are relatively large, which means that you can fit fewer songs on a computer hard drive or music server.

Lossy codecs, on the other hand, discard some part of the musical information in order to make the files smaller — for faster downloads on the Internet or to cram more music on a given size of computer storage device. These lossy codecs use sophisticated models of the human ear (and how it hears sounds) to throw away bits of musical information that are *less important* when you are listening to the music. You probably won't notice the difference when listening casually, but many people (especially folks with good hearing!) can hear a difference when a lossy and lossless version of the same music are played back over a high-quality home theater audio system.

The most common lossless codecs you'll run across are as follows:

- **Windows Media Lossless:** Part of Microsoft Windows Media Player 9 and 10, this codec is built into the Windows Media Player software and is supported by some of the media adapter systems we discuss in Chapter 10.

- **Apple Lossless:** Included with iTunes software, Apple's Lossless Encoder is Apple's competitor to Windows Media Lossless.

- **Free Lossless Audio Codec (FLAC):** Free Lossless Audio Codec is, as its name implies, a lossless codec that is free. It's part of an open source initiative, and you can find out more at `http://flac.sourceforge.net`. A few of the audio players we discuss in Chapter 10 are beginning to support the FLAC codec, including the Sonos Digital Music System and the Slim Devices Squeezebox.

Among the most popular lossy codecs are the following:

- **MP3:** MPEG (Motion Picture Experts Group) 1 Audio Layer 3 is the full name of the most common digital music format. MP3 audio files are the ones commonly traded (usually illegally) on the Net, and they are the most common digital music codec used on PCs and digital music systems in a wireless network.

  A limited number of systems and software applications also support the more advanced *mp3PRO* codec, which adds a technology called *SBR* (or Spectral Band Replication) to improve the sound quality over standard MP3-encoded music files.

- **WMA:** Windows Media Audio is the standard audio format used by the Windows Media Player and compatible hardware. A lossless version of WMA (discussed earlier) does exist, but most WMA files use a lossy compression system.

- **AAC:** Advanced Audio Codec is the format used by Apple Computer's popular iTunes Music Store and is the default codec used for music encoded using the iTunes application. Like WMA, AAC files are lossy (though within Apple's iTunes system there is a lossless codec as well, called Apple Lossless).

- **Ogg Vorbis:** Another free codec is Ogg Vorbis (`www.vorbis.com`). Ogg Vorbis is designed to be free from the licensing fees that software and hardware companies must pay for other codecs like MP3, while providing improved sound quality compared to other lossy codecs.

Your choice of codec will depend upon a couple of things:

- ✔ **Where you get your music from.** If you buy digital music at an on-line music store, you're stuck with the codec that they use. Most stores use WMA or AAC and not MP3 because these formats allow the record companies to stick *DRM* (digital rights management) software into the music files, which keeps buyers from sharing this music on the Internet. If you create your own music from CDs at home, your choice will be influenced by the software you use.

- ✔ **The devices you use to play your music in your home theater.** As we discuss in Chapter 10, there are a large number of devices (usually called *media players* or *adapters*) that you can use to get music from a computer into your home theater. Most of these devices support only a limited number of codecs, so you have to match the codec you use to create and store digital music with those supported by your media player.

- ✔ **Personal preference also comes into play.** Many folks simply find that they prefer a lossless codec or that they prefer a codec like AAC (which is "newer" and takes advantage of advances in codec technology) to one like MP3. We recommend that, after you've figured out the first two criteria, you "try out" a few different codecs and see if you can tell a difference.

We talk in great detail about the sources for digital music and also about the devices that you can use to integrate this music into your home theater in Chapter 10. The Media Center PCs we discuss in Chapter 8 are also a great way to get digital audio into your home theater.

Getting your hands on MP3s

We bet you've heard a lot about MP3 music, but where do all these MP3s come from, anyway? Is there an MP3 fairy out there who magically dumps them on the hard drives of good girls and boys?

Well, in fact, there used to be something pretty similar. Napster (which is now gone, due to legal actions) and other file-sharing services allowed people to put their music collections on-line and share them with the world. Of course, record companies weren't all that supportive of this grassroots music revolution, so most of these services got sued out of existence soon after starting.

Today, you can get your own MP3 files (and notice we call them files, because they're just that — computer data files on a hard drive) in two legal ways:

- ✔ **Rip your own:** You can convert your CDs to MP3s on your computer (this process is called *ripping*). To do this, you need a PC with a CD or DVD drive (which we bet you already have) and an MP3 program. Our favorite programs are MUSICMATCH Jukebox for Windows (www.musicmatch.com) and iTunes for the Mac and Windows (www.apple.com/itunes).

 ✔ **Download legally:** These days, it's really easy to find legal places to download the most popular music on MP3 (or in AAC or WMA formats). Some of our favorite on-line music stores include Apple's iTunes Music Store (available within Apple's iTunes software or at `www.apple.com/itunes/`) and Rhapsody (`www.rhapsody.com`). We talk about a bunch of these stores in Chapter 10.

Old-School Jams — Turntables

For most of the world, the LP has unfortunately gone the way of the dodo. But although LPs are far from the public eye, they've never really gone away. Many artists still release LP versions of their new records, and a handful of small manufacturers (and a few big ones) continue to crank out turntables.

In fact, the turntable has become hip again in some circles. And many audiophiles have long felt that LPs (at least when played on super-high-quality turntables) sound better than CDs.

Buying a turntable isn't as simple as buying a CD, DVD-A, or SACD player. It's a much more subjective process. In the digital world, it's easy to keep a checklist of features in mind, such as digital output or MP3 CD support. But when you start shopping for turntables, you're really getting into a whole different world. There's some really esoteric stuff out there, such as vacuum hold-down systems (which suck the record flat on the platter to alleviate warps), and there are what we call "religious wars" between proponents of different turntable design philosophies. Having said that, here are a few things to consider when buying a turntable:

 ✔ **Belt drive or direct drive:** The platter (the thing that the record sits and spins around on) can be spun in two ways. There are pros and cons for each.

 • **Belt drive:** In this setup, the motor is separated from the platter and spindle and turned by a rubber belt that runs around the outside of the platter. A belt drive tends to isolate the rest of the turntable from any vibrations coming from the motor (vibrations that the stylus or needle could pick up and transmit to the receiver and to your ears). On the downside, a belt drive tends to be less accurate than a direct drive in its playback speed, which can lead to changes in the pitch of your music.

 • **Direct drive:** An electric motor is directly attached to the spindle (the small cylinder that the platter rests upon). Direct drive turntables tend to be a bit more constant in their speed, so the turntable is more likely to turn 33⅓ times per minute without any speed variations (such variations tend to make your music sound warbly).

Some folks, however, feel that direct drive turntables are more susceptible to vibrations (both external, like footsteps, and internal, like the vibrations of the motor itself).

✔ **Suspended or unsuspended:** Vibrations are a big deal with a turntable because the stylus dragging through the grooves of the LP can pick up extraneous vibrations (like those caused by your feet walking across the floor) and transmit them along with your music. Some turntables have elaborate suspension systems designed to isolate the platter (and therefore the record) from these vibrations, whereas others rely on the user to isolate the *entire* turntable (by placing the whole thing on a very sturdy rack, for example).

✔ **Automatic, semiautomatic, or manual:** An automatic turntable lets you put a record on the platter, push a button, and listen. The turntable itself moves the tone arm over the record, drops it down before the first song, and then lifts it up and returns it to the resting position when the side of the record is done. High-end audiophiles *hate* these because they — well, we don't know why they hate them so much, though we guess they just love to drop that needle down. Manual turntables require you to manually move the tone arm over the record and then lower it onto and off the record. Semiautomatics do half your work for you — you lower the stylus onto the record, but when the record side is finished playing, the turntable lifts the tone arm and stylus up off the record automatically so you don't have to hear that repeating *fpppt fpppt fpppt* sound as the stylus does an endless loop at the end of the record.

In our opinion, good turntables can have any of the attributes we just mentioned. We've heard good automatic turntables and good manuals, good belt drives and good direct drives, and so on. If you're buying a turntable, think about what your needs are. Do you have a lot of records that you're going to play all the time? If so, invest $500 to $1,000 dollars in a nice turntable from a company such as Rega (www.rega.co.uk) or Pro-Ject (www.project-audio.com). Have just a couple of old favorites you can't get on CD? Check out some of the $150 to $200 models from Sony or Denon. Want to be a DJ (and do some scratching like the late, great Jam Master Jay)? Check out Panasonic's Technics brand of DJ turntables.

Whatever you do, don't leave a turntable out of the equation if you have a few boxes of records in the closet.

Because LPs are much less popular than they used to be, many new A/V receivers don't have the proper inputs to connect a turntable. So before you plunk down some cash on a new turntable, check to see whether your receiver even has a turntable connection (usually labeled "phono"). If it doesn't, you can use an external *phono preamp*, which connects between the turntable and the receiver. You simply plug the cables from the turntable into the phono preamp and then use a standard audio cable to connect the preamp to any open audio inputs on the receiver (most people use the ones labeled "aux"). Recoton (www.recoton.com) makes an inexpensive phono preamp for about $50, but you can buy more expensive (and better) preamps from some of the turntable manufacturers that we mention in this section. You can also build your own phono preamp from kits available on-line at places like www.bottlehead.com.

Catching up with cassettes

If you need a cassette deck because you have a ton of tapes filling shoeboxes in your closet, or because you want to make tapes for playing back in the car or in a portable headset, here are a few things you should look for:

- **Single or dual well:** If you think you might end up dubbing (or making copies of) a lot of cassettes, you need a *dual-well* tape deck that has this capability. If you plan to record only the radio or your own CDs, you can save money by getting yourself a single-well deck.

- **Noise reduction:** Before Dolby Labs became famous for its surround sound standards (like Dolby Digital), millions of audiophiles knew the company for its Cassette Noise Reduction standards. These standards (which go by the names Dolby B, C, and S) are electronic processes designed to increase the sound quality of cassettes by decreasing noise (like tape hiss — the sound you can hear when quiet passages are playing). The general rule for these systems is that the higher the name of the system, alphabetically, the better (so S is best, then C, then B). The key thing to keep in mind is that you must have the same system that you record the tape with on the tape deck you use for playback. If you record with Dolby C, you need to play your tape on a Dolby C deck. Dolby S is a slight exception to this rule; tapes recorded with this system can be played back on Dolby B decks with at least some of the benefits of S intact.

- **Number of heads:** Most tape decks have two heads (the heads are the electromagnetic devices that read and write audio signals onto the tape itself). The two-head design uses the same head for both playing back recorded music and for recording music on the tape (the other head is used for erasing the tape when you are recording). Fancier tape decks have a three-head design, which has separate playback and record heads. Because each head is used for only one function, each head can be designed for optimal functionality for its purpose.

- **Number of motors:** A tape is moved over the heads by means of a pair of spindles (which fit in the little wheels on the cassette) and — more importantly — by a pair of devices called a *capstan* and *pinch roller*. The capstan and pinch roller are the essential devices that keep the tape moving over the heads at the correct speed, without any speed fluctuations. Inexpensive tape decks use a single electric motor and a belt (like a radiator fan belt in a car) for this function, while higher-quality decks have a motor for each of the spindles and a third for the capstan/pinch roller combo.

Tuning In to Radio

Sometimes, you just can't be bothered to put in a CD or SACD or cue up an MP3 (not to mention pull out, clean off, and play a record). You know that couch potato lethargy we're talking about? If you're a music lover (and we bet you are), then nothing allows you to enjoy music with absolutely no involvement like turning on your favorite radio station and vegging out.

Local radio

In the home theater you don't usually have to think about much when it comes to radio. Unless you're buying separate components, you have a radio tuner built in to your A/V receiver.

If you *do* buy separate components instead of an A/V receiver (sneak over to Chapter 10 if you don't know what we're talking about), you probably will have to buy a radio tuner and plug it into your system as an audio source device, just as you plug a CD or DVD-Audio player into your system. AM/FM radio tuners usually range in price from about $150 to $500 (though, like any A/V component, you can buy high-end versions that cost ten times the average). Things to look for include the following:

- **AM and FM sensitivity:** Measured in the oh-so-familiar decibel femtowatt (dBf), this is a measurement of how well the tuner can pick up signals. The lower this number (it's usually in the range of 9 to 11 dBf), the better.

- **Adjustable selectivity:** Some tuners come with a switch on the front (or on the remote control) that lets you choose between wide and narrow selectivity. The wide mode gives you better reception and sound quality on powerful stations, whereas the narrow mode can tune in weak signals from distant stations while avoiding interference from stations on adjacent frequencies.

- **Antenna diversity:** Not a necessity, but some fancier tuners have *two* antenna inputs that you can manually or automatically have the tuner choose between when you're trying to pull in a radio station.

If you're lucky enough to live in an area with some good radio stations, you might want to invest in a high-quality tuner near the top of your price range.

Satellite radio

If you're like us, you live where there isn't a whole lot of programming you really want to listen to. In that case, you might check out satellite radio, which offers a huge number of stations (each of the two satellite radio providers offer over 100 channels) beamed to your house or car from a hand-ful of geostationary satellites hovering above the equator. We find that there's just a ton more diversity and just plain interesting stuff coming across these space-based airwaves than we find on our local radio today. Satellite radio services from XM Radio and Sirius require you to — gasp — *pay* for your radio (both start at $12.95 a month).

If you want to get into satellite radio, you need to first check out the Web sites of the two providers, www.xmradio.com and www.sirius.com, to see which one has programming that you prefer. Then, you need to get your hands on a satellite radio tuner (you can find a bunch of different models listed on each company's Web page). The majority of these satellite tuners are designed for in-car use (because people tend to listen to the radio most often while they're driving), but you can find radios suitable for in-home (and home theater!) use from both providers.

If you want to put satellite radio into your home theater, you have a few choices:

- ✔ You can get a dockable tuner. You can put these tuners in your car and, when you get home, pull them out and plug them into your A/V receiver via a simple docking station that provides power, an antenna connec-tion, and the proper connectors to hook into your receiver. This is usu-ally the cheapest and most convenient approach if you're going to be in the car a lot but still want satellite radio in the house.

- ✔ You can buy a dedicated in-home satellite tuner that looks like any other piece of A/V gear and sits on your equipment rack along with your receiver and DVD player. These models (like Polk Audio's XRt12 Reference Tuner — $299.99 list price, www.polkaudio.com) have bigger displays and higher-quality internal components for the best sound quality, but they aren't portable like dockable radios.

- ✔ You can buy an A/V receiver with a built-in satellite receiver. A growing number of A/V receivers (see Chapter 11 for the lowdown on these devices) have a built-in satellite receiver. Just add an antenna kit and a subscription and you're off to the races (or listening to Howard Stern if it's a Sirius radio!). A good example here is Denon's AVR-4306 (www.denon.com, $1,999.99), which includes a built-in XM radio receiver as well as dis-crete iPod and USB player inputs.

If you're using a dedicated indoor satellite tuner (or one inside your receiver) *and* you also want to listen to satellite radio in your car, you'll end up needing more than one subscription. Each individual tuner requires its own subscrip-tion. Luckily, the second subscription can be part of a package deal and will run you $6.99 per additional radio on either service.

These satellites are down by the equator, so no matter where you live in the United States, you need to be able to put the antenna in a south-facing window to pick up a good signal in your home.

Internet radio

If you set up a home theater PC in your A/V system, you can get lots of great radio programming from Internet radio broadcasts. Using an MP3 player, such as MUSICMATCH Jukebox or iTunes, or a streaming media player, such as Windows Media Player or Real Player (www.real.com), you can tune in to literally thousands of radio stations from around the world. With a broadband DSL or cable modem Internet connection, the quality is pretty decent, too.

So if you're like Pat, and you find that San Diego is just out of range of the great PBS station in Santa Monica (www.kcrw.org), you can just tune in on the Net. Pretty cool, and it doesn't cost you an extra penny. This is also a great way to get the radio broadcasts of your favorite college sports teams. Neither of us ever misses a Duke basketball game, even if we're on the road, because we can tune in on our laptops. Go Blue Devils!

In Chapter 10, we tell you about media players and adapters that can support Internet radio. You can also use a Media Center PC, as described in Chapter 8.

Chapter 6

Feeding Video into Your Theater

*I*f you're like us, watching movies is the main reason you decided to get a home theater in the first place. High-quality music reproduction and high-impact video gaming are just (awesome) side benefits. You can get movies (and TV shows and other video content) into your home theater system in many ways — such as plugging into a cable or satellite TV system or even hooking up an antenna for broadcast TV. (We talk about all of these TV systems in Chapter 7.) For most folks, however, watching a movie means watching a *prerecorded* movie (typically a movie on DVD that you've bought or rented from the local video store — or on-line through a service like Netflix).

In this chapter, we talk about the key sources of prerecorded video in your home theater. We spend most of our time discussing the source that's most important to us and most likely to you as well — the digital video disc, better known as the DVD. (They're also sometimes called *Digital Versatile Discs* because they don't just carry video.) We also introduce you to the two new (and competing) systems for delivering high-definition TV on DVD-like optical discs. Get ready for VHS versus Betamax, round two — with high definition as a reward this time! We also talk about the VCR, the personal video recorder (or PVR), and some other nonbroadcast sources of video.

DVD Rules the Roost

The DVD is a high-quality centerpiece to a home theater. Keep in mind the cardinal rule of any A/V system: Garbage in equals garbage out. The corollary of this states that no matter how good your video display and audio system are, if you put a junky, low-fidelity signal into them, you're going to see and hear junky, low-fidelity home theater. That's why DVD is so important — it's a cheap, easy-to-use, high-quality system for movies and movie soundtracks. And the better your display (like an HDTV), the more you'll appreciate a high-quality signal being fed to your display.

In this section, we spend a little time talking about the DVDs themselves and what they can do. Chances are good that you are already familiar with the DVD (after all, DVD has been one of the most — if not *the* most — rapidly adopted new technologies of all time). But DVD is a moving target — manufacturers of DVD players have continually improved their gear and added new features that both improve picture quality and make your DVD viewing more convenient. So read on and be prepared to discover something new!

Getting to know DVDs

The DVD is a 12cm optical disc (by the way, *optical* means that the data on the disc is read by a laser). From a distance, a DVD looks just like a CD. The big difference between the DVD and the CD is the format that each uses for burning those little digital pits into the disc (pits that turn into digital 1s and 0s when the laser reads them). Because the DVD uses a more complex formatting scheme, it has the capacity to store a lot more data than a CD. A DVD can hold a minimum of 4.7GB of data (dual layer DVDs, discussed later, can hold more), whereas a CD's limit is about 700MB (so a DVD can hold more than six times as much data).

A DVD's extra capacity is crucial to home theater because it lets the DVD store about two hours of high-quality digital video *and* digital audio signals using Dolby Digital or DTS (see Chapter 3 if you don't know what these are) *and* an analog two-channel stereo signal as well. A CD, well, it can't hold more than a few dozen minutes of this kind of home theater data.

You'll also hear, as you begin getting deeper into the home theater world, about *dual layer* and *double-sided* DVDs. These discs (which work just fine in any DVD player) hold even more data for long movies and cool extras, such as deleted scenes or director commentary. The additional space is made possible by putting the extra data on either — no surprise here — a different layer of the DVD or on the other side (so you just have to flip the disc, like an LP).

Like a CD, the DVD stores its information in a digital format (you probably guessed that from the name) and, for video, uses the MPEG format that we discuss in Chapter 4. The DVD can also hold the audio soundtracks that correspond to this video in a variety of Dolby and DTS formats, as well as cool extra features, such as additional foreign language soundtracks, subtitles, scene indexes (which let you skip to different scenes in a movie, just like you can skip to different songs on a CD), and more.

The DVD can also do something that most other home theater source devices (we talk about a few others later in this chapter) can't do. It can display *true* widescreen video.

Not all DVDs (the discs themselves, not the DVD player) give you a true widescreen anamorphic picture. Many DVDs have been formatted in the standard 4:3 aspect ratio instead. If you want widescreen, you need to pick DVDs with labels that say "anamorphic," "widescreen," "16:9," or something similar. Many movie companies put both versions on a single disc (using the dual-layer technology we just mentioned) or release both widescreen and Pan and Scan (frames cropped to fit a traditional television screen) DVD versions of an individual movie. See Chapter 4 for all the details about widescreen viewing — including a handy explanation of the term "anamorphic."

Choosing a DVD player

Well, we've talked a lot about why we think DVD players are so important in a home theater. Now comes the fun part — picking one out. There's some really good news here, especially if your budget is like ours (and most people's), which is to say, *limited.*

DVD technology has advanced incredibly in the few years that DVD players have been on the market, and the price drops have been stupendous. For example, Pat's not-quite-2-year-old somehow laid an impressive beating on his old DVD player. No worries though! He was able to buy a sweet new *upconverting* (we'll explain this in a moment) HDMI-equipped player for about half of what he had paid for the previous DVD player. (So thanks, Annabel, for letting Daddy get a new DVD player!) Bottom line is this: If you're still sitting on the DVD fence, get off it!

Like every single piece of A/V gear we discuss in this book, you can spend a fortune on a DVD player if you want to. And you may want to if you're building a really fancy, no-holds-barred, high-end home theater. Although you can get a great picture from that $59 model, if you have a high-end video projector and a top-of-the-line surround sound audio system, you might want to buy a fancier model. Such a system yearns for higher-quality electronic components and more powerful chips to convert the digital data on the DVD into video and sound. Just to give you an idea of the range of prices, as we write, the current prices of a single company (Denon) range from $150 to $3,500.

So what should you look for in a DVD player? We think the following items are the key things to put on your mental checklist as you start shopping:

✔ **Connections on the back:** We talk in detail about the "hierarchy of connections" in Chapter 16. For video, the best connection for DVD players is the component video connection, and just about all (but the very cheapest) DVD players have these (as do almost all displays these days — and all HDTV-capable TVs will). If you have a TV that can accept these connections, make sure you get a DVD player that can also use them. On the audio side of things, you'll find two kinds of digital connectors (for Dolby Digital and DTS digital surround sound) — the coaxial and optical (or Toslink) connections. The key thing here is to make sure that the connectors on your DVD player match up with those on your A/V receiver.

Some of the newest DVD players have moved on to digital video outputs. If your display supports an HDMI or DVI connection, consider a DVD player that has one of these outputs.

✔ **Single or multidisc capability:** DVD players come in single-disc and multidisc models. For just watching movies, a single-disc player is fine, but if you plan to use your DVD player as your only CD player, you might want to pay a bit more for a multidisc player that lets you provide hours of background music during, for example, a party.

✔ **Progressive or interlaced:** Progressive scan is becoming a really big deal because the video industry is gradually moving from interlaced video toward a progressive video future. We discuss progressive and interlaced scans in more detail in Chapter 4, so we don't bother you with that here. Bottom line: If you have an HDTV or other progressive-scan monitor, you want a DVD player that offers progressive-scan capabilities. Although most progressive-scan TVs have a built-in deinterlacer for playing interlaced material (DVDs are still interlaced), the deinterlacers in many progressive-scan DVD players are better. Even if you don't have a progressive-scan display but might someday, consider a progressive-scan DVD player as well, especially considering that prices on these DVD players have dropped so much that they're hardly more expensive than a regular DVD player — in fact, all but the cheapest DVD players these days have progressive-scan functionality.

✔ **Upconversion:** The "latest and greatest" feature found in many new DVD players is the ability to *upconvert* a DVD to a higher resolution for playback on your HDTV display. An upconverting DVD player has an internal *scaler* (see Chapter 13 for more on this device's functionality) that allows it to take the 480i resolution stored on DVDs and convert it to 480p (progressive scan) or (more significantly) to a 720p or 1080i signal. Essentially, an upconverting DVD player gives you a simulated high-definition version of the video on your DVD. Just as important, an upconverting DVD player uses the HDMI or DVI outputs we discuss previously to send this picture to your HDTV display — so you get all of the benefits of a digital connection *and* a picture that's designed for a high-definition display.

✔ **Support for other formats:** Many DVD players now support on-line video file formats like DivX or xvid. This can come in handy if you are downloading HDTV video clips from the Internet using these formats — you can burn DVDs on your computer and play them back on your DVD player.

✔ **Adjustability:** To get the best out of a home theater, you need to do more than just plug everything in properly. You also need to spend some time tweaking the audio and video settings to get the best picture in your room. Most of these adjustments are done on the TV or projector itself, not on the DVD player. But some DVD players allow you to adjust things such as brightness (or black level) in the DVD player.

✔ **Surround sound decoder:** If you are starting your home theater from scratch, we recommend that you buy a home theater receiver (or separate components decoder) that is capable of decoding (at a minimum) Dolby Digital 5.1 and DTS Digital surround sound signals. If, however, you are adding a DVD player into an existing home theater with an older receiver that doesn't support digital surround sound, you can buy a DVD player with a built-in surround sound decoder. The downside of this is that you need to use *six* analog audio cables to connect the DVD player to your receiver, instead of a single digital interconnect. Some of the older receivers were marketed as "Digital ready" with six preamp jacks on the back for just this purpose; if your receiver doesn't have a built-in Dolby Digital decoder and it doesn't have these six inputs (or its own Dolby Digital decoder), you can't play back digital 5.1-channel surround sound with it!

✔ **Audio disc support:** All DVD players can play back store-bought, prerecorded CDs. Not all, however, can play back homemade CD-R or CD-RW discs, nor can many DVD players play back CDs containing MP3 music files. If these features are important to you (and you don't have a CD player that can handle this for you), make sure your DVD player can handle all these formats before you buy.

✔ **Recording capability:** Just as the CD has moved from a factory-produced, read-only CD to a "make your own" medium (such as CD-Rs and CD-RWs), so has DVD recording started to become a truly consumer-friendly technology. We discuss the pitfalls of DVD recording (and there are pitfalls, due to some incompatible industry standards) in the sidebar, "Recording your own DVDs," later in this chapter.

✔ **Remote control:** Most people have too many remote controls when they get into home theater. To avoid remote overload, look at how other systems in your home theater can control your DVD player. For example, many A/V equipment vendors have special "system link" cables that let the receiver control the DVD player and other components. The down-side of such systems is that you must buy all your equipment from the same vendor to take advantage of them. The alternative (which we dis-cuss in Chapter 15) is to use a *universal remote control* to control every-thing. If you're going down this route, ask your dealer if there are any special codes or other things you need to consider before buying a spe-cific DVD player.

✔ **DVD extras:** Many DVDs include extra features that you'd never get on a VHS tape, laserdisc, or other (older) video source. For example, some DVDs have alternate camera angles — so you can click a button on the remote control and see the film from a different character's perspective. Most DVD players support this feature, but not all do. You can also find DVD players that have special features, such as a digital zoom that lets you enlarge part of the picture on your screen, or a frame-by-frame fast forward, so that you can watch that starship explode in excruciating detail. You can even buy DVD players that can display standard PC or Mac JPEG picture files from Kodak's PictureCDs or from your own home-made CD-R.

✔ **All-in-one functionality:** The DVD players with built-in surround sound decoding are a first step in this direction, but if space is limited in your home theater, you may want to take the full leap — DVD players and A/V receivers all-in-one slim chassis. Lots of these models are part of lower-priced "home theater in a box" systems, but you can also find very high quality (and expensive) all-in-ones. For example, the Scottish high-end A/V manufacturer Linn (www.linn.co.uk) has a very cool all-in-one system called the Classik Movie System.

If you're buying an inexpensive DVD player, it's probably okay to choose one based on features and reviews (we list a bunch of places to find these reviews in Chapter 23). But if you plan to spend $400 or more on a DVD player and are lucky enough to have a good home theater shop or dealer nearby, take the time to get a good audition of the DVD player. Do this in the showrooms of the dealer, at a minimum, and at home with a demo model, if possible. You're the one who's going to be watching movies on this machine, so make sure your eyes like what they see.

Playing DVDs on an HDTV

Many folks hear "widescreen" and "digital" and think "HDTV." Well, DVD is not HDTV. DVD is digital. It provides a great picture, but it isn't a true high-definition video source. Although DVD looks better than ever before when you play it back on an HDTV (using a progressive-scan DVD player we men-tion earlier in this chapter), DVD doesn't give you the same quality of picture that a full-on HDTV signal (coming in over a broadcast TV signal or from your cable or satellite provider) can give.

What's the region thing all about?

Region codes, which you may see in catalogs or on DVDs themselves, enable movie studios to control who can watch DVDs (the studios are like that about a lot of things). The codes are both embedded in the DVD itself and also coded into the circuitry of the DVD player primarily so that movie studios can release movies and DVDs at different times in different places. So a movie may be released theatrically in the United States first, and then, several months later, it is released theatrically in Europe and also released on DVD in North America. The region code prevents North American retailers from selling the DVD to European customers while the movie is still in theaters there.

If you dig around on the Internet, you can find region-free programs for the PC or modified, universal, region-free DVD players. We're generally supportive of this concept (especially when we find that some foreign movie we *really* want on DVD isn't available in our North American region code), but we're going to leave you to your own devices when it comes to region-free players. The movie studios are really down on this concept, and often aggressively pursue legal actions (including jail time) against people who try to crack the region codes. In fact, we're not going to say any more on the subject — jailhouse uniforms don't really fit either of our senses of fashion and style.

By the way, here are the regions:

- **Region 1:** North America

- **Region 2:** Western Europe, Middle East, Japan, and South Africa

- **Region 3:** South Korea, Taiwan, Hong Kong, and Southeast Asia

- **Region 4:** Australia, New Zealand, and Latin America

- **Region 5:** Eastern Europe, Africa, and India

- **Region 6:** China

- **Region 7:** Reserved (For the moon maybe? We're not too sure.)

- **Region 8:** Special international venues (such as cruise ships and airplanes)

Why don't traditional DVDs "do" HDTV? Well, for one reason, HDTV wasn't fully finalized and on the market when the DVD was developed, so DVD was designed to work with the TVs of the time (which are still the majority of TVs today). More importantly, HDTV requires a ton (literally, we measured) of digital data. Using the traditional NTSC signal, you can fit a two-hour movie comfortably onto a DVD, but you wouldn't be able to fit more than a fraction of that movie onto a DVD if it was encoded as an HDTV signal.

Upconverting DVD players give you something approaching HDTV, but the video being fed from these players into your display is *not* true HDTV. To get true HDTV, manufacturers have to go beyond the traditional DVD — and the next section spells out two paths the DVD industry is taking.

Putting the HD in DVD

What's really exciting in the DVD world is the development of a couple of new DVD formats that will allow true high-definition programming to be available on optical discs. A number of companies have banded together into two groups with *competing* standards for these next-generation, high-def disc formats:

- ✔ **Blu-ray:** Led by Sony, the Blu-ray camp has developed a high-definition-capable disc format that is also being supported by Apple, Dell, HP, Panasonic, Pioneer, Thompson, Philips — and a whole bunch of other companies. The really big deal for Blu-ray is that Sony has made it the disc format for their new PlayStation 3 gaming console — so the format will end up in millions of homes quickly.

- ✔ **HD-DVD:** The competing format championed by Toshiba, HD-DVD also has an illustrious list of companies behind it, including Microsoft, HP, Intel, NEC, and others.

Yep, it looks like we're heading into another *format war,* in which two competing groups of companies agree to disagree and push two different standards onto the market. This happened a few years ago with high-resolution audio discs (read about SACD and DVD-Audio in Chapter 5), and the results weren't pretty for anyone. With the audio discs, basically no one bought either format in significant numbers, though both are still plugging along. This isn't the first format war to hit the home theater industry either — if you recall the early days of VCRs, Sony and Matsushita duked it out over the Betamax and VHS formats.

Sometimes, one format wins out over another (for example, VHS over Betamax); other times, neither one becomes a clear winner. In the case of high-def DVDs, it's still way too early to tell because the first DVD players that can handle either of these disc formats are still very new and have sold only a few tens of thousands of units — a drop in the bucket compared to the millions of DVD players sold each year.

So we can't predict which format will win the hearts and minds of consumers at this point. An interesting thing to watch will be the actions of the movie studios who actually create and sell the discs themselves. Right now, most studios have chosen one or the other format — pretty much splitting down the middle, with a slight advantage to Blu-ray. (Sony owns a few motion picture studios itself, which helps here.)

We expect that if one or the other format really becomes dominant, all of the studios will eventually begin to sell movies in that format, no matter which camp they are in today. Heck, Sony sold a lot of movies in the VHS format, even though Betamax was its baby!

Betting on Blu-ray

The Blu-ray disc, as we mention above, was developed by Sony and is supported by a bunch of companies (including all of Sony's motion picture studios).

Blu-ray will be a very capable disc format — by which we mean that there will be *lots* of storage space on a Blu-ray disc. Storage space is the key for high-definition disc formats simply because HDTV takes up as much as nine or ten times the storage space (for any given length of video) than does a standard-definition DVD-quality video. So you really need to be able to cram a lot of bits on the disc to make high definition work.

The good news here is that Blu-ray *can* hold a *lot* of bits and bytes — up to 50GB of data (more than five or six times what a standard DVD can hold). That 50GB capacity is for a dual-layer disc; a single-layer disc can hold 25GB of data — enough space for at least two hours of high-definition programming. Blu-ray discs can hold even more data if the disc is encoded using a more efficient *codec* (like MPEG 4 instead of MPEG 2), which means you can potentially fit *four hours* of high def on a single-layer disc.

Blu-ray discs will support all of the same audio formats that a regular DVD supports but will also include the latest and greatest from Dolby — Dolby Digital Plus and Dolby TrueHD. (See Chapter 5 for more on these formats.) Because no A/V receivers include decoders for these new formats today, the first Blu-ray disc players will have a built-in surround sound decoder and will connect via analog cables for Dolby TrueHD. You can use a standard digital audio cable, however, for Dolby Digital, Digital Plus, or DTS.

Several manufacturers launched (or are launching) Blu-ray players at the end of 2006 and in early 2007, including Sony, Samsung, Panasonic, and Pioneer.

The Blu-ray disc has two big advantages in the coming market battle with HD-DVD. First, it has more storage space (which can be a huge deal with HDTV). Second, it's going to be sitting in millions of living rooms inside all of the PlayStation 3 game consoles that Sony began selling in late-2006.

Blu-ray gets its name from the *color* of the laser that reads the discs inside a Blu-ray player. Instead of the traditional red laser used by CDs and "regular" DVDs, Blu-ray uses a blue laser. (We bet you knew what we were going to say there, huh?) The blue laser has a smaller wavelength and is more suited to reading the physically smaller *spots* on the disc itself. This ability to focus in on smaller spots allows the disc to have *more* spots — and more spots means more data.

Heading toward high def with HD-DVD

Toshiba's competing format, HD-DVD (high-definition DVD) is in many ways similar to Blu-ray. Like Blu-ray, HD-DVD supports high-definition video. And like Blu-ray, it uses a blue laser to focus in on smaller spots on the DVD itself.

The big difference is that HD-DVD is more similar to a traditional DVD in the way that the disc itself is constructed and in the way that a movie (or other data) is stored on the disc. This similarity is a double-edged sword — it makes HD-DVD discs less expensive to manufacture, but at the same time it limits the absolute storage space on a single disc. HD-DVD discs can hold about 15GB of data on a single-layer disc and 30GB on a dual-layer disc. So you get about 40 percent less video on a disc with HD-DVD than you'd get with Blue-ray — though recently announced 45 GB *triple layer* discs will even the match, at least until Blu-ray goes to three layers too!

HD-DVD players were the first on the market in the United States, as Toshiba launched two models in the spring of 2006, starting at about $500, and has already moved on to its second generation (with similar pricing). Interestingly, there is also an HD-DVD game console angle similar to the Blu-ray PlayStation 3, as Microsoft has begun selling an external HD-DVD drive for the new Xbox 360. This drive isn't inside the box like the PS3's is, but it matches up nicely with the Xbox 360 unit itself.

When you look at the relatively smaller capacity of HD-DVDs, you might think that Blu-ray is a slam dunk, simply due to its apparent technical superiority. Well that may or may not end up being the case, for two reasons. First, because HD-DVD discs are quite similar to regular DVDs, they can actually be produced on the same manufacturing lines without too much retooling. This is a big deal, especially when you stop and think about how many DVD production lines there are in the world, pumping out hundreds of millions of DVDs every year. Blu-ray will require a much more expensive factory upgrade — something that may slow the availability of Blu-ray discs.

Second, HD-DVD will hit the market first. The Toshiba players will be on the market well ahead of the first mainstream Blu-ray players. (In Japan, you can already buy a Blu-ray player, but it costs in the multiples of thousands of dollars and isn't widely available.) This "first to market" advantage may give HD-DVD the momentum it needs to succeed.

Figuring out where to go from here

As we mention in the beginning of this section, it's just too soon to tell with Blu-ray and HD-DVD. Both formats produce *amazing* pictures (we've seen both and were blown away by both!). Both have an array of blue-chip companies behind them. (Sorry, we couldn't avoid the pun.) It could go either way, both ways, or neither way. We just can't tell.

We are pretty sure, however, that at least one of these formats will be very successful. As many as 10 percent of all homes in the United States have HDTVs these days, and there is essentially *no* prerecorded high-definition material to play on these expensive TVs. People are anxiously awaiting a solution.

The safest bet for someone building a home theater might be to wait for a *universal* disc player that can handle both formats. None are yet formally announced, but several manufacturers have hinted both in private and in public that they will build such a device. We can't wait!

VCRs Ain't (Quite) Dead Yet

We spend a lot of time talking about DVD players because we love them so much. But we realize that some movies just aren't available on DVD yet (or ever, in some cases). And you probably want to record TV shows that you won't be home for or watch home movies you've recorded with your camcorder. Or you've got a zillion VHS tapes that you're stuck with in a DVD age, like Danny. These are all areas in which a videocassette recorder (or VCR) comes in super handy.

You can buy three kinds of VCRs today:

- ✔ **VHS VCRs:** These are your standard, garden-variety VCRs that have been around for 40 years or so. They use VHS videocassettes and record a low-resolution TV signal (only about 240 lines of resolution). Most of these VHS VCRs are cheap (less than $100), and most include stereo audio capabilities (if so, they're labeled HiFi) and analog Dolby surround sound capabilities.

- ✔ **S-VHS VCRs:** The S-VHS (or Super VHS) VCR uses a special S-VHS tape to provide a higher-quality, higher-resolution (400 lines, instead of 240) picture. Regular VHS tapes work on these decks, but S-VHS videocassettes don't work on most regular VHS decks. (If you plan on trading tapes with someone or using a regular VHS VCR you have elsewhere, keep that in mind.) S-VHS VCRs start off at around $90.

- ✔ **D-VHS VCRs:** The latest and greatest in the VCR world, these are high-definition VCRs. D-VHS VCRs can play and record standard VHS and S-VHS videotapes. More importantly, D-VHS VCRs can also record all the HDTV formats (discussed in Chapter 5). You can get a limited number of movies on prerecorded D-VHS videocassettes, but it's a small number compared to what you can get on DVD. You can buy a D-VHS VCR for about $500 — if you can find one.

The D-VHS system has been out for over five years now and has essentially been a major flop on the market. These recorders actually work pretty well, with great picture quality, but folks have gotten used to the wonders of DVDs, with their almost instant access to any spot on the disc, their durability, and just the plain fact that you never need to rewind a tape (nothing worse than forgetting to rewind!). And PVRs (personal video recorders, discussed in the next section) have pretty much completely taken over the TV show "time shifting" role in most homes. So while a few manufacturers still make D-VHS recorders, they're all but gone from the market. We suspect that Blu-ray and/or HD-DVD will finally kill them off for good. We can't really recommend that you buy a D-VHS deck, but we won't try to stop you if you do — just be aware that there's probably not a lot of future in these devices.

When buying a VCR of any kind, look for the following things:

- ✔ **HiFi capability:** All the D-VHS and S-VHS VCRs have this, and most regular VHS decks have this feature as well. If you buy a model without it, you won't even get stereo sound — just crummy mono (one-channel) sound.

- ✔ **VCR Plus+:** This system enables the average human being to record a certain show at a certain time more easily. With this system, you simply punch in a special code that is listed in your paper's TV listings (or in *TV Guide*) next to the show you want to record. More-advanced versions of VCR Plus+ (called Silver and Gold) allow you to localize your VCR Plus+ settings for your area.

- ✔ **All-in-one units:** Some VCRs are incorporated into a single chassis with a DVD player or with a MiniDV or other camcorder tape player. These all-in-one units take up less room on your equipment rack, if space is a concern. And the VCR/camcorder tape combo units make it easy to make VCR copies of your home movies.

Even if your VCR is in the same chassis as a DVD player, you can't make tapes of your favorite DVD movies. A copy protection system called Macrovision keeps you from doing this, and it's built into all DVD players, all VCRs, and most commercial DVD discs. Even if you want to copy your favorite movie from DVD to VHS to play back on a VCR in your vacation home or somewhere else, you're just plain out of luck.

We're not all that enthusiastic about the VCR these days (although we think the D-VHS would be pretty cool if many people weren't restricted from using it for its intended purpose — recording HDTV shows for later playback). Even big movie rental places like Blockbuster are phasing out VHS tapes in favor of DVDs. But we do think it's worthwhile to have an inexpensive VCR in your home theater, just to have the capability of playing older movies that you can't find on DVD. We recommend you get an inexpensive S-VHS model — and don't spend too much money on it.

PVRs Rock!

One reason we're not all that interested in VCRs these days is because we've found the PVR, or personal video recorder, which offers a much better way to tape our favorite shows. PVRs are basically purpose-built computers that record video onto a standard computer hard drive. Think of it as a computer-based VCR. There are no tapes to wear out, break, or jam — just a fast, reliable computer hard drive.

Actually, the metaphor of a PVR being like a computer-based VCR really sells the PVR short. Using a PVR is *soooo* much better than using a VCR that it's actually hard to begin to describe the benefits of the PVR. Don't just take our word for it, look at these things you can do with a PVR (and not with a VCR!):

- ✔ You can play back one recorded show while simultaneously recording another.

- ✔ You can pause live TV (if you're recording it on your PVR).

- ✔ You can skip the commercials with the click of a button if you are recording the show and start watching a couple minutes past the start time. (Broadcasters *hate* this feature and are suing some PVR vendors.)

- ✔ You can let the PVR automatically record your favorite show every time it's on. (All PVRs connect to a program service, usually via a telephone line, that has a complete program guide for weeks at a time, customized for your area.)

- ✔ You can use the program service to help you find shows.

- ✔ You can connect some PVRs to a computer network (some models even have built-in wireless network connections) and the Internet so you can share recordings with your friends or send copies of shows you've recorded to your PVR at your vacation home (if you have one).

Traditionally, PVRs are sold as standalone boxes — generally the size and shape of a cable set-top box, a DVD player, or any other A/V component. These units start off at as little as $50 for a unit that has enough hard drive space to record 40 hours of programming, and they go up in price for larger-capacity units. You also need to pay a monthly fee (around $10 per month, though you can pay $250 for a lifetime subscription) to get the necessary programming guide service. The major manufacturer of standalone PVRs is TiVo (www.tivo.com). We talk about some of the neat features of TiVo's most recent PVRs (like the cool TiVo ToGo feature) in Chapter 10.

None of TiVo's PVRs can record or play back HDTV content. In our opinion, this is a major, major shortcoming. For standard definition, TiVo's PVRs are great devices, with the best software for controlling the recording and playback processes, but we really recommend them only for home theaters that don't have HDTV and that aren't using a set-top box for satellite or cable TV reception.

Beyond TiVo, the real action in the PVR world these days comes in the form of PVRs that are *integrated* into other devices. The most common place you'll see this is within a cable or satellite set-top box (and for those of you who can get TV services from the phone company, in their set-top boxes as well).

Integrating the PVR into the set-top box has a couple of huge advantages:

- ✔ **It makes setup and operation easier:** With the PVR hardware and software as part of the set-top box itself, you have nothing to hook up and nothing to configure; it's just there. That's huge, considering that getting a standalone PVR configured to control your set-top box or satellite receiver is a major pain in the rear end.

- ✔ **The whole experience is more integrated:** As we discuss in Chapter 7, most TV providers include on-screen programming guides, video on demand, and more. PVR becomes just another one of these functions and is tightly integrated into the experience — so setting up a recording is typically the work of one or two button pushes while you're looking at your on-screen guide.

- ✔ **They can support HDTV:** This is the biggest deal for us. Both satellite and cable providers are offering HDTV PVRs that can record and play back high-definition TV broadcasts, to which we can only say *thank you!*

- ✔ **They can support two-tuner operation:** Standalone PVRs can typically record only one show at a time, so you can watch a show while recording it, or watch a recording while recording another show, but that's it. Most cable or satellite PVRs are *two-tuner* models that allow you to view and/or record *two* shows at a time. This gives you the ability to watch one show while recording a different show or even record two shows at a time while watching a recording of a *third* show. You'd have to be a real TV junkie to miss anything with this capability.

- ✔ **They might not cost anything up-front:** While standalone PVRs require cash out of your pocket to buy the unit, most cable and many satellite PVRs don't cost you anything up-front. You simply pay a monthly service fee (which you also would pay for standalone PVRs), and you don't need to buy any equipment.

As we write, the cable and satellite PVRs have the upper hand in terms of functionality and practicality. But TiVo isn't standing still, and the TiVo folks may surprise us all with some must-have functionality when they release their third generation of PVRs sometime in 2006. All we know for sure is that we gotta have our PVRs (no matter who makes them). It's simply a *must* for our home theaters, and if you ever use a PVR, we are sure it will become a must for yours, too.

You can also use a PC as a PVR. We talk about this more in Chapter 8.

Recording your own DVDs

PVR hard drives, no matter how big, eventually run out of space, and home movies take up a lot of digital space, too. Eventually, you have to store your video somewhere — both to archive it so that you can use the hard drive or camcorder tape for new stuff, and also so that you can share your content with others. The best way to do this, in our minds, is by making your own DVDs.

Just as you can create your own CDs by using a CD *burner* (or recorder), you can now easily make your own DVDs by using a DVD recorder. There are two ways you can do this:

✔ **Buy a DVD recorder:** This is an A/V component, like a DVD player that has a built-in mechanism for recording DVDs as well.

✔ **Use a PC with a built-in DVD recorder:** Apple, Sony, and a few other PC vendors sell computers with built-in DVD recorders. You can also buy an internal or external (connected with a USB or FireWire cable) DVD burner for your existing PC.

In either case, you have a somewhat difficult decision to make because the makers of DVD recorders have decided that cooperating (for the sake of the consumer) is simply not something they have in them. So there are three *completely incompatible* systems out there for DVD recording: DVD-R/RW, DVD-RAM, and DVD+R/RW. Ugh — acronym soup. Although it's really ugly and very confusing to the consumer (look at the plus and minus signs closely), here's a little help.

DVD-R/RW systems are generally considered the most compatible with existing DVD *players* — so you have the best shot at having your homemade DVDs play back on your mom's or friend's or whomever's DVD player (though even with this standard, it only works on about 90 percent of DVD players). DVD-RAM is the least compatible; you basically need another DVD-RAM recorder or player to play back these discs. DVD+R/RW is close to DVD-R/RW, only slightly less compatible.

If you're making DVDs only for yourself, these distinctions might not be too important. You can play back your DVDs on the machine that made them no matter what. If you have sharing in mind, then we suggest the DVD-R/RW or DVD+R/RW recorders.

Homegrown Video Programming

You don't have to limit your home theater viewing to prerecorded DVDs and television broadcasts. You can also incorporate video from your own sources. Many folks like to make their own video programming — home movies and the like. We think that these videos deserve a proper playback system — and we think that the home theater is the right place. Another source of video in the home that a lot of people don't think of when designing their home theater is in-house closed circuit or surveillance video.

Camcorders

Although the topic of camcorders is beyond the scope of this book, we do want to put in a few words about fitting a camcorder into your home theater. (See *Digital Video For Dummies,* 2nd Edition, by Martin Doucette, published by Wiley Publishing, Inc., for details about camcorders.)

First off, we think that digital camcorders are the way to go (look for formats like Mini DV, MICROMV, or Digital 8 instead of an analog Hi8 format), for two reasons. First of all, these digital formats can take higher-quality, better-looking, higher-resolution video and digital audio (which will look and sound much better in your big-screen home theater). Second, digital camcorders can connect to your PC through a standard FireWire cable (also known as i.LINK or IEEE 1394) and transfer video to your computer's hard drive for editing. Editing is a key thing — no one wants to watch your "raw" video footage, they want to see a nice finished product, without any mistakes, and possibly with a soundtrack.

Connecting your camcorder to your home theater is really a simple process. All these digital camcorders use standard S-Video connectors (which we discuss in Chapter 16).

If you use a camcorder in your home theater, we recommend you choose an A/V receiver with a set of inputs for the camcorder on the front. With this setup, you don't have to monkey around behind the equipment rack when you want to plug in your camcorder.

If you're moving into the HDTV realm and you are a video camera enthusiast, we suggest you look into the new category of high-definition camcorders. There aren't a lot of HD models on the market yet — the "market" here meaning *consumer* HD camcorders. (There *are* a lot of professional models for TV studios, filmmakers, and the like.) The models we list here are mainly in the *prosumer* category, which means they are expensive and good enough for entry-level professional use, but not so expensive that enthusiastic amateurs won't buy them:

> ✔ **Sanyo's HD1:** Sanyo currently (as we write in early 2006) has the cheapest HD-capable camcorder on the market, the HD1. This model can support 720p video (the actual resolution is 1280 x 760 pixels). Like a growing number of video cameras, the HD1 does away with the tape and uses a solid-state memory card (like a digital camera uses) to record video. You can record up to 41 minutes of high-def video on this model using a 2GB *SD Card* memory card. With a list price of $799.99, this is the cheapest HD-capable camcorder yet. You can find out more about this model at the following URL:

```
www.sanyo.com/entertainment/cameracorder/index.cfm?pro
            ductID=1239
```

✔ **Sony's HDRFX1:** Sony's entry into the prosumer HD camcorder market is a bit more expensive (okay, a *big bit* listing at $4,999.99, but available on-line for closer to $3,200). This killer machine can record video at the full 1080i resolution and features a killer lens, 3 *CCDs* (charge-coupled devices — the chips that actually receive and digitize the image) for better color reproduction, and more. An awesome camcorder if you can swing the asking price.

Sony also has a cheaper model (with fewer bells and whistles, of course), the HDR-HC1, which retails for under $1,800.

✔ **JVC's GR-HD1US:** JVC offers a 1080i camcorder similar to Sony's HDRFX1 model, the GR-HD1US. (Don't worry, we won't have a pop quiz on model numbers at the end of the chapter!) With a list price of $3,499.95, this may not be on everyone's shopping list, but if you're looking for true high def, make sure you check out this model along with the Sony and Sanyo!

Video surveillance

Surveillance is kind of a scary word. We hesitate to use it because it sounds kind of paranoid and big-brotherish. But it's an accurate word for what we're talking about — video cameras mounted in and around your home that let you keep an eye on what's going on from the comfort of your home theater (or any room with a television).

Surveillance video is not high-quality, surround sound video. In fact, most surveillance video (often called closed circuit TV or CCTV) is pretty awful to look at. But if you want to know who's ringing the doorbell or keep an eye on the baby asleep in her room while you watch a movie in the home theater, then you probably don't need a high-quality picture. Heck, you might not even want a color picture . . . or sound. You just want to see what's going on.

There are a couple of ways to get this home surveillance video into your system:

✔ **You can use a wireless system like those offered by X10.** These systems (which start at around $80 at `www.x10.com`) use a 2.4 GHz radio signal (like those used by many cordless phones) to send video from a remote location to a small receiver that plugs into your home theater receiver or directly into your TV. You might put one of these cameras by your front door or use Danny's favorite, X10.com's FloodCam, which is built into a set of motion-sensitive floodlights on the side of your house.

✔ **You can use networked cameras that connect to your home's computer network.** These systems, from companies like Panasonic and D-Link, are a bit more expensive (starting at around $400 per camera) but are much more capable. Using a standard (wired) Ethernet network or a wireless computer network (802.11b/g or Wi-Fi), you can feed the video from these cameras into your home theater PC, and you can even view them from outside the home theater (if you have a broadband Internet connection) by using the built-in Web server on these cameras.

✔ **You can use a traditional "wired" CCTV system.** These cameras connect to your home's coaxial video cabling (the cable that brings antenna and cable TV connections to your home theater, as we discuss in Chapter 18) and use devices called *modulators* that let you turn this video into an in-house TV station. To view a modulated CCTV channel, you just need to tune your TV to the right channel. If you have a picture-in-picture system in your TV, you can even keep an eye on things in a small window while you watch something else on the rest of the screen.

These cameras are not only good for viewing, but for recording as well. Danny likes the FloodCam because it records when motion sets it off, day or night. You never know when you might need that.

Chapter 7

Feeding Your Home Theater from Outside Your Home

*I*n the previous two chapters, we talk about a bunch of different audio and video sources that let you enjoy prerecorded content (like movies on DVD or music on CD) or content that you've created yourself (like home movies and recordings you've made of broadcast TV). For most people, this kind of content is just part of the overall home theater experience. You may also want to use your cool A/V equipment to do standard couch potato stuff — watching the big game or sitcoms on TV. In this chapter, we discuss the different ways you can bring these "outside the house" sources into your home theater.

We talk about three primary ways you can get television into your home — satellite, cable, and over-the-air broadcasts. We don't think these three things need to be mutually exclusive. You might, for example, get a satellite TV system but also have an antenna to pick up local stations. Or you might get digital cable to pick up those mythical 500 stations but still hook up an antenna to pick up the local HDTV broadcasts. So keep an open mind as you plan your theater.

Some local phone companies are beginning to offer TV services, often using fiber optic cables, which are replacing regular copper phone lines. In most cases these services don't (currently) differ all that much from the services offered by cable TV providers — they connect to your TV the same way, use similar set-top boxes, and offer similar feature sets. In the future, however, these IPTV (Internet Protocol TV) services may offer a richer mix of channels — on demand — and more cool features than either satellite or cable. The biggest telephone company provider of TV services today is Verizon (with its FIOS fiber optic deployments), and AT&T (formerly SBC) is right behind them with something called *Project Lightspeed.* Keep an eye out for your own phone company — pretty soon, we expect they'll be competing directly with your cable and satellite TV services.

Digital Satellite Does It All

For many home theater enthusiasts, TV means one thing: satellite TV. DSS (Digital Satellite Service) is the way people do satellite today (many people also call it DBS, Direct Broadcast Satellite). If you wanted satellite TV 20 or so years ago, you were stuck with something called C-Band (named after the radio frequency on which these satellites operated), which required you to put a *huge* (9-foot or so) satellite dish in your backyard.

DSS is a much more user- and landscape-friendly version of satellite TV. DSS dishes can be as small as 18 inches across and are much easier to integrate into the average backyard. Despite this more compact size, DSS has all the advantages that drew people to those big dishes back in the '80s — tons of channels and interesting programming you can't get from your local broadcast channels.

If your cable company offers a digital cable service (which we discuss in an upcoming section), you can probably get just as many channels on that service as you can on a satellite service.

Signing up for digital satellite

In the United States, the two main providers of DSS services are DirecTV and Echostar (Echostar's service is called DISH Network), and they are pretty similar. Both services offer digital transmission of their video content using MPEG-2 (discussed in Chapter 4). This digital transmission has advantages for both the satellite companies (because it lets them fit more TV channels into the radio waves over which their satellites broadcast) and the customer (because it eliminates the distortions that often occur in nondigital transmissions).

Both DSS service providers are furiously launching new satellites into orbit, outfitted with systems that can support the newer *MPEG-4* system, which provides greater compression. After these new satellites are launched, both providers will be able to use this expanded capacity to offer more high-definition (HDTV) channels.

To pick up stations coming from these new MPEG-4 satellites, you need a new satellite receiver. For DirecTV — who has begun broadcasting in a few cities with MPEG-4 — this is the H20 receiver and the AT9 satellite dish, already available. As we write, DISH hasn't yet launched this service, so keep an eye out on the DISH Web site for more details.

We like both services. To decide between the two, shop for pricing and channels that are best for you. You can look at channel lineups and prices on-line at www.directv.com and www.dishnetwork.com.

Although DSS systems broadcast all their content using digital technology, the majority of the programming sent out over these systems is analog TV, or NTSC, which we discuss in Chapter 4. However, DSS systems still carry a relatively large number of HDTV stations, which is why many home theater owners choose DSS as their primary source of television. The total number carried is increasing month by month as new satellites come on-line, but is still limited to about 20 or 25 channels — just a small percentage of the hundreds of stations carried by these systems, but in many areas, that's more than are available by cable or broadcast.

Some of the key features of both DSS systems include

- ✔ Hundreds of channels, including movie, sports, and sometimes even local broadcast channels
- ✔ On-screen program guides that include all the current and upcoming (for a week or so) programming scheduled on the system
- ✔ Dozens of digital audio channels
- ✔ High-definition TV

Understanding the drawbacks

DSS services are pretty awesome, we think, but they *do* have a few drawbacks. If you decide to go the DSS route, keep a few things in mind:

- ✔ **You might not get local stations:** In some parts of the country, you can get a local package that includes most if not all of your local broadcast stations. In some smaller cities and more rural areas, you still need to get cable or set up a broadcast antenna to pick up local stations.

You won't get the local stations in HDTV unless you are lucky enough to be in one of the cities receiving the new MPEG-4 broadcasts discussed earlier in this section. Most HD-capable DSS satellite receivers have built-in over-the-air broadcast TV tuners that can pick up the HDTV signals being sent out by the TV stations in your town.

- ✔ **You need a special satellite receiver:** You can't just plug the cable from your satellite dish into a TV; you need a special satellite receiver. You can share this receiver with other TVs in your house, but if you want to watch different programs on different TVs, you need a receiver for each TV.

- ✔ **You need to hook into a phone line:** Your satellite receiver has to "talk" back to the service provider to maintain your pay-per-view account and to check for software upgrades. The receivers usually do this in the middle of the night, so they don't interfere with phone calls. If you never use pay-per-view or some of the premium sports channels, you may be able to skip the phone line entirely. Check with the provider before you buy in on this if getting a phone line in your home theater is an issue.

- ✔ **Your satellite dish antenna must be able to "see" the satellites:** It must have a clear line of sight to the satellites, which hover over the equator. Some folks in northern areas (or in Hawaii) might not be able to pick up all the satellites, so they get only some of the channels, not all. Even if you're in the right spot, geographically speaking, you still need to have a clear view to the south, without hills and trees (or even tall buildings) in the way.

- ✔ **You have to install the system:** This isn't a really big deal for most folks, particularly when free installation deals are constantly being advertised. If you don't own your home, however, installation could be a deal breaker, so check with your landlord first.

One more thing: You may run into some resistance from homeowners' associations, neighborhood covenants, and the like. Don't take this lying down. The FCC ruled in 2001 that these "local" regulations can't be used to prevent you from installing a DSS dish. The only big exceptions are for safety (for example, you can't be too close to a power line) and for homes in historic districts. You may also be restricted from attaching your dish to "common" areas like shared exterior walls in condos. Otherwise, no one can keep you from using a dish if you want to. Know your rights! Check out www.fcc.gov/mb/facts/otard.html for the actual, long-winded text of this ruling.

Getting the dish on the dish

On your roof (or on the side of your house, or on top of a big rock in your backyard — you can stick these things just about anywhere) goes an 18- to 30-inch round or oval satellite dish. This dish is your main link to those satellites floating around in space, so it has to be aimed properly to pick up the signals. (By the way, this aiming is really the hardest part of the whole installation — despite the existence of self-install kits, we think aiming is sufficiently hard that it warrants a professional installation.)

Don't buy the round dish if you're getting a new DirecTV system. Only the slightly larger oval dish picks up the HDTV signals available on that service. For DISH Network, you need a second dish for HDTV, so this caveat doesn't apply.

Within this dish assembly are devices called LNBs, or Low Noise Blockers — the horn-shaped dinguses that sit in front of the actual parabola of the dish. These devices sift the high-frequency satellite signals out from other radio signals and block out the extraneous signals. Dishes can have one or more LNBs, depending on what you want to do with them. (Dishes with more than one LNB are referred to as *dual-, triple-,* or *quadruple-*LNB dishes — the newest DirecTV dish, the AT9, has *five* LNBs.)

Deciding how many LNBs and what shape of antenna you want can be really confusing. It depends on where you live, what service you are subscribing to, and how many TVs you want your satellite to feed into. There's no simple formula because there are multiple variables (and we really hated that multiple variable stuff back when we were in school).

One key factor to remember is that single-LNB dishes can feed only a single DSS receiver. If you want to watch different programs on different TVs simultaneously, you need at least a dual-LNB dish. We recommend that you get at least a dual-LNB dish; it's a false economy to get the marginally cheaper single-LNB dish.

If you subscribe to DirecTV, you should consider the five-LNB dish if you want HDTV (or local channels in some parts of the country). DISH Network uses a second dish for HDTV, so you won't ever run into a triple-LNB dish for that service.

Choosing a receiver

The television signals feeding in from a dish (or dishes) and through an LNB (or LNBs) are in a format that basically no TV can decode and display. So between the dish/LNB and your TV, you need to install a DSS receiver.

Although many things about DirecTV and DISH Network are similar, the receiver is one area in which they diverge. DISH Network maintains tight control on the receiver business and sells its own brand of receivers directly to its customers. (You can choose from several models in different price ranges.) DirecTV has a more open outlook on the receiver business, so you can buy your receivers from a range of companies, such as Sony, Samsung, and RCA.

Regardless of how you get the receiver, you have a few decisions to make before you buy. Right at the top of the list, you're going to need to work out whether or not you want a receiver that's

- ✔ **HDTV-capable:** If you have an HDTV or an HDTV-ready monitor, you can get the awesome high-definition programming through your DSS system. If you don't have one of these HDTV-capable TVs, you gain nothing from an HDTV-capable DSS receiver. You may still want to buy one if a TV upgrade is in your near future, but if you don't plan to upgrade for several years, we suggest you wait. Receiver prices are always dropping, and you'll probably get a much better deal in two years, even if you have to get rid of your existing receiver.

- ✔ **Home theater–capable:** Any DSS receiver can be used in a home theater, but some of the cheaper receivers don't have the proper chips inside or connectors on the back to provide the highest quality home theater experience that DSS can offer. We highly recommend that you make sure your DSS receiver has at least an S-Video connector on the back (we talk about video connectors in Chapter 16), as well as a digital audio connector (coaxial or optical) for Dolby Digital surround sound (which some, but not all, DSS programs include).

- ✔ **PVR-equipped:** Some DSS receivers now come with a built-in hard drive–based PVR (personal video recorder). Although you can certainly add your own PVR to a DSS-fed home theater, the integration of these units is kind of nice because the program guide that lets you select what show you want to watch live is well-integrated into the PVR's recording scheduling system. See Chapter 6 for a discussion of PVRs.

You might also want to keep an eye out for more prosaic features when choosing a DSS receiver. For example, some receivers have better (and easier to use) parental "lockout" controls that keep the kids from watching stuff you don't want them to watch. Others have remote controls based on RF (radio frequencies) instead of IR (infrared), so you can control them without a direct line of sight to the receiver. It always pays to check out the little details when you're making these investments. (By the way, the investment isn't too steep. You can find complete dish and two-receiver packages for under $200, but the price can rise to $500 or more for each HDTV-capable receiver.)

A handful of TVs on the market don't need an external receiver to connect to a DSS dish. Several manufacturers, most notably Thompson, make HDTVs with built-in DSS receivers for DirecTV. (So far, DISH Network still requires a separate receiver.) We're not sure this setup is a good thing because it limits your upgrade path and gives you twice as much to break down in a single device. It does save room, however, if you're tight on space.

Cable Cornucopia

The biggest competitor to the DSS companies comes from local cable companies, such as Time Warner, Comcast, and Cox Communications. Until recently, most home theater buffs didn't really consider cable TV to be much of a competitor to DSS — old-fashioned *analog* cable systems didn't offer nearly as many channels (particularly when it came to movie channels) as the satellites did. That fact has changed, however, with the advent of *digital* cable systems. These systems use MPEG-2 compression technology to carry analog (NTSC) programming into your house, and many provide you with Dolby Digital signals for at least some of the programming.

Lots of people confuse digital cable with HDTV, but for the *vast majority* of channels, digital cable is not HDTV. Most cable companies offer a dozen or so channels of HDTV over their digital cable systems (for example, Pat's cable company offers him 20 HDTV channels, out of about 500 total channels). But the rest is just digitally compressed and transmitted analog NTSC TV.

Functionally, DSS and digital cable are very similar. Both offer hundreds of channels, including tons of movie channels, pay-per-view movies, and every iteration of the Discovery channel you can imagine (Discovery Brain Surgery Channel, anyone?). Like DSS, digital cable includes a pretty on-screen interface that lets you browse through TV listings, set reminder timers, and the like.

The way that digital cable connects to your A/V system is even very similar to DSS. Digital cable requires a set-top box (equivalent to the DSS receiver) that converts these digitally compressed MPEG-2 channels into analog NTSC signals for your TV. And like DSS, if you want to get HDTV signals over digital cable (if your cable company offers them), you need a special set-top box with HDTV capabilities and HDTV connectors on the back, such as HDMI or wideband component video.

A number of new HDTVs are coming with the equivalent of a built-in cable set-top box. These DCR (or digital cable–ready) TVs use a small *smartcard* known as the *CableCARD,* which you rent from your cable TV provider. With a CableCARD, you can skip the set-top box, but you lose some of its features like video on demand (VoD) and an on-screen cable guide. See the sidebar titled "Can I see your CableCARD please?" for more information.

The big difference between DSS and digital cable, in our minds, is the fact that DSS gives you a choice of receivers (that you have to pay for), whereas digital cable gives you no choice. You rent the digital cable set-top box as part of your monthly service fee, and you get what the cable company gives you. The advantage of this approach is that the cable company has to fix or replace your set-top box if it stops working, but the disadvantage is that you really can't pick a set-top box that has the features you want. Like Model Ts, they come in any color you want, as long as it's black.

Can I see your CableCARD please?

Many of the newest HDTVs are DCR, or digital cable–ready. When you buy one of these TVs, you can plug the coaxial cable right from your wall into the TV, entirely skipping the set-top box. In order to get premium channels (like HBO), you will need to rent a device from your cable company known as a *CableCARD,* which plugs into a CableCARD slot on your TV .

The CableCARD is a smartcard with an embedded chip that can decrypt or descramble premium channels. Essentially, your cable company uses the CableCARD as a "mini" set-top box, built right into your TV.

There are two variants of CableCARD technology — CableCARD 1.0 and 2.0. As we write in early 2006, only the 1.0 version is available. It's quite limited in its capabilities because it is a *one-way* system. That means that it can only descramble systems coming *into* your TV; it can't communicate back with the cable company, in other words. So you lose the on-screen program guide, video on demand (VoD), and other features that a true set-top box gives you. Version 2.0, however, will supposedly give you

the two-way communications you need to get these interactive TV features and will support program guides, VoD, and other enhanced digital cable features.

Version 2.0 of the CableCARD is expected to hit the market sometime in 2006 — though it's not clear how quickly it will be adopted.

We're of mixed feelings about CableCARD. On the one hand, we love the way it lets you streamline your home theater — removing yet another black or silver box from your equipment rack. On the other hand, as it works today — the 1.0 version — it's a bit limiting. For example, Pat uses his cable set-top box as a DVR (see Chapter 6), so there's no advantage to him of getting rid of the set-top box. (He'd just have to go out and buy a separate DVR.)

When CableCARD 2.0 comes to market (and the cable companies are only mildly interested — they'd prefer to rent you a set-top box) things will get more interesting. We can't wait to see CableCARD 2.0 TiVo DVRs and other devices that can really make use of the system.

The other big difference between DSS and digital cable is one that we can't measure ourselves (we'd need to invest much of our book royalties on the test gear), but which we've heard many industry experts tell us: Many cable companies *compress* the analog NTSC signals carried over digital cable more than the DSS providers do. Because MPEG-2 is what's known as a *lossy* compression technology (meaning that, when MPEG-2 files are uncompressed for viewing, some of the original data is lost), this extra compression means your picture is less sharp and detailed than it would be at a lower compression level.

It's not all bad news, however. There are two big advantages to going with digital cable over DSS:

  ✓ **Digital cable systems always carry all your local channels (they're required to by law).** You might even get local cable-only channels that you'd never get over DSS or with a broadcast TV antenna.

✔ **Digital cable systems are two-way systems, communicating back to the cable company over the same line that carries your cable TV to you.** So you don't need a phone line (like you do with DSS), and you can actually do neat interactive TV stuff with digital cable. In many areas, you can actually do video on demand (or VoD) over a digital cable system. (We talk about VoD in more detail at the end of this chapter).

Another great feature of cable is that it is — generally speaking — immune to weather phenomena that can cause DSS services to freeze up or blur. Obviously, a big storm could blow over the poles that carry your cable signal into your home, but you won't have to worry about heavy winds or rain affecting your signal as you do with satellite.

Making a decision between DSS and digital cable is really tough. In some parts of the country, it won't be tough at all. Digital cable may not be available, or it may be in a primitive state (for example, no HDTV channels, no VoD, and fewer channels than DSS). In these cases, it helps to have either a good dealer or a lot of friends with home theaters so that you can judge different systems with your own eyes.

What about analog cable?

Most cable companies now offer digital cable service. They have to if they want to compete with the DSS guys, and they can if they've upgraded their cable plants to two-way in order to offer cable modem Internet access (which most cable companies have done). In some areas, however, you're still stuck with analog cable. There's nothing inherently wrong with analog cable. It was good enough for the cable TV industry to convince about 70 percent of Americans to buy their service in the first place, but it's not a particularly sexy service. If you need or want to get analog cable into your home theater, there's not a lot that needs to be done.

Any TV purchased in the past five to ten years (and certainly any TV you may shop for when building a home theater) is cable ready, with one big exception: Some high-end TVs (such as plasmas and front-projection models) ship as monitors without any kind of TV tuner built in. Besides this small group, any modern TV should be able to plug directly into an analog cable system and work without any extra pieces or parts. In a few cable systems, you need a set-top converter box (the analog equivalent to digital set-top boxes) in order to get pay-per-view or certain movie channels — often called *premium channels*.

Although most home theater builders will move up to digital cable or DSS, there's still a place for analog cable. For example, a basic analog cable package (which might cost less than $20 a month) is a good way to add all the local channels you want to receive to your DSS-based home theater system — particularly if you live in an area where over-the-air broadcast is spotty, and you can't get your local channels via DSS. If Pat ever switches to DSS, he's going to keep his basic analog cable service for two reasons: He has a cable modem that he can't live without, and he gets all the Padres games on cable and can't get them anywhere else.

Antennas Make a Comeback

Remember the good old days? Yeah, neither do we, but we can remember a day (not so long ago) when all the homes in our neighborhood sported rooftop TV antennas, sort of like how many homes in our neighborhood now sport rooftop DSS dishes. For most of us, the rooftop TV antenna (and its close ally, the back-of-the-set rabbit ears) went the way of black and white TVs and dodos a long time ago. Tuning in to broadcast TV was just too much of a pain in the butt compared to the "plug and play" of cable (or the "have a professional aim and then play" of DSS).

But a funny thing happened on the way to obsolescence. Antennas became hip again. HDTV is the reason. (It's always the reason for us, but we're like that.)

Moving everyone to ATSC and HDTV

HDTV is the reason because our good buddies at the FCC (the Federal Communications Commission) came up with a ruling a few years back that made a huge deal with every single TV broadcaster in the nation. The deal was this: We'll give you an extra chunk of the airwaves for a second TV channel absolutely free, but you have to use it to broadcast digital TV (and eventually you have to give us back your old channel so we can use it for other purposes, like wireless Internet connections).

Now this deal was supposed to be totally complete by 2006. And when we say totally, we mean that by 2006, every single station in America was supposed to be broadcasting all of its programming digitally, using one of the many different digital TV (ATSC) formats. Well, as we write, that has not happened, but most stations across the U.S. are now broadcasting both digital and analog signals.

The next step in the digital TV transition is for the few remaining analog-only holdouts to begin transmitting digital TV and then — the big step — for all stations to turn off their analog broadcasts. The *new* deadline for this step is February 17, 2009. By that date, all of your older analog TVs will need a (hopefully inexpensive) digital TV tuner that will pick up the over-the-air digital signals and convert them to an analog signal the older TVs can pick up. In Chapter 13 we talk about TVs with built-in ATSC (digital TV) tuners — most new TVs these days have this feature, and before 2009, all TVs with any kind of tuner built-in will as well.

The government is helping the transition along. In the summer of 2002, the FCC made a ruling that, by 2007, every TV sold in America must have a receiver that can get ATSC broadcasts. Keep in mind, this doesn't mean that these TVs will be able to display HDTV (for example, they might not have a high enough resolution, or they may not be able to display widescreen content properly), but they will be able to receive it and display it at lower resolutions and at a 4:3 aspect ratio. Eventually, when enough of these TVs are in people's homes, analog TV as we know it will go away, replaced by ATSC and HDTV.

This transition has caused a revitalization of the TV antenna industry. DSS and (some) digital cable systems carry a few HDTV stations, but they each have severe limitations to how many they can fit on their systems because HDTV is a bandwidth hog. It uses a lot more bandwidth than NTSC programming does — especially when the NTSC has been compressed using MPEG-2 — and bandwidth is a limited commodity on cable and DSS systems. To give more to HDTV means taking some away from something else. It's a zero sum game.

Sorry for the long background discussion, but we really felt it was important to understand what's happening before we discuss what you can do today.

Picking up ATSC with an antenna

Today, if you live in or around a large city, you can pick up ATSC programming by hooking up an antenna and tuning it into your local broadcasters. If you live in a smaller town, you just may have to wait it out for a while. The costs of putting in the new transmission and other broadcast station equipment to do ATSC are pretty high, and small stations are going to need frequent and persistent applications of something like an electric cattle prod to their posteriors to get it done.

Before you start investing in an antenna, check with your local broadcasters and see who actually has their ATSC channels up and running. You can also look on-line at www.hdtvpub.com. Just type in your zip code and find out who's broadcasting in your area.

The law requires these TV stations to broadcast in ATSC, not HDTV. HDTV is a subset of ATSC (check back in Chapter 4 if you missed this distinction). Generally speaking, of the 18 formats allowed under ATSC, we consider only 2 of them, 720p and 1080i, to be HDTV.

We focus on ATSC antennas here, and not older NTSC antennas, but the same general characteristics apply to each.

You can choose from both indoor and outdoor antennas. Indoor antennas work just fine if you are lucky enough to live in an area with great signals coming over the air, but most people get better results with outdoor antennas. Outdoor antennas are further categorized by three features:

✔ **Size:** We won't spend too much time explaining the concept of size to you, but ATSC antennas fit into small, medium, and large groups.

✔ **Directionality:** Some antennas (multidirectional) can pick up signals coming from any point of the compass, whereas others (directional) need to be aimed toward the incoming signal.

✔ **Amplification:** Most antennas are unamplified (meaning they don't have an electronic signal booster), but for weak signals, some antennas use a small *preamplifier* to boost the signals and help your TV tuner decode them.

Tuning in over-the-air HDTV can be a tricky business. The good news is that digital broadcasts are free of the snow, fade, and other things that made broadcast analog TV so frustrating. The bad news is that in place of these distortions, digital broadcasts tend to be, well, digital. In other words, they're either on (working) or off (nothing, nada, zip). It's not even a matter of just being too far from the broadcast tower either. We've heard of people being too close, or people being in the right range, but behind a hill.

The Consumer Electronics Association (CEA) has developed a great system to help you figure out which kind of antenna you need to get ATSC signals in your home. Go to its Web site at www.antennaweb.org, type in some basic address information, and its database spits out an antenna recommendation for you. The CEA even has a color coding system that participating antenna manufacturers put on the outside of their boxes so you can choose the right one at the store. Very handy.

Neat Network-based Services

As service providers (such as cable companies) have spent their billions of dollars building broadband networks for Internet access and digital cable, they've come across one big issue: They need to make money to pay back this investment. So they are constantly looking for new services that take advantage of these high-speed networks — services they can charge users for.

Well, we're often leery when service providers try to charge us more (well, not really; our day job is helping them figure out what these services might be!), but we definitely think that these new services are a case in which the customer also wins. These companies are looking at offering lots of different entertainment services (including neat stuff such as video games on demand), but the two most interesting (in our minds) are the following:

✔ **Video on demand (VoD):** Like to watch movies, but hate to go to the video store? One alternative is to join a service that does movie rentals on-line (and via the U.S. mail), like Netflix (www.netflix.com). Another very cool way to watch movies is to use a VoD service (now being offered by many cable companies as a part of digital cable services). VoD is kinda like pay-per-view (PPV). You pay for individual movies and shows, and you watch them on your cable-connected TV. But the similarities end there because VoD movies aren't run as scheduled broadcasts (like every hour on the hour). Instead, VoD movies are stored on big computers (video servers) as MPEG-2 files. When you want to watch one, you simply select it on your on-screen guide and press Play on your remote. The movie gets streamed to your set-top box (just like movies you watch on the Internet, but at a much higher quality), and played back on your TV. You have complete control of the stream, so, just like using a VCR or DVD player, you can start, stop, pause, fast forward, and rewind — the works — all for the same cost as regular PPV. One other neat VoD service is called SVoD (subscription VoD), which allows you to subscribe to a certain channel or show, such as HBO, and get VoD access to all the episodes of a favorite show (such as *The Sopranos*).

✔ **Networked PVRs:** This is a more futuristic service, but it's on the verge of appearing on the market. Networked PVR is a cross between regular personal video recorders (PVRs), such as ReplayTVs, and VoD. Like a PVR, a networked PVR records the shows you want to save on a big computer hard drive. But like VoD, this big computer hard drive is located in the service provider's office, not in your home theater. So you tell the system what you want to save, and it saves it in a centralized location. When you want to watch, you just click a button on your remote, and the programming is streamed to your TV over the cable company's broadband network. You can still do all the fast forward and pause type stuff you do on a regular PVR, but you have no extra boxes in your home theater and nothing to buy (you will have to pay a monthly fee for this, of course).

You might even see your phone company (believe it or not) get into these services. Phone companies are investigating new high-speed technologies (such as faster versions of the DSL Internet service they offer now, and even faster fiber optic–based services) that will allow them to compete with the cable companies. It seems fair enough, considering that cable companies are now starting to offer Internet access and long distance services. We can't wait for some competition!

Chapter 8

Introducing the Home Theater PC

· ·

· ·

For years now, there has been a huge digital divide between the PC world and the consumer electronics world. You have no doubt been exposed to the concept of multimedia in a PC in the form of animations, video games, MP3 audio, and maybe even short movie clips. Indeed, the ability to play these forms of media is a basic requirement of a multimedia PC.

Similarly, consumer electronics devices have been enabling much of the same entertainment content (video games, audio, video, and so on), but within its domain — the home entertainment center or home theater.

What most people have been waiting for is a sensible, economical, standardized, and indeed mass-market way to link the two. Well, wait no more — the era of the home theater PC is here and now.

In this chapter, we talk about what a home theater PC is, what kinds of pieces and parts you need to create a home theater PC out of your present PC, and also how you can buy a home theater PC right off the shelf (or off a Web page). We also talk a little about the kinds of *content* (audio and video) that your home theater PC can feed into the rest of your A/V gear in your home theater (and vice versa).

Meet the Home Theater PC

You should think of a home theater PC (or *HTPC,* as all the cool kids refer to them) as a high-quality source device attached to your A/V system, just as you think of a DVD player as a high-quality source. In fact, if you go relatively high end, you can create an HTPC that funnels audio and video into your system at a higher quality level than many moderately priced, standalone components. HTPC can be that good.

Building an HTPC is not something you can expect to do without a fair amount of knowledge about PCs, including some skills at opening up a PC and installing new cards and drives and being able to install and troubleshoot *drivers* (the software that integrates hardware devices with the operating system of a PC) and other software. We simply don't have room in this book to give you all the nitty-gritty details, but we will give you a good grounding in the essential pieces and parts you need to build your own HTPC. If you don't want to build your own, you *can* buy a ready-to-go version of the HTPC off the shelf (and we explain how later in this chapter).

Sizing up a home theater PC

Depending on your needs, a home theater PC should be able to do some or all of the following things:

- ✔ **Store audio (music) files.** No matter the file type, HTPCs need hard drive space and software for audio files.

- ✔ **Store video clips.** Homemade camcorder movies, downloaded movie trailers, or even downloaded full movies and TV shows belong on the HTPC. You need (again) hard drive space and software to make this happen.

- ✔ **Play CDs and DVDs.** This is an easy requirement because most PCs can at least play back CDs, but DVD is also essential in a home theater environment.

- ✔ **Act as a DVR (digital video recorder).** This is an optional (but almost essential, we think) function that uses the HTPC's hard drive to record television shows — essentially making it act like a TiVo or your cable or satellite provider's DVR.

- ✔ **Let you play video games on the big screen.** With the right hardware, PCs are sometimes even better than gaming consoles (which we cover in Chapter 9) in terms of game-type stuff, such as frames per second (or things blown to bits per millisecond).

- ✔ **Tune in to on-line music and video content.** You can grab a lot of really awesome content on the Internet these days. If you pay for this content (and you do have to pay for the good stuff, legally speaking), why not enjoy it on the big screen and with the good audio equipment?

- ✔ **Provide a high-quality, progressive video signal to your display.** All PCs have a built-in video system that's designed to display on a PC monitor (which, by the way, is inherently progressive — check out Chapter 4 if you don't remember what this is). Most PCs, however, can't display on a TV, at least not at high quality. An HTPC needs special hardware — which doesn't cost too much money — to make this happen. (This investment also gives you better performance on your PC's monitor, which is never bad.)

✔ **Decode and send to your display HDTV content.** This is another optional function, but a really cool one. With the right hardware inside (an HDTV-capable video card and TV tuner card), HTPCs can provide a cheap way to decode over-the-air HDTV signals and send them to your home theater display.

Building an HTPC

If the idea of putting together your own HTPC puts a twinkle in your eye, then this section is for you (and the HTPC we describe here really involves a building process — although there's an increasing number of small, specialty PC builders, like the folks at www.digitalconnection.com, who will put one together for you). So what do you need besides steady hands, nerves of steel, and a handy dandy TORX screwdriver or two? Well, let us tell you. The key pieces and parts to any HTPC are the following:

✔ **Fast processor:** Generally, you need a fast Pentium IV processor (preferably 2.0 GHz or faster) or an equivalent AMD processor. You can get away with less, but you might have performance issues (such as DVDs having *artifacts,* or leftover or poorly presented pixels, on the screen because the PC can't keep up decoding the DVD's MPEG content).

✔ **Sufficient RAM:** For an HTPC, you need at least 512MB of RAM, and 1GB or more is a good idea.

✔ **A big hard drive:** If you're not planning on saving a lot of video on your HTPC (meaning you won't be using it as a PVR — personal video recorder), you can probably get by with an 80GB hard drive. If you are going to start doing the PVR thing (or if you're going to put a lot of MP3 files on the HTPC), we recommend a much bigger hard drive. You can buy a 250GB drive for about $150, and even go as big as 500GB for under $400 (that's huge!).

✔ **A powerful, high-quality video card with an appropriate TV interface:** This is perhaps the most important feature. You need a graphics card that has TV outputs (at least an S-Video output, preferably component video outputs). If you're using a front-projection TV system (see Chapter 13), you might be able to use a different interface (like a VGA or DVI cable) that is more common to PC applications than home video (because many projectors can also be used as PC projectors — in meeting rooms, for example). We like the graphics cards available from ATI (www.ati.com) and NVIDIA (www.nvidia.com). Some specific things to look for in a video card are the following:

- *Look for a card with a built-in* video processing engine *(or VPE).* These are specifically designed for video.

- *Don't look for a gaming card.* Super-high-end graphics cards designed for the ultimate in PC gaming are typically not optimized for video display. They work, but you can probably do better with a (cheaper) card designed for video.

- *Look for a card with a built-in TV tuner.* Some products, like ATI's "All-in-Wonder" series of cards, have a built-in cable-ready TV tuner, so you can plug your cable TV or broadcast antenna directly into the card for TV viewing. Many cards have built-in ATSC tuners (see Chapter 7 for more on this topic) so you can tune in high-definition TV channels. Unfortunately, we don't know of any cards that can handle DSS or digital cable. Sorry.

  With the launch of the Windows Vista operating system in 2007 (see the sidebar, "Looking forward to Vista"), Microsoft will be supporting the CableCARD standard (discussed in Chapter 7). With a CableCARD built into your HTPC, you will be able to subscribe to digital cable services (including HDTV services if your video card and tuner support HDTV) directly from your PC. We're definitely waiting with bated breath on this one.

- *Think about HDTV.* A growing number of HTPC video cards now have built-in TV tuners that are capable of capturing ATSC/HDTV over-the-air broadcasts. These cards are capable of sending video to your display at an HDTV resolution (such as 720p or 1080i). So if you want to feed HDTV into your HTPC (wow, acronyms galore — sorry!), you need to add an HDTV tuner card (like ones made by AccessDTV — www.accessdtv.com).

- *Check the resolutions of the card.* If you have a non-HDTV-ready display unit (like a regular NTSC direct-view TV), you need only a 480-line output (with progressive scan, if your TV can handle it). If you have a projection TV or a plasma flat-panel TV, it may have a *native* resolution (which we discuss in Chapters 13 and 14). Make sure your card can display video at this resolution (you normally set the resolution of the card by using software bundled with your video card).

✔ **A high-end audio card:** Because you'll probably be playing surround sound formats on your HTPC, you'll want an audio card that can support this. Audio cards may have either a coaxial or an optical output. (Make sure you get one that has the same kind as what you have on the back of your receiver.) Many sound card manufacturers call this an *S/PDIF* (Sony/Philips Digital Interface) interface.

✔ **A CD/DVD-ROM drive:** This one is kind of a no-brainer — you're going to want to listen to CDs and watch DVDs. You might, however, also want to create your own CDs and DVDs, so consider a DVD-RW/DVD+RW drive (that can record DVDs). If you have a slower PC, you might consider adding a hardware device called a *DVD decoder* — this device performs hardware-based decoding of the MPEG video on DVDs, leaving your computer's main processor free to do its thing (like running the operating system). You can get DVD decoders from companies like Creative Labs and Sigma Designs (www.sigmadesigns.com).

✔ **An appropriate operating system:** We recommend that you use a modern operating system, such as Windows XP/Vista or Macintosh OS X. (If you use Linux, you're on your own — though we give a few tips in the section titled "Got Linux?".)

✔ **Software for playing or recording content:** At a minimum, you need some MP3 jukebox software to take care of your CD/MP3 playing, storage, and organization needs, and a similar DVD player program. For music, we like MUSICMATCH Jukebox (www.musicmatch.com) or iTunes (www.apple.com), and for video, we like InterVideo WinDVD (www.intervideo.com) — and don't forget that Microsoft's built-into-the-system Windows Media Player does a great job with both audio and video. A great free option is the VLC Media Player (VideoLAN Client; www.videolan.org/vlc), available for Mac, Windows, and Linux! If you want to use your HTPC as a PVR, you need some software (and perhaps hardware) to make that work, which we talk about in the following section.

✔ **A remote control:** Now, very few PCs come out-of-the-box with a remote control, but many of the HTPC video and audio cards we've discussed do. The key attribute of any remote for an HTPC is that the accompanying software can control all your applications — MP3 jukebox, DVD player software, and so on. (All these remotes come with software that makes the PC recognize them.)

Getting a TV tuner in your PC

While many HTPC video cards include a built-in TV tuner, you can also add a TV tuner to your HTPC separately. In fact, even if your video card has a tuner, you may want to add an additional TV tuner to your PC so that you can record one program while watching another (or record two at once). Some folks even go beyond two and put three or more tuners in their HTPCs.

You can add tuners in two ways: You can install an internal card that fits into one of your PC's PCI card slots, or you can add an external tuner card that plugs into a USB 2.0 or FireWire port on your PC. If you're making a laptop PC into an HTPC, you'll probably need to use an external tuner card because most laptops don't have a PCI slot for internal cards.

Understanding Viiv

At the annual CES (consumer electronics show) in 2006, Intel began showing prototypes of devices built on its new Viiv architecture. Viiv is based on the new *dual core* Pentium chips, but it includes a whole range of hardware, software, and even *service* components (meaning that various entertainment providers are creating music, video, and other entertainment services that work specifically with Viiv-based equipment).

Viiv will be the technological underpinning of new Media Center PCs (discussed in the section titled "Getting an HTPC the Easy Way") and HTPCs, as well as new non-PC devices like home media servers, TV set-top boxes, and more. For more information on Viiv as well as a list of Viiv-enabled PCs, check out the following URL: `www.intel.com/products/viiv/index.htm`.

We're focusing on the Windows operating system here, but Apple Macintosh computers can also make great HTPCs, with the right accessories and software. See the section, "Putting a Mac in your home theater," for more information about Mac-based HTPCs. That's really all there is to say (at our high-level view) about HTPCs. In Chapter 17, we discuss what you need to do to get this beautiful, high-tech monster hooked into your home theater.

Getting an HTPC the Easy Way

What if you don't want to go through all this computer building? Well, your friends at Microsoft (really, they're your friends) got together with a handful of their closest PC hardware partners and came up with their own version of the HTPC called the Windows XP Media Center Edition (`www.microsoft.com/windowsxp/mediacenter`).

Media Center (we're just going to shorten the name to that) is both software (XP Media Center Edition 2005 operating system) and hardware (the Media Center PC). One big deal about Media Center is that it's like the old Frank Sinatra song, "Love and Marriage": You can't have one without the other. You can get the Media Center operating system only by purchasing a brand new PC that has been outfitted specifically to be a Media Center PC.

You can't go to Microsoft.com and buy a "media center upgrade" for your existing Windows XP PC. You gotta buy a new machine.

What do you get out of a Media Center PC? Well, the details (such as the exact model of graphics card) depend upon the vendor, but the basic features of a Media Center PC include the following:

- **A remote control:** All Media Center PCs come with an infrared remote control that lets you control the various A/V functions from across the room (including other devices, such as cable boxes).

- **An "advanced" graphics card:** We put *advanced* in quotes because that's Microsoft's official term for describing it. Can't argue with strong words like that! Most of the Media Center PCs we've seen use something like NVIDIA's GeForce 6600 GT or ATI's Radeon 9200 or 9800 PRO graphics cards (which are cards you might purchase if you were building your own HTPC). These "advanced" cards must include a TV tuner function and a TV output for connecting to your display.

- **A hardware encoder:** This turns video from your TV source (like cable TV) into MPEG digital video and turns your Media Center PC into a PVR.

- **A digital audio output:** As we discuss in the preceding section, this lets you connect your PC to your A/V receiver for surround sound purposes.

- **Software that makes it all work:** This is the cool part (well, the whole thing is cool, but this makes it even cooler). Software to play your MP3s, CDs, and DVDs, and to run your PVR is all included and well integrated. So you don't have to bend over backward to make it all work.

Looking forward to Vista

Microsoft will be launching the replacement for Windows XP — Windows Vista — sometime in 2007. When they do, the Media Center Edition name will be retired, but the functionality will remain. While we haven't seen any official product announcements as we write in early 2006, we have seen Microsoft's official Vista lineup.

There will be six different variants of Windows Vista (up from three for XP — professional, home, and Media Center Edition). The top two "consumer" variants of Vista will contain the functionality that is now included in Media Center Edition: Vista Home Premium (which adds Media Center to the rest of the standard "home" Vista features), and Vista Ultimate (which includes everything *and* the kitchen sink — all the business and home features of Windows Vista plus Media Center). We don't yet know how these software bundles will be packaged up for consumers, but we expect that if you don't currently have a Media Center Edition PC, you'll need to buy a new PC to get the Premium or Ultimate package. Even if an upgrade is offered, we expect that the hardware requirements of Premium and Ultimate will be pretty steep and will rule out all but the newest PCs.

Coming soon: Media servers

While HTPCs and Windows XP Media Center Edition PCs are really just what their names say they are — PCs — there's a new generation of computer-like devices hitting the market that will do many of the same things in a more consumer-friendly fashion. *Media servers* are what we call them (and what most people call them — we're not just making this stuff up). A media server is really just a souped-up version of a standalone PVR (such as a TiVo) or a standalone MP3 server (such as an Audio ReQuest). The media server doesn't run a PC operating system and doesn't do normal PC stuff. It just serves up media (hence the name). We expect consumer electronics companies, such as Sony and Toshiba, to start selling media servers any day now. You'll be able to hook them into your PC network *and* into your home theater and use them to store music, video, digital photographs, and more.

A Media Center PC acts just like a regular PC most of the time. You use it for e-mail, Web surfing, writing books, and whatever. But when you click the remote, the PC shifts over to Media Center mode, and your normal PC desktop is replaced by a simplified interface (designed to be read from across the room on either a PC display or a home theater display). You can perform all the HTPC functions we discuss earlier in the section, "Sizing up a home theater PC," and also play games, manage and display digital photographs, and more. Very cool.

There are dozens of Media Center PC vendors as we write, and more hit the market every month. The coolest model we've seen so far is the Alienware DH-5 (www.alienware.com). Check it out; this baby can support up to *three* TV tuners (so you can record two shows and watch a third at the same time!) and can record up to 500 hours of video on its internal hard drives. Plus, it looks just like a piece of home theater gear and not like a bland beige PC.

Other HTPC Software Packages

Media Center Edition is the most popular (and easiest) way to get a Media Center PC, but it's not the only such package out there. You can add HTPC software and hardware to a Windows PC, or even build an HTPC using a Macintosh or a Linux-powered PC.

Building a Windows HTPC

You can build a home theater PC by using one of the following solutions (and these aren't even the only ones out there, only the most popular!):

✔ **BeyondTV** (www.snapstream.com): BeyondTV is SnapStream's media center/DVR software system. It offers a free on-screen program guide, customized to your area, and support for multiple TV tuners (for recording more than one program at a time). BeyondTV supports HDTV viewing and recording. One really neat feature of BeyondTV is its remote recording feature that lets you log in and set up recordings from any Web browser, including those found on many mobile phones! An optional component, BeyondMedia, allows you to control all of the media on your PC via SnapStream's interface and your remote control. The price ranges from $69.99 for the basic BeyondTV application, up to $199.99 for the full bundle that includes the BeyondMedia software and a TV tuner card.

✔ **SageTV** (www.sagetv.com): SageTV is a cool media center application that can control your TV, DVR, music, video, and photos. One feature that we really like about SageTV is its ability to work across a home network — so you can easily access media located on any PC attached to your home's wired or wireless network. You can even access and control the TV tuners located on other networked computers, creating, in effect, a whole-home DVR system that spans all of your TV tuner–equipped PCs.

✔ **Pinnacle Media Center** (www.pinnaclesys.com): Pinnacle sells both hardware and software — TV tuners and DVR/media center software. Their top-of-the-line software system, Pinnacle Media Center, is included with their PCTV 110i and PCTV 100e tuners (these are internal and external USB tuners, respectively). The internal (110i) version runs $79.99, and the external version lists for $99.99.

Putting a Mac in your home theater

Apple has launched it's own answer to the Windows XP Media Center Edition. Called Front Row, it's a media center (in the generic sense) application built right into the Macintosh OS X (10.4 Tiger) operating system. Front Row is a combination of software (the Front Row software) and hardware (in particular, Apple's elegant new remote control) that works with the inherent media capabilities of Apple's hardware and software to present audio, pictures, downloaded and/or home video, and DVDs on your Mac's display or an attached TV.

What Front Row doesn't include is any functionality for watching or recording TV. For that, you need to add some hardware and software, like Miglia's Evolution TV ($279, www.miglia.com) or Elgato's EyeTV 500 ($349, www.elgato.com). These systems include external TV tuner and decoder hardware (which connect to your Mac's USB or FireWire ports) and DVR software that turn your Mac into a full-fledged DVR.

The Front Row software (everything minus the DVR, in other words) is available only from Apple — it's standard on several Mac models, including (as we write) the iMac, the Intel-powered MacBook Pro, and the Intel-powered Mac Mini. There's no additional charge for Front Row, it just comes as a standard feature of these models. We expect Apple will add Front Row to more models over time, and we also wouldn't be surprised to see Mac hardware that uses Front Row and adds in the DVR and TV capabilities that you have to add in today.

By the way, you don't have to stick just to Front Row. Straight from the folks at Elgato comes Elgato's EyeHome ($199), which includes a remote controlled hardware device that you can place anywhere on your home network and control from any Mac on your network. EyeHome includes all of the cool audio/video/photograph features you'd expect, and also includes a Web browser connection that lets you view Web sites on your big-screen TV in the home theater. Our tech editor uses EyeHome and he *loves* it. And he's a smart guy, so you should listen to him!

Got Linux?

If you are running a PC with the Linux operating system instead of Windows, you don't have to give up on creating an HTPC. In fact, one of the most popular HTPC media center software packages is available only for the Linux OS — MythTV (www.mythtv.org). Check the MythTV site to see if the software will work on your particular Linux distribution and hardware.

Like most Linux software, MythTV comes with a great price — it's free! And also like many Linux programs, it's updated constantly. While the basic MythTV software is designed solely for DVR TV control functionality, the open source nature of MythTV means that other folks can develop additional functionality for the product — and they have, creating plug-ins to do other HTPC/media center functions like photo viewing, music playback and management, and more.

The best place to get more info about MythTV is on the MythTV wiki, at the following URL: www.mythtv.org/wiki/index.php/Main_Page.

By the way, if you're not familiar with wikis, check out http://en.wikipedia.org/wiki/wiki. This site explains the concept and uses of the wiki, which is basically an on-line encyclopedia format that allows multiple users to add and edit entries — a community-maintained encyclopedia or data source. They can be really handy!

Chapter 9

Gaming Galore

*T*oday's video gaming systems are crammed full of high-powered audio and graphics chips that can put your home theater through its paces. With DVD-based games, you get audio that can use all the speakers in your surround sound system and video that can fill up your screen. Video games aren't just kids' toys anymore; they can be an integral part of your home theater experience!

In this chapter, we talk about how video consoles can fit into your home theater system. (Okay, we realize some folks think they shouldn't play any role whatsoever, but we disagree — as you'll soon discover.) We talk about the leading console systems as well as how you might bring PC gaming systems into your home theater. By the way, we think game consoles are the best way to bring gaming to the big screen, but if you're handy with your PC, you can get a great gaming experience with a gaming PC as well.

Integrating Cool Consoles into Your Home Theater

If you have (or are considering buying) a modern gaming console, such as an Xbox 360 or the forthcoming PlayStation 3, you really need to be thinking about how you plan to integrate it as a source device (in other words, a device that provides audio and video) into your home theater. Yeah, we know — some "high end" home theater folks might be cringing right now. Let 'em. We think video games fit into even top-of-the-line home theaters.

Game consoles are, of course, built for video games, but if you're not deep of pocket, you might even think about letting your game console do double duty as your DVD player (yep, they can do that), at least until you've saved up the money for a nice, new, upconverting, standalone DVD player (as discussed in Chapter 6). Most of the consoles we discuss here can replace a DVD and/or CD player in your home theater, and more importantly, all of them can be a heck of a lot of fun. In the following sections, we give you an overview of the different consoles and how you can integrate them into your home theater.

When we say a game console is fast, we're not talking about how many MHz the processor operates at or other computer-centric measures of speed (though these are very important). Rather, we're talking about how much information the console can push up onto the TV screen when it's playing a game. (Okay — when *you're* playing a game and the console is *processing* the game.) Most experts use the number of polygons per second as a measurement for speed, and that's a pretty good measure, although some gaming experts use other graphics measurements.

Playing with Sony's PlayStations

Sony has been leading the way in the game console world for years now, first with the its popular PlayStation, then with the PlayStation 2, and soon with the PlayStation 3. (The names don't get any more original as time goes by, but the performance remains truly exceptional!)

PlayStation 2

The most popular gaming console to date has been Sony's PlayStation 2 (known among the In Crowd as *PS2*). This cool black-and-purple box has a 300 MHz processor under the hood, which might not sound like much in PC terms, but this processor is especially designed for gaming and can really crank out the video. The processor includes secondary processors, called *floating point* processors, that help the PS2 do the math on all of a game's polygons (remember polygons from geometry?) at supercomputer speeds.

Besides this high-powered processor, the PS2 includes a bunch of additional features:

- **A powerful graphics chip:** The *Graphics Synthesizer* chip does the actual work of creating all the pixels (or colored dots) that show up on your TV screen as the game video. For you tech types out there, this is a 256-bit graphics chip.

- **32MB of RAMBUS:** RAMBUS is a high-speed type of RAM or computer memory, and it holds all the computer instructions and codes that make up the game.

- **A DVD-ROM drive:** This drive plays the optical discs containing the PS2 games and can also play PlayStation 1 games, movie DVDs, and CDs.

✔ **Lots of ports and connections:** You get the following:

- Two gaming controller ports (The controllers are the physical interface between you and the game.)

- Two USB ports

  USB stands for *Universal Serial Bus* — like on a PC.

- Two memory card slots (to store game data, such as your current level in a game), as well as an expansion bay that lets you install a computer hard drive for even more storage

- A single i.LINK port (Sony's name for IEEE 1394 or FireWire — a super-high-speed connection used for all sorts of computer-related devices, such as hard drives and digital video cameras) that lets you connect multiple PS2s together for head-to-head gaming

  We talk about these fancy connections in Chapter 16.

You can also buy an on-line gaming connection kit for the PS2 that lets you connect your PS2 console to the Internet to play games against other people who aren't *anywhere* near your home theater. Neat. See the section, "Playing games on-line."

You can find out more about the PS2 (and the hundreds of games available for it) on-line at www.playstation.com.

The latest and greatest: PlayStation 3

The really exciting news from Sony is the PlayStation 3 (or PS3).

The PS3 is Sony's next-generation gaming console designed specifically for high-performance gaming in a home theater with an HDTV display. (Say *that* three times fast.) The PS3 is built around an entirely new kind of CPU called the *Cell* processor, designed by IBM with a little help from Sony and Toshiba. The Cell processor has multiple independent processing sections (called *Synergistic Processing Elements*, if you want to get technical) that give the PS3 the ability to render video at rates previously unheard of for consumer-grade computing devices. You've probably heard various PC and gaming manufacturers describe their systems as "supercomputer-like" over the years — this one truly is.

The PS3 will also include a Blu-ray disc player (see Chapter 6), so it can support high-definition optical discs for playing movies, and the capacity of Blu-ray (well over 20GB of data per disc) will let game makers cram a ton of detail into their game software.

PS3 will also include built-in wireless networking (so you can easily connect to Internet on-line gaming services through your Wi-Fi network), a powerful graphics chip (developed by NVIDIA), and an array of outputs to hook into your home theater.

Most importantly, PS3 will have two HDMI outputs for connecting to your high-definition display and optical and coaxial digital audio outputs for connecting to your A/V receiver for Dolby Digital or DTS 5.1-channel surround sound.

We can't wait to get our own PS3s! Unfortunately, we have been waiting, as the PS3 is tough to get your hands on. It was launched in late 2006, but only in certain markets. By the middle of 2007, the PS3 should be available just about everywhere, for about $600.

Xbox marks the spot

Microsoft hasn't just let Sony own the gaming console business. In fact, they've quickly established themselves as the number-two console maker and may move ahead of Sony with their latest console, the Xbox 360 — which beat the PS3 to market by at least six months.

Xbox

Until late 2001, PS2 was the king of the hill, the A#1, the fastest game console you could wrap your mitts around. Nothing faster . . . anywhere.

In November 2001, however, Microsoft launched its own competing game console — the Xbox (www.xbox.com). If you've ever picked one up and tried to move it around, you probably already know that this is a serious chunk of hardware. But the Xbox isn't just a big lump of metal — it's a seriously fast gaming console with faster-than-the-PS2 chips that have made it a serious contender to the PS2.

When comparing the Xbox and the PS2, most gaming geeks have found that the Xbox is a *bit* faster and more powerful. Not a lot faster, but if you have a high-resolution display (such as an HDTV) and are playing the same game, you'll probably find the video on the Xbox to be a bit sharper.

Not surprisingly, because Microsoft is primarily a PC software company, the Xbox has a lot in common with a Windows PC. However, everything has been altered, modified, and tweaked for gaming, and you can't use an Xbox to write a book in Microsoft Word. Intel builds the main processor, which is a 733 MHz variant of the Pentium III PC processor. More PC hardware can be found in the Xbox in the form of the graphics processor, dubbed the *X Chip,* which NVIDIA builds and which is a variant of the company's GeForce 3 PC video cards.

Other cool features of the Xbox include

- **A built-in 8GB hard drive (like a PC hard drive):** You can use the drive to save game data or to store audio tracks ripped from your own CDs so that you can customize your game soundtracks with your own favorite music. (*Ripping* is the process of converting CD audio to files on the hard drive, like the creation of MP3 music files.)

✔ **64MB of high-speed RAM:** This is good for holding the game data that the Pentium processor and NVIDIA chip are processing.

✔ **A built-in Ethernet port:** Ethernet is the high-speed (10 Mbps) networking system that most computer networks use. Ethernet is also the connection found on the majority of DSL and cable modems for home high-speed Internet, and this port lets you connect your Xbox to the Internet for on-line gaming — as we discuss in the section, "Playing games on-line."

✔ **A DVD optical drive for games, CDs, and video DVDs:** Unlike the PS2, however, the Xbox can't play video DVD out-of-the-box — you need to pay about $30 for a remote control and adapter (which plugs into one of the controller ports) to make this work.

✔ **Ports and slots:** You get four USB-type game controller ports (two more than the PS2) for multiplayer games, as well as a slot for an 8MB memory card.

What's really cool about the Xbox from a home theater perspective is the fact that the Xbox is the first console that can display its games on 1080i high-definition TV. (It has been joined in this capability by the Xbox 360, which we discuss next — the PS3, whenever it comes out, will also have this ability.) This means that you can have some really awesome, high-resolution gaming going on in your theater. Keep in mind that not too many games on the market have been specially designed (as they must be) to really take advantage of HDTV, but more and more are being so designed. And even if games aren't 1080i games, they still work well with (and look good on) HDTVs.

Get your HDTV gaming on with the Xbox 360

Microsoft didn't just rest on its laurels with the Xbox; it went back to the drawing boards and came out with an entirely new, better, and faster console at the end of 2005: the Xbox 360.

The Xbox 360 uses a custom version of the IBM PowerPC chip, with three *cores* (or independent processing units) providing a huge speed boost over the older Intel chips in the original Xbox. The 360 also includes a much faster graphics processing unit from ATI that can support high-definition (1080i) video on your HDTV.

Other features of the Xbox 360 include

✔ **512 Megabytes of RAM:** Eight times the memory in the original Xbox for faster access to gaming software. (You always get better response times when you access your game in RAM rather than from the DVD or other optical drive.)

✔ **A 32-bit audio processor:** This supports 5.1-channel Dolby Digital surround sound.

✔ **A wireless controller system:** No need to worry about tripping over the cords; the Xbox 360 offers wireless controllers that operate in the 2.4 GHz frequency band (the same frequencies used by Wi-Fi). Note that this is an optional component — not all Xbox 360s include these controllers in the package. You can "connect" up to four controllers at once using the wireless system.

✔ **An optional hard drive:** Microsoft sells a 20GB hard drive for the Xbox 360 that can hold music, pictures, and other media.

✔ **Network capabilities:** The Xbox 360 includes an Ethernet networking port that lets you connect your console to a home network for on-line gaming and for media purposes (like playing video and audio files on your PC). Microsoft also sells an 802.11 (Wi-Fi) wireless networking adapter that lets you connect to a wireless network (802.11a or 802.11g).

When you read that the Xbox 360 has "built-in wireless" capabilities, remember that this is for the controllers. If you want to use the wireless networking capability to connect your Xbox 360 to a home network and the Internet, you need this optional 802.11 networking adapter.

✔ **Front USB ports:** The Xbox 360 has two USB ports hidden under a port on the front of the unit (and a third USB port on the back) that let you connect devices like an iPod, a Sony PSP (handheld gaming machine), or even a digital camera.

✔ **Media center capabilities:** This is one of our favorite features of the Xbox 360 — if you have a Windows XP Media Center Edition PC, you can use your Xbox 360 as a *Media Center Extender* that will allow you to access all of the TV, music, photos, and video functionality of your Media Center PC over your home's wired or wireless network. So you can have your media stored on the Media Center PC in your home office and use the Xbox 360 to access and enjoy the media in your home theater. Pretty darned cool if you ask us.

The Xbox 360 comes in two different versions: the Xbox 360 (the fancier package) and the Core Edition (which does without some of the niceties). The fully featured Xbox 360 includes the hard drive, a wireless controller, a headset for Xbox Live on-line gaming with voice communications, an Ethernet cable for networking, and a component video cable for high-definition TV hook-ups. The Core Edition does without these features (it has a wired controller, for example), but you can buy all of these accessories a la carte if and when you decide you need them. The Xbox 360 also includes a free Xbox Live on-line gaming subscription (the Silver package for free, and a month trial of the Gold package) — you need to add on an accessory hard drive to the Core Edition to get this feature. The full-featured Xbox 360 bundle lists for $399, while the Xbox 360 Core Edition is a hundred bucks cheaper at $299.

If you want to get a lot of detail about the Xbox 360, check out *Xbox 360 For Dummies,* by Brian Johnson and Duncan Mackenzie. Those guys have all the good insider scoop and can give you levels of detail that we simply don't have room to include.

Unlike PS3, the Xbox 360 does *not* have a built-in optical drive that can play high-definition movies (the PS3 has a Blu-ray disc drive built-in). Microsoft has, however, begun selling an accessory HD-DVD drive that can be plugged into the Xbox 360, enabling the 360 to be a full high-definition source device in your home theater.

Not Rubik's Cube; it's GameCube

Not to be outdone by Sony and Microsoft, the granddaddy of game consoles, Nintendo, has its own new, high-powered, home theater–ready gaming console called the GameCube. This is by far the cutest of the three. It's positively tiny, especially compared with the huge hunk of metal that holds in the innards of the Xbox. The GameCube (or GC to the gaming cognoscenti) is no slouch, performance-wise, despite its diminutive dimensions (the GC is only 4 inches high).

Inside of the GC is a 485 MHz PowerPC processor — just like the ones traditionally inside of Apple Macs and PowerBooks and used by the Xbox 360. (IBM, the maker of PowerPC chips, and Nintendo have code-named this chip "Gekko.")

Other features of the GameCube include

- ✔ **A powerful graphics processor:** This one is code-named "Flipper," like the dolphin (though you shouldn't get this Flipper wet). Built by ATI (a leader in the computer graphics chip market), Flipper can crank out up to 12 million polygons per second to fill your screen with gamey goodness.

- ✔ **40MB of system memory:** This includes 24MB of some superfast RAM called MoSys 1T-SRAM. (No, we're not sure what that name stands for either, but it *is* faster than regular memory chips.)

- ✔ **Four ports for gaming controllers:** These are for multiplayer games.

- ✔ **Two memory card slots:** You can use these to save game information.

- ✔ **A proprietary optical disc that's smaller than traditional DVDs or CDs:** This smaller disc helps keep the size of the GC down to a minimum, but it does have the unfortunate drawback of keeping the GC from doing double duty as your home DVD player.

It's a revolution; it's the Wii!

Just as Microsoft and Sony have launched (or will soon launch, in the case of Sony) replacements for the Xbox and PS2, so will Nintendo follow up the GC with a faster, sleeker, and more home theater–friendly "next-generation" gaming console.

The new Nintendo (previously code-named the Revolution) is the Nintendo Wii (pronounced *we,* or for fun, *wheeee!*). The Revolution will be powered by a new CPU, code-named "Broadway," built by IBM (part of the PowerPC family). ATI developed a new graphics chipset, code-named "Hollywood," for the Wii. (We're waiting for another component to be code-named "Bollywood," but so far no luck!)

Nintendo has taken a slightly different approach with the Wii, making it smaller and cheaper than the Xbox 360 or PS3. From the home theater perspective, the bad part of this approach is that the Wii does *not* support HDTV resolutions in its graphics display (no 720p or 1080p) — too bad. The Wii does support 480p progressive scan, if you use component video cables to connect it. It also supports 5.1 channel surround sound.

The coolest thing about the Wii, and in our minds this at least somewhat makes up for the home theater shortcomings, is the controller. Rather than a traditional game controller, the Wii has a controller (the Wii Remote, or as most folks call it, the *Wiimote)* that looks a lot like a TV remote control — with fewer buttons and a more vertical orientation, as opposed to the horizontal orientation of most game controllers. The neat part is that this controller includes some sensors that can detect the motion of the controller in your hand, so you can control action on the screen (or at least some of the actions) by simply moving the controller in space, without having to push buttons or press toggles. This is something we've been waiting for *someone* to add into gaming, so we're glad to see that Nintendo is on the case.

The Wii is also wireless-enabled, with built-in 802.11 Wi-Fi networking. This feature allows you to quickly and easily get your Wii "on the Net" for Internet on-line gaming. Very cool.

The GameCube lags behind the other two consoles in some ways. Namely, its performance is slightly lower (though still excellent), and it can't play DVDs or CDs, which is why we mention it last. It does have some advantages though. Its small size makes it quite portable if you want to move your GC to the kids' bedroom (or take it out of the kids' bedroom!). Nintendo has a lot of incredibly popular games (think *Mario*) that you can play only on the GC. And finally, the GC costs less than the other consoles. (We haven't talked about prices too much yet because they change all the time and because so many different packages are out there. But as we write this book, the basic console and one-controller package for a PS2 or an Xbox is $199, whereas the GameCube is only $99.)

If you or your kids have one of the handheld Nintendo Game Boy Advance units, you can buy a cable to hook it up to your GameCube to play head-to-head between the units or to view your Game Boy games on the big screen.

The currently shipping models of the GC don't include a digital audio output for discrete surround sound. That means you'll have to use your A/V receiver's Dolby Pro Logic IIx capabilities to create surround sound out of the two-channel stereo audio the GC does put out.

Playing games on-line

Playing a video game by yourself can be a lot of fun, but some games are just meant to be played head-to-head against a human opponent. It's really a lot more fun to blow up your friends than it is to bomb an artificial computer opponent. Unfortunately, your friends can't always come over to play — especially if, like Pat, you've bumped into the big "FOUR OH" and find yourself trying to convince your friends to come over to play games. ("Uh, no, you can't bring your baby.")

Luckily, the broadband revolution that's given so many of us high-speed Internet access at home (using cable modems or DSL) has come to the video game world. All three of the gaming consoles we discuss in this chapter now have optional on-line gaming kits that enable you to connect your console not only to the home theater, but also to the Internet.

This connection opens up a world of new opportunities in game play. Play head to head against your buddy across town — or across the country. Join on-line games with complete strangers. Whatever floats your boat.

If the Xbox is your game console of choice, you need to check out Xbox *Live* (www.xbox.com/live). For $69.99, you get the components you need to get on-line and a year of gaming service — additional years cost $49.99. Microsoft *doesn't* provide the broadband service for Xbox *Live*, just the gaming service itself, and Xbox *Live* is broadband only. The gaming service eliminates the need to subscribe to one service for Game A and another for Game B.

The Xbox 360 (the full-featured edition with the built-in hard drive) comes with on-line gaming capabilities as well — a "Silver" level is free and lets you join on-line gaming communities, download (or purchase) games on-line, set up a profile for yourself, and even communicate with others via voice (using the Xbox 360's headset). If you want to get involved in actually playing head-to-head against other gamers on-line, you need to upgrade to the "Gold" level. Everyone gets a free month of Gold with their Xbox 360 — if you like it and want to keep your Gold status, you must pay. There are several different subscription levels (depending on whether you buy in a store or on-line, and for how long) — the one year subscription purchased on-line is $49.99. Note that the Xbox Live service for Xbox 360 is part of the same overall service offered by Microsoft, but is designed specifically for the newer console — and that the subscription plans and hardware are different for the two different consoles.

If you use a PS2, you need to spend $40 on Sony's PlayStation 2 Network Adapter, which enables you to connect via broadband or dialup connections. We think you really need broadband to do on-line gaming right (otherwise the play is just too choppy and lagged), but if you can't get broadband, it's nice to have the option of dialup. Regardless of how you connect, with a PS2, you need to sign up for a separate gaming service for each game you have (through the game software companies like Sega and EA).

The Nintendo Wii can be connected to Nintendo's Wi-Fi Connection service by using either a wireless router on your home broadband connection, or by connecting to any of over 6,000 hot spots throughout the U.S. (and worldwide). You can find details about Wi-Fi connection at `www.nintendowifi.com`.

Sony's PS3 has a free (though game manufacturers can charge you a fee for online play of specific games) service called PlayStation Network. Connect your PS3 to your home's broadband connection using an Ethernet cable or Wi-Fi and you can log into the network and register yourself through the PS3 console itself.

Remember that the cost of getting into on-line gaming is higher than just the price of the kit or service. You also need to account for the costs of new, online-ready games (we expect to see a ton of new ones hit the market) and gaming services. If you're not using an Xbox and Xbox *Live,* you also need to keep in mind that there may be costs associated with the on-line gaming services that let you connect with others on-line — meaning you may have to pay some additional fees to the game software companies.

Consoles aren't just for games

A game console isn't just fun — it can also be a multipurpose device that does more than just games. In fact, all of the manufacturers of game consoles have scores of engineers in white lab coats squirreled away at their headquarters, developing new ways that game consoles can be the centerpiece of a home's media room. So, although we're about to mention a few of the things that game consoles can do in the here and now, there's more to come.

Let's stay in the present for a moment, however, and look at what game consoles can do today:

✔ **Play DVD movies:** The Xbox, Xbox 360, and PS2 can all do this, although neither the Xbox nor the PS2 has progressive-scan DVD functionality. (See Chapter 6 if you're not sure what that means.) The PS3, with its built-in Blu-ray disc drive, will be capable of playing high-definition movies as well as standard DVDs (as will the Xbox 360 with the accessory HD-DVD drive that Microsoft has announced) — you'll be able to view progressive-scan DVDs and TrueHD (720p or 1080i) with the PS3 or Xbox 360.

✔ **Play audio CDs:** Again, both the Xbox and the PS2 can play any of your audio CDs when connected to your home theater. The Xbox 360 goes further here by letting you integrate a USB-equipped portable music player like an iPod into the system — simply plug it in and access your music through the Xbox 360. And if you have a Media Center Edition PC or Windows XP PC, your Xbox 360 can access all of the music you've stored on that device.

✔ **Surf the Web:** Not for novices, but if you have a PS2, you can buy Sony's Linux Kit for the PS2 for about $200. Linux, in case you aren't familiar with it, is a UNIX-based computer operating system favored by many techies, and this kit (which includes a hard drive, mouse, keyboard, and network adapter) lets you run all sorts of Linux applications on the PS2. Find out more at www.playstation.com.

This last item isn't exactly mainstream, but it gives you a good idea of where consoles are heading — right into the PC mainstream.

Because video game consoles tend to display parts of their images in a *static* fashion — in other words, part of the picture never, or rarely, changes — you need to be careful when picking a television for your video game–enhanced home theater. Some projection televisions (mainly those that use CRT picture tubes) and some flat-panel TVs (plasma screen TVs) can experience "burn in" when you use video games on them a lot. This means that the thin phosphor layers that light up to show your picture on these TVs become permanently etched with the images from your video game. Check the TV manufacturer's instructions before you use a video game console with one of these TVs.

Integrating PC-based Gaming into Your Home Theater

Although most people think of console gaming as something you do in the living room (or home theater room) and PC gaming as something you do in the home office or at a desk somewhere, PC-based games actually do have a role in the home theater. Speaking even more generally, we think PCs have a place in — or connected to — your home theater for a lot of functions. (Read Chapter 8 for more on this, if you've skipped it.)

Gaming on the PC has evolved over the years to be as sophisticated, fast, and graphics-rich as console gaming. In fact, if you want the ultimate in gaming machines — the no-holds-barred, polygon-generating king of the hill — you need to look at a PC, not at a console. And PCs are inherently more networkable than a console; these days, you have to try hard to find a PC that doesn't have a modem, an Ethernet port, and a dozen other ways to connect to other devices and networks. So PC-based gaming can be a great alternative to the consoles we discuss earlier in this chapter. You're no longer limited to that Minesweeper game that comes loaded on all PCs.

We should mention right up front in this section that purpose-built gaming consoles make the most sense for most people in a home theater. They're ready to go out of the box; with Plug-and-Play, they're simple to connect, set up, and play. Most PCs, on the other hand, need some serious tweaking to do gaming in a home theater environment (and by that, we mean using the surround sound system and television/monitor of your home theater). So keep that in mind.

Upgrading to Windows XP Media Center

The easiest way to get your PC involved in your home theater is to go out and buy an entirely new PC — one that uses Microsoft's new Windows XP Media Center Edition operating system. You can find out a ton about this new evolution of Windows at Microsoft's "test drive" site: www.microsoft.com/windowsxp/mediacenter/default.mspx.

Media Center is all about the convergence of the PC and the TV (and other home theater components). It was designed from the ground up as an operating system *and* a set of PC hardware that lets you easily connect the PC to your home entertainment gear. For this reason, you can't (at least currently) just go out and buy a Media Center upgrade for your current PC. Instead, you need to buy a new PC that includes some hardware specifically designed around the new operating system and that will facilitate this new PC-to-TV connection.

Media Center Edition PCs usually include the following extra (or enhanced) components, compared to a regular PC:

- ✔ A graphics card (or controller) with a TV Out connection that uses component video, S-Video, or composite video (RCA) cables to connect to your TV or home theater receiver. (Check out Chapter 16 for more details on what these connections are.)

- ✔ A sound board that can output surround sound using Dolby Digital 5.1. (See Chapter 5 for details on Dolby.)

- ✔ A remote control that lets you sit on the couch and click away at your PC.

The only things you need to transform a Media Center PC into a full-fledged member of your home theater are the cables to plug things together and, of course, the games and controllers that you want to play with.

We talk a lot more about Media Center PCs in Chapter 8.

Building your own gaming PC

You don't *need* to get an XP Media Center PC to get your PC games hooked into your home theater. Creating your own Home Theater PC is a very valid approach — as long as you keep in mind that it might take a bit more PC expertise than just buying a new PC that was specially designed for such use. We talk at length in Chapter 8 about how to choose PCs and PC components and accessories as source devices and video recorders for your home theater, and exactly the same rules that apply there apply to using your PC as a gaming machine in your home theater.

You need just a couple of things:

✔ A graphics card that can

  • Connect to a television

  • Display properly on the television (meaning it can output the right resolution for your particular TV)

✔ A sound card that can connect to your home theater receiver using either analog (RCA) jacks or a digital connection, and that can provide the receiver with analog Dolby Pro Logic or (preferably) Dolby Digital signals

That's basically it. In Chapter 18, we talk more about setting up your PC and home Internet connection with your home theater.

Adding Extra Game Controllers

Whatever game system you choose — console or PC, Xbox or PS2 (or Xbox 360 or PS3) — you need to interface with it. That is the whole point of games: interactivity. Of course, by connecting your game system to your home theater, you've covered how your eyes and ears (and rear end, if you've got a big enough subwoofer) interface with the system. The other key interface is, of course, your hands (and sometimes feet), which connect to your games with a controller.

All game consoles come with one or two basic multipurpose controllers that usually have enough buttons and joysticks and four-way pointers to drive us adults crazy (though the kids seem to catch on to them right away). These controllers (sometimes called *gamepads*) allow you to play just about any game if you can twist your thumbs in the right direction and have the appropriate level of dexterity and coordination. You might, however, want to consider some specialized controllers if you have certain games that you simply love to play again and again. (You might save yourself from repetitive stress injuries this way — and increase your score!)

Some of the controllers you can buy include

- **Wireless controllers:** These are usually just like the general-purpose controllers, but they connect by using radio waves, not wires. If you have dogs, small kids, or are simply sick of tripping over wires, pick up a pair of these wireless wonders.

- **Wheel controllers:** The kids like *Mario,* but we like *Grand Turismo 3* (at least Pat does). In other words, we want to pretend that we're not stuck in traffic, that we're Colin McRae zipping through the World Rally Championship in our WRX. Thumb buttons don't cut it for this activity. Get a wheel controller that includes brake and accelerator pedals, a big fat racing wheel, and a nice short-throw shift knob. Racers, start your engines! Check out www.madcatz.com for our favorite wheels.

- **Joysticks:** Want to pretend you're "Cool Hand" Grafton's wing man in *Flight of the Intruder?* Well, then you need a joystick controller with enough buttons to "pickle" your bombs on target. Check out www. thrustmaster.com for some cool joysticks.

There are literally a ton of controllers out there you can buy (really, we bought one of each and weighed them! — okay, that's a lie), including some really funky ones. There are skateboard-shaped controllers that you stand on for skating, surfing, or boarding games, and even one that consists of a mat for replicating dance moves you see on-screen. You can find something for everyone, and groovy controllers are truly a way to maximize your home theater fun.

Chapter 10

Accessing Digital Content at Home and Over the Internet

*U*ntil recently, most of the content destined for your home theater came in the form of DVDs, camcorder tapes, VHS videos, burned MP3s, CDs, audio tapes, and other such content in and around the home. Not much of it came directly and in real time from Internet sources (except to those of you who figured out Napster before it got shut down!).

Believe it or not, soon, very soon, the Internet is going to be the main way you get content into your home theater. Believe us — we do this for a living. You are just seeing the earliest movements toward the flood of Internet content — buying music and TV shows from Apple's iTunes, searching for home videos at http://video.google.com, accessing streaming video of your local high school basketball team being filmed live by students . . . it's going to come from everywhere, and the vast majority of it is going to come from the Internet.

High-speed Internet connectivity — which again we argue is a baseline requirement for any home theater — will enable you to download a lot of content for viewing whenever you would like. This will put lots of pricing and product pressure on the cable, satellite, and telephone company TV offerings, and that does not bother us a bit!

A large number of diverse players are trying to make Internet-based content as easy for you to adopt as finding a sports score or weather forecast on any portal site. Yahoo!, MSN, Google, and others will be trying to convince you to search, view, and even buy content through their portals.

Having an Internet-based home theater is Step One. After you are plugged in, the World Wide Web is open to you. This means you'll have digital content around your house from all over the world to keep you busy at night! Whew, and you thought you were going to get some sleep!

Learning about Digital Content for Your Home Theater

Grabbing music and video off the Internet is likely not a new topic for you. Companies like Napster and KaZaA have been in the news for years, and online music and video stores like Apple's iTunes are an often-mentioned item in almost any magazine or newspaper.

But when you get right down to it, a few high-level constructs would be good to introduce, so you know what all the fuss is about.

Whether it's on a computer hard drive down the hall or on a server in Outer Mongolia, the concepts surrounding "content" are the same.

So here's a quick hit of the key concepts we want you to know about electronic content:

- **File Encoding:** Digital music and video files are *encoded* (converted to digital formats) using specific encoding formats. For audio, MP3 is most common, but there are many others out there, including Windows Media Audio (WMA), Advanced Audio Code (AAC), and even weirdly named ones like Ogg Vorbis. We discuss these audio formats in detail in Chapter 3. Similarly, there are a number of video formats (like WMV and MPEG), discussed in Chapter 4.

  The key thing you must keep in mind about the encoding format used for your audio or video is that whatever system you use for *decoding* that file to display it on your home theater must support the format you are using. For example, if your digital media adapter doesn't support Apple's encrypted AAC format, you won't be able to play music from the iTunes Music Store on your home theater system.

- **Streaming versus downloading:** Not all audio or video is delivered in the same fashion. In fact, there are two predominant ways of sending the content — streaming and downloading. *Streaming video* means that there is no local copy of the video on your device. It plays while it is delivered over your home network and/or the Internet. Most Internet connections aren't fast enough to play really high quality streaming video, so you find that many Internet movies are downloaded to your machine instead. *Downloaded video* is delivered as a file to be stored inside your set-top box, Media Center PC, or other device, and then played back from that local storage. So while downloaded video can deliver a TV-like quality viewing experience, complete with the ability to fast forward, pause, rewind, and so on, you have to wait a while — usually up to an hour or more — for full-length movies to download.

✔ **Internet radio:** *Internet radio* is exactly what it sounds like — radio stations broadcasting in a streaming fashion over the Internet. So if you are a college student and you miss your favorite radio station back home, you can still listen to it via streaming audio over the Internet.

We discuss Internet radio briefly in Chapter 5 in addition to later in this chapter.

✔ **Podcasts:** *Podcasts* are the equivalent of downloaded Internet radio. They are files that contain audio (and, more and more, video) that often are packaged like daily newscasts or commentary. Podcasts are so named because they initially were targeted toward easy dissemination of content to iPod users.

✔ **Video search:** *Video search* is catching on fast. Video search engines scour the Web and find content based on keywords and file formats and then make this available through some sort of on-screen interface. Google has perhaps the best-known search interface at `http://video.google.com`, but there are others, including Yahoo! (`http://video.search.yahoo.com`) and AltaVista (`www.altavista.com/video/default`). These search engines marry the best of non-X-rated amateur videos from the Web with the ability to buy videos of TV show series and movies as well.

✔ **File sharing:** *File-sharing* networks are networks set up for, not surprisingly, sharing files. In a very "free love" approach to content, early file-sharing networks adopted a "What's mine is yours, and vice versa" approach toward exchanging content. Basically, you were encouraged to make your music available to anyone who wanted it, and they would do the same with you. Napster, Grokster, and other early leaders in this space were taken to court by the music industry, proven to be in violation of Federal copyright laws in the United States, and shut down. Most of the large worldwide music-sharing services used *peer-to-peer* technologies, described below.

✔ **Peer-to-peer:** *Peer-to-peer* (P2P) is a concept often associated with music file sharing because it is the way most of the illegal music download services worked. Peer-to-peer simply means that you directly connect to other people's computers to download files, instead of going to a central file server. See, not only are central file servers expensive and require a lot of costly broadband bandwidth to support music and video downloading, they're also very easy to find and shut down.

Peer-to-peer networks operate without such central control, and allow multiple users to share files at the same time — you'll often be downloading and uploading different "chunks" of a file to and from numerous folks at the same time.

Peer-to-peer is not just used for file sharing — you also probably use it for some instant messaging services, too.

✔ **Digital rights management (DRM):** No initials in your Home Theater Glossary (you keep it under your pillow, don't you?) are more accursed than *DRM* — digital rights management. If you download a lot of iTunes songs, you've run into DRM restrictions when trying to load your songs to other devices. (Most portable music players — besides the iPod — simply can't play back iTunes Music Store downloads.) If you've ever tried to copy a DVD, you've encountered DRM. DRM is everywhere you don't want it to be.

To be fair, DRM exists for a reason — to protect the copyright interests of the music, movie, and other content owners. Managing who has rights to do what with which digital assets is a key function of any DRM system.

DRM is often in the news, but you may not hear it referenced as such. In late 2005/early 2006, when you saw all the hubbub over Sony putting DRM software on their CDs to protect against unauthorized copying — software that was resident in a PC's *rootkit* — that was a DRM issue. (Though the issue itself wasn't the activity of the DRM system, but rather the "secret" software that the CD installed onto people's hard drives.)

The rules for sharing content are defined both technically and legally. You can do a lot of stuff technically — that does not make it legal. You can safely assume that the law says you can't copy anything unless you are told you explicitly can. You also can pretty much assume you cannot rebroadcast or retransmit the content in any way. Indeed, some analysts question whether the Slingbox, mentioned later in this chapter (it's a device that sends your home theater TV signals across the Internet to your laptop or mobile phone), violates copyright rules by retransmitting the signals received by your set-top box. By the time you read this, this may have (or not) become a mainstream issue.

But we did say that *part* of sharing content is defined technically. This is true. In many instances, you cannot record or copy content because there is special coding in the content itself that prevents you from doing this.

Some of the music services will explicitly allow you to make one copy, or play the songs on up to five machines, or some such limitation. This will be part of your subscription contract and should be fairly obvious. For instance, if you download content from iTunes, you can house that content on up to five computers (and an unlimited number of iPods). Look for this when trying to decide which service to use.

We specifically talk about DRM issues throughout this book as we encounter DRM problems. For the sake of this chapter, know that the Internet content you download will have strong limits on where you can put it, and you will most likely be able to view/listen to the content only on the machine to which you download the content.

Gauging Your Network Requirements

Figuring out digital content's impact on your computing and network requirements is a lot like trying to figure out how much space you need in your living room for books. There are big books, small books, fat books, thin books. Depending on the size of what you like, that's what you need to plan for.

With music, videos, and even pictures, it is a little more predictable than book sizes because

- You can usually decide the quality of the content recording you are obtaining/making.
- You can determine how long you want to have the content.
- You can determine when you want to have it.

It goes without saying that if you want to download the biggest movie at the best quality *and* you want to keep it stored on your hard drive (you just love that *Rome* mini-series don't ya!) *and* you want it *now,* then you're going to need a lot more capacity than someone who merely wants to stream a movie to their small TV set in average-quality mode and be done with it.

Figuring out the basics

You'll hear companies talk about the number of songs or movies you can store on their MP3 players and other digital content media. To make these statements, the manufacturers have to make an assumption about your encoding format, and they will generally assume a lower-quality format to boost the number of songs they can brag can fit on their devices!

- For music, 384 Kbps encoding is very high quality to most people, and that implies that you can fit about 6,600 songs onto an 80GB hard drive.
- Many folks encode their songs at lower bit rates, like 192 Kbps or even 128 Kbps, allowing even more songs to fit on the drive. You'll have to make your own judgment about quality versus space. We think 384 Kbps is a good balance between audio quality and storage space; you may be happier with a higher or lower bit rate.
- For video, near-DVD quality is about 1.5 Mbps bit rate and about 4 Mbps is a good rule of thumb for full DVD quality. At these bit rates, you can fit about 50 or so "near-DVD" quality movies on an 80GB hard drive, or about 18 "full DVD" quality movies on the same sized drive.
- For photos, a high-resolution photo is about 2.5MB, and you can fit about 30,000 pictures onto an 80GB hard drive.

> ✔ If you're going to be streaming a lot of content from the Internet, then the minimum bandwidth we think you want to have from your broadband access service is a 2 Mbps download speed — though you can get by with less.

Broadband access *into* your home is typically asymmetrical, meaning that your download speeds are different — and almost always higher — than your upload speeds. The nature of the Internet has been that you ask for something, be it a Web page or anything else, and you get it. The size of your question uploaded to the Internet (a few bytes worth of "Show me `http://www.dummies.com`") and the size of the file that is downloaded in response (all the files that constitute the whole Web page) are drastically different, and the broadband network technologies were skewed toward larger download speeds for this reason.

Checking your in-home capabilities

In addition to the capabilities of your PC and of your Internet connection, you need to concern yourself with the capabilities of your *in-home* network connections — the wired or wireless networks that carry content between your broadband modem, your computers, and your home theater and networked source devices in the home theater.

The size of the network *within* your home is not as asymmetrical, and files are flying all over the place between computers, your modems, printers, scanners, cameras, and so on. So your home's computer network is considered symmetrical and is designed out of the box as such. Thus, you see home networking measured in terms of overall bidirectional capacity at any one time, such as 10 Mbps.

We discuss home networking for your home theater in detail in Chapter 18.

Making Your Content Digital

While you can obtain a lot of cool digital content for your home theater from the Internet and on-line services and stores, you'll probably find that a good deal of things you'd like to display in your home theater comes from sources *inside* of your home. You probably already have collections of movies, songs, and photographs that are not digital, but which you'd like to display in your theater. There's nothing wrong with just using analog source devices (like VCRs, cassette decks, and turntables) to get this content into your home theater, but many folks like to go "all digital."

Why is this the case? Well, first of all, digital media is typically much more durable than analog media. LP records scratch, tapes break and wear out, but digital files can be played over and over without any degradation. Second, digital media is *physically* very space efficient — you can cram a lot of video, music, and photos onto a small computer hard drive and then put the bulky tapes, records, and cassettes away in the attic. Finally, digital media is more convenient — instead of pulling out a tape (for example), you can simply "browse" for that video on a computer interface and instantly start playing it (and pause, rewind, and skip around much more easily too!).

If your content is not yet digitized — for instance, it's still on VHS tapes, paper photographs, photo negatives, cassette tapes, and so on — you can digitize it.

There's an art and a process to getting your content digitized and putting it on your network — much more than we can cover in this one book. But in a nutshell, here are some options for you to consider:

- ✔ **Photos:** Although you can use any scanner to scan your photos into an electronic file, we recommend that you use a scanner designed specifically to scan old photos and negatives. Most of the experts we know in this area point to Nikon's "CoolScan" family of slide and film scanners (`http://nikonimaging.com/global/products/scanner/index.htm`, $500–$2,000). You feed your negatives and slides into the scanner, and the system converts them into digital files. You will have to spend time reviewing the output, but with Nikon's raved-about software, the fixes made for dust and scratches are amazing. You can get cheaper scanners, but you get what you pay for. We advise you to spend the money and get the best you can get — there's a reason you are scanning all these pictures to begin with, so do it right.

- ✔ **Movies:** If you have shelves of VHS home movies you need to convert to DVD, this is actually a pretty straightforward and simple process. Unless you want to pay a lot of money for an all-in-one conversion device, you can get by with a PC, a VCR, a device that converts the VCR's analog signals into digital, and some editing software to make sure everything is just right. Pinnacle Systems (`www.pinnaclesys.com`, $50–$130) offers an easy-to-use line of products designed just for transferring tapes. Its top-of-the-line Digital Video Creator 150 ($130) comes with the hardware and software to do the conversion. (The cable has RCA jacks on one end for connecting to your VCR and a USB 2.0 jack on other for connecting to your PC.) If you don't have a DVD burner in your home theater, you can get an add-on burner that will connect to your PC starting around $75 at any PC store.

  Mac users might consider El Gato's EyeTV system, which does most of the same things that Digital Video Creator 150 does, only on the Apple Mac OS. Check it out at `www.elgato.com`.

- ✔ **Music:** If you have shoeboxes full of old cassettes and peach crates full of vinyl LPs, these too can be converted to digital. You don't really need any special hardware — just your old turntable or tape player. Grab a cable with two RCA plugs at one end and a mini ⅛-inch stereo plug at the other, which you can get at RadioShack. Connect the RCA plugs to the Tape Out jacks on your preamplifier or receiver and connect the other end to the Line In jack on your PC sound card. Then you load equalization/sound processing software, such as Nero 7 Ultra Edition (www.nero.com, $80), turn on your source player, and the software will clean up your vinyl and cassette recordings, lifting out any annoying scratches and pops along the way. If you want, it will break the long taped recording into smaller music files so you can have each song isolated on the CD. When it's ready, it will help you burn the results to CD. If you have a LightScribe burner, it will even help you label the CD. (See the "Burning labels onto your discs in your PC!" sidebar.)

If your content is already digital — on mini-DV tapes in a FireWire-accessible camcorder, in a Wi-Fi outfitted digital camera, on secure digital (SD) storage cards from your cellphone camera, digital camera, or video camera, or something similar — getting it into your home theater merely involves a simple file transfer.

If you don't have an SD (or other digital card) reader in your home theater, get a "universal" or "all-in-one" card reader device that can access a wide range of memory cards and process them into your home theater gear. Transferring files directly off your digital devices really eats into the battery charge, which in turn, over time, reduces the life of the battery unnecessarily. Just pop out the card and stick it in these readers, and your files automatically transfer to the reader's parent device. If you get devices with a USB connection, make sure it supports the faster USB 2.0 version. Dazzle's Universal 10-in-1 Memory Card Reader/Writer (available from www.radioshack.com, $40) is a great example: It reads the ten most popular memory cards from one device. That should cover all your memory card–outfitted digital devices in your home.

Burning labels onto your discs in your PC!

You might encounter a really cool new technology when shopping for a CD or DVD burner. *LightScribe Direct Disc Labeling* enables you to burn professional, silkscreen-quality labels directly on your CDs and DVDs — if you have a LightScribe-enabled optical disc drive and LightScribe-compatible media. With LightScribe, you create or download the label of your choice. Then, after you burn your data, music, or video onto a CD or DVD, simply flip the disc over, put it back into the drive, and burn your newly created label design directly onto the disc. It looks professional and way cool. Look for LightScribe when buying a burner.

You can save a few bucks (and get results almost as good as LightScribe) by combining "printable" CDs and DVDs (look on the label when you buy) with a printer like Epson's R340 — this combination lets you pop the disc right into a slot on the printer to create high-quality labels using the inkjet printer.

When it comes to getting camcorder movies into your home theater, check out Microsoft's Movie Maker software, which resides on most Windows XP PCs. (If by chance your PC lacks a copy, you can download it for free from the Microsoft site at `www.microsoft.com/windowsxp/using/moviemaker/default.mspx`.) This will help you get your movie onto your PC, where you can add music, move scenes around, and add on-screen text. A bit too techie for you? Then consider Muvee's autoProducer software (`www.muvee.com`, $75). With autoProducer, you select your video file, plus the music you like and style of movie you want to create, and press a button — autoProducer will create the movie for you. It selects the scenes with the most apparent action and best shots and dubs in the music, resulting in a more concise view of your hours of home film footage. Your neighbors and friends will thank you. If you've got a Mac running OS X, you can use Apple's iMovie software. It comes standard on most new Macs, or you can buy it as part of the Apple iLife software bundle (`www.apple.com/ilife`). It's considered by many to be the easiest-to-use movie-making software system, but this ease-of-use doesn't come at the expense of capabilities. (It's got all of the features most nonprofessional movie makers need, and works well with Apple's iDVD software to create DVD movies you can bring with you.)

Finding Sources of Content On-line

Finding on-line digital content can be hard if you don't know where to look. More than 2,500 radio stations broadcast over the Internet, for instance. Most mainstream FM stations also simulcast over the Internet. On the video side, CNN, MSNBC, Yahoo!, and others offer up lots of Internet video content; Google's video search capability gives surfers access to amateur video as well as Hollywood fare. Content is simply all over the place.

Lucky for you, lots of industry players have stepped up to the challenge of organizing all of this content for you through *content portals*.

When it comes to buying or accessing on-line content, there are three main forms of content services:

- ✔ **Download:** You download a file and it's yours to use forever. Music downloads tend to fall into this category. Downloads may be free or paid for.

- ✔ **Rental:** You download a file, and it's yours to use for a limited time. Many movie rentals allow you a certain number of days to view the movie before it expires and is no longer viewable. Rentals are usually paid for, but can be free on promotion.

- ✔ **Subscription:** You subscribe to a service that gives you access to unlimited use of the content as it is presented on the portal, such as subscribing to 120 channels of streaming audio for a monthly fee.

In this section, we'll look at a few of these portals offering downloads, rentals, and subscriptions for audio and video content.

Audio content

Audio preceded video in terms of portals on the Internet, largely because audio could be listened to via dialup Internet connections because of the much smaller file sizes relative to video. Video had to wait for mass broadband deployment to really take off.

Some of the most popular on-line audio content providers (with Web addresses conveniently appended) are shown below:

- ✔ Apple's iTunes Music Store (`www.apple.com/itunes`)
- ✔ Yahoo! Music (`music.yahoo.com`)
- ✔ Rhapsody (`www.rhapsody.com`)
- ✔ eMusic (`www.emusic.com`)
- ✔ Napster (`www.napster.com`)

The pricing and options for the services listed above change rapidly, and we'd be doing both you and us a disservice if we tried to describe all these services in detail. Instead, we'll give you advice about how to find the best service to match your needs:

- ✔ **Number of songs:** The bigger services offer you more choices — simple as that. If you are very much concerned about the variety and depth of content, then you should be aware that there is a big variance in the number of songs — and the number of songs from high-profile artists — each service makes available. Apple claims more than 2 million songs; Rhapsody has more than 1 million; MusicMatch more than 900,000. Urge, which was announced as we write this, says it has 2 million songs ready, too. In general, the wider your tastes, the more you want to go with the larger services.

- ✔ **Flexibility in use:** If you want to own all your own tracks and movies and have no problem limiting your player choice to iPod models, then iTunes is a great option for you. It's simple, has an extensive catalog, is leading the pack with video purchase options, and allows things like sharing over your LAN and on multiple PCs. However, the downside of iTunes is that you are married for life to the proprietary Apple world, and that world, as of the time of this writing, is very closed. You simply can't play your iTunes-purchased music or video on alternate players, set-top boxes, and so on — only Apple's own Airport Express will play iTunes Music Store–purchased songs remotely. On the other hand, if you go with the more widely accessible Microsoft Windows Media Audio (WMA)–based systems, you open up your entire home to a range of players, set-top boxes, and other platforms to access your digital content. The most flexible, for music at least, is eMusic, which does not use any sort of DRM (Digital Rights Management, discussed earlier in the chapter) system, so you can use them on anything that plays the MP3 format. But eMusic does not have as complete a catalog as iTunes or other services. So there are trade-offs.

✔ **Quality desired:** There is a range of quality in the digital content as well, mostly based on the encoding sampling rate used. None of the on-line digital content services store content in a lossless fashion, so all of them end up compromising the original recordings to some extent. You can truly notice a difference between tracks encoded at 128 Kbps, 160 Kbps, and 192 Kbps, for instance. (The higher the number, the better the quality, for those keeping track.) You do trade off the amount of music you can store on your player, though, because the file sizes are larger for higher sampling rates. But we think going for the higher sampling rate — 192 Kbps — is the appropriate trade-off.

✔ **Try before you buy:** If you are the type who likes to try out lots of new bands and watch all the new indie movies, then you should look at subscription services because you can listen and watch to your heart's content and buy what you like. If you go the download route, you'll buy a lot of content you end up not liking — and that's simply a waste of money. (You could buy more of our books with all that wasted money.) Of the subscription services, we like Rhapsody the most because of its user interface.

✔ **"On the go" services:** If you are constantly downloading your content and then hitting the road, you need to look at the available "To Go" services, such as Napster To Go and Rhapsody To Go, which take their subscription services and package them for road warriors. For about the cost of a CD each month, you can grab your music player, download anything in their full catalog, and hit the road. That's well worth it in our book. Only specific music and video players are supported, so check their sites.

We're not so sure you can make much of a decision based on sheer numbers — if you care about certain types of music or specific artists, then we suggest you avail yourself of the free trials and check them out. It's the best way to get a comfort level with the services.

Some services limit access to downloaded content to a specific number of computers, often called *authorized computers*. Be sure to understand where you can play your downloaded content because there usually are lots of restrictions.

If you like audio books, check out www.audible.com for audio content you can download to your portable music player to hear your latest book on tape. Also, if you like Internet radio, be sure to check out the following Internet radio hosting or search sites for cool stations:

- **SHOUTcast:** www.shoutcast.com
- **Live365:** www.live365.com
- **Radio-Locator:** www.radio-locator.com

Pat's favorite Internet-only radio station is Radio Paradise (www.radioparadise.com). You should check it out!

Video content

Many of the audio portals and services are getting into the movie act as well. Danny downloaded the first eight episodes of the second season of *Lost* from iTunes to catch up with what he'd missed on air. Some of the most popular on-line video sources (again, with handy Web addresses appended) are listed below:

- Movielink (www.movielink.com)
- CinemaNow (www.cinemanow.com)
- Vongo (www.vongo.com)
- Apple iTunes Music Store (www.apple.com/itunes) — yes, they have video, too!

The video search engines we discussed earlier in the chapter (like Google's and Yahoo!'s) can also be great sources of downloadable or streaming video content.

Video services change quickly as well. When looking at video services, you come up against some of the same issues you see with audio services:

- **Content:** Not all video services have the same content. As we write, iTunes has some TV shows and movie videos. CinemaNow and MovieLink focus on Hollywood movie fare. Over time, all of these players will move toward offering the same lineup of video content, with probably some exclusive showings here and there. But if you really want to catch up on old TV shows (Danny *really* wants to watch the *Rome* series he missed), then look specifically for such offers.

- **Subscriptions versus downloads:** For the most part, Internet-based video is offered as pay-as-you-go downloads. But some services, such as

Akimbo (see the "Standalone media devices" section, later in this chapter), have subscription-based services for certain types of content. So if you like to watch old History Channel episodes, you might be better off getting an Akimbo device.

✔ **Terms of use:** Some video download services let you watch a show once. Some let you start and stop it as often as you want, but you have to finish within three days. Some let you keep it forever. The models are all over the place. Be sure to check out what you are buying. The price might be the same, but the terms could be very different.

Video content is a developing market, and lots of the involved players are trying to figure it out. Video is starting to take up more and more traffic on the networks, and at some point, there will be internal pressures on the cable and telephone companies to put limits on their unlimited broadband Internet access subscribers — in other words, they'll probably figure out a way to charge more to those users downloading a lot of content from the Internet. Watch for any announcements along these lines if you are a big video downloader.

Using an MCE PC to Access Content

In Chapter 8, we discuss home theater PCs (HTPCs) and Microsoft's XP Media Center Edition (MCE) software for your home theater. In this section, we discuss how you might use such a PC as a source device in your home theater — specifically, how you'd use it to access Internet content.

HTPCs are good as an alternative to other home theater source devices — for example, as a high-quality way to play back DVDs. But for most folks, they're not worth the trouble just for that purpose. What really makes an HTPC useful is its ability to provide a *portal* to all sorts of great Internet-based content. Now, if you're a real PC aficionado, you might build an HTPC just for fun. But if you're like us, you're going to go down this road only if there's something in it for you. There is!

Most HTPCs and Microsoft's MCE systems enable users to seek out and find all digital content within the home's network. So it will scan all attached computers for songs, videos, photos, and other content and then make it available to you in a consolidated portal interface, where you can view photo slideshows, home movies, or just play music from your library.

Microsoft's Media Center Edition software has a special section for accessing Internet content — Online Spotlight (`www.microsoft.com/windowsxp/mediacenter/evaluation/onlinespotlight.mspx`). This is an area designed to display products and services from Microsoft's content partners.

Some of the partners are ones mentioned earlier in the chapter — CinemaNow, MovieLink, and Napster, to name a few — and others are just more products to help with digital content, like Ofoto's photosharing service or ABC's Enhanced TV for interactive entertainment from that network. Selecting any Spotlight partner is as simple as clicking their icon in MCE and working within their MCE-compatible portal.

While it doesn't specifically include an Online Spotlight equivalent, Apple's Front Row software (included on most new Macs including the iMac, the Mac Mini, and the latest PowerBooks) will let Mac users gain access to downloaded Internet content in their home theater. And El Gato's EyeHome software/hardware combo (discussed in Chapter 8) provides full access to a Web browser on your home theater's display, meaning you can access just about any Internet content through a networked Mac.

For more details on HTPCs, check out Chapter 8.

Using a Media Server or Adapter to Access Content On-line

You don't have to own a home theater PC to access Internet content — some companies make it really easy for you to download Internet content to your TV via a special unit that you connect to your TV set.

There are two main types of devices on the market:

- ✔ **Media adapters/servers:** Media adapters communicate with a PC and facilitate the flow of content from and through your Internet-connected PC to your home theater.

- ✔ **Standalone devices:** Standalone devices connect directly to the Internet and do not require an intermediary PC. While they usually can catalogue and access PC-stored content, it's not the main focus of these devices — so you don't need an actively running PC to gain access to Internet content with these devices.

Media adapters and servers

Many leading consumer electronics manufacturers offer media adapters, and capabilities and quality can vary substantially among these products. Media adapters "adapt" the PC content to the home theater environment, offering up content to common stereo interfaces such as RCA and digital audio jacks, instead of the more computer-oriented USB and Ethernet jacks.

The typical media adapter is wireless, supports 802.11a or b/g, has RCA interfaces and a remote control, and has some sort of on-screen or LCD interface for selecting among the content choices on your linked PC.

The list of media adapter players is long. The following list gives you a flavor for what's out there:

- **Roku Labs SoundBridge:** Roku Labs (www.rokulabs.com, $150–$400) makes some of the sexiest products on the market. Their SoundBridge series elegantly links your home theater to a remote PC via 802.11g wireless. It supports Apple's Bonjour technology (formerly known as Rendezvous) and iTunes, as well as Windows Media Connect, Windows Media Player 10, and Windows Media DRM 10 — it's the most compatible music player around.

  Remember, Apple does not allow streaming of its purchased music yet (except through their own Airport Express device), so any songs bought in iTunes cannot be played through the SoundBridge, but it does support the AAC format so that when Apple does open this up, Roku will support it — the SoundBridge *does* support any music that you've imported (ripped) into iTunes on your own.

- **Squeezebox:** Mama's got a Squeezebox, and it's made by Slim Devices (www.slimdevices.com, $249). It has standard analog as well as digital optical and coax outputs, so you can link this into your stereo directly with high-quality inputs if you like. The Squeezebox has "always-on" Internet Radio, powered by its own SqueezeNetwork, that lets you tune in to Internet radio streams even when the home PC is switched off. It features Ethernet and 802.11g connections. (The wireless-capable version costs a bit more, listing at $299.) Overall, very nice.

- **Apple AirPort Express:** Aside from being the only device we know of that can stream Apple songs purchased in the iTunes Music Store (because it's made by Apple, of course), the AirPort Express (www.apple.com, $129) is a small, funky little device that serves multiple roles: media adapter, travel router, print server, Wi-Fi repeater, and more. You don't get a remote control, LCD, or on-screen display. For that, you'll want to upgrade to a Mac Mini running its Front Row software. We expect that by the time you read this, Apple will have launched its full digital media hub with Front Row and DVR functionality on board. We can't wait for that, personally. Be sure to look on Apple's Web site (www.apple.com) for that media adapter/set-top box.

- **Other media adapters:** Media adapters are all over the place and include

  - D-Link's MediaLounge products (www.dlink.com, $150–$250), including the DSM-520 Wireless HD Media Player and the DSM-120 Wireless Music Player

- Netgear's Wireless Digital Media Players (www.netgear.com, $80–$150), including the MP115 and MP101

- Linksys's wireless entertainment products (www.linksys.com, $75–$85), including the WMB54G Wireless-G Music Bridge and the WMCE54AG Dual-Band Wireless A/G Media Center Extender

- Actiontec's Wireless Digital Media Player (www.actiontec.com, $130)

Standalone media devices

Whereas media adapters were first out of the gate with lots of units, stand-alone media devices are growing rapidly. Here's a sampling of what's on the market:

✔ **Akimbo (www.akimbo.com, $70):** Akimbo offers an Internet content delivery service of TV shows, movies, and other video content. Akimbo can be accessed with an Akimbo set-top box or a Windows XP Media Center Edition PC via Online Spotlight. Akimbo offers a wide range of content, from the History Channel to Naked News. Akimbo offers two service levels:

  - **Basic:** For $9.99 per month, you can watch and download unlimited views of the basic content in Akimbo. Basic content includes fare such as a Turner Classic Movie of the Week, rock music videos from PlayMusic, and lots of National Geographic episodes, as well as trial subscriptions to paid content.

  - **Premium:** For an extra fee, typically $0.99–$3.99, you can watch other content on demand, just like cable video on demand if you have ever bought a movie on cable. BBC episodes of *Little Women* run $0.99, and movies from MovieLink can run about $3.99 or more.

  Some content has no viewing limit, and some has a 30-day allowable viewing period. Akimbo is adding content partners each month, and expects to have one of the largest collections of on-demand downloads in the industry.

✔ **TiVo (www.tivo.com, starts around $50):** While TiVo is definitely known for its personal video recording functionality, it is moving well beyond that space with deals with Yahoo!, Live365, Netflix, and others that in aggregate will open up the TiVo box to the whole Internet. Under the Netflix deal, for instance, you would not have to wait a day to get your disc — it would be downloaded in an hour to your unit. With your Live365 subscription, you can access thousands of radio stations on Live365's network through your home theater setup without even needing a PC.

✔ **Acoustic Energy's Wi-Fi Internet Radio (www.acoustic-energy.co.uk, $350):** The AE Wi-Fi Internet Radio is compatible with all three major streaming formats — Real Audio, MP3, and Windows Media streams — making it compatible with nearly all the world's broadcasters. It also supports 802.11b and 802.11g Wi-Fi connectivity, which frees you from having to be near a broadband connection.

✔ **LUKAS MP3 Internet Radio (www.stream-it.nl, $250):** The Lukas MP3 Internet Radio allows you to listen to thousands of free and subscription Internet radio stations without having to use a computer. This simple device allows you to change channels between stations you select when you set up the radio. A single loudspeaker outputs the sound — you can also plug the Internet Radio into a receiver and external speakers using its analog audio outputs (RCA jacks). Volume up/down buttons let you change the sound levels. It supports MP3 only.

✔ **PenguinRadio (www.penguinradio.com, $250):** This Internet radio outputs to a built-in 3-inch speaker or to RCA outputs. It supports MP3 only.

Taking Your Video with You

Getting Internet and computer-based content *into* your home theater is a neat trick (and one that we highly recommend you explore). But what's even neater is being able to access your home theater content *away* from your home theater. Imagine watching a show that you've recorded on your DVR and having to hop on the train to work before it's over. Well, with the right hardware and software, you can take that content with you and watch it on a laptop or handheld device wherever you are (as long as you have Internet connectivity).

This is a new area in home theater, and one that still has some bugs to work out, both technical and legal — digital rights management (DRM) raises its ugly head *again!* But it's something that you can do today, and that will become even more common in the future. In the following section, we tell you about the first few fruits of this new category of home entertainment gear:

✔ **TiVoToGo:** If you have a Series 2 TiVo DVR, you can use the TiVoToGo software built into the product to take your recorded shows on the road with you. This isn't an Internet-based product (like the Slingbox, which we discuss next). Instead, it uses your home network to transfer recordings from your TiVo to a Windows 2000 or XP laptop, or to a Windows Mobile handheld device *before you leave home.* When the transfer is done, you can use TiVo's software (a free download from TiVo's Web site) on that device to watch your recorded programs whenever and wherever you like. Check out www.tivo.com for more info.

✔ **Slingbox:** The Slingbox ($249 list price) is perhaps the coolest thing to come along the home theater and Internet pike in many years. It's a funky-looking box that you connect to your home theater and to your home network/Internet connection. Slingbox hooks into your TV source devices (like a cable or satellite set-top box, a DVD player, or a DVR) and allows you to *remotely* control, record, and watch video content. You can use a Slingbox to tune into live TV (for example, catch the local baseball game while you're on the road in your broadband-equipped hotel room) or to access recorded content on your DVR or DVD player. The companion to Slingbox is SlingPlayer software, which resides on a Windows 2000 or XP computer, and which controls the Slingbox and let's you view content across an Internet connection. SlingPlayer optimizes the content you're viewing to the speed of your connection, so if you're on a broadband connection, you can get a high-quality picture. SlingPlayer Mobile is also becoming available (from Sling's Web site for $29.99), and it will allow this capability to work on any Windows Mobile device as well. Check it out at www.slingbox.com).

- **Sony LocationFree:** Sony's $349 answer to the Slingbox, the LocationFree player, performs similar tasks, sending live TV and content from various DVRs across an Internet connection to remote PCs. Like the Slingbox, LocationFree let's you access your home TV programming — both live broadcasts and shows you've recorded on your DVR — from any remote location with a broadband Internet connection (like a hotel or your office). The biggest difference between the two is that Sony's system supports playing back content on the PSP handheld gaming device (which can connect to Wi-Fi wireless networks). As we write, there's no mobile device capability here (beyond the PSP, that is), but we wouldn't be surprised to see that added in over time. You can find out more at http://products.sel.sony.com/locationfreetv/.

Part III
Watching and Listening: Display and Control Devices

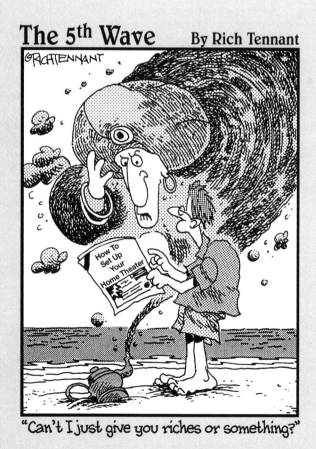

The 5th Wave   By Rich Tennant

"Can't I just give you riches or something?"

In this part . . .

Your journey through Home Theater Land continues with a look at the heart of your system — the receiver and controller devices. We start off this part by looking at what's really important about these systems in terms of interfaces, power levels, multizone capabilities, and so on. We also help you decide if you want an integrated box (a receiver) or separate components. We even talk some about power amplifiers, which is an area of conversation that makes lots of guys — yes, 99 percent of guys, sorry — very excited.

Then we walk you though a discussion of everything you've ever wanted to know about speakers, building off the surround sound knowledge from Part I.

The next chapter delves into your TV display options. Your home theater's display often overwhelms the home theater with its presence — not to mention that, with displays that can go to 120 inches and higher, the options can get really overwhelming. You can go in lots of directions, and we talk about HDTV, LCDs, plasma screens, and other display choices.

Then we get to the projectors. We talk about all the latest technologies and devices — including all-in-one projectors — and the pros and cons for each. CRT, LCD, DLP, LCoS — we've got all the hot acronyms here.

And then finally, we help you make your way through the myriad of options for remotely controlling your system. Find out about the best solutions on the market today.

Chapter 11

The Heart of a Home Theater: The A/V Receiver

*T*he A/V receiver is the hub of your home theater. It's the device that has both the brains and the brawn to control and drive your home theater experience. A growing home theater market, intense competition, and computer industry–like efficiencies at making electronic components have all benefited the A/V receiver. It's no longer a rarefied, esoteric piece of equipment. In fact, you can get a good one for quite a reasonable price. Picking through the lingo and marketing speak and choosing a good one can still be difficult, but that's why you bought this book!

In this chapter, we talk about the features and specifications that are important to keep in mind as you evaluate A/V receivers. We also talk about a different approach to controlling your system — using separate A/V controllers and power amplifier systems.

Digging In to the A/V Receiver

Think of the A/V receiver as the digital and electronic hub of your home theater. An A/V receiver does a bunch of things, all in one nice and relatively compact package. (It's sort of the Swiss army knife of the home theater, except you can't fit one in your pocket.) Among the tasks assigned to the A/V receiver are the following:

✓ **Connects and switches your audio sources:** Every audio source in your home theater should connect to your A/V receiver. The preamplifier section of the receiver allows you to easily switch to (or select) the audio source that you want to listen to.

✓ **Connects and switches your video sources:** With a few exceptions (which we discuss later), all your video source devices are also connected directly to the A/V receiver, which is in turn connected to your display device. This setup greatly simplifies the selection of video sources when you want to play a DVD, a show recorded on a PVR (like a TiVo), or anything else. In most cases, you select what you want to watch on the receiver's remote and don't have to adjust anything on the display.

Some folks feel that they can get the highest video quality by *not* connecting video sources through the receiver. With the advent of high-quality component video and even HDMI (High-Definition Multimedia Interface) switching (see Chapter 16 for more on these connections), we feel that there's a lot to gain by switching your video through the receiver, and little, if any, degradation in the quality of your video picture.

✓ **Tunes in radio programming:** Part of the definition of a receiver is that it includes a radio tuner so you can tune in PBS or Kanye West (or whatever floats your boat between those two extremes).

A few A/V receivers are beginning to include satellite radio receivers for XM or Sirius radio (see Chapter 5 for more on this). So if you want to get Howard Stern, sports programming, or other satellite-exclusive content, you might want to consider getting this capability built right into your A/V receiver. You will, however, have to pay extra for the subscription.

✓ **Decodes surround sound formats:** The ability to decode analog and digital surround sound formats (we talk about these in Chapter 3) is one of two features that distinguish an A/V receiver from a more traditional stereo receiver (the plain old stereo you've had around for years).

✓ **Amplifies audio signals to drive multiple speakers:** Another distinguishing characteristic of an A/V receiver is the fact that it contains at least five channels of amplification to *drive* (or provide power to) your surround sound speaker system.

✓ **Provides the user interface for your home theater:** The interface includes the receiver's remote control (or your own favorite remote, as we discuss in Chapter 15), the displays on the receiver's face, and (in many cases) an on-screen display on your television. All these elements enable you, the human (or your dog, if he's very talented), to command all the electronic components in your home theater.

In the following sections, we discuss each of these A/V receiver responsibilities in more detail.

Counting the inputs

Most people like to *ooh* and *ahh* at the bells and whistles — pretty design, big macho power ratings, and the like. When evaluating any A/V receiver, however, we think a good place to begin is by counting the inputs that let you connect source devices to the receiver. After all, if you have a DVD player, a cassette deck, a satellite receiver, an SACD (Super Audio Compact Disc) player, a turntable, a PVR (personal video recorder), an Xbox 360, and a VCR, you want to hook all these devices into your home theater.

To use all your components, you'd better have enough inputs on the back of your receiver. A receiver may have enough power to wake up people across town and a design so beautiful that your home theater skeptic spouse *begs* you to buy it, but that beauty won't do you much good if have to climb behind it and switch wires every time you want to switch sources. So before you buy anything, think about the components you have (and what you'll soon be getting) and make sure the receiver has enough inputs.

Most A/V receivers have enough inputs for most people. We don't want to scare you. In fact, most have enough jacks on the back to make your head swim. But many inexpensive receivers don't have enough of the *right kind* of jacks for some folks. This is particularly true for digital audio and video jacks but can also be true for the analog audio inputs if you've decided to go down the SACD or DVD-Audio path, which we cover in Chapter 5.

Deciphering digital audio inputs

Digital audio inputs (we show examples of these in Chapter 16) on an A/V receiver let you connect the audio outputs of DVD players, CD players, game consoles, HDTV tuners, Media Center PCs (Chapter 8), digital audio players for MP3 and other computer audio (Chapter 10), and many newer digital cable set-top boxes or DSS satellite receivers. Connecting these audio sources by using digital inputs (instead of the traditional analog inputs) is always a good idea because the digital signals are much less prone to electrical interference than analog signals. A more important consideration is that digital inputs are *required* to get digital surround sound formats, such as Dolby Digital and DTS, into your receiver. (The two-channel analog outputs on DVD players and other devices move you down to the lesser Dolby Pro Logic surround sound system. You can't get digital surround sound from these connections.)

The one exception to this rule involves devices (mainly DVD players) that have a built-in Dolby Digital or DTS surround sound decoder. You *can* connect these to your receiver using analog audio connections, but this may not be the optimal solution for the following reasons:

✔ You need to use six cables instead of one.

✔ You may lose some signal quality due to interference in the analog signal.

✔ You need a receiver that has the necessary six analog inputs on the back — and even if you have these, they may be "taken up" by the six channel outputs of a DVD-Audio or SACD player.

There are two types of digital audio connections (which we discuss in more detail in Chapter 16): coaxial and optical. Some high-end audio folks believe that the coaxial sounds better; it may have a slight sonic benefit, but not so much that regular people can tell. Just make sure that you don't buy a receiver with three optical connections and one coaxial connection and then find you have three source devices with coaxial connections only. Oops. (If you don't know what these look like, again look in Chapter 16.)

There's actually a third type of digital connection that can carry digital audio signals — the HDMI connection, which is increasingly used for HDTV tuners/satellite receivers and set-top boxes, and which is also moving its way into other devices like DVD players (both regular DVD players and the next-generation high-definition players we discuss in Chapter 6), and even in the newest game consoles like the Xbox 360. If you use HDMI to connect these devices to your home theater receiver, you don't need to use a separate digital audio connection — the audio and video are both carried over the HDMI connection.

Most A/V receivers — even new models — don't support HDMI switching. So if you want to use HDMI to connect your video, you'll run an HDMI cable from your source device directly to the TV, not to the receiver. In cases like this, you'll want to use a coaxial or optical digital audio connection to handle the surround sound connection into your receiver. We discuss this in more detail in Chapter 17.

The key measurement here is the total number of connections — as long as the types of connections match up with your other equipment, which is usually not a problem because most source devices have both kinds of connectors on back. Look again at the devices with digital connections mentioned at the beginning of this section. Count how many of those devices with digital outputs you have. Do the math. Many inexpensive receivers have only three digital inputs (some even fewer). If all you have is a DVD player, you'll be fine.

After a few years of home theatering, however, we bet you'll have multiple devices with digital outputs, so plan ahead.

It's not just the *number* of digital inputs, but also the *type* of inputs. Most A/V devices offer both a coaxial and an optical audio output, but some offer only one or the other. Make sure that, when you are counting up your digital input requirements, you account for the number of coaxial and optical inputs you need and choose a receiver accordingly.

Analyzing analog audio inputs

Now that we spent all that time telling you that digital inputs are so much better than analog inputs, why are we emphasizing analog inputs' importance now? Well, first of all, they're not really that awful. We think digital connections are the way to go when they're available, but analog is just fine when it's all you can get. Devices that use analog audio connections include the following:

- Older CD players (without a digital output)
- External radio tuners
- Analog VCRs
- Cable set-top and DSS receivers without digital outputs
- Cassette recorders
- Older game consoles (such as Nintendo 64 and the original PlayStation)
- The newest digital audio sources, SACD and DVD-A, which we discuss in Chapter 5

A move is afoot in the consumer electronics industry to allow digital connections for these last two devices. The connection would use FireWire, a computer technology often used for connecting portable hard drives, camcorders, iPods, and other devices to computers. As we write, a few receiver manufacturers have begun putting these FireWire ports on their receivers, but when and if this will ever take off is unclear.

Just about any device that uses a digital audio connection into your receiver — discussed in the previous section — can also use analog audio connections. We recommend using digital connections to your receiver when they're available, but if they're not, don't forget the fact that you *can* go analog. It may just get that piece of gear connected and save the day!

All the devices we mention in this list — except for SACD and DVD-Audio — use a simple pair of analog audio connections, one for the left channel and one for the right. It's not hard to figure these out. Just count up your inputs on the receiver and count up your devices. The inputs on the receiver are labeled, and these labels correspond to the buttons on the front of the console and on your remote control. It's always nice if the names on the receiver's inputs match input names on the device that you're connecting the receiver to, but it's not essential. It may not even be possible if you have some funky device that no one ever thought of when your receiver was designed.

The one exception to this flexibility in making connections are the inputs on your receiver marked *phono*. These are for your record player (phonograph) and are not standard inputs. If you have a record player, use these inputs for it. If you don't have a record player, don't use these inputs for anything else. If you do use them, it won't blow anything up, but it will sound amazingly awful, and your dog will hide under the bed until you turn it off.

For DVD-Audio and SACD players, you need a special set of analog inputs with six connectors. These formats can support multichannel audio (five channels plus a subwoofer for bass) and therefore need the extra inputs. Many newer receivers have a six-input section (called a *5.1 analog input*), so you can use an SACD or DVD-A player.

Some receivers also have a section on the back with six (or more!) inputs for an *external decoder*. These allow you to hook up a newer decoder in the future. The idea is that the future decoder will handle surround sound formats that weren't even thought of when the receiver was designed — a nice bit of futureproofing.

The multichannel input for DVD-A/SACD and the input for an external decoder are functionally identical. Some receivers will have one set of multichannel inputs labeled for DVD-A/SACD and another labeled for an external decoder. Others have only one set. In the majority of cases, you can use these inputs for either purpose.

Some receivers also have a set of six (or more) similar-looking *outputs*. These allow you to bypass the internal amplifiers in the receiver and use a set of separate, more powerful amplifiers to drive your speakers. Again, this is a nice feature to look for if you think you might need more power some time in the future.

Verifying video inputs

When hooking up a home theater, some folks try to connect all their video devices directly to the TV or display, but they usually don't succeed because most displays have a rather limited set of inputs on the back (though some have a ton). We prefer to connect all our video devices directly to the receiver and let the receiver *switch* (that is, select) which video source goes to the display. It's just easier, neater, and simpler that way.

We're talking about the video signal coming out of these devices here. They all have an audio signal as well (for the soundtrack), and that should also be connected to the receiver using one of the two methods described in the previous sections. You won't get any surround sound if you don't perform that basic step.

As we discuss in Chapter 16, there are four common types of video connections (in order of worst to best): coaxial (also called baseband — rarely found in a receiver), composite, S-Video, and component. (There are also digital connections for *some* HDTV tuners and sources, but these connections are designed to connect directly into the TV.) Virtually every A/V receiver has yellow color-coded composite video inputs on the back. (They're usually right next to the audio inputs for a source device, so they're labeled *DVD* or *VCR,* and so on.) Coaxial is the pits, so the less said about it the better. Composite video basically stinks (relative to S-video and component), so use it only for low-resolution video sources, such as low-end VCRs; otherwise, just leave those composite plugs unused.

What you want to look for in a receiver are S-Video connections (at a minimum) or component video connections (on fancier, more expensive receivers). The picture quality you get when using these connections is almost always better than what you get with a composite video connection. S-Video connections can be found on better VCRs (the S-VHS models), most DVD players, DSS receivers, digital cable set-top boxes, PVRs, and on modern gaming consoles (Xbox 360, PlayStation 3, or Wii, for example). Component video connections can be found on most DVD players (they're required for progressive-scan DVD), HDTV tuners, the gaming consoles we just mentioned, and even on the latest PVRs (such as the ReplayTV 5000).

HDTV signals need a special kind of component video connection called a *wideband component video* connection. Some receivers have component video connections but can't handle the higher frequencies of HDTV. If a specification is given, look for something higher than 25 MHz.

Until quite recently, component video inputs were a rarity on inexpensive and even moderately priced receivers. Because the popularity of DVD and other sources that can use component video (particularly HDTV) has risen, however, component video has moved into the mainstream. You'll still have a hard time finding a $500 receiver with more than two sets of component inputs, but for many people, that's enough. You can use S-Video for non-progressive or non-HDTV sources (such as a PlayStation 2) and reserve the component inputs for your progressive-scan DVD and your HDTV tuner.

Many otherwise excellent displays have only a single-component video input, and few displays have enough S-Video inputs for everything you might want to connect to them. This is a strong argument for finding a receiver that has a sufficient number of inputs. Like the audio inputs discussed earlier, this is a pretty simple thing to factor in while you are shopping. Count up what you have that uses S-Video or component video and start eliminating A/V receivers that don't have what you need from your shopping list.

Switching sources

With all these inputs, an A/V receiver can do all the source switching for your home theater system. Plug all your source devices into the receiver, connect your speakers and display to the receiver's outputs, and let the receiver do the work of sending audio and video to these devices — rather than having a bunch of individual cables running to your display. As we mention earlier, most displays simply don't have enough inputs (particularly on the video side) to allow you to connect the myriad video sources you have (or will soon have) directly into them. Allowing the A/V receiver to concentrate and switch between all these sources just plain makes sense.

As you audition receivers, check out the quality of their video switching. We can't give you a quantitative piece of advice here, but we can tell you to do some research. Read the reviews. Most good reviewers comment on the video switching capabilities. If you can, do your own quick test. Watch a bit of video on a DVD player hooked up through the receiver and then try watching the same video using the same type of connection plugged directly into the display. Hopefully, you won't see a difference, but if the picture is softer or less detailed when running through the receiver, then maybe it's not the receiver you want.

Another factor to keep in mind regarding video switching is how the A/V receiver itself connects to the display. You may have a mixture of composite, S-Video, and component video connections running into the receiver from your source devices. It's very likely that you will, in fact. Some more capable receivers convert signals from lower-quality to higher-quality connections. For example, a receiver may convert all composite and S-Video incoming connections to component video. This doesn't make the picture any better, but it does enable you to use a single output connection from the receiver to the display. It also enables you to set the display on its component input and then just leave it there and forget it, which is pretty handy.

Many receivers use the home theater display to provide on-screen system controls. If your system converts composite or S-Video to a higher-quality connection, make sure it also sends the on-screen display over that connection. Switching the display back to the composite video input just to tweak a control is a real pain in the tonsils (as Pat's mom says — though he's not sure what that means).

Understanding upconversion

A feature that has hit the market recently (and that we think can be really handy) is video *upconversion*. Essentially, a receiver with upconversion takes lower-resolution video input (like composite or S-video) and converts it to a higher-resolution format, like component video or even HDMI.

Uh oh, too few inputs on your receiver?

Sometimes, you do your homework and buy a receiver with enough inputs, and then some new video source plops into your life unannounced, leaving you an input or two short. (Or maybe you just plain fell in love with a receiver that didn't have enough inputs. We forgive you.) What to do?

Well, first check your display for extra inputs on the back (or front). Using these isn't quite as neat and integrated as using the receiver, but doing so won't hurt your quality at all.

If you're still running short, look into an external video switcher. You can get your hands on a cheap one at any electronics or home theater store. You usually switch this device manually (meaning you walk up to it and push a button).

Switchers accept composite or S-Video connections and have a single output on the back to run to your display. If you want to go for quality (and can afford to spend a bit more), check out the Monster Cable's Entech line of products (www.monstercable.com/entech). For about $350, you can get a system that accepts composite or S-Video connections from up to four devices and converts them into a single S-Video output for connecting to your A/V receiver (or directly to the display). This system also connects the corresponding analog audio signals and features an automatic switching system. Whichever source is actively playing is switched to the output connections (you can manually override this, too).

There are two primary reasons to consider video upconversion in a receiver:

✔ Fewer cables

✔ Improved picture quality

You'll see two types of upconversion when you're shopping for receivers:

✔ Component upconversion

✔ HDMI upconversion

Assessing your amplifier

Another essential job for any A/V receiver involves amplifying outgoing audio signals so that your speakers can do their thing. We discuss in greater detail how speakers work in the following chapter, but for now let's just say that they are based on electromagnetic systems that need a lot of electricity. The electrical signals coming out of audio source devices, however, are relatively low-powered. The amplifier does what its name says; it increases this power level.

Unscrambling power ratings

The first thing most folks look at when they see a shiny new receiver sitting on display is the power rating. The rating is measured in watts per channel (usually measured as RMS, or root mean square, instead of peak, which means that it is a measure of sustained power, not the highest possible instantaneous peak). The problem is that you can't take these ratings at face value because manufacturers play a lot of interesting tricks when they give these watt ratings. The result is that a receiver can be more or less powerful than another receiver with the same rating. To really get a feel for a receiver's power, examine the following four things closely:

✔ **Distortion:** Power is measured at a certain number of watts at a certain level of *distortion* (noise created by the amplifier). You want low distortion (of course). The tricky part comes in when you examine how the amplifier's power output is measured — specifically at what distortion level it's measured. An amp that is measured, for example, at 100 watts per channel at 0.02 percent THD (*total harmonic distortion,* the standard measurement) is quieter and is probably more powerful than one that is measured at 100 watts per channel at 0.2 percent THD. You can really do a direct comparison only if both are measured at the same THD percentage. Another way of looking at this issue is this fact: If manufacturers measure power at a higher distortion rating, they can squeeze more "on paper" power out of the receiver.

✔ **Impedance:** Almost all amplifiers are rated at 8 ohms impedance (a measure of electrical resistance, discussed in Chapter 12), so you can compare ratings this way, but a few are also measured at 6 or even 4 ohms. These lower resistances can give an artificially high power rating — be suspicious.

Not all amplifiers built into receivers (or even in separate power amplifiers) can power 4-ohm speakers without overheating, popping a circuit breaker, or just plain breaking down. Check to see whether a receiver can support these lower impedances if you choose speakers that require it. This is rare unless you are buying some really high-end gear — most home theater speaker systems are rated at 8 ohms of impedance (though the actual number varies as the speakers reproduce different frequencies).

✔ **Frequency range:** Lower frequencies (the bass frequencies) require more amplifier power than higher frequencies. Because of this, some receiver manufacturers test their systems not at the full 20 to 20,000 Hz range (which is what we call *full range*), but with a limited range (such as 40 to 20,000 Hz). This can also create an artificially high power rating. Receivers that are measured at full range are often called *full bandwidth rated.*

✔ **Number of channels driven:** Home theater receivers should be capable of driving at least five speakers (some have amplifiers for six, seven, or more speakers for extra surround channels). Power ratings should state how many speakers are actually being driven when the system is tested. Preferably, all channels are driven simultaneously at the stated power. Some systems give power ratings in *stereo* mode (with only the front left and right speakers driven), which means that the power with all speakers being driven is less than the stated amount.

Determining how much receiver power you need

How much power do you need in your receiver? Well, we're going to weasel out by saying, "It depends." Which speakers you choose plays a key role here. Different speakers have different *sensitivities,* a measure of how loud they are, given a certain amount of power. The standard measure for this is how many decibels they produce with 1 watt of power at 1 meter's distance from the speaker. A more sensitive speaker requires less amplification to reach the same volume level.

You also need to consider the size of your home theater and how loudly you plan on playing your movies and music. If you want to create permanent hearing loss, or if you have a room the size of the Taj Mahal, you might need a receiver that can pump out 150 watts per channel. If you have relatively sensitive speakers, a moderately sized home theater, and don't plan on testing the thickness of your window glass with really loud music, then a receiver with 70 watts per channel (or less) might do the trick. We think that receivers with about 100 watts per channel (honestly measured) will do the trick in just about any home theater.

Amplifiers (whether separate or in a receiver) make their power by using transistors. In the old days, amplifiers used vacuum tubes, and some really expensive high-end amps still use tubes because some audio enthusiasts prefer their sound. Inexpensive receivers use an IC (integrated circuit), which provides the power-generating transistors for several audio channels on a single chip. Better receivers have *discrete* amplifier output transistors — separate transistors for each channel. Typically, you get more power and better sound from a discrete design.

Zoning out to the rest of the house

Many home theater receivers — particularly when you start hitting about $1,000 or higher in price — include a *multizone* functionality. This lets your receiver not only control your home theater, but also provide music to other rooms in your house. A multizone receiver is a good way to get started down the whole-home theater path.

The simplest multizone receivers have a pair of stereo audio outputs (not speaker connectors or amplifier channels, just outputs). These outputs enable you to run an audio cable to another room and connect to a separate amplifier and speakers in that room (or to a pair of *active* speakers that have a built-in amplifier). The key feature to look for here is that this second zone is truly a second zone. That is to say, the receiver lets you send a *different* audio source to the second room, not just the one you are playing in the home theater. So the kids can listen to Barney the dinosaur sing, "I love you," in the den, while you watch *Memento* in the home theater.

As you get into more sophisticated systems, you can find receivers with extra built-in amplifiers (so you don't need an amp in the extra room) and with extra zones (so you can send different audio sources to a third or fourth room). You may even find multizone A/V receivers that send out a composite video signal. With this signal, you can watch the video from a home theater video source elsewhere in the home.

In Chapter 18, we get into more detail about sharing home theater sources throughout the home. If you want to get really sophisticated with a true "every room in the house" system, you might need some more gear (which we discuss in that chapter).

Having fun with DSPs and decoders

Another key responsibility of the A/V receiver is to decode surround sound formats in your audio and video programming so that sound can be sent to those six or more speakers in your theater. Two kinds of chips in the receiver handle all this digital magic: the DSP and the DAC.

Digital Signal Processors

The DSP (Digital Signal Processor) is the brains of the decoding process. This chip handles all the *steering* of surround sound, sending musical signals to the correct channels. The DSP also can provide its own sound field enhancements — essentially electronic changes in tone and timing (echoes) — though some people hate them and wouldn't use the term *enhancement* to describe them! These enhancements are called *DSP Modes,* which are modifications to the signal to create delays in the sound. The delays can make your home theater sound like something else — for example, a cathedral or a smoky jazzy club (you have to provide your own smoke).

One feature that DSPs enable (and that we love!) is the ability to *dynamically compress* music and, more importantly, movie soundtracks. Dynamic compression makes the louds less loud and also makes the quiet parts not quite so quiet. When someone is sleeping two rooms over while you watch a movie at night, you don't necessarily want that *Top Gun* F-14 flying overhead at full roar. (Pat was in the Navy and spent too much time in the Persian Gulf with jets taking off about 15 feet over his head and doesn't ever want to hear that again, but that's a different story.) This feature, often called *nighttime mode,* is really great for family harmony.

Many receiver manufacturers make a big deal about which DSP they use. It does make a difference, and some aficionados have their own preferences. The key is that the DSP can support the decoding of the surround sound formats you want and need in your home theater. At a minimum, you should pick a receiver that can decode Dolby Digital and DTS (the plain-Jane 5.1 versions of these standards) and Dolby Pro Logic II (for VHS and other nondigital sources). We like receivers that can also decode Dolby Pro Logic IIx, which does a much better job on VHS and regular TV — luckily Pro Logic IIx is becoming pretty much standard these days.

If you're getting into a six- or seven-channel system, then you want a receiver that can support DTS-ES or Dolby Digital EX (or THX Surround EX). We don't think that's necessary for an entry-level home theater, but if you're getting fancy, why not?

And as the high-definition DVD formats (Blu-ray and HD-DVD) start hitting the market, you'll want to support them with a receiver that can handle Dolby's *TrueHD* and *Digital Plus* as well as DTS's *DTS HD* formats, all discussed in Chapter 3. As we go to press, these new standards haven't hit the mainstream, but we expect them to become common in the near future.

Digital Analog Converters

DACs (or Digital Analog Converters) take the digitally encoded musical signals (from a Dolby Digital or DTS DVD soundtrack or the PCM — short for Pulse Code Modulation, a standard way of storing digital audio — from a compact disc connected digitally) and convert these digital signals into analog signals that the receiver's amplifier and the speakers can understand. Receiver vendors seem to be going through some kind of a race with DACs these days. Each vendor is coming out with models that have new DACs with even higher capacities.

DACs are rated by the frequency of digital signal and the number of bits they can decode (for example, 96 kHz and 24 bits). We've seen receivers with *multiple* DACs (up to 16 in a single receiver) rated at 192 kHz and 24 bits. You should choose a receiver with at least 96 kHz/24-bit DACs. If digital connections for systems such as SACD or DVD-Audio ever become common, those higher-capacity DACs will become a minimum recommendation (today, they are not, in our minds).

Sometimes, you don't want to mess with all that digital stuff. Analog signals coming into the receiver are typically converted to digital signals (using ADCs — the opposite of DACs). The digital signals run through the DSP and are then converted back to analog signals with the DACs. Many audio purists feel that all this conversion can create minor (but to them, not insignificant) distortions in the audio. If your receiver has *analog bypass,* you can stay in straight, old-fashioned, pure analog all the way to the amplifier section. We recommend analog bypass for the analog inputs from an SACD or DVD-Audio player, as well as for turntable inputs. Some receivers automatically bypass the digital stuff for these inputs, whereas others have a switch on the remote. Some don't bypass it at all; so if you want this feature, check to see if your receiver will give it to you.

Dealing with bass

Connecting a subwoofer (or more than one if you love the bass) to your home theater is an essential part of providing the sound for your movies and TV. The majority of subwoofers are *active* (they have their own built-in ampli-fiers). You need an output on your A/V receiver to connect a standard analog audio cable to the subwoofer. On most receivers, this output is labeled the *LFE* (Low Frequency Effects) channel and is indicated by the ".1" part of 5.1-, 6.1-, and 7.1-channel surround sound formats. We highly recommend you get a receiver with this output, and most will have one — it's pretty much assured if you buy a Dolby Digital– or DTS-equipped receiver.

The other subwoofer-related thing to look for is an *adjustable crossover* that lets you select which audio frequencies go to the subwoofer and which go to the main front speakers. Different speaker systems sound better with the crossover set at different frequencies. If you have small bookshelf speakers in the front, you might set the crossover to a higher frequency. If you have a set of huge tower speakers with giant woofers (bass speakers) of their own, you might set the crossover to a lower frequency and let the subwoofer concen-trate on only the really deep sounds.

We discuss speakers in more detail in Chapter 12.

Interfacing with your receiver

A/V receivers control a lot of things in your system, such as selection of audio and video sources, volume, surround sound formats, relative volume levels for surround speakers, and more. You interface with the receiver through the buttons and knobs on the front and, more importantly, through the remote control.

The receiver gives you feedback on your control actions through one or both of two means: lights and displays on the face of the receiver and an on-screen display on your television set. We like on-screen displays (they're easier to read), and we'd be willing to bet you will, too. However, you're not going to find this feature on most inexpensive receivers.

Whether or not you have an on-screen display, we think that checking out how the receiver's interface works is important. For example, most receivers use menu-driven controls (like the menus in a computer program). In some cases, you need to push a lot of buttons and navigate through several menus to get to important controls. That's okay for things you set once and forget about (such as your initial setup), but such controls are a real pain for procedures you do over and over again (such as selecting a video or audio source). We like systems that have easy-to-understand menus and *direct access* to key functions (meaning you have to press only one button to get to them).

When evaluating a receiver's interface, you also want to check out the remote control. These days, most A/V receivers can control other devices (such as DVD players). Many remotes are *learning* or *programmable* ones that can control devices from other manufacturers. Cheaper programmable remotes work only with equipment from the same manufacturer. When you start getting fancy, you find remotes that are backlit (so you can see them in the dark) or even *touch screen* remotes (with a touch-sensitive LCD panel instead of a million tiny little buttons). We talk about remotes in much more detail in Chapter 15.

Making the Separates Decision

As you start moving up the price scale, you begin to reach a decision point: Do you want to stick with a (very very good) all-in-one high-end A/V receiver, or do you want to move into separates? *Separates* break down the functions of the receiver into three (you guessed it) separate components: a radio tuner, a power amplifier (or power amplifiers), and an A/V controller. You can probably guess what the tuner and amplifiers do; the controller performs the switching and *preamplification* tasks (basically, adjusting the levels of audio signals to control your volume) and includes the DSPs and DACs that do surround sound decoding and conversion of digital audio into analog audio.

You might go with separates for a couple of reasons:

✔ **More flexibility:** A separates system lets you choose exactly which components you want. Like the amplifiers from Brand X, but the controller functions from Brand Y? Mix and match! Separates give you a more flexible upgrade path, too. If you buy a Dolby Digital and DTS 5.1 decoder but someday want to move up to Dolby Digital Plus (or some future surround sound format), you only need to upgrade the decoder, not the whole system. Keep in mind that you might have to buy extra amplifiers for extra surround sound channels, but that's easy to do.

✔ **Better performance:** A/V receivers can offer really excellent sound quality, but for that last little bit of sonic realism, separates can offer the ultimate in sound. Putting all the electronics for your A/V components in separate chassis can reduce the possibility of these electronic gizmos interfering with each other and causing distortions in your sound. For example, many folks going the separates route buy fancy *mono* power amplifiers — a separate amplifier (with its own power supply and other internal components) for each channel. Most people don't have the space, budget, or (to be realistic) the need for such a setup. But it's a nice possibility to consider.

We talk about separate components in more detail in Chapter 21, where we talk about moving up to the high end of home theater. If you can afford the additional expense, you might want to consider using separates. If you don't want to spend any more than you have to and prefer the simplicity (and space savings) of an all-in-one solution, stick with an A/V receiver.

Chapter 12

Speaker of the House

- -

In This Chapter

▶ Understanding speaker bits and pieces

▶ Flanking your system to the left and right

▶ Surrounding yourself with a diffuse sound field

▶ Managing bass expectations

- -

Although your video display often hogs all the attention in your home theater, the speaker system is what really makes your theater sing — literally.

Speaker systems don't get the attention they deserve. Many people actually see the speaker system as almost an afterthought — something that is bundled with the receiver or other equipment. Speakers have a double curse: They lack oodles of fancy features and display screens, and the features they *do* have are tied up with very technical descriptions that most people can't decipher.

Not paying enough attention to your speaker system is a huge mistake. People notice bad audio a lot faster than they notice bad video. In this chapter, we explain how to evaluate your speakers, and we discuss issues to think about when buying speakers for your home theater. In Chapters 17 and 19, we talk about how to install your speakers and tweak them to perfection.

Understanding How Speakers Work

Unlike other components in your system, speakers are differentiated (more than anything else) by somewhat obscure technical characteristics. So an understanding of how speakers actually work may be just what you need in order to stay un-glassy-eyed when we go on and on about making sure your speakers are *in phase* and things like that.

Drivers

Speakers are actually relatively simple devices. Basically, you have an enclosure (typically a box) into which speaker drivers are attached. The *drivers* are the round elements that many people call the actual speakers (they're not). The drivers look like cones or horns (or even ribbons or domes), and in fact, the large surface area of the drivers is called the *cone* or *diaphragm*. These surfaces move back and forth to make the sound. If you have ever pulled the front screen off your speakers or have seen speakers without their front grille on, you've seen speaker drivers *au naturelle.*

Driver sizes

Drivers come in different sizes and modes, but generally speaking, you'll find three types, based on the frequencies they handle:

- **Tweeter driver:** These handle the high-frequency treble range (above 2,000 Hz).

- **Midrange driver:** These, not surprisingly, handle the midrange frequencies (200 Hz to 2,000 Hz).

- **Woofer driver:** These handle the low-frequency bass range (below 200 Hz).

No single driver is well suited to handle all sounds from 20 Hz to 20,000 Hz; multiple drivers are commonly used to be able to span the full spectrum. A speaker that handles the full frequency is called, not surprisingly, a *full-range* speaker.

How drivers work

Speaker driver cones are typically made from paper, plastic, or metal. This material moves back and forth and creates changes in the air pressure (sound waves) that ultimately arrive at your eardrum and cause it to move back and forth in a corresponding fashion. This causes you to hear the sound. The cone is moved by an electromagnetic process that's caused by a coil of wire, called the *voice coil,* at the base of the cone. The electrical impulses coming from the amplifier (or the amplifiers built in to your receiver) drive the voice coil, and the voice coil interacts with a permanent magnet attached to the speaker's cone (or dome or whatever shape it may take). (If you want a great explanation of how speakers work in more detail, check out `www.howstuffworks.com/speaker.htm`.)

Drivers come in all sorts of different sizes, but (again) generally speaking, the larger the driver is, the lower the frequencies it was designed for. Because higher frequencies require sound waves that have high and low pressure points close together, the cone must be smaller to be able to move back and forth fast enough to keep up. Lower frequencies have to move back and forth more slowly, and smaller drivers have a hard time with these. So you find that drivers are designed for specific audio frequency ranges.

Most speakers that have multiple drivers in their speaker enclosure have electronic circuits known as *crossovers,* which divide up inbound speaker signals and distribute them to the appropriate driver.

Drivers in speaker-market lingo

You'll most often run into two types of speakers on the market:

- **Two-way:** These have a woofer and a tweeter in one speaker enclosure.
- **Three-way:** These have a woofer, tweeter, and a midrange driver in the same enclosure.

You'll also run into speakers with multiple tweeters or midrange drivers, and occasionally *four-way* speakers with two of the frequencies divided up among four different drivers (or four different sets of drivers — for example two tweeters and two pairs of different sized midrange drivers). You can even find some speakers (typically smaller *satellite* speakers designed for wall mounting) with only *one* driver to handle both the bass and the treble. There's a huge amount of variety out there.

More drivers doesn't always mean better sound, but often speakers with multiple drivers sound better because each of the individual woofer, midrange, and tweeter drivers can be optimized to reproduce a very specific range of frequencies. Keep in mind that it's hard for a driver to reproduce the whole range of audio frequencies equally well.

The use of the cone-shaped diaphragm and electromagnetic-powered movement is specific to *dynamic speakers,* the class of speakers we've been discussing so far in this chapter. Generally, these are the speakers we recommend for home theater. We should tell you, though, that you may run across other speakers when touring your local audio showroom or electronics superstore — speakers that are more expensive and that are used for specific purposes. In most cases, we don't recommend the following speakers for home theater use:

- **Electrostatic speakers:** These are used primarily for stereo audio listening and are rare in home theater systems. They can't handle bass and are rather limited in where and how you position them.
- **Planar-magnetic speakers:** For similar reasons, these are not likely to be useful for your home theater application because they are best used for the higher frequencies only.

We mention electrostatic and planar-magnetic speakers in case someone tries to sell you some; unless you really know what you're doing with these types of speakers, you're better off spending your money on quality dynamic speakers.

The pole position

You'll also run into speakers with more than one set of speaker drivers, facing in different directions:

- **Monopole:** These speakers have all the drivers on one face of the enclosure and are known as *direct radiating* speakers. These can be used anywhere in your home theater.

- **Bipole:** These speakers have drivers on two faces, opposite each other. These are designed for the side/rear surround speaker applications.

- **Dipole:** These speakers have drivers on two faces, opposite each other. These are designed for the side/rear surround speaker applications.

  Bipole and dipole speakers sound pretty much the same, huh? Well, physically they are quite alike, but we'll discuss in the following section how the differ *functionally*.

- **Omnipole:** These speakers radiate their sound in all directions, in a 360-degree fashion, and are popular for outdoor applications. We won't talk much about these here, but know they exist.

To understand the difference between bipole and dipole speakers, we have to get technical for a minute, but it's an important tangent discussion.

Harken back to your science class days when you studied topics of *phase,* specifically being *in phase* and *out of phase.* If you recall, in a general sense, something is in phase when it acts in the same pattern and time session as something else, and out of phase when it doesn't. Because controlling the way sound waves interact with each other is a key component of home theater, you have to deal with the concept of phase.

Bipole and dipole speakers are designed specifically to help contribute to your surround sound field. All you need to know for now, however, are some basics about how they work. Bipole speakers fire their cones to the front and rear (remember, they have drivers on two planes) at the same time and in phase. In other words, the cones go out or in together, in the same direction (both out or both in) and at the same time. Dipole speakers are out of phase with each other. When one side's drivers are pushing out, the other side's drivers are pulling in. See the section, "Surround speakers," later in this chapter, for an explanation of how these speakers help create surround sound.

Although the electrical phase in bipoles and dipoles is different, the basic construction of bipoles and dipoles is very similar. You can find speakers on the market that can be both bipoles and dipoles. Most of these speakers have a switch that lets you switch the mode they operate in. Some people prefer music played back through bipoles and movies through dipoles, and these speakers let you make that choice on the fly.

Enclosed for your convenience

Your speaker enclosure, it turns out, is pretty critical. You see, with all the shaking your drivers do, if you have a rather flimsy speaker encasement, then it's either going to make a lot of noise, fall apart, or both. Your enclosure should be able to handle the vibrations with ease and should add little sound interference to the sound emanating from the drivers.

You'll run into two major types of enclosures: sealed (also known as *acoustic suspension*) enclosures and ported (also known as *bass reflex*) enclosures. A *sealed enclosure* is what it sounds like; it's an airtight case. As your driver moves back and forth, the air pressure in the speaker constantly changes. This puts extra pressure from behind on the diaphragm as it moves in and out, and that takes extra power to overcome. On the positive side, however, that extra pressure makes the cone snap back and forth faster and with more precision, giving you a crisper, more accurate sound.

A more efficient speaker design is the *ported* or *bass reflex enclosure.* In the front of these enclosures is a hole (port) that equalizes pressure between the inside and outside of the speaker. When the diaphragm moves back into the speaker, it increases the internal pressure, which is funneled out through the front port of the speaker. This augments the sound waves traveling from the speaker, and increases the efficiency tremendously. The downside is that, from a reproductive sound perspective, you may get less accurate results from bass reflex enclosures. That's because they don't have the benefit of the extra pressure influencing the reverberating diaphragm. So the speaker sound might reproduce bass notes less precisely — substituting a louder boominess for a more realistic reproduction of the low notes. (Less realistic reproduction here means that your low notes don't have as much house-shaking "oomph" as they should.)

Bass reflex enclosures can dramatically decrease your power requirements because they increase the bass output of a speaker by around 3 dB compared to a sealed enclosure. To match a 3 dB output boost through amplification, the power applied to the speaker needs to be doubled. So if a bass reflex enclosure speaker was powered with a 150-watt amplifier, a sealed enclosure speaker would require a 300-watt amplifier to produce the same output. That's a pretty awesome improvement.

In the end, you can be happy with either sealed or bass reflex designs. Just keep in mind that these units handle bass differently and that good design and construction can minimize problems associated with either speaker design.

Inside, outside, upside down?

As if all this were not enough, you'll probably run into four generic shape and size categories of speakers for your home entertainment system:

- **Floorstanding:** These speakers can be as tall as you are, can handle the full range of frequencies, and may or may not own the low-bass frequencies often taken over by the subwoofer.

- **Bookshelf:** These aptly named speakers are designed for smaller footprints (the amount of space they take up). You often find them on a bookshelf or discreetly mounted on the wall. Sometimes, you see them on speaker stands to bring them up to ear-level (which is the best way to install these types of speakers, in our opinion). They are usually designed to handle the midrange and high-end frequencies and are typically mated to a subwoofer in your installation. You may hear bookshelf speakers described as *satellite speakers.*

  Many manufacturers have designed special bookshelf-style speakers with mounting brackets and a sleek (and *thin*) enclosure designed for wall mounting next to a flat-panel plasma or LCD display. These speakers are usually referred to as *wall mounts.*

- **Subwoofer:** These speakers are larger and heavier than the bookshelf models and are usually kept on the floor due to their size and weight. These contain the large drivers for low-frequency use.

- **In-wall:** In-wall speakers share most of their characteristics with the bookshelf models; these are smaller speakers designed more for the midrange and high-end frequencies. Although some have enclosures that are mounted into the wall, the majority of these systems use the wall's own enclosed nature as its enclosure. The drivers and other pieces and parts (like the crossovers) are mounted in a frame mounted flush with the wall or ceiling.

  In general, in-wall speakers are more for whole-home background music and to contribute to the surround sound of a home theater. For the most part, the benefit of these speakers is their ability to be installed in places that have more aesthetic than acoustic appeal. They stay tucked away in corners or low on walls, but their acoustical contribution is mainly for background and surround types of sound. Also, depending on the construction of the walls themselves, in-wall speakers that lack their own enclosure may spread sound along the wall rather than direct sound forward. If you find yourself planning in-wall speakers, take some extra time to study up on the best ways to optimize their location and performance. This is not to say that there aren't good-sounding in-wall speakers — there are, and many high-end manufacturers make in-wall speakers these days. But good in-walls are typically more expensive than otherwise comparable bookshelf or floorstanding speakers.

Stereostone Age

If you decide to extend your home theater outside the boundaries of your home theater room, you may consider outdoor speakers because they are pertinent for your gardens, pool areas, and soon-to-be-outdoor theater greens.

All the discussion in this speaker section is pertinent to shopping for outdoor speakers. One of the leading vendors is Stereostone (www.stereostone.com), which makes speakers in all sorts of simulated rock forms and colors, like brown sandstone and black lava. There are omni-directional speakers, subwoofers, and even stereo fountains. You can get them with or without visible grills in the layers of the rock, and with volume controls for individual speaker control. All this in weatherproof enclosures that start as low as $150 and go up to $1,000 for the most sophisticated models.

Active and passive speakers

Finally, all speakers, regardless of the number of drivers, pole type, enclosure type, or whatever, fall into one of two categories: active or passive. How they're classified depends on their relationship to the amplifier driving them.

The vast majority of speakers are passive. A *passive* speaker doesn't have a built-in amplifier; it needs to be connected to your amplifier through normal speaker wire. This speaker-level signal has been amplified enough to drive the speakers sufficiently.

Active speakers, on the other hand, have a built-in amplifier and are fed by a low-level (line-level) signal passed along an interconnect cable originating at your preamplifier or controller. Because the amplifier is an active electronic device, it needs power, and so you have to put any active speakers near power outlets.

Connections are everything

When connecting your receiver or amplifier to your speakers, you're pretty much going to find two types of connectors: spring clips and five-way binding posts. Spring clips are considered the lower end of the two, and most audiophiles tend to put them down. You see, spring clips have more exposed wiring, less surface contact, and greater likelihood of signal degradation over time due to this exposed wiring. Five-way binding posts, on the other hand, have a much more flexible connection structure. Not surprisingly, you can connect at least five ways. There are pin-form connectors, spade lugs, banana plugs, and a large washer-like area at the base that allows for more extensive contact with bare wire. There's too much to try to put into words here; we recommend that you get someone at a stereo store to show you a five-way binding post. Just know that the five-way binding posts are the way to go if you have a choice.

For most home theaters, the subwoofer is probably going to be your only active speaker (though you can also find passive subwoofers, and some high-end home theater systems use these). There's no practical reason for any of your other speakers to be active. Active speakers limit your ability to pick amplifiers tailored to your home theater and are generally more expensive options than what we've been talking about. They are also much harder to find. Most active speakers either fall into the low price/low-end category (designed for hooking into PCs or portable CD/MP3 players), or the really high end (where the speakers cost $5,000 to $10,000 *each*).

Setting Up Surround Sound

Whew. You still with us? Well, if you are, the worst is behind you. Now you can apply all this newfound knowledge to a discussion of your surround sound system. In this section, we talk about the different speakers found in any home theater system — the center channel speaker, the left and right front speakers, the surround channel speakers, and the subwoofer. (To see what a surround sound setup looks like, see Figure 12-1.)

Figure 12-1:
A typical surround sound speaker layout.

Center speakers

We start with the center speaker. On the one hand, the center speaker is probably the most important speaker in your system; on the other hand, it's (supposedly) optional. How can that be, you ask?

Well, many people say the center speaker is optional because the left and right speakers can handle the sound that comes from the center speaker. However, we think that you miss out on a lot, and we don't recommend this setup at all. The front center speaker, we feel, is critical and not at all optional, but some budget crunchers will try to convince you that it is.

Now, why is it critical? Ah, our favorite subject. The center speaker anchors your on-screen dialog and serves as a seamless connection between your left and right speakers. As that boat zooms by from left to right, you don't want to have a gap in the middle of your sound field (a concern as screens get larger and larger). Center speakers are usually located behind the screen or above or below displays so that you can localize the on-screen sound as much as possible.

To achieve this seamless harmony with the left and right front speakers, your choice of center speaker is important. Don't skimp on the center speaker in favor of your other front speakers. Each speaker (left, center, and right) is equally important and should be of similar size, similar capability, and preferably come from the same manufacturer. In fact, if you can use an identical model speaker for the center, left, and right speakers (we talk about them in just a second), do it. Many folks can't do this because they've chosen tower speakers for their left and right speakers, and can't possibly install a tower speaker on top of their display as a center channel speaker. (And if you're not using dipole or bipole speakers for your surround channels, you should consider using another identical pair of speakers for your surrounds as well.)

Make sure any speakers that will be close to a cathode ray tube (direct-view) video display are *video shielded* — especially the center speaker. If not, the speakers will cause video distortion on your screen. This is most important for your center speaker (which may rest directly on top of your display), but can also be an issue for your left and right speakers if they are close to the display as well.

Left and right speakers

We've cheated somewhat by talking a lot about the front left and right speakers already in this chapter. If possible, these speakers should be

✔ **Full-range speakers:** Yes, even if you plan on using a subwoofer.

✔ **Ear-level:** We'd recommend this level even for your bookshelf-style speakers. If the speakers are large, try to arrange it so that the tweeters are at ear level.

✔ **Of similar performance capability as the center speaker:** We'd even say they should come from the same manufacturer.

We talk in Chapter 2 about whether you can use your existing speakers with your home theater, and the bottom line is that if you do, try to buy a center speaker from the same manufacturer and class for the best results.

In an ideal world, you use exactly the same model of speaker for your center, left, and right speakers — all your front speakers. This isn't always practical, but we highly recommend you buy all three of these speakers from the same manufacturer and make sure that the manufacturer has designed them to be *timbre matched* — in other words, that they sound alike. This ensures that you get a more seamless listening experience.

Surround speakers

No matter what the setup of your speakers for surround sound — whether you have two, three, four, or more side and back speakers — your surround speakers play a fundamentally different role than your front speakers. You want things highly localized in the front part of your sound field, but the surround field is more diffuse.

Now we can get back to the bipole/dipole speakers we discuss earlier in the chapter. Recall that the purpose of the center speaker is to provide highly localized speaker information; it's coming from the center of the screen. There's a high correlation between what you see on the screen and where the sound comes from.

And likewise, the left and right speakers are to provide more lateral, but still highly localized and directed, sound. Together, the three represent the frontal face of your home theater sound experience. When there is a specific sound — the clash of swords, the shout of the main character, the click of a trigger being pulled back — the sound comes predominantly from these speakers.

The surround speakers have almost the opposite duty. Although you will hear discrete sounds from your surround speakers, their main duty is to create the sense of environment, the background, the unobvious. So if there is a howling wind, the pitter-patter of a rainstorm, or the background of a busy city, it comes from these speakers.

Reviewers tend to talk about the *diffuse sound* of the surround sound speakers because they often are not really making any specific sound per se, but a cacophony of sounds that together create an atmosphere. And where the front speakers (the center, left, and right) are arrayed at or around your ear level, the surround sounds tend to work higher, to the sides, and behind you, enveloping you in the surround sound field.

Surround sounds tend to rely less on direct radiated sound and more on reflected and indirect sound. Just like in a city where sounds bounce off buildings, or in a stadium where it's sometimes hard to localize a specific noise.

Bipole and dipole speakers, mounted on the sides of your room with front and rear facing drivers, contribute to this diffuse and reflected sound. Dipole speakers tend to be preferred for home theater applications because, relative to bipole speakers, they bleed out less sound to the sides and therefore are better at nonlocalized sounds. In comparison, bipole speakers tend to have more sound seep out from the sides, which makes them less diffuse.

Recall from Chapter 3 that there are several different modes of surround sound, often dependent on the encoding of your source input. There is a fair amount of debate about the appropriate speaker to use to create surround sound. For instance, Dolby Pro Logic encoders have a monophonic surround channel with a limited range of frequencies supported; by comparison, Dolby Digital encoders plan for full-range speakers. So do you use full-range speakers that are more directional, in order to take advantage of the newly enabled signals of Dolby Digital? Or, do you use more diffuse speakers to add to the shared atmosphere of the "surround"?

The choice isn't clear-cut. In general, we advise you to focus on creating a broad, diffuse sound field to the sides, back, and top of the room. A good installation uses dipole speakers to help provide localization where needed. For the higher-end encoding, such as THX Surround or DTS-ES, where there are at least four surround sound speakers, we suggest four dipole speakers — two on the sides and two in the back. You set up your two back surround speakers so that their drivers are in phase with one another. This maximizes the ability to create a specific sound image right behind you and serves as a good solution for home theater surround sound issues.

Some folks (typically on the high end of the home theater spectrum) recommend using direct radiating speakers for your surrounds. (In fact, DTS recommends this for DVDs encoded with their surround sound system.) We think that, for most people, dipoles are a better bet, mainly because, for most films, audio engineers mix the sound specifically for the diffuse speaker arrays used in theaters. So the majority of DVDs have been designed specifically for dipole-style speakers for your surrounds.

Going virtual

In a perfect world, we'd all have room in our home theaters for eight separate speakers (including the subwoofer), and we'd have all of our speaker cables neatly hidden inside the walls. In other words, we'd have a butt-kicking but aesthetically pleasing 7.1-channel surround sound system.

Sometimes, however, reality intrudes upon our perfect home theater world. Some folks just don't have the room for a full surround sound setup, or they have issues with the layout or construction of their room that keeps them from installing the full complement of surround speakers.

Many folks in this predicament are forced to stick with two-channel (stereo) audio and thus forgo surround sound. There is an alternative though — several manufacturers produce virtual surround sound speaker systems that incorporate multiple speaker drivers and some fancy electronics in a single speaker unit, which you place in the front of the room (usually right above or below your display).

These virtual systems use a combination of physical "aiming" and electronic trickery to introduce timing delays in the sound coming out of the speakers' drivers, which makes the sound "bounce" off your walls in a coordinated fashion. The result — while typically not as "immersive" as a full set of surround speakers — can come a lot closer to real surround sound than a pair of stereo speakers.

One example of these virtual systems is Yamaha's YSP-800. (It runs about $800 at most on-line retailers.) This system replaces not only all of your speakers, but also takes over the job of the A/V receiver. Connect your audio and video sources (like a DVD player) into the back of the YSP-800, plug it into the wall, and (with a little setup) you have convincing surround sound from a single speaker. It's a great setup for a quick and easy surround system for a smaller room or an apartment home theater.

Subwoofers in the mix

Most subwoofers have floor-based enclosures with active speaker systems (that is, with built-in amplifiers) for driving the low bass frequency ranges. Your biggest decision comes in *bass management*. That is, how do you want the bass signals in your system to be handled? You have a couple of options:

- The subwoofer can complement your full-range front speakers, providing for an even fuller bass signal.
- The subwoofer can handle all the bass, giving your front speakers the ability to focus on the mid- and high-range frequencies.

Most home theater experts will advise you to move all bass to the subwoofer. This results in more power and attention to the mid- and high-frequency drivers and less strain on the amplifier and speaker systems. This setup also gives you a more dynamic range, because the bass can go lower than most full-range speaker woofers can themselves (hence the term *sub*woofer).

If you have a modern A/V receiver, you use a standard line-level audio interconnect cable to connect your subwoofer to the receiver. (We talk about these cables in Chapter 16.) If you're using an older receiver as a stopgap until you purchase that nice new Dolby Digital A/V receiver, look for a subwoofer that also accepts *speaker level* connections. These connections enable you to run the speaker wires from your receiver to the subwoofer and then on to your front right and left speakers. In this case, there's no direct connection between your receiver and your front speakers — your front speaker *outputs* on the receiver are connected directly into the subwoofer, which is then connected with another set of speaker cables to the front speakers themselves. This type of connection isn't as good as a line level one, but it works.

Many subwoofers come with an Auto On/Off function that turns the active subwoofer's amplifier on and off with the presence of a signal. So the amplifier turns itself on when you're playing music or a movie soundtrack and then off again a few minutes after you're done. Pretty handy.

Recall that the subwoofer is usually powered by its own amplifier. As such, it has a volume control and a phase adjustment switch. You adjust the volume when fine-tuning your system and pretty much leave it at that setting. Your phase adjustment switch is sometimes a +/–180 degree switch and sometimes a continuously variable switch from 0 to +/–180 degrees (preferable). This comes into play when trying to fine-tune your system vis-à-vis your front left and right speakers. You adjust this so that the sound coming from each is relatively in alignment, despite the fact that the subwoofer and front speakers may be located at different distances from the listeners. By adjusting the phase, you can move the timing of the sound coming from the subwoofer.

In Chapter 21, we explain how to link your bass with *transducers* to provide a truly ground-shaking home theater experience.

Getting heady(phones) at home

You will see advertisements for surround sound headphones. Hopefully, you've understood enough in this chapter to say, "How can you cram five speakers and a subwoofer into a set of two-speaker headphones?" Hey, good question!

It's simple. No matter how many speakers you use in your system, you are still listening with two ears. These "surround sound" headphones basically try to reproduce what is arriving at your ears by using digital signal processors (DSPs). Dolby has gone one step further with a Dolby

Headphone encoder (www.dolby.com/dolbyheadphone) that can be built right into a receiver and that simulates Dolby Digital 5.1 over the two headphone channels. With Dolby Headphone, you don't use special headphones — any old pair of high-quality headphones will do the trick. Pretty cool, if you ask us.

If you plan on using headphones a lot (perhaps because your spouse does not like the movies you watch, eh, Pat?), check whether your receiver supports Dolby Headphone.

Chapter 13

Understanding Your Display Options

*W*e spend a lot of time in this part of the book talking about the audio systems that envelop you in surround sound and aurally immerse you in a movie. But let's face facts — we call it *watching* a movie because that's what we do. The audio creates the ambience, but the display is what you focus on. So choosing a high-quality video system that can properly display the content you want to watch — whether that content comes from traditional broadcast/ cable/satellite TV, from DVD, or even from HDTV — is essential.

In this chapter, we talk about the lingo of the TV world as our way of helping you make sense of all the terms and jargon you hear when you're shopping for a new display. We also talk about what it means for a display to be considered an *HDTV* (or high-definition TV) — which, by the way, we highly recommend you choose for your home theater. Finally, we discuss the different types of displays you can run into in a home theater and give you the lowdown on each type.

In Chapter 14, we talk in depth about each of the major categories of home theater displays, discussing the pros and cons of each type. So, if you already have a good feeling for what a comb filter does, for example, as well as the difference between an HDTV and an HDTV monitor, you probably don't need to linger here. Go ahead and skip right to Chapter 14 to get to the nitty-gritty — our recommendations on what type of TV to buy.

Learning the Lingo

If you're shopping for a TV for your home theater, you're probably going to run into salespeople, Web sites, and brochures full of acronyms and unfamiliar terms. Unfortunately, the technology industry tends to market its products with a list of features that are designed to bludgeon you upside the head and leave you with glassy eyes and a maxed-out credit card in your hand.

We're here to help. The following sections cover some of the most significant features and performance stats that you'll hear as you shop, and, more importantly, we explain what they mean!

Screen size

We won't insult your intelligence by telling you what *screen size* means, but we will tell you how it's measured. With a single exception (screens for front-projector systems), displays are measured diagonally. This is important to keep in mind because 16:9 and 4:3 screen sizes can't be directly compared diagonally — it's an apples and oranges thing. For example, a 16:9 32-inch screen is about 28 inches wide and a bit less than 16 inches high, while a 4:3 32-inch screen is 25.6 inches wide and a hair over 19 inches high.

Before you buy any television, you need to consider the size of your room and your expected seating distance from the display. As a gut reaction, most people think bigger is better when it comes to TV, but in fact, that's not really the case. Just as a TV can be obviously too small for a room (try sitting 15 feet back from a 27-inch TV), the opposite can be equally true. (Yes, Virginia, a TV can in fact be too darn big for a room.) And we're not just talking about being physically too big to fit in the room (or to look acceptable to your spouse, décor-wise), but also being visually too big.

Every video display has some sort of line structure (or in the case of flat-panel displays, pixel structure). The picture you see on your screen is made up of a series of individual points of light. Generally speaking, the bigger the screen, the bigger these individual points are. When you sit back a reasonable distance, your eyes can't discern these individual items, but if you get too close, they can. (Don't believe us? Turn on any TV in your house and walk right up to it. Take a look. See?)

Because line or pixel size depends on the size of the screen, the distance at which you can make out this structure varies by screen size. (The number of lines or pixels being displayed plays a part, too, which makes this effect slightly less noticeable on HDTVs that fit 720 or more vertically measured lines on the screen, instead of 480.)

Generally, we recommend that you sit two and a half screen size measurements from an HDTV-capable display and three screen sizes away from a non-HDTV. Note that we said you can sit *closer* to an HDTV than you can to a traditional TV simply because there are more lines and pixels on the screen (which makes them smaller and harder to see individually). The real goal of these measurements is to make sure that, for any particular viewing distance, your screen is close enough to give you a truly immersive "big screen" experience without being so big that you can make out the individual elements that make up the picture.

Lots of folks just want a gigantic TV. Nothing wrong with that in our minds, but do pay a little attention to these formulas so you don't end up with a screen so big that you can make out the individual pixels and lines — it makes the picture much less realistic, and it can really be kind of annoying. Certain types of displays, such as LCD (liquid crystal display) flat panels and LCD projection TVs, have pixels with physical characteristics that make them even more noticeable when you're close up — keep this in mind when you're choosing a display.

You can turn this equation around (ah, the wonders of math, huh?). If you have a good idea of how big your home theater room is going to be (we bet that you do) and also how far your primary seating area is going to be from the screen, you can use these guidelines to determine how big a display you need. If you're going for a widescreen HDTV, measure the distance to your seating area and divide by 2.5 — then multiply this number by 12 to determine your optimal screen size in inches (measured diagonally). Substitute a 3 for the 2.5 if you're going with an old-fashioned non-HDTV set.

Some of the newest high-definition TVs — fully capable of 1080p display resolutions, meaning they can show up to 1,080 lines running across the screen, as opposed to the 720 that most HDTVs are capable of — can be comfortably viewed at even closer distances than the 720p HDTVs. So if you want a huge screen (relative to your viewing distance), you might want to choose one of these displays. You're much less likely to see the individual picture elements with these displays, even if you're considerably closer than 2.5 times the screen size.

Table 13-1 is a rough guideline for screen size versus distance from the screen. Keep in mind that you don't have to be *exact* here — these are guidelines. If you want to go up or down a screen size from these recommendations, feel free — it shouldn't cause you any real viewing issues.

Table 13-1	Screen Size and Viewing Distance		
Analog TV Size	*Analog TV Viewing Distance*	*HDTV Size*	*HDTV Viewing Distance*
27 inch	6 feet, 9 inches	30 inch	6 feet, 3 inches
32 inch	8 feet	34 inch	7 feet, 1 inch
36 inch	9 feet	42 inch	8 feet, 6 inches
40 inch	10 feet	50 inch	10 feet, 5 inches
50 inch	12 feet, 6 inches	55 inch	11 feet, 6 inches
55 inch	13 feet, 9 inches	60 inch	12 feet, 6 inches
60 inch	15 feet	65 inch	13 feet, 6 inches

Aspect ratio

We already let the cat out of the bag on this subject (several times throughout the book), but let's repeat it because it's important — displays can be shaped for widescreen material (16:9) or for traditional TV viewing (4:3).

Although you can still find plenty of 4:3 displays on the market, for home theater purposes, we think you need to go with a widescreen (16:9) display — that's the right aspect ratio for DVDs, high-definition TV programming, and even many video games. If you're just buying a TV for the kitchen or guest bedroom, you might choose to go with 4:3, but for theater viewing, you really need to go widescreen.

In the past, we recommended that folks buying CRT (tube) TVs consider a 4:3 aspect ratio, as long as the TV could be optimized (the beam "re-aimed" in other words) for 16:9. That recommendation was mainly because there weren't a lot of widescreen tube TVs on the market. But these days, a number of manufacturers sell widescreen tube TVs.

Picture adjustability

Any display allows you to adjust the specific settings for your picture (and this is something we highly recommend you do). To do so, you typically use an on-screen display and your remote control.

Most people think of these settings as something to do once and never change. In fact, different environments might call for different settings. You might have one setting for the darkened-room home theater environment and another setting (that deals with ambient light better) for the brightly lit Super Bowl party.

Some systems let you save these settings as presets so that you can quickly access a certain group of settings without having to manually readjust every setting each time you want to re-create your settings. It's nice to be able to press a few quick buttons and get things back to the optimal movie-watching settings without readjusting your picture manually.

We recommend that you choose a display that lets you set the picture separately for each input or source device. That way, you can customize your settings individually — one setting for the HDTV cable box on your HDMI input, for example, and another for the DVD player and other devices coming into one of your display's component video inputs from your A/V receiver. We talk more about these settings in Chapter 20.

Connections on the back

When you get down to the business of connecting your A/V gear to your display, you need to make sure that your display has the right inputs to connect the source devices that will feed video into your home theater. Keep in mind that most video source devices have multiple types of video outputs, and that you can get the best picture quality if you use the right connection methods. So when you evaluate displays, remember that it's not just the *number* of inputs that's important, but rather the *type*. In fact, we'd argue in most cases that type is *more important* than the number of inputs.

We recommend that you connect most or all of your source devices directly to your A/V receiver, not your display, to simplify both hook-up and operation. So it's typically not all that important to have, for example, four different S-video inputs on the back of your TV. You'll connect all of your S-video sources directly to your receiver and will need only a single S-video cable connecting the receiver to your TV.

You should make sure that your display has at least one of each of the following types of inputs (check out Figure 13-1; we discuss these inputs in detail in Chapter 16):

- ✔ Composite video
- ✔ S-Video (Just like in the comic books, "S" here stands for Super, as in Super-Video)

✔ Component video

✔ HDMI — short for High-Definition Multimedia Interface

You should also expect to have a pair of analog audio inputs for each of these inputs (except for HDMI, which carries the audio on the same cable as it carries the video, which is very handy!).

You may also find the following inputs on your display:

✔ DVI — Okay, it's really Digital Video Interface, which can be used for PC connections

✔ VGA (the old standby, Video Graphics Array, used, like DVI, for connections to a PC)

✔ FireWire (not common, but found on a few brands of HDTVs)

While we find that having multiple numbers of each of these connection types can be a bit of overkill if you're connecting your sources through the receiver (as we recommend), there are some situations in which you'll be very happy to have multiples of certain types of inputs:

✔ **Component video:** If your A/V receiver can't handle high-definition signals through its component video inputs (almost all new home theater receivers can, but many older models can only handle DVD and not HDTV), you'll want to have at least two sets of component video inputs on your display.

✔ **HDMI:** HDMI, as we discuss in Chapter 16, is rapidly becoming *the* method for connecting source components to high-definition TVs. Most A/V receivers don't have HDMI video switching capabilities (see Chapter 11 to learn more about video switching), and many that do can accept only a couple of HDMI inputs.

Figure 13-1:
That's a lot
of inputs!

We highly recommend that if you're buying a new display, you choose one that has two HDMI inputs, just to increase your options and give you some more flexibility when you add new components like an HD-DVD or Blu-ray disc player to your home theater.

If you don't have enough HDMI inputs on your TV, you can always add an external HDMI video switch, as we discuss in Chapter 21.

Connections on the front

If you own a camcorder or some other portable video source device (such as a laptop computer that you may wish to occasionally connect to your home theater display), you may want to choose a display with a set of A/V connectors on the front of the unit. It's a lot easier to make quick, temporary connections this way than it is to try to climb behind your display and hook things up.

Look for a display that has at least one set of analog audio and video (preferably both composite and S-Video) connections on the front. Note that many flat-panel TVs, as well as the thinner microdisplay rear-projection models, hide these inputs on the side or even bottom (for wall mounted displays) of the TV.

Monitor versus television

When a display comes with a built-in TV tuner (so you can plug in an antenna or a cable connection and immediately watch TV), we call it a *television.* Some displays — for example, many projectors and plasma displays — come without any built-in TV tuning capabilities; we call these displays *monitors* or *HD-ready displays.* In fact, some monitors don't have a built-in audio speaker, so they don't offer even a minimal audio capacity. (We don't think this is a huge deal because any home theater worth its salt already has a good audio system, but for casual viewing, like watching the news, you may not want to fire up your audio system.)

Contrast ratio

If you look at TVs on a showroom floor, you might not ever realize this (because the displays have their brightness cranked up), but displays should be capable of showing both dark and light scenes. For example, you want to be able to see the flash of the artillery in *Saving Private Ryan* as well as the soldiers seeking cover in the shadows.

There's a measurement for how well a display can show both bright brights and nuanced darks: *contrast ratio.* You'll see this as a numeric ratio, something like 1000:1, representing the whitest white compared to the blackest black. Typically, direct-view (tube) displays and projector systems that use CRTs have the highest contrast ratios, whereas systems that use plasma or LCD technologies have the lowest. When it comes to contrast ratio, a higher ratio is better.

There isn't a standardized, approved way of measuring contrast ratios, so one manufacturer's 800:1 may not be the same as another's. You need to rely on magazine and on-line reviews and use your own eyes in a thorough test drive at a dealer's showroom. We like reviews that include a professional calibration of the display because that shows the display's true "ultimate" capabilities. When you do a test drive, use some of your own DVDs that you know well.

Comb filter

Many video sources (such as broadcast NTSC television or composite video connections from other source devices) send both the color (chrominance) and brightness (luminance) parts of the video signal as a single, combined (or composite) signal. Inside the TV, either a *notch filter* or a *comb filter* separates these signals into their component parts. If signals aren't properly separated, you see moving dots of color around the edges of images, a phenomenon called *dot crawl.*

Notch filters are the least effective at this process, whereas the various kinds of comb filters do a better job. You'll find three kinds of comb filters in direct-view displays:

- ✔ **2-D comb filter:** This is the least effective (and least expensive) kind of comb filter, though it is better than a notch filter.

- ✔ **3-D comb filter:** We're talking middle ground here — better than 2-D, but not as good as the digital comb filter.

- ✔ **Digital comb filter (sometimes called 3-D Y/C):** Found in more expensive direct-view sets, the digital comb filter uses more sophisticated (and digital!) signal processing to separate chrominance and luminance. This is the king of the hill when it comes to comb filters.

When you connect sources to your display with S-Video or component video cables (discussed in Chapter 16), chrominance and luminance are separated in the source device, not in your TV. In this case, your display's built-in comb filter is bypassed.

Resolution

As we discuss in Chapter 4, *display resolution* is a measure of how precise and sharp a picture a display can create. For standard-definition programming — such as NTSC television and, to a degree, DVD — this isn't a really huge deal. (Any display can handle the 480 vertical lines of resolution of these formats — which is not to say they'll all look the same!) As you start getting into HDTV sources (and even widescreen "anamorphic" DVDs), however, resolution becomes a really big deal.

Generally, display vendors spend most of their time talking about the *vertical* resolution of their sets, which corresponds to the most commonly discussed resolutions of HDTV, 720 and 1080. Some displays (particularly those that have a fixed-pixel system, such as LCD or plasma) give resolution in terms of both horizontal and vertical numbers (similar to the way resolutions are discussed in the computer display world). So you might see, for example, a plasma display with a resolution of 1280 x 720p (which corresponds to 720p). In this case, the 1280 refers to the horizontal resolution (the number of pixels, or individual points, across the screen) and 720 refers to the vertical number (like the scan lines on a conventional TV).

As we mention in Chapter 4, displays are also classified by the *input resolutions* that they can handle. These input resolutions simply are the resolutions that the display can accept from source devices. The circuitry inside the display itself converts (if necessary) these signals to the display's own native display resolution. Read the fine print closely — some displays (the EDTVs we talk about in Chapter 4, for example) can accept high-definition resolutions like 720p, but they display it at a lower (not high-definition) resolution.

When you get into high-definition digital displays, you'll find out that your display holds some circuitry that handles this conversion from *input resolution* to *display resolution*. This circuitry is known as the *scaler* because it scales the image from one size to another. When you're reading reviews of different displays you are considering, pay close attention to the capabilities of this scaler; it will manipulate most of the video signals you send into your TV. (There aren't necessarily going to be any hard, cold, objective numbers to describe scaler performance, but instead the reviews will talk about the absence of "jagged lines" and other visible picture distortions for scaled images.) All else being equal, a display with a better scaler will have a better picture, especially when it displays video sources that aren't created in the display's native display resolution.

Interlaced and progressive scan

In Chapter 4 (it's a chapter you shouldn't skip!), we talk about the two *scanning* methods that video displays use — interlaced and progressive. Traditional TV systems (such as NTSC, the standard TV system in the

United States) use an *interlaced* scan, where half the picture appears on the screen at a time. The other half follows an instant later (¹⁄₆₀th of a second, to be precise). The interlaced system relies on the fact that your eyes can't really detect this procedure in action — at least not explicitly. In a progressive-scan system, the entire picture is painted at once, which greatly reduces the flickering that people notice when watching TV. Progressive scan is available throughout the range of TV types we're about to discuss. We highly recommend progressive scan if it fits into your budget because the picture appears much smoother and more like a film. (You can get direct-view progressive-scan TVs for under $500 these days.)

Any HDTV display can handle progressive scan.

Scan frequency

Scan frequency is something you might not hear much about unless you're buying an HDTV or a high-end projector system, but if you're shopping in the higher end of the market, you should know what scan frequency is. In general terms, scan frequency (which is measured in kHz — thousands of cycles per second) is directly related to the interlaced and progressive-scan types that we discuss in the preceding section. Standard NTSC video, which is interlaced, puts out 15,734 scan lines per second. 15.75 kHz is the common rounded version of this number. When you start getting into progressive-scan video (using, for example, a progressive-scan DVD player), you effectively double this scan frequency to 31.5 kHz. HDTV systems can go even higher. If you're looking into CRT projector systems (which we discuss in the following chapter), you'll hear a lot about scan frequencies.

If you're choosing a digital display (LCD, plasma, or DLP [Digital Light Processor]), you will probably never run into any mention of scan frequency. This is something that really only comes into play for CRT projections (and, to a lesser extent, direct-view CRT displays). For the most part, you won't have to worry about scan frequency unless you are buying one of these displays.

Getting Equipped for HDTV

Before we start talking about the physical differences between the various categories of displays (differences such as picture tube or no picture tube), we want to cover one even higher-level distinction. That distinction is the following: Is the display capable of playing back HDTV at full resolution?

We talk a lot about what HDTV *is* in Chapter 4, including the fact that next-generation digital TV (also called ATSC) has a bunch of different formats. Two of those formats, 1080i and 720p, qualify as high-definition television, or HDTV.

Deciding on HDTV or a traditional NTSC TV is probably the most important decision you can make if you're buying a new display unit for your home theater, but we think home theater shoppers won't need to agonize over this decision any longer. That's because we think almost all displays that are appropriate for home theaters should be capable of displaying HDTV. At the very least, we feel that moving up to HDTV capabilities won't be much of a price jump. If you can afford it today (and you can get HDTV-ready sets for under $1,000), we highly recommend that you get an HDTV or HDTV-ready display now.

You can buy an HDTV for well under $1,000 these days, so unless your budget is quite tight, we really think you should make an HDTV-capable display the centerpiece of your home theater. With HDTV programming becoming commonplace (see Chapter 7), and HDTV discs also hitting the market (see Chapter 6), there's plenty of great HDTV content to watch on your big screen. So if you can swing it, we urge you to go the HDTV route!

We talk about HDTV back in Chapter 4. Now, we want to talk about the characteristics of TVs and displays that can play back HDTV programming. The first layer of the HDTV onion that we should peel back is the concept of an *HDTV* versus an *HDTV-ready* system. An HDTV has the following key characteristics:

- ✔ **Resolution:** Can display true high-definition signals with at least 720 lines of horizontal resolution (in other words, 720 lines of picture data stacked on top of each other vertically on the screen).

    The latest and greatest HDTVs can display the full 1920 x 1080 pixels of 1080i HDTV signals (and do so in a progressive scan fashion). Such HDTVs are often called *1080p HDTVs.*

- ✔ **Aspect ratio:** Has a widescreen aspect ratio of 16:9.

- ✔ **Tuner:** Has a built-in TV tuner, which is capable of decoding any over-the-air broadcast format within the ATSC digital television standard. (HDTVs that get their HDTV programming from an internal DSS receiver are also called HDTVs, even though they don't strictly fit this definition.)

An HDTV-ready set, often called an *HDTV monitor,* must meet only the first two requirements. Many direct-view (tube) HDTV-ready sets meet the second requirement only because of an "anamorphic squeeze" mode (discussed in Chapter 14), not because the sets are physically shaped in the 16:9 aspect ratio.

Will my HDTV work next year?

Seems impossible to even consider, doesn't it? HDTV is the newest thing around, just barely on the market, and already we're asking a question like this? Well, although it would take a degree of contempt for (or ignorance of) the customer, which we don't think the HDTV industry will let happen, it *is* possible that some buyers of HDTV technology may find their sets unable to connect in the not-so-distant future.

The issue is copy protection. Many movie and TV studios want to have some control over your ability to make copies of digital content sent to your HDTV (not all, to be fair — a few actually support technologies like the D-VHS we discuss in Chapter 6). So a new type of connection technology called *HDMI* (High-Definition Multimedia Interface), which supports a copy-protection system called *HDCP* (High Definition Content Protection), has been developed for HDTV-ready TVs, set-top boxes, and HDTV tuners. Not every HDTV comes with an HDMI interface. If you don't have HDMI (or it's older cousin DVI, which also supports HDCP) on your HDTV, you'll connect to your HDTV sources with analog component video cables (in the vast majority of cases).

There's nothing wrong with component video, but the TV and movie industries don't like analog connections because they can't easily apply their copy protection systems to these connections like they can to digital connections like HDMI. So there exists a possibility that in the future, HDTV sources will only be displayed in their full resolution when using a digital (HDMI) connection and will be converted down to a lower resolution when sent over analog cables.

Could happen. Probably won't. But we wanted to mention it as something to think about before you make an investment in HDTV. Keep in mind that this issue (not having an HDCP-enabled HDMI or DVI connection on your HDTV-ready display) won't keep you from using any HDTV tuner you buy along with the display (or the built-in tuner if you buy a true HDTV). It'll just keep you from having all the flexibility you might want. We highly recommend getting a unit with HDMI connections (even though we're not all that keen on the concept of HDCP).

(By the way, the FireWire digital connection system can also support copy protection and should provide you with a safe investment as well, but not too many display vendors have chosen to put FireWire on their displays.)

All four types of displays we discuss in this book — direct-view, flat-panel, front-projection, and rear-projection systems — can be built as an HDTV or HDTV-ready system. And just like non-HDTV versions of these displays, a huge range of sizes and shapes is on the market. You can buy a 14-inch LCD (liquid crystal display — which we talk about in depth in Chapter 14) HDTV for a bedroom or kitchen, or you can buy a $30,000 HDTV-ready projector that requires professional mounting and calibration and gives you an HDTV picture the size of some movie theater screens. You can find a vast range of options in the HDTV world.

As we discuss the different types of displays in this chapter (and in the following chapter when we discuss projectors), we talk about the strengths and weaknesses of each type of display in overall terms (HDTV, NTSC, DVD playback, you name it — when we say overall, we mean overall). Remember that *any* of these systems can be used for HDTV (of course, not *every* or even most models within these groups can display HDTV signals). We mention any special HDTV considerations as we discuss each type of display.

Choosing a TV

As you shop for a display, you'll find that, beyond all the brand and size choices, you need to make some high-level decisions about what kind of display you want. For many people, a display (or TV) means the traditional tube television that's been around for decades, but new technologies have made flat-panel screens (which have no tube and are only a few inches deep) into a viable choice as well — and projection TVs (which shoot the picture onto a screen) have never been better, cheaper, or bigger. In this section, we give you an overview of the primary technologies that underlie different types of TVs. (In the following chapter, we talk about each of these TV types in depth, so you can understand the pros and cons of each type.)

The first distinction to be made in the world of home theater displays revolves around how the picture gets to your eyeballs.

- With some displays, you are directly viewing the image created by the imaging hardware within the TV. In other words, the image is created on the screen you are watching. These displays are known as *direct view*. The most common type of direct-view display is the old-fashioned "tube" TV, but flat-panel (hang-on-the-wall) plasma and LCD TVs can also be considered direct-view displays.

- Other displays create the image in one place and then *project* it onto a screen elsewhere. These *projector* displays work much like a movie projector in a theater (and better than that noisy one in your third-grade social studies class) and can offer the biggest image size of any type of display. There are two types of projectors:

  - Rear-projection systems, which display an image on the *back* of the screen, which you then view from the front.

  - Front-projection systems, which display an image on the *front* of a screen (the same side you view the image on).

Beyond this initial categorization, displays are also categorized by the underlying technology that creates the image. There are a few dominant technologies here. Note that most of these technologies can be used for either direct-view or projection displays, depending on how they are implemented.

- ✔ **CRT:** CRT, or cathode ray tube, is the traditional technology behind TVs and home theater displays (for a long time, the *only* technology, but that has changed a lot in the past ten years). CRTs can be used in both direct-view and projector applications.

- ✔ **Plasma:** Plasma (sometimes called PDP, or *plasma display panel*) displays use a grid of electrical circuits sandwiched between two plates of glass to electrically excite a gas and cause it to put out light. Plasma displays are the thin (often less than 4 inches thick) TVs that everyone's dying to hang on their walls.

- ✔ **LCD:** LCDs do exactly what their name implies — they have liquid crystal particles within them that can be aligned in different ways to create different colors. When a bright light shines through these crystals, you get a video picture. LCDs can be flat-panel TVs (like a plasma display), or they can be used in projection TVs (see the bullet on microdisplays below). If you've seen a laptop computer (or a desktop PC with a flat-panel display), you've seen an LCD.

- ✔ **Microdisplays:** Traditionally, projection systems used CRT tubes to create the projected image. Most current projection systems use a microdisplay technology to do so instead. A microdisplay is exactly what the name says it is — basically a tiny display that uses some sort of miniaturized display technology to create an image that is then enlarged when it is beamed onto the projection screen. There are several different technologies within the microdisplay family:

  - **LCD:** The same LCD technology used for flat-panel screens can be shrunken down and used within a projector.

  - **DLP:** A DLP, or *digital light processor,* uses a special video chip from Texas Instruments that includes millions of microscopic mirrors that are moved by computer command (sort of like the Robot in *Lost in Space,* only smaller!) to create an image.

  - **LCoS:** *Liquid Crystal on Silicon* microdisplays use a special variant of LCD technology that's shrunken down to the chip level.

As we mentioned, some of these technologies can be used in either direct-view or projection applications (CRT and LCD in particular), which can make things a bit confusing for the casual shopper. If you're shopping on-line (or just comparing prices), and you don't actually see the TV in front of you, make sure you read *all* of the details. We'd hate for you to think you were getting an LCD flat panel to hang on the wall when you were actually pricing out an LCD front-projection system that goes on the ceiling and needs a separate screen!

Chapter 14

Comparing Display Technologies

· ·

· ·

Choosing the right display for *your* home theater is one of the most important tasks you'll face when you begin building your home theater. Your display is the most visible (no pun intended) part of your home theater, and a great high-definition widescreen picture can really knock folks' socks off. So choose the right display for your particular home theater, and you'll be that much closer to the "being there" experience that you get at the movies.

In Chapter 13, we talk about all of the things you should understand about displays in general, including the features and capabilities to look for when shopping for a new TV or display. Those discussions apply across all sorts of display types — you'll want, for example, an HDMI input whether you are buying a plasma or a DLP rear-projection unit.

In this chapter, we take the discussion to the next level by examining each of the common types of displays you might choose for a home theater — CRT "tube" TVs, plasma and LCD flat panels, and the whole array of front- and rear-projection TVs — and give you some insight into the pros and cons of each type. Combine this with the knowledge you gain by reading Chapter 13, and you'll be ready to start shopping!

Sticking with the Tried-and-True Tube

Admit it. You say it, too: "What's on the tube?" C'mon, we all say it, and for good reason — the vast majority of TVs are *direct-view CRT* (or cathode ray *tube*) models. You know what they look like — kind of big and bulky, with a big (and relatively heavy) glass tube inside.

The CRT itself is a vacuum tube (so don't drop it — well, don't drop any television, if you can help it, especially not on your foot) with an electron gun at the back and a *phosphor* coating on the inside of the screen (the part you look at). When a CRT operates, the electron gun shoots a beam of electrons on that phosphor coating, as shown in Figure 14-1. In reaction to being bombarded by these electrons, the phosphor coating lights up. A color CRT actually has three electron guns — one each for red, green, and blue. This combination of colors (often called *RGB*) can be combined on the screen to produce any color you want.

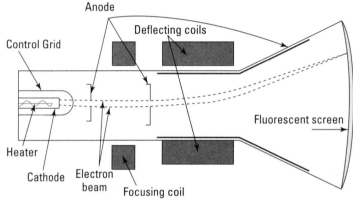

Figure 14-1: Faster than a speeding electron!

Anode

Deflecting coils

Control Grid

Fluorescent screen

Heater

Cathode   Electron beam

Focusing coil

Because CRT TVs are an old technology, many people skip right past them as they shop for a home theater display. We're not *entirely* convinced that's a good idea. CRT TVs have a few significant things going for them:

✓ **They're cheap:** Because the factories and machines and technologies behind CRT are old (though constantly refined), CRTs are rather inexpensive to build (HDTV models are not nearly as cheap). This gets passed on to the consumer in the form of lower prices (capitalism at work!), making CRT televisions the cheapest you can buy.

You can buy a 26-inch HDTV-ready CRT television for about $500 — about as cheap as you're likely to see in the near future for an HDTV-ready display.

✓ **They work well in a bright room:** The contrast ratios and overall ability to crank out the light are typically highest on CRT displays. If you can't create a dark environment for your home theater (something we think is really important, but that we realize isn't always possible), a direct-view TV may be your best choice. Another reason to choose direct-view is because you like to have your buddies over for the big game in the middle of a bright day.

✔ **They have excellent viewing angles:** You can sit (or stand — we don't care how you watch your home theater system!) pretty well off the "center axis" of a CRT and still see a good picture. There's not a small "sweet spot" centered around the perpendicular from your screen with a CRT (as there is with many projection TVs, for example).

✔ **They're better at black:** Not only are CRTs brighter than other display types, they're also better at creating dark images than most other kinds of displays. So if you like to watch a lot of *film noir* or anything that has dark scenes (with people lurking in the shadows), you'll appreciate the fact that CRT displays let you see details that can be lost on other sets.

Like anything else, getting a CRT TV has some drawbacks. Whether these drawbacks are enough to drive you to a different display type really depends on how important the strengths we just listed are to you. Here's what to keep in mind as you make this decision:

✔ **Limited size:** Although CRTs are relatively easy and cheap to make, the manufacturing process does become difficult when CRTs reach a certain size. Huge vacuum tubes aren't easy to create, and as the screen gets bigger, keeping the electron guns properly aimed is also a big issue for display designers. When you start looking at displays bigger than about 40 inches, you won't find CRTs in your size range.

✔ **Heavy and bulky:** You certainly can't hang a CRT on the wall (like you can with the plasma displays we discuss in a moment). In fact, if you go for a bigger screen size, you can't even lift your CRT TV (CRTs bigger than 36 inches often weigh over 200 pounds). And weight isn't the only issue — CRT sets usually have 2 or 3 feet of electronics and tube behind the screen. So if you're tight on space but desire a big screen, don't be surprised if a CRT doesn't work for you.

✔ **Lower resolution:** For NTSC and DVD viewing, CRT displays (at least high-quality models) can meet the resolution demands of the source material. But when you start getting into HDTV sources, you'll find that CRTs can't keep up. They *can* provide excellent pictures, but if you were to compare them side by side with a plasma or projection TV, you'd find that most direct-view HDTVs don't match up, at least in terms of resolution.

If you have the money to spend (and it won't be cheap), you can get many of the benefits of a direct-view TV, without the drawbacks, by investing in a CRT-based projection TV. We discuss such models later in this chapter.

If a tube TV fits into your budget, room, and lifestyle, there are a few things you should look for. (As an aside, one of Pat's college professors automatically gave an F to anyone who used the word *lifestyle* in a paper, so he loves to sprinkle it in his writing now.) Consider this a checklist of sorts, but keep in mind that some TVs can have all these things and still not be all that great. Others can be great even though they're missing a feature or two. So the following items are recommended but not essential:

✔ **Flat-screen:** Older TVs had a curved screen surface (the actual front of the screen that you watch), but many newer models have a truly flat screen surface. (This is different than a flat-panel, where the whole display is flat and thin.) The biggest advantage of a flat-screen direct-view TV is the fact that this screen is much less susceptible to reflections and glare.

✔ **Aspect ratio:** For most display types, we *only* recommend a 16:9 aspect ratio that is optimized for widescreen movie viewing. We also recommend that you consider a widescreen model if you're buying a tube TV, but you may find that your budget works better with a 4:3 tube TV (the widescreen models are typically a bit more expensive). If you do buy a 4:3 tube TV, be sure that it supports the *anamorphic squeeze* or *16:9 mode* discussed in the next bullet, or you'll suffer from a significant loss of resolution when playing DVDs, HDTV, and other widescreen content.

✔ **Anamorphic squeeze:** Often called *raster squeeze,* this is a neat trick that lets you watch anamorphic DVDs at full resolution on 4:3 aspect ratio, direct-view TVs. (This isn't a feature you find or need on fixed-pixel displays, such as LCD or plasma.) The squeeze basically re-aims the electron guns' beams (the raster) to create a 16:9 window within the 4:3 screen. At first glance, this looks a lot like a letterboxed video picture on your screen, but instead of wasting lines of resolution to draw black bars, this refocused beam uses the entire 480 lines to create the video you're watching. The result is a sharper, brighter, and better-looking picture. Some displays have an automatic system for detecting 16:9 sources and turning on this mode, and others have a button on the remote to activate it.

If you use this mode, make sure you've set your DVD player to "think" it's connected to a 16:9 TV. Otherwise, you don't get anything out of your display's anamorphic squeeze function.

The bottom line with tube TVs is this — they have a number of advantages and a number of disadvantages. Most folks starting a new home theater today will choose one of the newer (but more expensive) technologies we discuss throughout the rest of the chapter. If you decide that you want a tube display, act soon — many manufacturers are cutting back production and using this technology only for the most inexpensive "throwaway" TVs that people put in their guest bedrooms or garages. For example, as we were writing this chapter, Sony announced that it was closing its huge Trinitron picture tube factory in Pat's neighborhood of San Diego. It's starting to become the end of an era for the tube TV.

The replacement for the CRT?

As the era of the tube draws to a close, a new and somewhat similar technology called SED *(surface-conduction electron-emitter display)* has begun to trickle out of the labs. Toshiba and Canon are the two big proponents of this technology, which is in many ways a hybrid of the CRT and the plasma display.

SED displays (none are in production as we write, but we've seen demonstrations of some hand-built prototypes) are designed to be thin and flat, like a plasma TV, but at the same time provide the bright picture and the deep, deep blacks of a CRT. Essentially, an SED display takes the electron gun of a CRT and turns it into a big flat panel that sends the electrons across a small vacuum to the phosphors on another flat panel of glass. It looks like a plasma display (because it's thin and flat), but because it uses electrons hitting a phosphor layer, it has all the picture benefits of a CRT. (Plasma also uses electrons, but the process involves exciting a gas with an electrical charge, causing the gas to emit electrons, rather than just shooting them out of an electron "gun.") And the great thing is that an SED can be high resolution (easily meeting the 1920 x 1080 resolution of the highest HDTV standards) while using less than half the power that a plasma or LCD flat panel uses.

We were blown away by the demos we saw, and predict that SED will be the next big thing in flat-panel displays (unless the LCD and plasma manufacturers can keep up!). Expect to see the first SED sets hitting the market by the end of 2008. Keep your eyes peeled!

And if that's not enough to anticipate, another technology called O-LED (Organic LED), originally thought up by the folks at Kodak, is on the way. This technology is similar to LCD, but uses an organic material that can generate its own light — LCDs require a backlight to shine through the LCD — and which will be cheaper, thinner, and brighter than O-LED.

Personally, we have a love/hate relationship with these kinds of new technologies. We love them (LOVE THEM!) for their performance and how they improve the state of the home theater art. We hate that we know about them and then have to consider whether to buy new gear now or to wait for that "next big thing." Our advice to you is that there will *always be* a next big thing just around the corner. So if you're ready to buy now, don't wait for these technologies. But if they start to hit the market when you're in the market yourself, by all means check them out!

Thin Is In — Flat-panel TVs

The coolest development in the TV world in years and years has been the advent of the flat-panel (notice we didn't say *flat-screen*) display. These are TVs that you can literally hang on the wall. Flat-panel TVs use technologies such as LCD and plasma to create a TV that is barely bigger than the screen itself. These displays have a small frame around the edges of the screen and are about 3 or 4 inches deep. There are some tradeoffs to flat-panel displays, but if you can live with them, you can definitely find a place in your home theater for a flat-panel — literally!

Demystifying LCD

If you have a laptop computer, a digital watch, a handheld computer, or just about anything electronic, you've probably seen, touched, felt, and used a liquid crystal display, or LCD. We first saw LCDs on digital watches back when we were kids (we thought they were cool) and never imagined the size they'd grow to. We certainly never thought LCDs would one day display high-resolution images with millions of gradations of color. But that's exactly what they can do, and are doing, in an increasing number of homes and home theaters.

You may be wondering how LCD displays actually work. Well here's the short answer. (There are armies of lab-coated PhDs working at the manufacturers of these things who can give you the long answer!) An LCD display consists of a large number of pixels (or picture elements) consisting of liquid crystal molecules being held between two sets of transparent electrodes. These liquid crystals react in predictable ways when the electrical charge running between those electrodes is changed — meaning they twist and move in ways that let different amounts (and colors) of light through the crystals. The LCD has a control system that translates your video signals into the proper charges for each of those electrodes. A light source (usually a fluorescent bulb, though LED bulbs are starting to hit the market) shines *through* the LCD panel (it's built into your display, and is typically there for the life of the display) and creates your picture.

Because the light shines through the liquid crystals, rather than reflecting off of them or being created *by* them, an LCD is what is known as a *transmissive* display. Generally speaking, transmissive displays are slightly less bright — you lose some of the bulb's brightness going through the crystals — but LCD makers can make up for this by using a really bright bulb for the backlight.

Despite these amazing changes, LCDs tend to be the smallest displays — or at least smaller per dollar spent. Put a different way, LCD displays tend to cost the most for a given screen size — a plasma of the same size will typically cost about 30 percent less than an LCD unit.

This price difference is a result of the process of "growing" LCD crystals. Unfortunately for us consumers, that process is quite complicated — and the bigger the crystal, the harder (and more expensive) it is to make. Most of the LCD displays top out at about 45 inches, and the typical LCD is smaller still, at about 37 inches. (See Figure 14-2.) So most folks will use an LCD in a smaller home theater setting — where a 37-inch display makes sense — and move up to a plasma or projection unit if they need a larger display.

We're talking about direct-view LCDs here (where you look directly at the LCD, just as you look directly at the picture tube with direct-view tube TV). LCDs can also be used in projector TVs (both front and rear), and we talk about them later in this chapter — in the "Getting Into Projection TVs" section, if you want us to be specific.

Figure 14-2:
Liquid crystals put the HD in your TV.

A few companies make mega-big LCD displays. As we write (early 2006), we've seen prototypes for LCD displays as big as 82 inches diagonally. And new technologies, such as O-LED (Organic LED), promise LCD-like displays in even bigger sizes in the future. We've even seen prototype systems that seamlessly combine three smaller (and easier-to-build) LCD panels into a larger single panel — making a cheaper big LCD.

Most LCD television monitors are built in the widescreen 16:9 aspect ratio, although some vendors sell 4:3 versions (which are more typical for PC screens). We prefer the widescreen versions of LCDs because 16:9 LCDs don't tend to "wear out" unevenly (like direct-view CRTs do) when used to display 4:3 video programming.

LCD displays have a couple of particular strong points when it comes to playing video:

- **Extremely high resolutions:** LCDs can easily reach HDTV resolutions (in fact, most LCD displays do). You can easily find a 1080p-capable LCD display — most plasma displays are 720p instead.

- **Excellent color:** LCDs offer exceptional reproduction of colors, with the potential for beautifully re-created colors across the spectrum. This differs from other flat-panel displays (such as plasma systems), which often tend to inaccurately display certain colors.

- **Great picture:** The newest (and most expensive) LCDs use an LED (light emitting diode) instead of a traditional bulb for their light source. These LEDs produce a higher-quality picture because the LED itself emits a more natural (closer to daylight) light than does a bulb (which tends to be yellowish, not true white).

- **PC monitor–capable:** This probably won't surprise you because you're probably familiar with LCD computer monitors. Most LCD television displays can also do double-duty as a PC monitor, plugging directly into any PC with a standard PC video cable.

✔ **No *burn-in*:** If you play a lot of video games, watch the stock ticker on MSNBC, or do other things with your display that involve a lot of *static* content (images that don't change or move around) on a CRT display, you can end up with those images permanently burned into the phosphors on your screen. When these images become permanently etched into the phosphor, you see them even when you're watching something else. Because LCDs use a separate backlight instead of creating their own light with phosphors, they are immune to this problem (plasmas are not, by the way).

You can get a *stuck pixel* on an LCD screen, where a single pixel always emits a color (often red). This can be annoying, so check your manufacturer's warranty to see whether they will repair a display if it has stuck pixels. This is a pretty rare occurrence, but it can happen. Most people don't even notice it, but if you're sharp-eyed, it might drive you crazy.

✔ **Inherently progressive:** Unlike direct-view systems, LCDs don't display their picture using electron guns scanning lines across a screen. Instead, LCDs use millions of tiny transistors that can be individually controlled by the "brains" inside the display. This means that LCDs can easily handle progressive-scan sources, such as progressive-scan DVD and HDTV — unlike some direct-view systems that simply can't scan fast enough to display progressive video.

Besides the size limitation we discuss earlier in this section, consider a few other problem areas before you buy an LCD system as your primary display in a home theater:

✔ **Expensive for their size:** Inch for viewing inch, LCDs tend to be a bit more expensive than the plasma flat-panels we discuss next, and much more expensive than CRT displays. At the beginning of 2006, you could expect to pay about $1,700 for an HDTV-ready, 37-inch LCD display. For the same price, you could buy an HDTV-ready, 42-inch plasma set — in other words, get a bigger monitor for the same price.

✔ **Poor reproduction of blacks:** Compared with direct-view tube displays, LCDs do a poor job of reproducing black images. Darker screen images never show up as true black, but rather as various shades of gray, and actions happening in these darker areas are difficult to discern.

✔ **Poor response time:** Some LCD displays suffer from a poor *response time* — meaning it takes a while for the pixels to change colors in response to a rapidly changing scene in your video program. This can bug the living daylights out of some people, particularly when you're watching sports (you might see a trail of a moving ball on the screen, for example).

Most new LCD TVs have this problem licked — to be sure, look for a response time of less than 16 milliseconds.

✔ **Limited viewing angle:** Although they are getting better (due to some intensive efforts by manufacturers), LCDs typically have a poor viewing angle. If you are not sitting almost directly in front of the screen, you don't get a good picture.

✔ **Limited brightness:** Because LCDs use a backlight shining through the liquid crystal, most of the light is absorbed. As a result, the LCD displays have lower contrast and are harder to view in a brightly lit room (the picture appears washed out), compared with CRT TVs.

Staying on the cutting edge with plasma

Perhaps the coolest thing to come down the home theater pike in quite some time (maybe ever!) is the larger, flat-screen monitor that uses plasma technology. A plasma screen contains literally millions of gas-filled cells (or pixels) wedged between two pieces of glass. An electrical grid zaps these pixels and causes the gases to ionize (the ionized gas is plasma — hence the name). The ionized gases, in turn, cause a layer of phosphor on the outside layer of glass to light up (just like the electron gun in a CRT causes the phosphor to light up on the front of the tube).

Plasma displays have really captured the attention of the home theater industry (and of home theater consumers) because of the sheer size and quality of the picture they can produce. They're also known for their compact size. Plasma displays are available in 42-, 50-, and even 60-inch sizes — and they can get even bigger. (Panasonic showed off a 103-inch plasma at the 2006 Consumer Electronics show — don't even ask about the price!) Even at the larger sizes, the display itself is usually no more than 5 or 6 inches deep — and suitable for wall hanging! All the plasma displays in these sizes (which are by far the most common, at least in the U.S. market) have a 16:9 aspect ratio.

Other benefits of plasma displays include the following:

✔ **Excellent brightness:** Because plasma displays use the direct lighting of phosphors (instead of a backlighting system like LCDs), they can have an extremely bright and crisp picture, just like a direct-view CRT TV. In fact, because each pixel is controlled directly by the electrical grid behind the plasma cells, the brightness tends to be extremely even across the screen. In a CRT, the electron guns shoot at the phosphors from differing angles depending upon which part of the screen the gun is creating, which can cause uneven brightness in badly designed CRTs.

✔ **High resolution:** Although not all plasma displays can reach HDTV levels of resolution (many "inexpensive" $2,000 plasma models can't show true HDTV), they do typically provide greater resolution than CRT displays. This is especially true of the more expensive HDTV plasmas, which can often reach higher horizontal resolutions that CRT sets can't match. Just about all plasma displays on the market are 16:9 aspect ratio sets, which is also essential for HDTV viewing.

✔ **PC monitor–capable:** Like LCD screens, most plasma displays can be plugged directly into any PC (not just home theater PCs with special TV video cards) to act as a gigantic PC monitor.

✔ **No geometric distortion:** In a CRT display, the electron guns that shoot their beams on the phosphor screen are in a fixed location (the center/back of the tube). The angle at which these beams hit the phosphor varies; in the middle of the screen, the angle is perpendicular, but the angle is quite different at the corners of the screen. This can cause distortions in the picture — *geometric distortions* caused by this changing angle. In a plasma display, each gas pocket is at an identical angle (and distance) to the phosphor it lights up, so you don't get distortions around the edge of the picture.

✔ **Progressive by nature:** Like LCDs, plasma systems don't use a scanning electron beam to create a picture. Instead, all the pixels on the screen are lit up simultaneously. So progressive video sources display progressively on any plasma system; you don't need to buy a special progressive set like you do with CRT displays.

✔ **A wide viewing angle:** Unlike LCDs (which often have problems in this regard), plasma displays have a good picture even when you are sitting "off axis" (not perpendicular to the screen surface). In a smaller room, where some of the seating might be at a rather acute angle from the screen, the wide viewing angle can be a big plus.

Of course, the plasma equation has a few downsides (besides the fact that a lot of us can't afford the $3,000 it costs for an HDTV plasma):

✔ **Susceptible to burn-in:** Any system that uses a phosphor screen to display video can fall victim to the phosphor burn-in mentioned earlier in this chapter. If you do a lot of video gaming or stock/news ticker viewing, you need to be aware of this fact. Although burn-in can also be an issue with a CRT set, it's an even bigger issue with a plasma, considering the price. You can't remove burn-in after it's happened; you need to either live with it or replace the display.

You can minimize burn-in on any display by calibrating the set properly and by reducing the brightness from its (usually too high) factory setting.

✔ **Shorter lifespan:** Another phenomenon of any phosphor-based display system is that eventually the phosphors "wear out" or lose their brightness. Like burn-in, this degradation also happens to CRT-based direct-view displays, but it often happens faster with plasma displays. Given the considerably higher cost of a plasma, your cost per hour of viewing is much higher. Before you buy, check the manufacturer's specifications on *hours to half brightness* (the point at which the display is only half as bright as it was when new). For example, if this specification is 20,000 hours, and you watch the set for 6 hours a day, it will be effectively worn out in about 9 years. If you have kids, keep in mind that 6 hours a day is *not* an excessive estimate for how long the television may be turned on every day.

✔ **Not as high resolution as LCD:** Even though many (and soon, we expect, most) plasma TVs can display high-definition TV, they do so at the 720p resolution. Only a few, very expensive plasmas are capable of 1080p resolutions — though an increasing number will be in the near future.

✔ **Less than perfect color reproduction:** Although plasma displays are capable of producing a breathtaking array of colors, all the sets built to date have had an unfortunate tendency to make red colors look more orange than true red. This has held true on just about every plasma set out there. Only a few factories in the whole world make some key components for plasma screens, so all these sets share certain characteristics, and this is unfortunately one of them. We're sure that this problem will be solved over time, but it is something to keep in mind (particularly if you're a Cincinnati Reds fan!).

✔ **Poor reproduction of black:** Although plasma displays are an equal to CRT sets in terms of absolute brightness, they fall short in the contrast ratio comparison. Like LCDs, plasma displays have a really hard time reproducing black, so black scenes end up being reproduced as shades of gray.

We think that these shortcomings are far from fatal. We love plasma displays, but we realize that they aren't for everyone. In many home theaters, perhaps the biggest factor supporting the plasma display (besides the undeniable wow factor that comes out every time you look at one in action) is their amazing compactness relative to screen size.

There's an acronym in the industry, SAF (spousal acceptance factor), that absolutely applies to the plasma display. (Actually, the term is WAF, but we're being politically correct here.) If your spouse isn't really into the concept of a home theater and hates the idea of a huge TV cluttering up the family or living room, a plasma may be your home theater salvation. You don't even have to tell him or her you wanted one anyway (because of the awesome picture). Grumble a little bit and get some brownie points out of your purchase!

Getting Into Projection TVs

When you go to the movies, the images you see are projected onto that big screen in front of you. If size matters to you (and if you have the room in your home theater — and seats far enough away from the screen), then you too should consider a projector for your home theater's display system. Even if size isn't a huge deal to you, you may decide to go with a front-projection system because they can offer the ultimate in home theater image quality.

Going all-in-one

Typically, front-projection displays are the "high end" of the market. Folks considering one of these in their theater will often spend $4,000 or more for the combination of the projector and screen. As a result, many folks who want to spend $2,000 or so for a big-screen system will choose a rear-projection TV (something we recommend). There's a new category of projection systems on the market that turns this formula on its head — front-projection displays in a very inexpensive form that anyone can afford.

These "all-in-one" front-projection systems are the display equivalent of the "home theater in a box" solutions for audio that we discuss in Chapter 2. Essentially, these include a DLP-powered front projector, a DVD player, and even (in most cases) a pair of speakers. They're no substitute for a full home theater system, but an easy way to get up and running. We think the best use for these devices is as a home theater solution for the kids' playroom, for the vacation home, or anywhere besides your true home theater. They're also great for gamers — plug in an Xbox or PlayStation, shine the projector on the wall, and you're ready for some truly big-screen Halo or Gran Turismo action!

None of these all-in-one systems supports HDTV resolutions (though we expect that newer versions will), but you get a lot for your money (typically just a shade more than $1,000). Check out Radio Shack's Cinego 1000 ($1,300) and Optoma's DV-10 ($1,500 list, less on-line) for some good examples of these systems.

In this section, we talk about the two types of projectors available for home theater: all-in-one rear-projection systems and movie projector–like front-projection systems. We also talk about the different kinds of projector systems found in both front and rear projectors. And, finally, we get into the choices you'll find for separate screens (needed if you buy a front-projection system).

For many home theater enthusiasts, a theater isn't really a theater unless you have a projector. Until the advent of the plasma flat panel (discussed in the previous chapter), projectors were really the only choice for big screens (bigger than the approximately 40-inch limit of CRT direct-view TVs, at least). And while 60-inch plasmas are now on the market, you still need a projector system to get a *really* big picture. (Front-projection screens can be as big as 10 feet or more *across!*)

But projection systems don't need to break the bank either. Rear-projection systems (RPTVs) are perhaps the best value in home theater, at least in terms of bang for the buck. For a few thousand bucks — or even less, as new technologies like DLP (Digital Light Processor) begin to saturate the market — you can get a picture as big as a plasma, in full HDTV glory. You can't hang one of these units on the wall, but visually, the picture is at least as good as (and often better than) plasma, for thousands less. In particular, RPTVs are much better than most plasma displays at reproducing blacks on-screen, which means you get superior reproduction of darker scenes when you're watching movies or television.

Choosing between front and rear projection

The first big decision to make when evaluating projection systems is, for most people, the easiest: front or rear projection. We say this is the easiest decision to make because we find that most people choose a rear-projection system. They are cheaper (generally speaking, though high-end rear projectors can definitely cost more than low-end front-projection systems), and they are easier to set up and integrate into your home theater.

Having said that, let's define the difference between these systems. It's quite simple, really:

- **Front projection:** A front projector is very similar to a movie projector (except it doesn't use film). It includes a projector unit (which is usually mounted on your ceiling but can also be on a lift, on a floor mount, or in the rear wall) and a separate screen. Video sources (such as DVDs, cable, and satellite TV) are routed into the projector, which then turns these signals into light. Then, the light is (ding ding ding, you guessed it) *projected* onto a separate screen that's mounted on a wall at the front of your home theater. Figure 14-3 shows a front-projection system.

- **Rear-projection:** These are the traditional big-screen TVs that have been sold for years and years. If your Uncle Vinnie got a big screen back in 1987 for Superbowl XXI, this is what he has. Now some people, having seen the lousy, washed-out picture on Uncle Vinnie's TV, think that rear projectors trade picture quality for size. Nothing can be further from the truth. A good-quality, well-set-up rear projector can offer an awesome picture. A rear-projection TV (or RPTV) has both parts of the front projector (the projector and the screen) in a single, all-in-one box, and the projector illuminates the *back* of the screen instead of the front. Figure 14-4 shows a rear-projection system.

Figure 14-3:
A front-projection system.

Figure 14-4:
The all-in-one rear-projection system.

RPTVs are great. In fact, we think they may be the best value in home theater big-screen displays. But they do have two limitations: a limited viewing angle and size. Because of the way video is internally reflected toward the screen in these sets, you need to be perpendicular (or near-perpendicular) to the display to see a good picture. Keep that limitation in mind as you consider an RPTV. If your home theater room is set up with widely dispersed seating, an RPTV may not be your best choice. Also, rear-projection TVs can be very deep and overwhelm a room with their size. For some, this is a limitation.

If you have a really big room, and you can keep it dark enough to use a front-projection system, then front projection is the way to get that truly movie theater–sized picture. But the dark room is a major *must* to get the most out of a front-projection system. Don't think you can set up a front projector in your family room (you know, the room with the picture window on one wall and the sliding glass door on the other — oh yeah, and the skylight too!) and get a good picture. You *can,* but only if you spend a lot of time and effort blocking out the light. You *need* a dark room to get the most out of front projection — that's why we recommend rear-projection systems for the average home theater builder who doesn't have a dedicated room and who wants to be able to watch TV in the broad daylight.

It may sound obvious, but don't forget that you'll need to have an unimpeded path between the projector and the screen in a front projection system. Unless you're just a huge fan of MST3k (`www.mst3kinfo.org`) and want to see people's head's silhouetted on the screen, you'll need to be able to keep the air between your projector and screen clear of all objects.

Now, we've already come right out and said that for most people — *most* people, not *all* people — rear-projection systems are probably the best choice. As we mention earlier, the lower cost and easier setup make rear projectors more consumer-friendly. (You don't have to spend nearly as much time getting the projector properly aligned and aimed at the screen with a rear projector — though you do have to spend *some* time doing this.) But with the advent of new, computer-based technologies such as DLP (Digital Light Processor) chips, front projectors have begun to drop in price from the stratospheric ($20,000 to $60,000) to the reasonable (well under $2,000), and the setup of these new systems is easier, too (which we explain in a minute). Rather than take up your valuable reading time with a long-winded description of the relative benefits and shortcomings of these two types of projectors, we've created the handy-dandy Table 14-1 to enlighten, educate, and energize the home theater portion of your brain.

Table 14-1	Comparing Front and Rear Projectors	
Characteristic	*Front Projector*	*Rear Projector*
Screen size	Gigantic	Merely huge
Price	Moderate to astronomical	Moderate to high
Aspect ratio (4:3 or 16:9)	Fixed or flexible (depends on technology)	Fixed
Picture quality	Great to astonishing	Great to astonishing
Setup	Moderate to complicated	Easy to moderate
Installation	Moderate to complicated	Easy

Selecting a projection method

As you move past the rear- versus front-projection decision, you'll find that you really haven't decided anything at all. Four main technologies that are currently on the market do the actual work of converting electrical video source signals into light that can be projected onto the screen. Each of these can be found in either front- or rear-projection units. Keep in mind, however, that new variants of these technologies, as well as entirely new ways of projecting video, are being invented all the time.

Catching on to the cathode ray

We cover the CRT, or cathode ray tube, in the first section of this chapter, so we're not going to get into a long discussion about what they are or how they work here. However, that good, old-fashioned tube is not only the heart of most conventional TVs, but also the centerpiece of the most sophisticated, highest-quality projector systems (which is to say, the most sophisticated, highest-quality displays, period).

CRT projectors, particularly front-projection systems, can provide the highest resolution (including full HDTV support), the most excellent color, and a bright picture with a superb contrast ratio. (If any of these terms seems unfamiliar to you, refer to Chapter 13.) CRT projectors also provide the best reproduction of black tints — significantly better than any of the other projector types available.

Unlike direct-view CRT displays, which use a single picture tube, CRT projectors use three separate tubes — one each for red, green, and blue. The extra tubes make the setup and calibration more complex because the light projection from these three CRTs must be *converged* (aligned so that they each hit the screen at the same place). If you've seen bad projection TV before, with inaccurate color reproduction and colored "halos" around objects, you've probably seen a system that has not been properly converged. It's not pretty. Convergence on projection systems tends to drift over time, so you need to think about resetting the convergence a couple of times a year. Luckily, many RPTVs now include an automatic convergence system that simplifies this process. In Chapter 19, we discuss how you can do your own calibration or hire a professional to calibrate your projection system.

Perhaps the biggest factor to consider when comparing CRT projectors is tube size. In the RPTV realm, this isn't a huge deal. Almost all RPTVs have the same size (7-inch) tubes, but front projectors have tubes in the 7-, 8-, and 9-inch ranges. Bigger tubes bring with them sharper, more detailed pictures, but at a considerably higher price. In fact, the price differential between a 7- or 8-inch projector and a 9-inch model can be striking. You can get a decent 7-inch front projector for under $10,000 (still a lot), but 9-inch CRT projectors usually start off in the $30,000 range.

Keep in mind three things about any CRT projector system (front or RPTV):

✔ **Brightness can be an issue:** This isn't a major problem for RPTVs, where the tube is relatively close to the screen, but in a front projector environment, the CRT is the least bright of all the alternatives. Imagine trying to light up a screen across the room with your old direct-view TV (not really a fair comparison, but the technology is very similar), and you'll understand that a CRT doesn't throw off a ton of light. The other systems we discuss use a separate (high-powered) light source, which gives them greater brightness. So a CRT front projector works best in a room with very little ambient light; in fact, near total darkness works best. (Total darkness gives you the best picture with any front-projection system.)

✔ **Tubes wear out:** Just as direct-view CRTs lose brightness over time, so do CRT projectors. In fact, because CRT projectors need to be set up to project more light than a direct-view TV (especially front projectors), CRT tubes in a projector tend to wear out even faster. Check the manufacturer's specifications for how quickly its tubes lose brightness and plan on budgeting some home theater money for new tubes based on those specifications. This isn't a cheap fix. You can spend thousands of dollars on new tubes every time you need to replace them, so read the fine print.

✔ **Tubes can get burn-in:** *Burn-in* occurs when static content, such as video games, permanently alters the phosphors on your CRT, so that you always see, for example, a ghost image of Halo's weapons status on your screen. If you (or your kids) play a ton of video games, we suggest you look at one of the other projector technologies we're about to discuss. Burn-in can also be a problem when the CRTs have a fixed aspect ratio. For example, if you have 16:9 (widescreen) tubes and watch a ton of 4:3 (traditional square screen) content, you can end up with uneven brightness on the tubes. This occurs because the center of the tube is constantly in use, but the edges are used only occasionally. (We discuss burn-in earlier in this chapter.)

We've given you a quick overview of CRT projectors. CRT RPTVs are the kind of product you can buy, install, and set up on your own, if you want to. We think that a CRT front projector is something you *need* professional help with. That includes help choosing the right model and an associated screen and help installing, configuring, and maintaining the projector. It's a huge investment, and you should find a dealer you're comfortable with who can help you down this path.

The success of the next three projection technologies we discuss (LCD, DLP, and LCoS) have pretty much taken the wind out of the CRT projection TV market. You can still buy CRT-based projectors, but they are increasingly rare. Microdisplay projectors using these newer technologies just have too many advantages for the average home theater builder, so sales of the CRT-based models have plummeted.

Projecting with LCDs

LCD technologies have been used for years and years for relatively low-quality projectors — the kind you might have in the conference room at work for projecting those ubiquitous PowerPoint slides on the white board during mind-numbingly boring meetings.

Well, the LCD has come of age in the era of home theater, and now you can buy front-projection systems based on the LCD that provide a high-quality (often HDTV) picture at a price that is typically lower than that of CRT front-projection systems. (Note that LCD RPTVs aren't much cheaper than CRT RPTVs and may even cost more, simply because the small tubes used in RPTVs are dirt cheap.)

LCD projectors typically use three small LCD panels (a couple of inches across at most) — one each for red, green, and blue picture information. Behind these panel is a strong lamp that provides the light. LCDs (and the DLP and LCoS projectors we discuss next) are *fixed-pixel* displays, meaning that they display video at a certain resolution. For example, Sony's most recent LCD RPTV displays at 1,366 pixels horizontally and 768 pixels vertically (this exceeds the 720 vertical pixels required for 720i, so the set is HDTV-ready). An internal device called an *image scaler* converts the incoming signal (such as 480p from progressive scan DVDs or 1080i from an HDTV broadcast) to the 1366 x 768 resolution for display. LCD projectors are inherently progressive, so even standard NTSC broadcasts are converted to a progressive-scan mode for display.

The quality of the image scaler — how well it converts other signals to the fixed-pixel resolution *native* to the LCD — is a key factor in a projector's picture quality. In Chapter 21, we talk about external image scalers (and related devices such as line doublers and quadruplers) that can improve the picture quality of a projection system — and not just for fixed-pixel displays, but also for CRT projection systems as well.

Because you never know who'll come up with a better system the month after this book is printed, we generally avoid dropping brand name recommendations. However, we find that scalers from one company, Faroudja (now owned by Genesis Microchip — www.gnss.com), are always excellent. You can find many different brands of projectors (and HDTVs in general) that use Faroudja chips (notably the *DCDI* chip) to scale, or *upconvert,* images.

LCD projector systems have a couple of big advantages, when compared with CRT projectors:

✔ **Lower-cost front projectors:** Although CRT front projectors can cost an arm and three legs, you can buy a quality LCD front projector for less than $2,000.

✔ **More-compact RPTVs:** Because the LCD panels and the lamp are small, LCD RPTVs can be much thinner than CRT RPTVs. Although many CRT systems can be 3 or more feet deep, LCD systems can be less than 15 inches deep. That helps a lot both in small rooms and with the SAF (spousal acceptance factor).

✔ **Brighter than CRT:** The separate lamp used in CRT projectors puts out a ton of light. (You wouldn't want to have someone shine one in your eyes close up!) The result is a brighter picture that can tolerate more ambient light in your home theater.

For the best brightness and color reproduction, look for LCD projectors (typically only RPTVs) that use LED backlights instead of traditional bulbs.

✔ **Don't need to be converged:** Despite the fact that an LCD projector contains three LCD panels, it has only one light source. So you don't need to converge the picture like you do with a CRT projector. This makes the setup much easier for mere mortals.

✔ **Burn-in isn't a big issue:** Plug in that Xbox or PlayStation and play all the games you want. Because LCD systems don't use phosphors, they can't get permanent burn-in like CRTs (or flat-panel plasma systems) can.

Of course, there's got to be a downside, right? LCD projectors don't do a couple of things well:

✔ **Relatively poor black performance:** LCD projectors, like LCD direct-view sets, can't display true black tints well. Dark scenes end up being gray instead. So when the Orcs are sneaking up on Frodo from the mouth of that dark cave, you can't see them all that well.

✔ **Limited resolution:** Today's LCD panels can reach HDTV resolutions (at least 720p resolutions), but most can't display the full resolution of 1080i content. To do so, the LCD panels need a resolution of 1920 x 1080, and none we know of are there yet.

✔ **The lamp will wear out:** Nothing lasts forever, and the high-output lamps on LCD projectors tend to wear out after a few thousand hours of use. That lifespan is a lot less than the one for tubes on a CRT, but LCD projector lamps cost a lot less to replace (hundreds instead of thousands of dollars).

✔ **The "stuck pixel" problem:** If you own a laptop computer (or a desktop computer with an LCD display), you may be familiar with the issue of *stuck pixels.* These are usually minor manufacturing defects that cause individual pixels to not light up when the display tells them to. Because the relative size of pixels in a projection system is large, you may notice a dead pixel on your screen (and be very annoyed by it). Many manufacturers think that having a few stuck pixels is just part of doing business, and they will not replace your LCD panels except in extreme cases. As a result, it is a good idea to find out the manufacturer's "dead pixel policy" before you buy.

✔ **The "screen door":** When LCD images are projected onto big screens (like the ones you find in a front-projector system), you can begin to see the pixel structure of the LCD itself. By this we mean the physical structure of the LCD that separates the individual pixels. Because of the way LCDs are constructed, you can look closely at a large projected image and see dots of lighter and darker areas — like you're looking at the world through a metal screen door. We should emphasize that this isn't a huge issue. This "screen door" effect is sort of like the scan lines on a CRT system in that you really notice it only if you're too close to a big image.

For more information on LCD projection displays, a listing of current models, and more good old-fashioned marketing talk than you can shake a stick at, check out 3LCD.com, a consortium of manufacturers of LCD projection systems.

Deciding on a DLP

Texas Instruments has developed (over the course of many years) a completely new way of projecting video called the DLP (short for *Digital Light Processor*). DLP has created a whole new category of inexpensive projector systems and has also led to a digital revolution in those old-fashioned movie theaters you used to go to before you got a home theater. If you were lucky enough to see *Star Wars: Episode III — Revenge of the Sith* in a digital theater, you have already seen DLP (a super-high-end, expensive version) in action.

The DLP is an entirely digital process that utilizes a semiconductor generically called the *DMD* (*digital micromirror device*). The DMD contains over a million incredibly tiny, hinged mirrors. Each of these mirrors represents a single pixel on your video image. The DLP chip's electronic logic controls the hinges on the mirrors, turning them so that they either reflect light (onto your screen) or block it (creating a dark spot on the screen). When the DLP's "brains" turn these mirrors on and off, the mirrors create different levels of light between black and white that result in a *grayscale* version of your image. A device called a *color wheel* filters light from a lamp (like the lamps found in LCD projectors), reflects this off the mirrors on the DLP chip, and provides the color in your image. This is really a Mach III fly-by of the details of DLP; if you want to know the nitty gritty, check out Texas Instruments' site at www.dlp.com.

The DLP system we just described, with the color wheel, is called a *single-chip* DLP solution, and is by far the most common in consumer DLP projectors. Movie theater projectors (and a few ultra-expensive home theater models) dispense with the color wheel, and use three DLP chips (one for red, one for green, and one for blue). These three-chip projectors can produce more gradations of color than a single-chip system but cost a heck of a lot more.

Weebles wobble

Texas Instruments got together with computer/technology behemoth Hewlett Packard and incorporated one of HP's technologies into some of its DLP chips. Called *wobbulation,* this technology allows each of the individual mirrors within a DLP chip to address (or beam its reflected light at) two different pixels. What this does is allow a chip with a resolution of 960 x 1080 to effectively have a resolution of 1920 x 1080 (the full resolution of 1080i/p high definition). TI calls this technology *smooth picture.*

Many 1080p-capable DLP TVs use this technology to achieve their full resolution. Nothing wrong with that, but testing has found that some displays using wobbulation don't quite achieve the full resolution in the real world. The latest DLP displays (announced as we write, but not yet on the market) will offer true 1080p resolution without this wobbulation technique — which promises to provide a better picture.

When looking at DLP projectors, the most important factor to consider is the capabilities of the DLP chip, which is the heart of the system. Like LCDs, DLPs are fixed-pixel displays, and Texas Instruments has a couple of chips on the market with different aspect ratios and different resolutions. Early DLP chips were designed for 4:3 video reproduction (with a lower-resolution 16:9 mode), but current models are designed for 16:9 aspect ratios.

Most DLP chips can reproduce HDTV resolutions. However, some less expensive versions cannot. All DLP chips that we know of can reproduce 16:9 widescreen progressive scan video (which is 848 x 480 pixels), but the fancier versions can reproduce 720p and even 1080p HDTV signals. The latest and greatest DLP chip (given the nature of the computer industry, this will change relatively soon) is called the xHD4, which offers a 16:9 aspect ratio and a 1920 x 1080 pixel resolution.

 There's a lot of discussion in various Internet forums about all of the different DLP chips that TI makes and sells to display manufacturers. If you dig deep enough, you can usually find some info about a specific chip and a specific TV, but in fact this information is usually pretty well hidden. TI (and the display manufacturers) tend not to speak about individual chips (like xHD3 or xHD4), but rather about the resolution of the chips (720p or 1080p).

DLP projectors share many of the advantages of LCD models: low price, compact size (with particularly thin RPTVs possible), and immunity from image burn-in. They also share what many find to be the biggest of the same drawbacks: less-than-perfect reproduction of blacks (but better than most LCD projectors). But DLPs don't have the screen door issue we mention earlier and, additionally, have one big advantage over the other types of projectors we've discussed so far: They are brighter (and therefore better in rooms that aren't too dark). In a DLP chip, light from the lamp is reflected off the mirrors, but in an LCD, light is transmitted through the liquid crystals, which causes a decrease in brightness.

One issue that some folks have with DLP projectors is something called the *rainbow effect.* During a highly contrasted scene (such as white on a black background), some folks can see a shimmery colored image (like a rainbow, naturally!) in their peripheral vision. Not everyone can see this, but some small percentage of the population sees it and is annoyed (to the point of headaches or even dizziness!). You can minimize the rainbow effect by choosing a three-chip DLP set with individual DLP chips for red, green, and blue — many folks believe that the color wheel in single-chip projectors causes the effect.

The newest trend in DLP is to use a single chip, but to replace the color wheel and single light source with three LED light sources (red, blue, and green). This helps get rid of the rainbow effect and has the additional benefit of improving the color reproduction of the DLP projector. LEDs are really cool things — we think you'll start seeing them more and more in home theater displays (as well as in everyday objects like flashlights, car headlights, and other lighting systems). They have the advantage, when compared with incandescent lighting, of truer colors, lower energy consumption, and greatly increased life spans.

We love the future of DLP projectors (both front and rear). They have great pictures, are relatively inexpensive, and are a snap to set up. As the technology matures, we think this may end up being the predominant projection system of the future — already over 75 manufacturers use the technology in their projector systems. Given the nature of the microprocessor business, we think that DLP chips will get much cheaper and much more capable faster than you can bat an eye. You can already buy a good-quality HDTV-ready front-projection DLP system for under $3,000. And DLP RPTVs typically offer the best "bang for the buck," providing the best mixture of price and picture quality — better picture quality than most LCD RPTVs for the same price, and almost as good as the LCoS displays we discuss in the next section, for less.

Looking at LCoS

Another "projector-on-a-chip" system that has hit the market in recent years is the LCoS (Liquid Crystal on Silicon) system. A couple of different manufacturers are making LCoS systems, but the most prominent to date have been JVC, with a system called D-ILA (Digital Direct Drive Image Light Amplifier) — we're puzzled by the acronym, but we guess DDDILA is too hard to remember — and Sony, with its SXRD (Silicon Crystal X-tal — for acronym purposes — Reflective Display) projection TVs.

LCoS systems are basically a new variant of LCDs. LCoS systems still use liquid crystals, but instead of transmitting light through the liquid crystal (like an LCD does), LCoS reflects the light like a DLP, resulting in a significantly brighter image.

There aren't a lot of LCoS projectors on the market yet, but those that are available — that is to say, JVC's D-ILA models, Sony's SXRD models, and a few others — have perhaps the finest picture quality of any projection displays available.

LCoS systems offer true 1080p resolution (with no tricks like the *wobbulation* we discuss in the "Weebles wobble" sidebar) and an incredibly smooth, film-like image. LCoS beats out LCD projection systems in the brightness game, while avoiding the rainbow effects found in DLPs.

LCoS is also known for exceptional black reproduction, rivaling, if not quite matching, the blacks displayed by the super-expensive CRT projection systems that used to be the high end of the market.

What's the catch? Well, LCoS projectors are more expensive than LCD or DLP projectors — there simply isn't the kind of volume production of the LCoS microdisplay components to bring the prices down to those levels yet. You can expect to pay about 30 percent more for a 1080p LCoS display than you would for an identically sized DLP display.

The good news here is that the prices are coming down rapidly. For example, Sony's first generation of SXRD RPTVs cost about twice what a similarly sized DLP projector would have cost. The models currently shipping as we write (less than a year into the technology's life span) are only about $1,000 more than a similarly sized DLP and offer a better picture. So keep your eye on LCoS, as it may very well give DLP a run for its (and your) money!

Keeping other features in mind

Regardless of technology, keep in mind a few other things when evaluating projection systems:

- **Fixed versus variable focal length (front projectors only):** Some front-projection systems (including many fancy CRT models) have what's known as a *fixed focal length.* This means that, for a given screen size, the projector must be placed a fixed and predetermined distance away. This can limit your placement in the room. If a heating duct on the ceiling is right where the projector needs to be, that's too bad. Projectors with variable focal length can be placed in different spots to fit your room's layout and then adjusted to focus on the screen properly.

- **Light output (front-projection only):** We've already discussed the various projector types with regards to their relative brightness. But within these categories, projectors vary from model to model in their overall brightness. This is measured in *ANSI lumens* and is a good measure of how well a system will work in a bright room. Brighter, high-end projectors are often rated at 1,000 or more lumens, whereas cheaper ones are often below 500. We don't recommend that you use any projector in a brightly lit room, but if you simply can't make the room dark, go for a brighter unit.

Just because you can crank your amp up to 11, doesn't mean that you should. (Please excuse the shameless, pop culture, *Spinal Tap* reference.) As we explain in the first section of this chapter, you shouldn't leave the brightness on your direct-view CRT system cranked up all the way, and the same rule applies to a projection system. In Chapter 19, we talk about how to set up your brightness settings (and a bunch of other settings) on your display.

- **Aspect ratio:** In the RPTV world, systems have a fixed aspect ratio. They're either 4:3 (standard squarish TV) or 16:9 (widescreen). We recommend you get the widescreen version unless *all* you watch is *Leave It to Beaver* reruns. Some front projectors also have a fixed native aspect ratio, but many systems can be adjusted to work at either aspect ratio. If you don't have a choice, go with the widescreen, and if you pick a system with an adjustable aspect ratio, enjoy it!

- **Projector noise:** Many front-projection TVs employ a cooling fan — particularly LCD and DLP systems, which need bright (and hot!) lamps to create the picture. DLP systems may also make an audible noise when the color wheel spins. Keep in mind the fact that, in a small room, you may hear these noises, which can be annoying. Try to audition your projector in your dealer's showroom and pay attention to the noise it makes. You have to live with it after you buy it!

- **Everything we discuss in Chapter 13:** This is our convenient catch-all category. In Chapter 13, we list a ton of things to consider when evaluating a display system, such as the number of inputs, the adjustability of the system, and so on. We really don't feel like repeating ourselves, and we don't like typing that much (or even cutting and pasting!) either. So go read Chapter 13 because it all applies here, too.

Selecting your silver screen

As they say in the ginsu knife ads, "But wait, there's more!" We've talked about the projectors themselves, but in the case of front-projection systems, we've only talked about half the equation. You gotta shine that nice, high-def image onto something, and we definitely don't recommend an old bed sheet or the wall. You need a real screen — just like a movie theater.

Screens come in a couple different forms:

- ✔ **Portable screens that sit on a tripod:** You can fold these up and put them away when you're done (but who's ever done with a home theater?). These are a bit less than optimal (if you take them down, you need to get them back in *exactly* the same spot or refocus the projector — if it can even be focused!). We don't recommend these at all.

- ✔ **Retractable screens:** These can be manually or electrically powered. Although nothing is cooler than pressing a button on the remote and having the screen come down, this setup will cost you more than the manual version. You also need to make sure these systems are properly installed so that they are flat (otherwise the image can be distorted), and periodically check to make sure they haven't become misaligned with use.

- ✔ **Fixed wall- and ceiling-mounted screens:** If you have a dedicated home theater and you'll never want to hide the screen, these are probably the best way to go.

Even more important than the form are the technical characteristics of the screen. The big four are the following:

- ✔ **Gain:** Gain is a measure of how reflective the screen is — how much of the projector's light gets bounced back to your eyeballs. There's a standard industry reference for gain, and systems that have exactly as much gain as that reference are rated at a gain of 1. More-reflective (high-gain) screens are rated greater than 1 (say 1.2), while less-reflective (low-gain) screens are rated below 1 (many are rated at 0.8). Generally speaking, match CRT projectors with high-gain screens (between 1 and 1.3, though you can go higher if needed). Brighter, fixed-pixel systems like LCD or DLP can use a low-gain screen (0.8 or lower).

- ✔ **Viewing angle:** Most display systems have a limited angle (from perpendicular) in which they look best. Sit outside that angle, and the picture becomes very dim. For front-projector screens, this viewing angle is inversely proportional to gain. In other words, the higher the gain, the smaller the angle in which viewers will get a good picture. For this reason, you are best off choosing the lowest gain screen that works with your projector in your room. This is why low-gain screens are recommended for fixed-pixel projectors; LCD, DLP, and LCoS projectors have light to spare, so why not trade some of it for a wider viewing angle? Viewing angles are usually listed in a number of degrees (like 90). Your viewing angle is half this amount (45, in this case) on either side of perpendicular.

- ✔ **Hotspotting:** One reason you shouldn't use a screen with too high a gain for your projector is the *hotspotting* phenomenon. When this occurs, one part of the screen is brighter than the other parts. Typically, the center of the screen gets too bright, relative to the edges, which makes the picture on the edges appear washed out.

- ✔ **Aspect ratio:** Screens are available in either the 16:9 widescreen or 4:3 aspect ratios. You should, of course, choose the same aspect ratio as that of your projector. You can buy (or make your own, if you're crafty) *masks* to cover the unlit portions of the screen when you're watching material of a different aspect ratio, so you can cover the sides of the screen with a mask when you're watching a 4:3 TV show (more *Leave It to Beaver?)* on your 16:9 screen.

Choosing a screen is not something for the faint of heart. Find out what screens your projector manufacturer recommends, ask your dealer what he or she recommends, and if at all possible, look at your projector (or the identical model) on the screen before you buy.

There are three major manufacturers of screens for front-projection displays: Da-Lite (www.da-lite.com), Draper (www.draperinc.com), and Stewart Filmscreen (www.stewartfilmscreen.com).

Chapter 15

Remote Controlling Your Home Theater

*R*emote controls have come a long way since the first clunky universal remote controls let you manipulate multiple devices from one gadget. Today, you have all sorts of options: tiny, large, color, touch-sensitive, voice-controlled, time-controlled, and on and on. You can spend $19 on a great remote or $5,000 on a "gold plated" touch screen, whole-home remote control that not only controls all of the devices in your home theater, but that can also run *all* of the electronics in your home. Decisions, decisions.

Sifting through Remote Control Options

The remote control is nothing more than a means to tell your system what to do. The term *remote* just means you don't control your home theater equipment manually (by getting up and pushing buttons). Just to show that we all can be as high-tech as the next guy, let's treat the remote control as an *interface,* and say that you can interface with your system in multiple ways.

Types of remotes

Hundreds upon hundreds of remotes are out there. Generically, they fall into the following categories, which are presented in increasing order of functionality and desirability:

- ✔ **Standard/dedicated remotes:** These are the device-specific remotes that come with your system. If you stopped here, you might have ten or so remotes on your coffee table!

- ✔ **Brand-based remotes that come with a component:** Brand-based remotes work with all sorts of devices from the same manufacturer. For instance, the RCA remote you get with an RCA DSS receiver usually has buttons for your RCA TV and your RCA VCR. There are buttons for each of the devices supported.

- ✔ **Third-party universal remote controls:** Many leading electronics brands sell so-called *universal remote controls.* These remotes supposedly work with any electronics device by way of onboard code databases. These remotes generally come with manuals that walk you through setting up your remote for your specific components. This environment is ever-changing, however, and we've found that you get what you pay for. We've never been happy with cheap universal remotes (like the $20 "do everything" universal remotes you see at the mega-sized electronics stores). Some capability is always missing. We prefer the slightly more expensive *learning remotes.*

  Most A/V receivers and TVs and many DVD players come with a universal remote, but many don't have a lot of functionality on other brands of equipment — just the basics.

- ✔ **Learning remotes:** Learning remotes can learn codes from your existing remote controls. You simply point your remotes at each other, go through a listing of commands, and the remote codes are transferred from one to the other. These remotes have a higher success rate than universal remotes because you are essentially using the same codes as your present remote — not codes that a database says *should* work. Some learning remotes have an onboard, preprogrammed database against which they try to match the codes being learned; others are completely learning-based. The downside of a completely learning-based remote is that, if you lose your original remote, it's almost impossible to train this one.

- ✔ **Programmable remotes:** Programmable remotes allow you to create *macros,* which are sequential code combinations that do a lot of things at once. So say you want to watch a movie on a DVD. You could program a macro to turn on your TV, receiver, and DVD player; set the receiver to the appropriate source and output modes; and start the DVD in the tray — all from one button. Now, if it could only pop the popcorn, too. . . .

✔ **Computer-based remotes:** Computer-based remotes take advantage of the growing number of computing devices around the home to provide remote control capabilities. This category includes PDAs, Web tablets, portable touch screens, and PCs. Home control software that can drive your lighting, heating, and other environmental controls in addition to your home theater needs is also in this group.

✔ **Proprietary systems:** A number of closed-system control devices enable you to integrate control of all your home theater devices on a single control system. Companies such as Niles Audio (www.nilesaudio.com) and Crestron (www.crestron.com) are renowned for their control systems.

Remote control features

As simple as a remote control seems to be, the world of remotes is insanely complex. This section discusses some ways in which remotes have gotten more complex lately.

Radio frequency (RF) versus infrared (IR)

It used to be that all remotes were infrared-based. Now, many are touting RF connectivity, which is in many ways better than IR. First, RF signals tend to travel farther than IR. Second, you don't need to point the remote at the TV set; RF can go in all directions, even through walls and cabinet doors. The biggest downside of RF remotes is that you can't easily integrate them into one remote (such as a learning remote) — at least not yet. Still, we prefer RF to IR if we can get it.

The only real downside of RF remotes is that there is the possibility that you could find yourself unintentionally controlling devices in other rooms. In the vast majority of cases, you won't run into this issue, as those other devices won't be using the same remote codes as the ones in your home theater room.

Most home theater equipment uses an IR remote control system, so if you use an RF system, you need some equipment to convert the RF signals to IR to control these IR-only devices. We talk about how to do this in Chapter 18.

Touch screen displays

Color and grayscale displays are replacing hard buttons on remotes, enabling them to be far more programmable and customizable for your system. It's not unusual that your remote would connect to your PC today in order to customize the "soft buttons" on your remote's screen. We are finding that standalone touch screens are even replacing remotes.

New control options

A lot of new stuff is coming down the pike, but we think two-way operation and voice control are innovations that will grow in popularity. With two-way operation, higher-end remotes can interact with the controlled unit to determine its *state*. So, for instance, if a unit is already on, your programmed macro won't turn it off at the start of its session. And with two-way operation, you can check your actions to make sure they were carried out, too.

Nice, but not earth-shaking enough in its newness for you? Then try voice control, which lets you bark out orders to your remote control (and even to other microphones in your home theater). Want the volume turned up? No problem: "Higher volume please." (Have we reached a new threshold when a couch potato doesn't even have to lift a thumb?) Voice control functionality is making its way into a lot of devices, including PDAs and standalone Web tablets, making voice control a key future item in your home theater.

Another interesting innovation is the docking cradle. A cradle might enable your remote to charge up, to access the Internet for revised programming schedules, or to update its internal code databases. (We think docking cradles are really a covert plot to make sure you always know where your remote is located.)

IR (infrared) emitters/blasters

When one IR device wants to control another device, it often sends signals to the other device's IR port through an *IR blaster* — a small device that sits some distance from (or in the instance of very small versions called *emitters,* is taped to) the IR port. Many PC applications interface with your home theater system through an IR blaster (to do things such as change the channel on your satellite receiver to start recording a program). You might find you have several IR blasters for different devices in your system. No one feels this is the best long-term approach because newer devices allow for direct data interface via Ethernet, low-speed data connections, or even RF. But for now, IR blasters are the only option for many older systems.

Within specific brands of A/V gear, you will find IR ports for interconnecting and sharing IR data directly into the motherboard — bypassing the IR port. This is one of the benefits of using a single manufacturer for your gear. Examples of this include systems like Sony's S-Link, which uses a special cable to connect Sony devices to each other.

For the rest of this chapter, we focus on some of the highlights of this section — the things that we think you'll likely run into or want to have.

Going Universal

Universal remotes are constantly changing and vary in price from about $20 on up. They can have backlit buttons, touch screens, color screens, voice commands, and so on. A lot of it depends on what you really want out of a remote control. The more you spend on your entertainment system, the more you'll probably spend on your remote control.

Here are examples of some of the neater remotes you can get:

- **X10 Universal 5-in-1 Remote** ($49, www.x10.com): This IR-based remote not only controls your home theater system devices, but any X10-driven devices as well (using RF for the X-10 stuff only). Want to turn down all the lights prior to your "show"? No problem — connect them to X10 outlets and control them remotely with one button.

If you're not familiar with X10 (the technology, as opposed to the company with the same name), it is a *powerline* control and automation technology, meaning it uses your electrical outlets. Essentially, X10 lets you send commands to devices in your home (like light switches) that have X10 communications capabilities built-in or added on via a small device called an *X10 module.* X10 lets you turn things on and off and also lets you dim lights, adjust fan speeds, and more!

- **ATI Remote Wonder Plus** ($39, www.ati.com): The ATI Remote Wonder was originally packaged only with ATI's great All-in-Wonder PC cards. (See Chapter 8 for more All-in-Wonder info.) Now, you can use this remote for any PC application. It is RF-based and comes with a small RF receiver that plugs into any Windows-compatible PC's USB port and even works with OS X Macintosh computers. A great low-cost way to control your PC, Remote Wonder Plus even offers precise "mouse control," so you aren't limited to just skipping between songs, but you can use it just like a wireless mouse to use your PC's cursor.

- **Universal URC-300** ($169, www.universalremote.com): Universal's URC-300 is one of the least expensive remotes with a touch screen controller. This touch screen allows you to create customized commands on the screen, so you can create macro commands with names that you understand (like "Play a DVD") and access them by simply pressing that part of the LCD screen. This is a whole heck of a lot easier than trying to hit all of the component commands individually, or even trying to remember *which* macro you want to use. (Many programmable remotes make you press something like Macro + 1 to access a command — which is fine, as long as you remember which macro number you're looking for — but it's significantly more user friendly to be able to just press a touch screen with the command you want labeled in plain English.)

Remotes for the rest of the family

Got kids? Try the weemote from Fobis ($24.95 from www.weemote.com). This is a remote designed just for 3- to 8-year-olds, so you can limit the channels they watch and make them responsible for their own remotes (in other words, keep their paws off yours). A typical setup with a cable-ready TV takes about five minutes. Fobis also has a cheaper weemote (the weemote dV, $19.95) that's especially made for letting kids navigate interactive components of DVDs or digital TV services. There's even a "Senior" weemote (the weemote SR, $24.95) that's designed for older folks who might not have great eyesight or manual dexterity and therefore can't handle the 97 or so buttons on the typical universal or learning remote.

✔ **Philips Pronto line of remotes** ($199 to over $1,000, www.pronto.philips.com): Philips has a solid line of remote controls that have defined the leading edge of home theater remotes in a lot of ways. The $199 (list price) fully programmable and learning Pronto NEO is the entry level to the Pronto range, but it has a lot of features, including a big (but not color) touch screen, 4MB of memory, and the ability to program your remote using your PC. Plus, with IR/RF capability, the unit allows the user to control infrared devices in cabinets or in other rooms with the simple addition of a Philips RF receiver, available as an option for $149.

Of course, many more remotes are on the market. A great site to check out remote control options is Remote Central (www.remotecentral.com). They have great reviews and track the newest remotes on the market.

You can go universal with your remote in another sense: You can control your home theater from anywhere in the home! We talk more about these capabilities in Chapter 18.

Programming on Your Remote

We mention earlier that remotes are becoming learning-friendly and programmable. Nothing exemplifies this more than the $249 Logitech Harmony 880 Remote Control (www.logitech.com). The 880 helps you do more than control different devices; it helps you control different actions. Harmony's remote has an LCD screen and links to your PC or Mac via a USB connection to program the remote to tie together multiple actions at once, in order.

Say you want to listen to a CD on your AudioReQuest CD server. You have to turn on the TV, set it to video mode, turn on receiver one, set it to CD, turn on receiver two, set it to CD, scroll down to your desired playlist, and press Play. Harmony reduces this to a simple one-click task. It makes schedules and listings available on your remote's screen, and when you click it, all the requisite actions on your CD player, receivers, TV set, and so on are done in one quick series of signals from the remote to the devices. So Harmony is designed to help you perform activities such as watch TV, play a CD, play a DVD, and so on. That's what we call click and play!

The really cool feature is Logitech's on-line configuration tools. Simply plug the 880 into your Mac or PC with the supplied USB cable and go to Logitech's Harmony Web site. As you answer a series of questions on-screen about which equipment you are trying to control and how it's all hooked together, the "logic" of your remote's macros is automatically built for you. So you don't have to laboriously (okay, it's not labor, but it *is* a real time waster), manually, program a macro to (to pull an example out of our hats) "select receiver, select menu, down arrow twice, select enter, up arrow once, select enter again," or whatever arcane combination of keystrokes will make your equipment do what you want it to do. The Logitech database already "knows" all of this and simply downloads the right instructions to your remote over the Internet. So you just press the "DVD" command, and your remote will tell your DVD player, your receiver, your TV, your . . . well, whatever . . . what to do. We like it when technology works for us, rather than the other way around.

Harmony is also a learning remote, and the latest version has added number buttons, a docking and recharging station, and more. Très cool. For the price and simplicity, every home theater owner should check out these Harmony remotes.

For about $150 more, Logitech offers the Harmony 890, which adds RF remote capabilities to control devices that are out of range of your IR signal.

Getting super fancy

A number of manufacturers build touchpad controllers that are not just simple remote controls but rather whole-home control systems, which let you tap into lighting, HVAC (heating, ventilation, and air conditioning), drapery controls, alarm systems, automation systems, and more.

An example here is Crestron (www.crestron.com), a company that develops incredibly cool (and incredibly expensive) home automation, control, and entertainment systems. This is the stuff of *MTV Cribs* that can be found in those $20 million dream homes that we all wish to buy when we win the lottery. Crestron rules the upper end of touch screen options, as discussed in detail in Chapter 21. Crestron's color touchpad systems are to die for, or at least second mortgage for.

Part IV
Putting It All Together

"Wait a minute... This is a movie, not a game?! I thought I was the one making Keanu Reeves jump kick in slow motion."

In this part . . .

So you know what stuff you need to buy to get into home theater, and you may have even bought it. Well, if you're like us, buying stuff is a reflexive act. We could do it in our sleep. The hard part is figuring out how to hook it all up. Fear not — Part IV to the rescue.

First, we talk about the cables and connectors you can use to connect the components of your home theater. This is really an important section to read because in many cases, you can use more than one kind of cable, and there's definitely a hierarchy. Some of these cables are simply much better than others in terms of creating a home theater that looks and sounds like it should.

Next, we talk you through the "insert tab A into slot A" aspect of connecting a home theater. Now, remember that this advice is generic. Home theater equipment vendors are always coming up with their own little "modifications," making it hard for us to give concrete advice that applies in every single situation. But we get you 99 percent of the way there.

We also talk about how to do some nontraditional things with your home theater. First, we discuss how to connect your home theater components into a whole-home network that lets you view, listen to, and control expensive home theater gear anywhere in your home. We also give you some details about how to hook up the home theater PCs we talk about in Part II, so that you can bring the power of the PC (and the Internet) to your home theater!

Chapter 16

Home Theater Cable Basics

. . . .

In This Chapter

▶ Making short run connections

▶ Connecting speakers

▶ Choosing a digital connection

▶ Connecting the rest of the house

▶ Looking at cabling odds and ends

. . . .

*O*ne of the most puzzling, infuriating, blood-pressure-raising tasks in assembling a home theater is finding the right kind, size, shape, and length of cables. Someday in the not-so-distant future, if the copyright lawyers don't get in the way, there may be a single type of digital cable that can connect everything together — this is the holy grail of the consumer electronics industry. All that's needed is some widespread agreement among *all* parties to make this happen.

There's hope here — a cable system called *HDMI,* capable of carrying both audio and video, is becoming very popular. (Those in the know know that HDMI stands for High-Definition Multimedia Interface.) It won't solve the problem for your older gear, but it's becoming almost standard on new equipment. We discuss HDMI in the section titled "Employing digital video connections."

We may soon see an even better solution to the cabling problem: no cabling at all. The day is coming when inexpensive yet high-performance wireless systems will let you connect your components together without worrying about which plug goes where — or which throw rug to buy to hide that tangle of speaker wire.

We can dream of the day when complex cabling is no longer necessary, but it has not yet arrived. In this chapter, we discuss the different kinds of cables required to hook up the common components in a home theater as well as those needed to share your theater with the rest of the house. In many cases, there's more than one way to hook one component to another; we tell you which cable is best.

Working with Short Run Cables

Most of the connections you make in a home theater are *short runs* — that is, connections between components that are sitting just a few feet from each other (or are at least in the same room). The cables you use for these connections are typically called *interconnects*. Later in this chapter, we talk about the long run cables that make up the infrastructure of a whole-home audio and video network.

Choosing quality cables

We should take a moment here to talk about cable quality — right up front, in the beginning of the chapter. You can get audio cable (or most any kind of cable) for free in the box when you buy new equipment. Or you can pay literally $1,000 a foot for the double-secret-mojo, cold-fusion-reactor-type cables. In case you think we're kidding, we're not. (Well, we are about the cold-fusion part.) Some people pay thousands of dollars for each cable in their system. Our take on the matter is this: Don't use the free *el cheapo* cables that came in the box — because you *do* get what you pay for — but don't pay $1,000+ per cable either unless you are both rich and absolutely convinced that you can hear an improvement in your sound or see an improvement in your video. There's a happy medium. Bottom line: Yes, there is a difference in cables, but no, you don't have to pay a ton for good cables.

Look for cables that use oxygen-free copper (OFC) conductors and have gold-plated surfaces on the jacks. Oxygen-free copper is a purer form of copper, and the gold-plated surfaces resist corrosion. Use the shortest run of cable possible because the longer that audio signal travels over the cable, the more likely the signal will be audibly degraded by interference or *attenuation* (the weakening of the signal as it travels over any cable).

Dozens of companies make high-quality cables at a wide range of prices. Right off the bat, we can name Monster Cable (www.monstercable.com), Kimber Kable (www.kimber.com), and AudioQuest (www.audioquest.com). (By the way, there are so many good cables out on the market, please don't feel like our short list is anywhere near exhaustive. We could have filled a page with company names.)

Joining the RCA mania

The most common type of connector in any home theater is the standard analog *audio interconnect*. Traditionally, these cables came in pairs for two-channel (stereo) audio connections, but in the realm of the home theater, with its multiple surround sound channels, cables don't always work in neat pairs. You may find yourself using these cables individually (like the cable that connects a subwoofer to the receiver or controller) or in big bunches (like the six cables that connect an SACD [Super Audio CD] or DVD-Audio player to the receiver).

Audio interconnects use a standardized jack known as an *RCA jack,* which is nice because any audio interconnect with RCA jacks will plug into any corresponding RCA plug on a piece of A/V equipment. Figure 16-1 shows an RCA plug on a stereo (dual) pair of audio interconnects.

If you go shopping for audio interconnects, you'll find a huge array of different cable constructions. The typical audio interconnect is a *coaxial* cable, which means that it has two electrical conductors surrounded by a shielded jacket within the cable. This jacket is called *shielded* because it is designed to keep stray electromagnetic energy from getting into the conductors and causing interference with the audio signal. But you'll find a lot of variation out there, and some cables are unshielded but twisted. (Twisting has a similar effect to shielding — due to the black art of physics, twisted cables can *cancel out* interferences.)

Figure 16-1:
The
ubiquitous
RCA jack
and plug.

Connecting your speakers

Another cable that you'll find in every home theater (except for those that use active loudspeaker systems, which we discuss in Chapter 12) is the speaker cable. Speaker cables connect the outputs of the power amplifier or the amplifier section of the receiver to the speaker. These cables carry the high-powered electrical currents required to move the internal components of the speaker (the magnets that move the drivers, as described in Chapter 12). You need one pair of speaker cables for each speaker in your system (except for the subwoofer if it's an active system — which most are — and which uses an analog audio interconnect cable instead).

Some expensive speaker systems can use two pairs of speaker wires per speaker. These systems are either biwired or biamped:

- ✔ **Biwired:** Two sets of speaker wire connect to the same output on the receiver or power amplifier, and you plug them into two sets of terminals on the speaker itself.

- ✔ **Biamped:** The speaker uses two separate amplifiers — one for the low-frequency drivers and one for the high-frequency drivers.

Biwiring is one of those "audiophile" tricks that most people don't really hear. If it works for you, and you have speakers with such a setup, by all means use it. But for us, it's just not worth the expense of the extra set of speaker cables.

Because they typically go for longer distances (especially in the case of surround speakers) and carry more electrical current than interconnects, speaker cables are considerably beefier and thicker than interconnects. The thickness of speaker cables (or the conductors within, to be precise) is referred to as *gauge* (using the standard AWG, or American Wire Gauge, system). The lower the gauge, the thicker the conductors.

Thicker conductors have less electrical *resistance* to the current flowing through them. Too much resistance is a bad thing (it can alter the audio signal), and the longer the cable, the greater the resistance the signal faces while traveling over the cable. We recommend cables of no higher than 16-gauge thickness, and prefer 14-gauge cables. For longer runs of 40 feet or more, such as runs to surround sound speakers in a large room, we recommend moving down to 12-gauge cables if they fit your budget.

If you want to hide your speaker cables in the wall (or if you're running speaker cables through the wall for a multizone audio system), you need to get cables that are specially designed for this purpose and that meet electrical code requirements. You should choose cables that have been certified for this purpose by Underwriters Laboratories (UL-certified) and that meet the *CL3* specification (which relates to the insulation on the wires and helps prevent fires — a good thing in our opinion).

Unlike audio interconnects, which share the common RCA connector, you have a ton of connector choices when it comes to speaker cables (these connectors are sometimes called *terminations*). The most bare-bones approach is to just use the bare wire itself (stripped of any insulation), but we highly recommend you don't do this. You typically don't get as good a connection, and the bare wire ends can corrode over time, making the connection even worse (and impacting your sound quality).

You'll see three main types of connectors (besides the bare wire) on the market:

- ✔ **Pin connectors:** These look like they sound — a straight or angled pin at the end of the wire (though it's not sharp, so you won't put your eye out). These work best with the spring-loaded clip type of speaker connectors, which you find on less expensive receivers and speakers. Pin connectors also work with the preferred five-way binding posts found on better models. (We talk about five-way binding posts in Chapter 12.)

- ✔ **Spade lugs:** These U-shaped connectors fit behind the screws on a five-way binding post (you slide the open part of the U over the post and then screw down the plastic nut). Spade lugs can provide the tightest, most reliable connection you can get (because of that screwing down). Some spade lugs go beyond the "U" shape and are shaped like three-quarters of a circle, to hook around your binding post. These "hooked" connectors tend to be even more secure.

- ✔ **Banana plugs:** If you squint really hard, these plugs may actually look like bananas, but they look more like pin connectors that are fat in the middle. By bowing out in the middle, they provide a tight fit into the binding post. Banana plugs come in single and dual configurations. The dual variety is just two banana plugs (one for each wire in the pair of speaker wires) stuck together in the same housing.

Figure 16-2 shows the pin, spade lug, and banana plug, and Figure 16-3 shows a five-way binding post.

Although the spade lug provides the ultimate in speaker wire connections, we think the banana plug provides a connection that's very close in quality. The banana plug is also much easier to use because the banana just slides into the binding post (nothing to tighten or adjust).

Your choice of speaker cable connectors is largely driven by the receiver and speaker choices you make. While ideally manufacturers would create gear that could accept any of these connectors, the real world of designing and manufacturing A/V gear often makes that difficult. When you look at the sheer number of speaker connections that sprout on the back of a 7.1-channel receiver (at least 14 individual connectors just for the speakers — not to mention all of the audio and video interconnects), there's often just not enough room to accept many of the larger connectors (like spade lugs). When you're purchasing speaker cables, try to be sure that the connectors will fit — and make sure you can return the cables if they simply won't fit on your gear.

Figure 16-2:
From left to right, a pin connector, a spade lug, and a banana plug.

Figure 16-3:
The five-way binding post is your friend (it's most versatile).

Using digital audio interconnects

With the advent of computer-chip-laden receivers and DVD players, home theater has moved home A/V gear into the digital age. True, CD players have been digital for years, but for the majority of people, all the digital stuff happened *inside* the CD. The connections between the CD player and the receiver were all analog. Surround sound (specifically digital surround sound systems, such as Dolby Digital and DTS) has made the digital interconnect commonplace.

As we mention throughout the book, digital audio interconnects (to connect DVD players, HDTV tuners, video game consoles, and more to the A/V receiver or controller) are divided into two main types: coaxial and optical (or Toslink).

The HDMI connection (discussed later in this chapter, in the section called "Employing digital video connections") is primarily used as a method for making digital video connections, but HDMI can also carry up to eight channels of digital audio. As A/V receivers begin to include HDMI connections (and a growing number are), you'll be able to use a single cable to connect a source device like a DVD player or set-top box to your receiver, and also a single cable to connect the receiver to your display. Home theater cable nirvana is within sight! (At least for new equipment that includes HDMI.)

Coaxial digital interconnects

The *coaxial interconnect* looks an awful lot like a single (mono) audio interconnect. It has standard RCA jacks on both ends and a coaxial cable between them. Put the analog audio and coaxial interconnects side by side on a table (unlabeled of course), and you really can't tell them apart. But the conductors inside coaxial cables are of a different construction that's designed to handle the higher frequencies of digital signals. You shouldn't use standard audio interconnects in place of a coaxial digital cable. It's tough to explain the difference in sound you may experience if you use the wrong kind of cable here, but if your digital audio just doesn't sound *right,* check to see whether you have the correct digital interconnect hooked up.

Coaxial digital interconnects are not the only example of cables that use RCA plugs and look like audio interconnects but are not. Both the composite and the component video cables we discuss shortly also appear to be identical to audio interconnects, but in fact use different internal conductors and designs.

Also keep in mind that the term "coax" is typically used to describe the cables used to connect antennas, cable TV feeds, and satellite dishes to your home theater. That type of coax (using the "F connector) is a *completely* different kettle of fish from a coaxial digital audio cable.

Optical digital interconnects

The Toslink optical connector uses fiber optics instead of copper cabling and carries the digital signal as pulses of light instead of as an electrical signal. The connector on a Toslink interconnect, viewed head-on, looks like a nice little house in suburbia — except most houses don't have a laser flashing out of the side of them. (Well at least ours don't — we won't presume to speak for you.) Figure 16-4 shows the Toslink cable connector.

The *female* Toslink connector (on your receiver or DVD player or wherever you're plugging a Toslink into) is usually covered by a little removable dust cap. If you don't take off this cap, you're going to curse like a sailor trying to plug in that cable.

Some folks argue strongly either for Toslink or for coaxial digital audio connectors — we don't have any qualms recommending them both. Our basic advice is to use whichever is available to you — if they're both available, they're both equally good, assuming you don't use cables that fell off the back of a speeding van in your neighborhood.

Using analog video connections

The majority of video connections in a home theater are made using analog connections (though an increasing number of devices can use the newer digital video interconnects we discuss in the following section). You'll find three types of *short run* analog video connections in a home theater.

To truly understand the differences between the types of connections, you need to first understand what kinds of signals these cables carry. There are two components to a video signal — the *luminance* and the *chrominance*. The luminance provides the video display with the brightness information that determines which parts of the screen are darker or lighter. The chrominance adds information about what color each segment of the screen should be.

There is a definite hierarchy among video connections. One is visibly worse (in terms of picture quality) than the other two, and of the two superior methods, one is better (though not as significantly) than the other. In ascending order (worst to best), these connection types are as follows:

 ✔ **Composite video:** Both luminance and chrominance are combined into a single signal. The *comb filter* inside the display (discussed in Chapter 13) separates these two components and sends them to the appropriate internal circuitry.

- ✔ **S-Video:** In S-Video, luminance and chrominance are separated onto two separate signal paths, so the signal can bypass the comb filter in the TV. This usually results in a much clearer picture, with more defined colors and images.

- ✔ **Component video:** Component video separates the signal even further, providing one path for luminance information, and then providing two separate paths for chrominance information. Component video connections can be further enhanced in a *wideband* component video connection, which allows the higher frequencies needed for HDTV to travel from the source (such as an HDTV tuner) to the HDTV monitor.

So the big difference between composite (the lower-quality video signal), S-Video, and component video connections is the fact that the better connections carry luminance and chrominance information separately. Why is this a big deal? After all, the display *does* have a comb filter to take care of that problem. Well, here's a dirty little secret: Comb filters do an imperfect job of separating these two signals and can leave visible *artifacts* in your picture. You want the sharpest, most colorful picture you can get, don't you?

In some cases, you might not choose the highest-quality connection available to you. We talk about such cases in Chapter 17, when we discuss hooking up your home theater.

Both component and composite cables use standard RCA connectors and bear a striking resemblance to the analog audio interconnect (and the digital coaxial interconnect, for that matter). Composite video cables are loners (you need just one), and component video cables travel in small packs of three (often labeled Y, Pr, and Pb).

Composite video cables are usually color-coded yellow (that is to say, the connector usually has a yellow ring around it, or the rubber boot around the connector is yellow). Component video cables are also typically color-coded with red, green, and blue connectors.

S-Video is an unmistakable beast, with its own special connector (the S-Video connector of course). This connector has four small pins that correspond with four small holes on the S-Video plug on your gear. Figure 16-5 shows an S-Video connector.

S-Video connectors can be a real pain in the butt to line up and connect. One set of pins is slightly more widely spaced than the other (the bottom ones are farther apart). If you're really killing yourself, check to see that you aren't pushing this cable in upside down. A little plastic doohickey keeps you from really messing things up, but bent pins are far from unknown to first-time S-Video users.

Figure 16-5:
Separate that chrominance and luminance with S-Video.

Employing digital video connections

The consumer electronics industry (in association with the content providers) has been working overtime to develop some digital video interconnection systems that satisfy the following requirements:

- **Preserve the digital signal:** The video connection systems we discuss in the previous section are all analog systems. They carry analog video signals, not digital ones. Nothing is inherently wrong with analog connections, but they are more susceptible to interferences and other losses of signal quality when compared to digital connections. And in the case of digital signals (such as HDTV and other ATSC digital television broadcasts), there's really no reason to convert to analog until the very last minute (inside of the display itself). As Dick Vitale would say, "Keep it digital, baby!"

- **Minimize cables:** Some of these analog connections (particularly component video) also require multiple cables per connection. So if you want to connect the component video output of your HDTV tuner to your receiver and then to your display, you need six cables (three for each link). Add a DVD player using component video into the mix, and you have six more cables. Pretty soon, you have spaghetti. And this doesn't even include the cables you'll require for audio!

✔ **Provide copy protection:** These analog connections don't have any inherent copy protection systems. If there's one thing that content providers (movie and television studios) want to prevent, it's people copying their content. They don't even really want to let you make copies for personal use, such as copying *CSI* when you're out of town on business so that you can watch it after you come home.

We discuss the most common digital video connection options in the following sections.

FireWire

One of the first systems for digital video crossed over from the computer industry. *FireWire,* which is also called IEEE 1394 or i.LINK, depending on who's talking, was originally developed by Apple Computer for connecting peripheral devices to Macintosh computers. Companies such as Sony picked up on the technology and began incorporating FireWire into their camcorders and PCs, and FireWire grew from there. (The FireWire in camcorders is often called *DV.*)

Some HDTV tuners and HDTV-ready displays include FireWire connections, as do a few other devices (such as JVC's D-VHS), but as we write, FireWire appears to be becoming less common as a means of connecting HDTV devices together.

So why do we mention it? Well, for starters, you can still buy HDTV systems that use FireWire. Additionally, FireWire is beginning to become more common in the *audio* side of the home theater. The DVD Forum (a coalition of companies that helps develop the DVD standard) has recently approved FireWire as a connection method for the audio output of DVD-Audio players. When these players (and compatible receivers or controllers) hit the market, you'll be able to replace those six analog audio interconnects with a single cable. That will be nice!

Although DVI and particularly HDMI, FireWire's biggest competitors in the digital video connection world, appear to be winning the war of digital video interconnects, battles are still being fought, and the tide may turn. In fact, a new group called HANA (High-definition Audio-Video Networking Alliance, www.hanaalliance.org) was formed to create yet another set of standards for connecting your A/V gear together, and FireWire is a big part of that system. So don't count FireWire out completely yet. But don't be surprised if you don't see FireWire anywhere in your home theater either!

Digital Visual Interface

One reason that FireWire never really took off in the world of home theater was the success of its competitor, DVI (Digital Visual Interface). DVI is another technology adopted from the computer world, where it was originally developed as a means of connecting computers to digital LCD screens and projectors. Along the way, DVI picked up a strong copy protection system called HDCP (discussed in Chapter 13) and became a favorite of the HDTV industry.

HDCP makes DVI a relatively *dumb* connection — all it does is send video in one direction (for example, from the tuner to the display), and HDCP can limit your ability to make a digital copy of what you're watching. Figure 16-6 shows a DVI connector.

Figure 16-6:
A DVI
connector
for yummy
digital video
quality.

Not all devices with a DVI connector incorporate HDCP. For example, LCD computer monitors may use DVI without HDCP. If you connect an HDCP-enabled HDTV tuner to a non-HDCP display using a DVI cable, you can't get a full HDTV signal. Instead, the signal is converted to a lower resolution.

DVI is a great way to make digital video connections, and it is available on many displays and a number of source devices (like HDTV tuners), but it is rapidly being replaced by HDMI, which not only uses a smaller and simpler connector but can also carry digital audio signals.

The state of the art in digital video connections: HDMI

The latest and greatest in digital video (and audio) connections is the HDMI cable. HDMI stands for High-Definition Multimedia Interface, and you can find out more about the technology at the HDMI Web site at www.hdmi.org.

HDMI is being included in a variety of devices these days, including HDTVs, DVD players (both the current generation of DVD players and the forthcoming high-definition Blu-ray and HD-DVD players), cable and satellite set-top boxes, and Media Center Edition PCs, and it is even expected to show up in the Sony PlayStation 3 gaming console (which hasn't hit the market as we write).

What's so great about HDMI? Well, a few things:

- ✔ **It's all-digital.** Like DVI and FireWire, HDMI provides an all-digital path for your standard and high-definition video signals.

- ✔ **It's high-bandwidth.** HDMI can support data signals as fast as 5Gb per second. That means it can handle HDTV with plenty of room to spare. (In fact, HDTV uses less than half of this bandwidth — so the HDTV signals don't have to be compressed.) FireWire, by comparison, tops out at 400Mb per second (there is an 800Mb per second variant, but it's not very common) — less than $\frac{1}{12}$ of the bandwidth.

- ✔ **It can support all variants of HDTV.** 720p, 1080i, even 1080p can run over an HDMI cable.

- ✔ **It can carry up to eight channels of digital audio.** So a single HDMI cable can carry your HDTV *and* your 7.1-channel surround sound. Nothing like reducing the tangle of cables behind your system, huh?

As you shop for HDMI cables, you might consider consulting a cardiologist simply because the "big name" HDMI cables in your average electronics store are incredibly expensive and may cause your heart to palpitate. Don't fear, though — HDMI cables don't have to be super-expensive. In fact, certified HDMI cables can be relatively cheap, and there are many good on-line sources.

For example, Pat recently installed some HDMI cables in his wall that were about one-fifth the price of those at his local retail store, and they work *great!* We highly recommend that you spend a few moments perusing some of the other sources of information we discuss in Chapter 23 (like AVS Forum) and see what the home theater enthusiasts are using and where they're getting it on-line. You'll probably get a great bargain.

As long as your HDMI cable runs are less than 10 meters, you can buy one of these inexpensive cables and expect excellent results. When you get past 10 meters (that's over 30 feet — a long way!), we recommend that you consult a specialist because you might need some special active components to boost the signal level. But we're confident that most folks won't need to go more than 30 feet!

We think HDMI is the way to go. If you're shopping for a new TV, a new receiver, or a new DVD player, or choosing an HDTV set-top box or satellite receiver, go with HDMI if you can. HDMI can provide the highest quality video signal and throws your multichannel surround sound audio in on the same cable. You really can't go wrong here!

HDMI is fully *backward compatible* with DVI. What that means is that you can interconnect HDMI and DVI devices. So you can connect, for example, a DVI connector on your HDTV cable set-top box to an HDMI input on your new plasma (or vice versa). Keep in mind that such connections will carry only video signals — DVI doesn't support audio. If you're buying all new gear, it's best to choose HDMI all around, but if you're upgrading, the good news is that HDMI won't strand your investment in DVI-equipped gear. All you need is an inexpensive (about $20) adapter, or you can easily find HDMI-to-DVI cables, which have an HDMI connector on one end and a DVI connector on the other. We love it when something new doesn't make us have to throw away our old gear — don't you?

Working with Long Run Cables

When you start thinking about connecting your home theater to the rest of your home (perhaps to share a video source device with TVs in other rooms), you will run into a new set of cables. These *long run* cables are designed to minimize signal loss and get your audio and video to any spot in the house. Although you can distribute audio and video around the home in many ways, the three most common ways are the following:

- **RG6 coaxial cabling for video:** This cable (which we describe later in this chapter) carries video signals (and the associated audio tracks) from antennas, satellite dishes, and cable TV feeds from the street. With devices called *modulators,* you can actually create in-house TV channels and use this cable to share your own video sources with other TVs in the house.

- **Speaker cabling for whole-home audio:** We discuss speaker wires (appropriately rated for in-wall use) in the section, "Connecting your speakers," earlier in this chapter. You can use this same speaker wire to connect a multizone receiver (or a separate whole-home audio system) to speakers throughout the house.

- **Category 5e (CAT-5e) or Category 6 (CAT-6) network cabling:** This is the cable used for computer networks — the stuff you put in your walls if you are creating a whole-home network. With the appropriate gear on the ends of these cables (we discuss this in Chapter 18), you can use this cable to carry audio and video signals.

Going with RG6

Coaxial cable (usually just called *coax*) is a metallic cable most often used for transmitting radio frequency (RF) signals, such as broadband television video and radio signals. Coaxial cable contains two conductors, or *axes*, to carry data. A layer of dielectric insulating material surrounds a single, center conductor. The other conductor is a metal shield, usually made of a braided metallic wiring, that goes around the dielectric (insulating) layer. The outermost layer of coax cable is an insulating jacket. The connectors on an RG6 cable are known as *F connectors.*

You may encounter coaxial cables labeled RG6QS or RG6 Quad Shield, which means that the cable has additional shielding beneath the cable jacket — four layers, as the *quad* implies. These layers provide additional protection against interference from external sources. Because of this extra shielding, we recommend you use Quad Shield coax. It doesn't cost a lot more, and it's worth the investment.

CAT-5e/CAT-6 cabling systems

If you've ever spent any time building, designing, or just using a computer network, you've encountered CAT-5e or CAT-6 cabling — often generically called *Ethernet cables.* (These are two very similar types of data cables — CAT-5e is the most common, so we refer to it below, but both will work just fine.) CAT-5e is a type of UTP (unshielded twisted pair) copper cabling and can be used for phones, computer networks, home automation networks, and audio/video distribution systems. CAT-5e cables typically consist of four pairs of wire (eight total conductors) wrapped in a single jacket. The ends of CAT-5e cables are terminated in connectors known as *RJ-45 jacks,* which look exactly like the common RJ-11 phone jack, only wider.

CAT-5e cabling can be used to connect your home theater to your computer LAN (local area network) and through this LAN to the Internet. For example, CAT-5e connectors are commonly found on MP3 servers, PVRs, and increasingly on audio source devices that are designed to play back Internet radio stations or MP3 files located on a computer in your house. CAT-5e cabling may also be used to connect the A/V source components in your home theater to other rooms in the house. (We discuss systems that do this in Chapter 19.)

There is actually a range of category-rated UTP cables (for example, CAT-3 cabling is often used for telephone wiring). CAT-6 is the current "top-of-the-line" UTP cabling, suitable for very fast computer networks, but CAT-5e cable is the most common for home use, and is more than adequate for your home's wiring.

Each piece of a CAT-5e system (the cables themselves, the RJ-45 jacks, and so on) is subject to the CAT-5e rating system. If you use CAT-5e, make sure *all* the pieces and parts are rated CAT-5e. The "weakest link in the chain" rule applies here. Any piece that's rated below CAT-5e brings the whole system down to that lower rating. Many A/V-over-UTP systems require CAT-5e and don't work well on identical-looking but lower-rated cables. All CAT-5e cables and connectors will be clearly marked with a label of some sort, so just read the fine print (on the cable itself) to be sure.

Identifying Other Cable Odds and Ends

We end this chapter with a hodgepodge listing of other cables and connectors that may show up in your home theater. These connection systems are less common than the ones discussed in preceding sections, but none of them is a complete stranger to the world of home theater. This is particularly true if you are hooking your home theater into a whole-home network or when you are connecting PCs and other computer-like devices (such as PVRs and MP3 servers) into your home theater.

Wireless connections

Wireless networking technologies have made a huge splash in the computer networking world — everyone, it seems, has gone crazy for a system called *802.11* or *Wi-Fi* (a type of wireless computer LAN). (Read our books *Smart Homes For Dummies* and *Wireless Home Networking For Dummies,* both published by Wiley Publishing, Inc., for a ton of information about this technology — and you Mac folks might want to check out *Airport & Mac Wireless Networking For Dummies,* by Michael Cohen, as well.)

As more people begin to use PCs and the Internet in their home theaters, this technology is increasingly moving from the computer world to the consumer electronics world. Many manufacturers, such as NETGEAR (www.netgear. com) and D-Link (www.dlink.com), are creating devices called *Wi-Fi Ethernet Bridges* specifically for home entertainment/home theater gear. These bridges make it easy to connect Internet-capable home theater gear to your home's Wi-Fi network with the help of an Ethernet port. (Ethernet is the common computer network that uses CAT-5e cabling and RJ-45 jacks.) For about $100, you can buy one of these bridges and use a short length of CAT-5e cabling to connect it to your PVR (personal video recorder), MP3 server, home theater PC, or even your gaming console (such as Xbox or PlayStation 2). The bridge then connects wirelessly (using radio waves) to your DSL or cable modem through a device called an *access point.*

In Chapter 10, we discuss a number of Wi-Fi enabled systems that let you get content into your home theater.

RS-232

If you've ever connected a modem to an older PC, you've probably used an RS-232 connector and not even known it. RS-232 is a standard computer communications system that's more commonly known as a *serial* connection. Until the advent of the USB system (discussed in the following section), RS-232 was the standard connection for modems, handheld computer cradles, and many other PC peripheral devices.

In the home theater world, RS-232 is *not* used for carrying audio and video. It is, however, often used for connecting A/V components to automation and control systems (such as the Crestron systems we discuss in Chapter 15). You can also find RS-232 ports on the back of many advanced A/V receivers, where they can be used to connect the receiver to a PC for upgrading the software system within the receiver.

USB

USB (or Universal Serial Bus) has pretty much replaced RS-232 in the PC world. These days, most printers, external modems, handheld computers, portable MP3 players, and other PC peripheral devices connect to PCs via USB. In the home theater world, USB can be found on the back of many computer-like source devices (such as MP3 servers and PVRs). USB has not yet replaced RS-232 for connections to automation and control systems, but probably will eventually.

The most common use for USB in a home theater is in conjunction with a Wi-Fi system. You can outfit source devices that can connect to the Internet with a USB Wi-Fi network adapter. This adapter enables you to connect back to the access point and out to the Internet. USB is also used for remote control connections for PCs. The remote control receiver for the PC connects to the PC via a USB cable.

There are multiple types of USB devices out there. (With more than 1 billion USB-enabled devices in use around the world, that's probably no surprise.) The latest and greatest variant of USB is *USB 2.0 High-speed,* which supports data transfers at speeds of up to 480 Mbits per second. The older and slower USB 1.1 standard really doesn't cut it for home theater use, as it can barely handle audio signals and just plain can't do high-quality video.

You can also find a few A/V receivers (like JVC's RX-D201S — www.jvc.com) that have a USB connection that lets you connect to a nearby PC to feed digital audio signals (like MP3 files) from the PC to the receiver without using one of the media adapter devices we discuss in Chapter 10.

IR connections

In Chapter 18, we talk about ways that you can connect your home theater to speakers and displays in other parts of your home by using a whole-home entertainment network. As we discuss earlier in this chapter, you use RG6 coaxial cable, speaker wire, and/or CAT-5e cabling to carry your audio and video around the house. There's one other piece to this whole-home puzzle, however. You need some sort of system for controlling remote devices when you are watching them (or listening to them) in a different part of the house. If the phone rings, you want to be able to turn down the music or pause the movie.

Most A/V systems use IR (infrared) systems for their remote controls. IR is a great system, but because it uses a beam of light to carry control signals, it can't penetrate walls (unless you have a glass house, we suppose). So you need some sort of wired system that can carry IR signals from remote locations back to your home theater. (You can also find wireless alternatives from companies such as X10 — www.x10.com.) You can set up an infrared system in four ways:

✔ **IR cabling:** Many home networking vendors sell cables specially designed for carrying IR signals from remote locations back to the home theater.

✔ **CAT-5e cabling:** If you're using CAT-5e cabling for audio and video distribution (using some of the systems we discuss in Chapter 19), you'll find that these systems have a built-in capability to carry IR signals for remote controls. If you're not using one of these systems but have put CAT-5e cabling in your walls when building your home, you can use extra (unused) CAT-5e cables in place of the IR cabling we just mentioned.

✔ **RG6 coaxial cabling:** Using special devices called *IR injectors* (available from vendors such as ChannelPlus, www.channelplus.com), you can carry IR signals over the RG6 coax that you use for distributing cable or broadcast antenna TV signals.

You can't use an IR injector on the RG6 cables used to connect a DSS dish to DSS receivers.

✔ **Proprietary systems:** If you opt to install a high-end automation system, such as those from Crestron (www.crestron.com), you need to use special proprietary cables from the manufacturer. For example, Crestron uses its own special cable called CrestNet.

Chapter 17

Hooking Up Your A/V System

* *

* *

*Y*ou've picked a room, collected all your A/V gear, opened the boxes, and *oohed* and *aahed* at your shiny new stuff. Now it's time to get down to the work of hooking up your home theater. At first glance, this can seem like a daunting task. You have a lot of cables and connectors to deal with, and even experienced home theater folks may find the back of an A/V receiver confusing at first. The key is to take a methodical approach. With a few key concepts in mind, hooking up an A/V system can be easy and even fun!

In this chapter, we talk about where the various pieces and parts of an A/V system should go in your home theater and how they should be connected to each other. However, the advice we give in this chapter is *generic.* Although the majority of home theater components connect in a similar fashion with identical cables and connectors, there are always a few differences among different brands and models. For example, what we call CD Audio In might be labeled CD Line In or even Aux In on your receiver. For the exact terms and procedures that apply to your system, you need to read your manual.

Planning the Room Layout

After you've read those oh-so-fun manuals, you might think it's time to start plugging away. The temptation is to get things hooked up and working. You want to watch a movie *right now,* admit it . . . so would we. But by devoting a few minutes to planning out your next steps, you can make the process easier and get better results when the time comes to watch and listen to your system.

At a minimum, your home theater has six speakers (including the subwoofer). Each of these speakers plays a role in creating the illusion of being "in the action" when you watch movies or shows (or listen to multichannel audio on DVD-A or SACD). So you have to get the speakers in the right spots relative to your listening position. Incorrectly positioning your speakers creates gaps in the sound field that surrounds you. These gaps can be distracting or down-right annoying and can also cause room interactions that reduce the fidelity of the audio you are re-creating.

No matter what you do, your speakers are going to interact with your room, creating echoes and reflections that have some impact on the sound. The key is to reduce the negative effects of these interactions and, instead, use them to your advantage.

Getting the front speakers in place

The front speakers — left, right, and center — provide the bulk of the sound you listen to while watching a movie. One of the key jobs of these front speakers is to provide a realistic reproduction of dialogue — you want people in the middle of the display to sound like they're right in front of you, and those on the left and right to sound like that's where they are. Proper placement of these three front speakers is essential in creating this effect and minimizing any gaps in the speakers' coverage (so when dialogue moves from side to side, it does so seamlessly). Keep the following points in mind when setting up your front speakers:

- ✔ **Set up your center channel speaker first.** The placement of the left and right speakers is dependent upon the position of your center speaker.

- ✔ **Make sure the front surface of the center channel speaker is flush with the display.** Most center channel speakers are designed to be placed directly on top of the display. Keep the front surfaces of both flush with each other to minimize reflections. If your equipment physically permits, you might try to get the front of the speaker (the baffle) *in front of* the surface of the screen. (This is really hard to pull off in the real world, which is why we recommend just making them flush.)

  If you have a wall-mounted display (like a flat-panel plasma or LCD TV), you might have a hard time getting your center channel speaker flush with the display (unless you're using wall-mounted speakers especially designed for such applications — which are becoming quite popular these days). Don't sweat it; just try to keep the front of your center channel relatively close to the same vertical plane as the front of your display — don't stick it too far out in front if you can avoid it.

✔ **Keep the right and left channel speakers the same distance from your listening position as the front speaker.** Some people place the three front speakers in a straight line across the front of the room. This actually makes the center speaker closer to you than the others, meaning that sounds from the center speaker reach you sooner than sounds from the others. Instead of a line, the front speakers should form an *arc* in front of you, in which each speaker is the same distance from your primary viewing position (or the middle of the viewing position, such as the center of a couch or the middle of a group of seats).

If you're using wall-mount speakers with a wall-mounted flat panel, you're not going to be able to do this. Again, don't sweat it; it's not a huge deal, as long as you take the time to "teach" your receiver where your speakers are when you configure it. Because these speakers will be a bit farther away from you than the center channel when you're sitting directly in front of the display, you'll simply have the receiver introduce a bit of *delay* in the signals sent to these speakers, so the sound arrives at your ears at the right time.

✔ *Toe-in* **the left and right speakers.** The front panels of the left and right speakers should be placed so that they are aimed directly at (or immediately behind) your seating position. Many wall mounts allow you to angle the speakers this way.

Some speakers are designed such that their front panels are already toed-in when the speakers are placed parallel to the wall. Check the manual that comes with your speakers to see if there are any specific recommendations on toe-in.

✔ **Place the left and right speakers at a 45- to 60-degree angle from the listening position.** Start off with the speakers at the wider angle. Place each speaker 30 degrees to the right or left of the center speaker from your viewing position. If you find, while listening to movie soundtracks, that sounds seem unnatural and too widely spaced, you can move the right and left speakers closer to the screen. Conversely, if it's hard to distinguish right from left from most seating positions, spread them a bit farther apart. When you do so, maintain the arc we just mentioned.

✔ **Place the speakers' tweeters at or near the viewers' ear level.** Keep in mind the seated height of your viewers in the seating you've selected and adjust your speakers accordingly when selecting stands or wall mounting. Even if you have floorstanding speakers, you can buy small stands to raise the height, if necessary. If your center speaker is above you (maybe you put it on top of a gigantic RPTV), you can at least aim it down toward your listening position. Our technical editor (who's a genius at this stuff) likes to use rubber wedge-shaped doorstops under the backside of the center speaker to do this aiming.

Dealing with surrounds

Many people think of their surround sound speakers as their rear speakers. Indeed, many receivers label the surround outputs as Rear, so people imagine that these speakers need to be along the back wall, behind the listening position. This isn't always the case — particularly with the bipole or dipole surround speakers, which are the most common kinds (we prefer dipoles).

5.1-channel surround sound

For 5.1-channel surround sound, we recommend you place bipole or dipole surround speakers along the side walls (preferably mounted on the side wall). Position them even to or slightly behind your home theater seating, and about 2 feet above the listeners' seated ear level. If you are using direct-radiating speakers for your surrounds, the best placement is behind the listeners, aimed so that they radiate (face, in other words) toward the *back wall.* That might sound a bit counter-intuitive, but if you face them directly toward the listening position, you don't get the diffuse surround sound that you're looking for.

If your room layout supports it, you should place your surround speakers on either side of your primary viewing/listening position so that they are each within a 90 to 110 degree angle from your head — where straight ahead (looking at the screen) is 0 degrees.

Other types of surround sound

If you're using Dolby Digital EX or DTS ES, you have an extra speaker (or two) to deal with. These systems have side surrounds (which are placed like 5.1-channel side surrounds) and *center surround* channel speakers (one or two, depending on whether you're using a 6.1- or 7.1-channel setup).

These center surround speakers should be placed behind the listener. In a 6.1-channel setup, they go directly behind the listening position. In a 7.1-channel system, the two center surround speakers should be placed along the rear wall, on either side of the seating position.

In a 7.1 system, you should put each of the rear surrounds at an angle of 130 to 150 degrees from your main listening position — again relative to your display being 0 degrees.

Placing the subwoofer for optimal bass

You'll often hear people talk about low-frequency sounds being *nondirectional,* which is a fancy way of saying that you can't really locate where they are coming from by ear. Proponents of this concept will tell you that your subwoofer can be hidden well out of the way — under the proverbial end table, far away from the action. Subwoofers are nondirectional, to a degree, but putting your subwoofer too far away from the rest of your speakers (and from your listening position) can lead to situations in which you do hear where the bass is coming from. Indeed, if you move your subwoofer too far to the left or right, the bass isn't well integrated with the sound coming from the other speakers. In most cases, it's actually better to not hide the subwoofer. Treat it like any other speaker — show it off!

Many vendors recommend that you place your subwoofer in a corner. This placement reinforces the bass significantly, and we think this is a good place to start. However, in some rooms, you can get too much reinforcement of your bass in the corner, and you end up with boomy bass. What we mean by *boomy* is that the bass notes become indistinct; you just hear a low-frequency sound and can't really distinguish between the different frequencies. So if you're listening to a recording of someone playing a Bach fugue on a pipe organ, you don't hear the distinct notes in the lower register. If this happens to you, try moving the subwoofer out from the corner a bit.

One good (if slightly unscientific) way of finding a place for your subwoofer (after you've got it hooked up, of course) is to swap places with it. Put the subwoofer right up where you sit and turn on some bass-heavy music (or a bass-heavy movie soundtrack). Walk around the room until you find the place where the bass sounds best. Now, swap back by putting the subwoofer in the spot where the bass sounded best.

Figure 17-1 shows a typical 5.1-channel surround sound speaker configuration. As we discuss in the previous sections, the center and front left and right speakers are equidistant from the viewing position, with the left and right speakers 45 to 60 degrees apart (or 22 to 30 degrees on either side of the display from your main viewing position). The surrounds are beside or slightly behind the comfy home theater seats, and the subwoofer is placed along the front wall of the room.

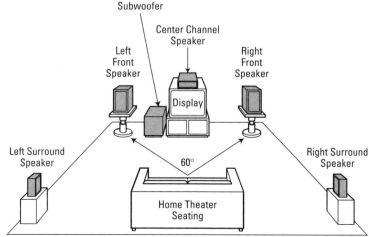

Figure 17-1: A 5.1-channel surround sound speaker configuration.

In a typical 7.1-channel configuration, the center, front, and surround speakers are in the same location as they are in a 5.1 layout, but you've added two additional rear surrounds located farther behind the main listening position.

Hiding Unsightly Cables

One drawback of a surround sound audio system is that having those speakers alongside or behind your seating position makes hiding the speaker cables difficult. Now, some people out there love the look of fancy speaker wires. (Pat has a set of Kimber speaker cables that he just loves to stare at, though his 2-year-old likes them for entirely unsafe play purposes.) But for most people, speaker cables are an unsightly reminder of all the work they've put into building their home theaters, and hiding these wires is a good thing.

The best way to hide cables, if you can pull it off, is to put them inside the wall. If you have a basement or attic under or over, respectively, your home theater room, using in-wall speaker cabling is pretty easy. Just make sure that you have the proper kind of speaker cable (UL-rated CL3 or higher) and that you use a thicker cable (lower gauge), such as 14- or even 12-gauge. See Chapter 16 for details about cables.

Sometimes, you just can't get your cables in the wall. For example, Pat's house (like many in southern California) doesn't have a basement, and the ceiling over his home theater is raised to the roof (no attic access). In these cases, you can try to hide your cables under carpets or rugs. If that doesn't work, you might consider installing a *raceway* along the baseboards of your room that can contain the wires (the raceway can, in fact, even be the baseboard itself, as long as there's room for cables behind it), or even consider using thin (but wide) flat cables. For example, Monster Cable (`www.monster cable.com`) sells flat speaker cables in its "Invisible out of wall" series. Taperwire (`www.taperwire.com`) also offers flattened versions of most wiring you find in the house — including speaker cables — so it's easy to hide. These flat cables are pretty hard to see when placed along your baseboards and can even be painted to match your wall colors.

Attaching Components to the A/V Receiver

Getting your speaker cables and speakers mounted in place is a good first step. Hooking up the rest of your A/V gear is the next step. (Keep in mind that you might have to go back to the speakers and tweak the placement of at least some of your speakers after everything is up and running.)

Spaghetti isn't just what's for dinner. It's also what you get when you pull out all the cables you bought for your home theater components. There sure is a lot of wire behind the scenes in today's home theater. (We hope that this will decrease over time as digital connections, such as HDMI, become more popular.) Luckily, any home theater worth its salt has a device — the A/V receiver or controller — that provides a central connection point for all these wires. Also, if you have a rack for your gear, the rack should have a good cable management system to help you out. We talk about racks in Chapter 20.

At the highest level, connecting components into your home theater is as simple as using the right cables to connect them to the back of your A/V receiver (or controller). With very few exceptions, you don't connect other components directly to each other. Let your A/V receiver do its job!

Some folks believe that you get the highest-quality video signal by connecting your components' video cables directly to the inputs on the back of display itself, bypassing the video source switching functionality of the receiver. (Video switching is when you run all video into the back of the receiver and then let the receiver send the signal you want to view to your display.) For most folks, we think this isn't worth the inconvenience — today's receivers typically have very high quality video switching circuitry, and most displays simply don't have enough inputs anyway. We particularly believe that you should take advantage of your receiver's HDMI switching and *upconversion* facilities if you have these features on your receiver. (Upconversion takes standard-definition signals and coverts them to a higher resolution for display on a high-definition TV.)

If your DVD player, set-top box, or satellite receiver (or other video source component) offers a digital video connection like HDMI, and your display accepts these connections, but your receiver doesn't offer HDMI switching (as we write in early 2006, this is still a relatively rare feature), we recommend that you ignore our previous advice and make those video connections directly, bypassing the receiver. In many cases, the quality of an HDMI signal is worth ignoring the convenience of receiver video switching.

Hooking up your speakers

The next step is to connect your speaker wires to the appropriate speaker outlets on your A/V receiver. This is a pretty simple process, but there are a few things to keep in mind:

> ✔ **Keep your speakers in phase.** Each speaker wire consists of two conductors, a positive and a negative. If you connect these out of phase (that is, the positive on the receiver to the negative on the speaker, and vice versa), you'll hear a definite impact on your sound. Specifically, your speakers can't create the appropriate *soundstage,* so sounds that

are supposed to clearly come from the right or the left won't. (By the way, *right* in this context means to the listener's right when facing the display or the front of the room.) Most speaker cables are also color-coded red and black to make this job easier (or you may have a white stripe on the jacket of one of the conductors in the speaker wire).

✔ **Make sure you have a tight connection.** For the best sound quality and for a connection that won't stop working over time, make sure your speaker connections are solid. We like banana plugs or spade lugs on five-way binding posts because you can get these suckers nice and tight. Make a good connection the first time, and you won't need to touch it again for years. We discuss these different connections in more detail in Chapter 16.

✔ **Don't forget to connect the subwoofer.** Most subwoofers are *active* speakers (they have their own built-in amplifiers), so you don't use speaker wires to connect them. You need a long analog audio interconnect cable, which runs between the Subwoofer Out or LFE output on the back of your receiver and the input on the subwoofer itself. Make sure you get a cable that's long enough to let you move the subwoofer around because you may need to reposition your subwoofer as you discover how it interacts with your home theater's room.

Connecting to the A/V receiver

Take a look at the back of any typical A/V receiver, like the one shown in Figure 17-2. Wow, that's a lot of jacks, huh? Well, they're not all back there for show or to make the designer happy. They're there to give you a flexible home theater system that can do what you need it to do.

Five composite and S-video inputs

Two component video inputs

Figure 17-2: Jack overkill.

Three optical inputs and one coaxial input

Each component in your A/V system has a set of audio and/or video connections to your A/V receiver. The receiver itself connects to your speakers and to your display (with another set of audio and video cables).

First, connect audio interconnects and video cables to each of your source devices. Keep the following things in mind:

✔ **Keep your right and left in mind with audio cables.** Any device that connects with analog audio cables has two connections (the cables themselves usually, but not always, come in attached stereo pairs). One jack (the right) is usually colored red, and the other white. Make sure that you connect the left output on the source device to the corresponding left input on the back of your receiver.

✔ **Use digital audio connections whenever possible.** Use coaxial or optical digital audio cables to connect DVD players, game consoles, DSS receivers, or any source that has a digital audio output. If you want to use Dolby Digital or DTS with any of these sources, you *must* use the digital audio connection.

Some folks feel that optical (Toslink) digital audio connections sound better than coaxial ones. We're not convinced of this, and recommend that you don't get too wrapped around the axle on this — use what you have. If you have both types of connections available to you on the device and the receiver and you have a preference, go with it. Otherwise, don't sweat this too much.

✔ **Keep track of which connections you use on your receiver.** One nice thing about the standardized connections used in home theaters is the fact that you don't have to plug sources into jacks that correspond with that device on your receiver. For example, if you have a video game console (but no corresponding "Game" inputs on your receiver), you can plug the game console into those "Laser Disc Player" inputs — assuming, of course, that you don't have a laser disc player in your system. This is where keeping track of your connections comes in handy. In order to send the audio and video from the game console to your speakers and display, you have to select the laser disc input on your receiver. You might even want to make a little cheat sheet to keep near your system (with all your little home theater quirks written down), so the rest of your family can run the system.

Fancy A/V receivers and controllers often have *assignable* inputs that let you select the names that correspond with each set of inputs on the back of the receiver or controller. In many cases, you can even "type" custom input names into your receiver's display by using your remote so that you can see the right input name on the front of your receiver or on your on-screen display. A very handy feature to have, especially when someone unfamiliar with the system is using it.

✔ **Use an extra set of audio and video cables to connect your recording systems.** Your receiver has an extra set of A/V output connectors that correspond with its VCR inputs (usually labeled VCR1, VCR2, and so on). When you connect your VCR or PVR (personal video recorder) to these inputs, use an extra set of cables to connect the receiver back to the inputs on these sources (labeled Audio In and Video In on the back of the source). This lets you route audio and video through the receiver for recording purposes. (You may not be able to record DVDs this way because of DVD's Macrovision copy protection system, which we discuss in Chapter 6.)

✔ **Use the highest-quality video connections available to you.** If you can use digital video connections (HDMI, DVI, or FireWire), do! Otherwise, use component video if your sources have these connections. If you must, use S-Video for sources, such as DSS receivers, that don't have component video connections. Some sources (such as many VCRs) have only composite video connections.

After you've connected all your sources to the receiver, you can connect the receiver to your display unit by using one or more video cables (we discuss this shortly) and a set of analog audio interconnects.

Using this set of audio cables between the receiver and the display may seem to be a bit of cabling overkill. After all, you already have a surround sound audio system connected to the receiver. We find that, sometimes, we just want to use the built-in speakers in our display, like when we flip on ESPN to catch the college basketball scores, and then turn the TV back off. If you don't think you'll ever do something like this, you can skip this step.

If you're using an HDMI connection between your receiver and display, you might be able to skip the step of adding an analog audio connection to the display. HDMI cables can also carry digital audio, so there's no need for separate audio connections. You can only skip the analog connection, however, if your receiver is only connected to HDMI sources *or* if the receiver has an *upconversion* feature that takes non-HDMI sources and sends them to the display over the HDMI connection.

A step you won't want to skip is connecting the receiver to your display with video cables. This can be a somewhat tricky proposition — the first step you need to take here is to understand whether your receiver has any *upconversion* capabilities. Many receivers these days will upconvert composite and S-Video sources (like non-HDTV cable boxes and VCRs) so that their signals can be sent to your display over component video cables. A growing number of receivers will even upconvert composite, S-Video, and component video signals to HDMI (which is a really cool feature!).

If your receiver *can* upconvert, you can simply connect the receiver's video outputs to the inputs on your display by using component video or HDMI cables (depending, of course, on which kind of upconversion — component or HDMI — your receiver offers).

If your receiver doesn't handle upconversion, you need to have one set of video cables for *each kind* of input you make into the receiver. So, for example, if you have a VCR connected via composite video, a game console connected via S-Video, and a DVD player connected via component video, you need to have one of each of these types of connections running *out* from your receiver to the display.

If you connect a source to your receiver with an S-Video or composite video cable but use only a component video cable to connect the receiver to your display, you'll find that you get sound but no picture when you try to play that source.

You don't need multiples of these video connections between the receiver and the display — just one connection for each type of connection you have *coming into* your receiver. So if you have three component video sources running into the back of your receiver, you need only one set of component video cables running to your display.

Getting television signals

TV comes into your system from a cable TV service, a DSS satellite dish, or an antenna for broadcast TV (or in some cases, from a combination of these devices). Regardless of the system, an RG6 coaxial cable connects these TV sources into your system.

If you use an antenna for non-HDTV over-the-air broadcast TV (or for nondigital cable without a converter box), this connection is usually pretty simple. Simply connect the coaxial cable coming out of your wall outlet to the Antenna/Cable In input on the back of your display. (**Note:** Your cable company may have installed a similar RG59 cable instead of an RG6 cable; if you're running your own cable, we recommend you use RG6.) If you've got a PVR or VCR, run the cable coming out of the wall to it first, and then to the inputs on the back of your TV.

If you have digital cable, analog cable with a converter, or a DSS dish, or if you're picking up over-the-air broadcast HDTV signals, you need to run the RG6 cable to the appropriate set-top box, DSS receiver, or HDTV tuner. These devices are connected through your A/V receiver, just like any other source device. You can use the receiver to send the video from these sources to your VCR for recording (if it's allowed).

If you're using broadcast HDTV and you have a true HDTV (with an integrated tuner), you can connect the coaxial cable running from this antenna directly to the back of your display.

Similarly, if your display is *digital cable–ready* (or DCR) and can use a *CableCARD,* you can connect the coaxial cable from your cable TV feed directly into your TV and forgo the cable set-top box. As we discuss in Chapter 7, this is very convenient but means that you won't be able to access some of digital cable's features, like video on demand (VoD) or the on-screen program guide.

If you have digital cable, you may want to route your cable signal through the PVR or VCR before you connect it to your set-top box. Many digital cable systems transmit a number of standard analog channels that your PVR or VCR can tune into. Routing this cable through the PVR/VCR lets you record those analog channels while your set-top box is tuned to a different channel (analog or digital) for simultaneous viewing.

Adding your gaming console or Home Theater PC

Very few A/V receivers have made provisions for connections from game consoles or Home Theater PCs (HTPCs). Although these devices are too new to have been incorporated into most receiver designs, that's no reason to give up hope. You can still get these devices hooked into your surround sound system and display.

The key thing to keep in mind is that HTPCs and game consoles are really no different from any other source device. They have analog and digital audio connections. They have composite, S-Video, and (in many cases) component video outputs. Your receiver doesn't care whether these signals come from a DVD player or an HTPC. Neither does your display.

So connect these devices just as you connect any of the other source devices we mention earlier in this chapter. Keep the same rules in mind: Use digital audio connections, if you can, and use the highest-quality video connection system that the device supports.

As we hint at earlier in this chapter, you probably won't find any inputs on the back of your receiver marked HTPC or Xbox. So find an unused set of inputs and use them.

If you have one of those fancy touch screen remote controls that we discuss in Chapter 15, you may be able to program the remote to use the actual name of the device you are using. So even if the HTPC is connected to the VCR2 input on your receiver, you can make the remote button say "HTPC." With this setup, the babysitter can easily use your home theater. (We're not sure whether or not that's a good thing.)

Powering the Network

After you've made all the connections, the temptation to plug everything into the wall and get going is strong. Hold off for one more step: making the power connections safely. We're not talking about your personal safety here, but the safety of your equipment. You probably forgot about power cables, but you should have some plans for these, too. There are lots of them, and they certainly get in the way a lot.

You'll have to confront two big issues: the number of connections and the quality of the connections (or, put another way, where to plug them in and how to keep your gear from getting fried).

You will simply have way more power cables than you think. The great thing about power management is that you can add connections as you need more with few issues. So if you need more outlets, no problem — just add some more outlets in the form of power strips. The overall power usage of your home theater is relatively light compared with, say, a dishwasher, so in general, connecting several home theater devices into one outlet is not a huge problem.

Some home theater components — high-powered receivers or power amplifiers and large displays — do draw a lot of current. It's always best to plug these items directly into your surge protector (which we discuss next). Other items, such as DVD players or CD players, can safely be plugged into either the surge protector or into one of the auxiliary outlets on the back of another piece of equipment (many receivers have such outlets).

Two kinds of outlets are used on the back of receivers: *switched* and *unswitched.* Switched outlets turn on and off with the receiver, while unswitched outlets are always on. Keep that distinction in mind if you have something plugged into your receiver's power outlets that you want to use even when the receiver is turned off.

The bigger issue is surge protection. Electrical currents are like water currents; they flow up and down, and if they get too high (a surge), it's a problem. (If they get too low [a brown-out], that's a problem, too.) You need to consider professional-class surge protection (not what you buy at Wal-Mart).

One good lightning strike can toast your home theater (and not in a good way). Leviton (www.leviton.com), for example, has a Home Theater Surge Protector that has nine outlets plus a neat expandable modular outlet that can handle surge protection for telephones, modems, faxes, DSL modems, cable modems, computer LANs, and satellite and cable TV systems.

If you are building from scratch or have the luxury of adding some outlets, put in electrical lines that are dedicated to your home theater and that go straight to your electrical panel so that no intermediate devices can cause in-home surges on your lines.

In general, we also advocate whole-home power protectors that can help groom the power coming from the street. That's where some of the big surges can come from, and these surges can hit not only your home theater, but also everything else in your home. We consider these $300 to $800 "first line of defense" units a must for any home. They sit between all the electrical lines coming in and your electrical panel, truly stopping any problems before they get to your house. You can find models that also protect your satellite and cable connections at the home level, too. You can get these from Leviton and other electrical suppliers.

We talk more in Chapter 21 about power conditioning, which is the next step up after surge protection. Power conditioners use various techniques to restore your A/C power to a true 60 Hz, 120-volt signal and can offer better audio and video performance.

Chapter 18

Plugging into a Whole-Home Entertainment Network

. . . .

In This Chapter

▶ Going whole-home with your home theater

▶ Staying sane with multizone audio

▶ Creating a CAT-5e network infrastructure

▶ Sharing video components through a whole-home network

▶ Tapping into your computer network

. . . .

We strongly believe that you should spend time thinking about how to exploit your investment in your home theater by taking it whole-home. In many instances, you've already done the hard part by deciding that a home theater is worth the big investment to begin with. Now, telling you to take it to the limit (oops, Eagles pop culture reference) by going whole-home (expanding your home theater's audio and video capabilities to other parts of your house) should not be so rough.

The point of this chapter is to expose you to some of the varied ways you can accomplish whole-home networking of your audio and video gear. If you are serious about this (and you know what's coming here — shameless self-promotion time!), we absolutely insist you think about getting our *Smart Homes For Dummies* book (Wiley) because it goes into all the requisite details for you to do this by yourself.

In this chapter, we talk in detail about some whole-home wiring systems that we recommend you install when you build or remodel your house. For most folks, the installation of whole-home wiring is *not* a casual project. If you don't have a whole-home wiring system in place and can't put one in, don't freak out! We also talk about some solutions that use wireless networks or existing wires in your wall to expand the reach of your home theater components.

Introducing Whole-Home Entertainment

Let's talk about what it means to go whole home. If you read Chapter 2, you may recall that you need to plan around two major concentrations of equipment:

- **Wiring hub:** This is generally that place where nearly everything comes into the house from the outside. The electrical panel is likely there, along with your incoming telephone lines, your cable or satellite service connections, and maybe your cable or DSL modem if you were smart and planned ahead. Ideally, most of your in-home communications and information services are connected together in this area, with *home run* wires running throughout the house in a hub-and-spoke fashion. (In a home run wiring system, each outlet has a dedicated wire running directly to it from the wiring hub.)

- **Media hub:** You can consider the main home theater to be your media hub. Most of the gear we discuss in this book resides in the media hub, either on shelves out in the open or in a configuration where you have some gear in the open and some in a nearby equipment closet or rack.

When you go whole home, equipment also resides in your media hub and in other rooms around your house. For example, Danny has a kids' computer lab where four computers are clustered together so that his two sets of twins (he has always been an overachiever) cannot fight over the computers to do their homework on-line. (Actually, Pat knows they are secretly playing *Civilization* and *MathBlaster.*)

In most cases, you are likely to have gear spread all over the house, particularly in the master bedroom, where you might have another TV, VCR, and cable/satellite receiver (maybe even another surround sound system), and potentially something in the kids' rooms.

So the question — and opportunity — is how can you link all your gear to minimize your costs (yes, you can *save* money by not having to buy a PVR or a satellite receiver for each room) and exploit your investment in your media hub? Well, have we got some ideas for you!

Think about what *whole-home* means for you; although you can grow your whole-home network, you can save money in the long run if you have a better idea of what you want to do up front. After you've already built the network, adding things can be more expensive. There's a world of difference between running an extra set of speakers to the bedroom or dining room for your audio and wanting to have background music in every room. If your whole-home plans are relatively limited, you can almost always get inexpensive (under $100) devices from Radio Shack (www.radioshack.com), X10 (www.x10.com), and SmartHome (www.smarthome.com) that can meet these needs.

But if you want to have more flexibility to mix and match in any room, or to have higher-quality connections, you may want to think about looking into a whole-home *distribution panel* for your signals. These panels, also called *structured cabling systems,* can support voice, data, and video distribution in the home relatively cheaply. You can get a good panel for under $1,000 and then add jacks and wiring accordingly.

Not all distribution panels are alike. Some are for one specific application (such as video), and others allow you to select whatever you want to put on any connection. For example, a CAT-5e-based system (using that standard computer-network cabling) might let you put phone, computer data, video, or audio on any line. You merely change out the outlets at the terminating end according to your needs in that room.

You can find a list of structured cabling vendors on the Web site for our book, *Smart Homes For Dummies.* Check it out at www.digitaldummies.com.

At a bare minimum, a structured cabling system should provide

- ✔ **A flexible telephone network** using high-quality, unshielded twisted-pair (UTP) phone cabling and a modular, configurable termination system in the wiring closet (the central location where all of these systems are connected together)

- ✔ **A computer network** of CAT-5e (the standard for Ethernet computer network cabling) UTP cabling for data networking

- ✔ **A centrally distributed coaxial cable (usually RG6 — the standard video cabling) network** for distributing video signals

- ✔ **An all-in-one modular termination panel** to neatly terminate all this network wiring in your wiring closet

- ✔ **Customized wall outlet plates** to provide connectors for your phone, data, audio, and video outlets that can be easily changed and reconfigured

Connecting to a Whole-Home Audio System

Whole-home audio is a pretty simple baseline that a lot of people consider when moving out of the home theater and into the other parts of the house. After all, the first step can be as easy as merely stringing another set of speaker wires from your multizone-capable A/V receiver (we talk about these in Chapter 11) in your home theater to, say, remote speakers located in the dining room. Keep in mind, however, that the limitations of a whole-home audio network are based on your A/V receiver. Most A/V receivers that have multizone capabilities can support audio in only one or two other rooms — not zones in every room in the house.

So if you want a true whole-home audio system, you probably need to consider installing additional equipment in the media hub (or nearby). With this equipment in place (and the appropriate wires in the wall), you can share the audio source devices in your home theater with any room in the house. In almost all cases, this system provides *stereo* (two-channel) audio, not surround sound (multichannel) audio, in rooms outside your home theater. The sidebar, "The trouble with whole-home surround sound," talks about this issue a bit more.

You can get audio from your home theater to other rooms in the house in four primary ways:

✔ **Use your receiver:** As we mention earlier, many receivers (at least above the $500–$600 price range) include multizone functionality that lets you run speaker wires or a long audio interconnect. You can really run these only into an adjacent room, not the entire length of the house, due to signal loss. This is the simplest way to get audio elsewhere in the home.

✔ **Buy a whole-home audio distribution system:** These systems come in both multizone and single-zone versions (we explain the difference later in this chapter) and use their own amplifiers and control systems to send audio to any room in the house. You can buy whole-home audio systems that support up to eight or more rooms.

✔ **Use a CAT-5e audio distribution system:** These systems can distribute line-level stereo audio signals over standard CAT-5e computer network cabling. Many of these systems are designed to carry both audio and video. Some (such as the SVC-10 from ChannelPlus, www.channelplus.com) can even carry the higher-quality S-Video signals and digital audio signals (such as Dolby Digital) over this network cabling. Most of these systems, however, can carry only composite video and stereo audio.

✔ **Use a wireless audio distribution system:** These are typically simple systems designed to go from point to point (rather than cover the whole home). Many people use them to send audio from their PC to their home theater, but they can also be used to get audio from a source in the home theater to other parts of the house.

Most of the CAT-5e and many of the wireless audio distribution systems we are about to discuss can also carry video signals.

Some of the whole-home audio network systems that we talk about use CAT-5e cabling, and we expect (in the not so distant future) to see systems that can distribute surround sound audio around the house digitally using this cable. Until these systems become available, however, we think it's best to stick with good old-fashioned two-channel stereo for whole-home audio networks.

The trouble with whole-home surround sound

The stereo audio standard, in which sound is separated into two channels (left and right), still dominates music production. With the advent of home theater, however, music can now be produced using multiple channels to drive a multitude of speakers.

For the average home (read that as a non-millionaire home), we recommend that you don't add multichannel capabilities to your whole-home audio network — at least not right now. Although you can build an audio network that goes beyond the two-channel (stereo) limit today, the network quickly becomes extremely complicated and prohibitively expensive. We think the best way to create a second multichannel surround system is to simply install a second, standalone surround sound system in that other room. If you're just trying to get surround sound in a bedroom or kid's room, you might consider an inexpensive home-theater-in-a-box solution that will give you surround sound for only a few hundred dollars.

Zoning out: Single-zone versus multizone systems

After you start sending audio to a whole-home audio network, you have some decisions to make. The biggest decision is what you want to listen to in different parts of your house. No, we're not talking about what CDs you're going to play, but rather what kind of flexibility your system has to play *different* audio sources in different parts of the house simultaneously.

In a *single-zone audio system,* you have only one audio source distributed to every endpoint across the network at any given time. You can turn various sets of speakers on or off, but you don't have the ability to listen to different audio sources in different parts of your house at the same time. A *multizone audio system,* such as the one shown in Figure 18-1, on the other hand, allows one family member to listen to, say, a CD in the family room while another person listens to the audio channel of a DVD in his or her bedroom. Some multizone systems will let you get really fancy and will let you share source devices in multiple locations throughout the home, while others will distribute audio sources from one location to multiple places within the home — in other words, some will play equipment from your home theater anywhere, while others will play equipment from all over the home in any room you choose.

Single-zone systems are easier and cheaper to build, but obviously less flexible than multizone systems. The good news is that the basic architecture (the wires you put in your walls) is usually the same for both types of systems. So you can install an inexpensive single-zone system and then upgrade your equipment to multizone later on.

Figure 18-1:
A simple,
multizone
audio
network.

Using speaker wires to build an audio network

The traditional way to expand an audio network is to simply extend in-the-wall speaker wires from your home theater or media center to remote locations in your house (anywhere you want to have audio). Remember that you need to use UL-rated CL3 speaker wires — given the distances traversed by these wires, we recommend 14-gauge or smaller wires. Refer to Figure 18-1 for a look at a simple multizone audio system. Chapter 16 explains cables and wires in more detail.

If your A/V receiver has multiroom capability, you can connect these speaker wires directly to your receiver by using a device called an *impedance matching system* (which we describe in more detail in the sidebar, "A word about impedance matching systems"). This device is necessary when you are connecting more than one pair of speakers to a single pair of speaker terminals on a receiver or amplifier — if you're just hooking up one set of speakers to that multiroom output, you can skip the impedance matching system.

A better way to use those speaker wire connections to multiple remote rooms is to use a special-purpose, multiroom, integrated amplifier. These devices contain individual pairs of amplifiers for each remote pair of speakers, so you don't need an impedance matching system, and you get plenty of power (and volume) in remote rooms. You can get multiroom integrated amplifiers in both single-zone and multizone configurations. These integrated amplifiers are available from companies such as Niles Audio (www.nilesaudio.com).

How do I connect source devices to my multiroom system?

Most audio source devices (such as CD players) have only one set of audio outputs on the back, and you probably already have this set connected to your A/V receiver. So how can you also feed this audio into a separate multi-room amplifier system? There are two options (besides buying a second CD player).

The easiest (and cheapest) way to do this is to use a Y-splitter audio cable that splits a single pair of stereo audio signals into two pairs. One branch of the Y goes to your A/V receiver, and the other to your multiroom system. You can buy these cables at Radio Shack and similar retailers.

Some multiroom installations use separate amplifiers for each zone. In these systems, you need more than a simple two-for-one split from a Y-splitter. The solution here is to use a *signal distribution amplifier*. This device takes the output of a source device, splits it into multiple outputs, and then amplifies these outputs to ensure that your signal is not degraded (if you split the signal without amplifying it, it could be too weak and would cause distortion that you would hear as a background noise or hiss). This is the best approach if you are using separate amplifiers for each remote pair of speakers.

 If you want to create a relatively inexpensive two-zone audio system, look for a multizone A/V receiver that has *line-level* outputs, instead of speaker-level outputs, for the second zone. With these systems, you can simply plug the receiver into a single-zone, multiroom, integrated amplifier using a pair of standard audio interconnect cables. Your home theater is Zone 1, and the rest of your house is Zone 2. It's not as good as a true multizone system, but a lot cheaper and easier to set up.

Besides a centralized amplifier/control system and speaker wires in the wall, you, of course, need to install speakers in the remote rooms. Most folks decide to use *in-wall* speaker systems (often placing these speakers in the ceiling), but you can also install speaker terminal wall jacks and then use standard loudspeakers. You connect the loudspeakers to these wall jacks just as you might connect them to the back of a receiver.

Controlling whole-home audio with IR

The other big challenge for a whole-home audio system is controlling your A/V components from remote rooms. Remember that most A/V components use IR (infrared) remote control systems, and that IR doesn't travel through walls and other obstacles. So you'll need a remote control system that can carry IR signals from IR sensors (that you simply aim a remote control at) or wall-mounted volume controls and keypads in your remote rooms. These whole-home IR systems typically require special three-conductor IR cabling, but can also be carried over other cables, such as CAT-5e computer network cables or even over the RG6 coaxial cables that carry video signals around the house from an antenna or cable TV service.

You need a few components to connect a whole-home IR system together:

✔ **IR sensors or keypads in remote rooms:** These are the end of the line for your IR network. Each run of IR cable terminates in one of these devices. IR sensors and keypads send IR control signals over the IR cabling as electrical signals.

✔ **An IR connecting block in your media hub:** This device connects to the other end of the IR cable runs and *concentrates* the IR signals they carry into outputs that can control your A/V components. You need a connecting block because you want only one IR input connected to each component in your system, but you have IR sensors or keypads in multiple rooms. The connecting block allows, for example, the IR signals coming from five different rooms to be sent to a single CD player.

✔ **IR emitters (IR blasters):** These devices run from the connecting block to the components themselves. IR emitters have only one function in life: They convert the electrical control signals back into IR (light) signals that A/V components can understand.

Building a whole-home IR distribution system is a relatively complicated process. The hardest part is programming keypads and getting the right IR signals to the right A/V components. We highly recommend that you work with a professional installer if you want to implement a whole-home IR network.

CAT-5e or wireless audio distribution systems can often carry IR control signals for you, so you won't need a separate IR network.

Plugging into CAT-5e

Aside from speaker cabling, you have other whole-home audio cabling options, such as CAT-5e. Systems from a variety of manufacturers can successfully carry line-level audio signals (the signals carried over audio interconnects) over CAT-5e cables in your walls. On the inexpensive end, you can get systems that convert the left and right line-level outputs of an audio device into a balanced signal. If high-end is your thing, go all the way with full-fledged, expensive audio (and video!) distribution systems that provide true multizone audio over CAT-5e.

You can distribute audio signals around the home using CAT-5e in three major ways, which we discuss in the following sections.

Point to point with baluns

Baluns are deployed in pairs for point-to-point use — meaning that it sends a signal from one place to a single other location (as opposed to a *point-to-multipoint* system, which can send a signal to multiple different locations). A *balun* is just a little passive device (meaning it doesn't need any external power), about the size of a deck of cards, with receptacles on both sides (an RJ-45 on one side and two or more RCA jacks on the other). One balun is associated with the source device (such as a CD player or the Audio Out ports of a receiver). This balun connects through an RCA audio interconnect to the left and right Audio Out channels. Then, you plug the balun into the CAT-5e cable by using a CAT-5e patch cable. At the other end of the network — down another leg of your home's CAT-5e that you've dedicated to audio — the process is reversed. The second balun plugs into the RJ-45 outlet on your wall (again using a patch cable), and then plugs into the left and right Audio In jacks of the remote amplifier or receiver that you're feeding the signal to. An example of one of these products is MuxLab's Stereo Hi-Fi Balun (www.muxlab.com).

You can also find baluns that can distribute digital audio signals — like the *bitstream* outputs of DVD players and other Dolby Digital or DTS sources — over CAT-5e cables. In many cases, these baluns can carry high-quality component video signals as well. An example of such a product is Intelix's (www.intelix.com) V3AD HDTV Component Video and Digital Audio over CAT-5 Balun. These units can connect to any source device with component video and coaxial digital audio outputs and send the signal over up to 1,000 feet of CAT-5e cabling.

Most folks find that these sort of baluns are most useful not for sending signals to a second room, but rather for use *within* a larger home theater room. For example, if you are trying to hide your source components within a closet or equipment room on one side of a large home theater room and are installing a display and speakers rather far away, you can use inexpensive CAT-5e cabling and baluns rather than running more expensive audio and video cables.

Single-zone CAT-5e audio-distribution systems

In the world of audio and CAT-5e, the next step up moves beyond the point-to-point limitation of baluns and provides a single-zone audio distribution network to multiple locations throughout the home. These systems, from vendors such as Russound (www.russound.com) and Leviton (www.leviton.com), typically use custom faceplates (the plastic plates that cover standard wall outlets) that replace standard RJ-45 faceplates in each room. These faceplates have a pair of female RCA audio jacks that can connect to any standard audio source device or amplifier/receiver. In the room containing the source device you want to share throughout the home, you simply plug a stereo audio patch cable between the device and the faceplate.

A word about impedance matching systems

When we talk about A/V receivers, and particularly about their amplifier sections, in Chapter 11, we mention that many receivers have trouble dealing with speakers with an impedance (a measure of electrical resistance) of 4 ohms or less. This really comes into play in whole-home audio systems. That's because when you try to drive two sets of speakers from the same stereo amplifier, the impedance of the speakers is effectively halved. That is to say, if you plug two sets of 8-ohm speakers into a *single* stereo amplifier, you end up with an effective impedance of 4 ohms. Add a third set, and you're in the danger zone for most receivers.

If you have a multizone audio distribution system, impedance isn't an issue (each pair of speakers has its own amplifier), but in a single-zone system, many folks try to cram multiple pairs of speakers onto a single amplifier. The safe way to do this is to use an *impedance matching* system. These systems let you hook up two, three, four, or more pairs of speakers to a single stereo amplifier without the impedance dropping to an unsafe level. Keep in mind that the amplifier power provided to these remote speakers will be reduced as you add extra sets of speakers onto the system. So the impedance matching system will protect your amplifier, but you may not get enough power to reach the volume levels you want.

In remote rooms, you use an audio patch cable to connect the faceplate to the inputs of a local receiver or amplifier. Connecting these remote outlets is a special CAT-5e audio hub located in your wiring closet. This hub takes the source signal and distributes it to every other CAT-5e outlet connected to the hub.

Multizone CAT-5e audio-distribution systems

If you want the utmost in flexibility and capability in a CAT-5e-based audio-distribution system, you need a system that can carry different audio programs to different parts of the house simultaneously — a multizone, multisource system. Like the multizone speaker-level systems discussed earlier in the chapter, multizone CAT-5e systems are high-end solutions that don't come cheap, but they can offer the utmost in sound quality and convenience. Because sending audio over CAT-5e is still new, it's not cheap. You'll probably end up paying $1,000 or more for the components alone, and that doesn't include the speakers and amplifiers or receivers in each room. And that's for the (relatively) cheap versions of these systems. Some high-end systems can cost tens of thousands of dollars. You can get systems from players such as Crestron (www.crestron.com), Russound (www.russound.com), and Niles Audio (www.nilesaudio.com).

Going wireless

The most popular way of getting audio around the house without a dedicated network is with an RF (radio frequency) wireless system. These come in two main flavors:

- ✔ **Wireless speaker systems** connect to the line-level outputs of a source device or preamplifier and send the signal over a 900 MHz or 2.4 GHz channel to a pair of self-amplified stereo speakers.

- ✔ **Wireless line-level distribution systems** hook up to your source components in the same fashion but send their signals to a receiver that hooks into your own amplifier and speakers on the far end.

One major potential difficulty with many wireless systems is that they use a line-level input — something that most source devices have only one of. So you may run into trouble hooking up a CD player, for example, to both your A/V receiver (or controller) for local listening and to one of these devices for remote listening. Luckily, many of these units also accept the output of your receiver or amp's headphone jack, so you can avoid this problem if you have a headphone jack available. Alternatively, you can use one of the Y-splitter audio cables we mention in the sidebar, "How do I connect source devices to my multiroom system?" earlier in this chapter. Prices for these wireless systems range from about $75 to $200. Major manufacturers include

- ✔ Recoton (www.recoton.com)
- ✔ RCA (www.rca.com)
- ✔ Logitech (www.logitech.com)

Another cool wireless product comes from the X10 Wireless Technologies folks (www.x10.com). (You probably know them from their infamous Internet pop-up ads on many popular Web sites.) X10's MP3 Anywhere system ($79.99) works like the other systems we describe, but it's available with a feature that we think is pretty cool: X10's BOOM! software. This software runs on your Windows PC and lets you remotely control and access the PC's MP3 music files as well as CDs and DVDs played back in the PC's internal drive. RCA (www.rca.com) has a $99 Lyra Wireless RD900W that lets you play PC-based music through the stereo, too.

The current state-of-the-art in wireless audio distribution systems involve those systems that use 802.11 (Wi-Fi) wireless networking to distribute audio around the home. Our current favorite system is the Sonos Digital Music System (www.sonos.com). The baseline Sonos system (the "introductory bundle") starts at $1,195 and supports two rooms.

This technogeek's dream system consists of a controller (the brains of the system), a "zone" player (the endpoints of the system where all the speaker and system interfaces are housed, as well as a four-port switch so that you can network other items in the vicinity — nice!), and matching speakers you can use if you want everything to match.

Most buyers of the Sonos system also buy a local NAS (Network Attached Storage) hard drive because the Sonos itself doesn't have one — a non-NAS system just plays music found elsewhere, like on your PC. You can also have more than one Sonos zone player; the players talk to each other and the controller in a "mesh" fashion (meaning the signal can hop from station to station, rather than only radiating out from the main base station), so if you have a really long house, you can still use the Sonos system. In such instances, the Sonos system synchronizes the music so that it all plays at the same time, avoiding any weird echo-type sounds around the house. Sonos uses 802.11g for its wireless protocol — but doesn't connect to your Wi-Fi access points (it creates its own "mesh" network) — hopping from Sonos to Sonos throughout your home.

Sharing Video Components throughout the Home

Sharing video in the home used to be a lot simpler a few years ago than it is today. This is largely due to the advent of all sorts of signal encryption as well as the introduction of digital transmissions into the mix. These have added their unique flies in the whole-home networking ointment.

You can share home theater video signals within your home (speaking generally here, of course) in four major ways:

- ✔ Use *modulators* to send your video over the coaxial cable carrying your antenna or cable TV signal
- ✔ Use a CAT-5e audio/video distribution system
- ✔ Use a wireless audio/video distribution system
- ✔ Use a system that carries audio and video over your existing phone wires

As the price of video source devices (like DVD players) plummets, the economics of creating a video distribution network in your home turns on its head. A few years ago, when DVD players cost $500 apiece, it made sense to create a system that could share the DVD player in your home theater with TVs in other rooms. Now that you can buy a good quality *upconverting* DVD player for well under $100, most folks simply choose to have an extra set of video source devices in remote locations. You may, however, run into a situation in which you'd like to share some sources in your home theater with displays in other parts of the home — in the following section, we tell you how to do so.

Using your TV cables

Most structured cabling systems (complete prepackaged home wiring products) include a centralized video distribution system. This system differs from the standard cable company installations in one big way. Most cable installations use a *branch and tree* architecture, with the cable coming into your house from the street and then being fed into a series of *splitters* — little "one in, two out" devices that split a cable signal into two branches. A centralized video distribution system uses a special splitter, called a *video distribution panel,* that splits the incoming cable (or antenna) signal into multiple lines running to all of your TVs — each a home run cable in a hub-and-spoke architecture.

With a central video distribution panel, you can create your own in-house television channels using modulators over your in-home coax cables. Simply put, a *modulator* takes the composite or S-Video output of a video source device (as well as the stereo analog audio outputs) and transforms it into an RF (radio frequency) signal — just like a television station does. You simply set the modulator to broadcast over an unused channel and connect it to your video distribution panel. When you want to watch that source somewhere else in the house, you just need to tune your remote TV to that station, and voilà!

Figure 18-2 shows a modulated signal (in this case, a VCR, but it can be any video source, such as a DVD player or a DSS satellite receiver).

Figure 18-2:
Watching a
VCR in
another
room.

Modulator systems don't work for everybody. New digital cable systems are designed to use all or most of the available spectrum on your home's coax network, so carving out bandwidth for your piggyback data transmission is not so easy. In many instances, it's almost impossible. You are likely better off pursuing some of the nonmodulator alternatives we're about to discuss instead.

CAT-5e and wireless systems

Many of the CAT-5e and wireless systems we discuss earlier in the chapter can carry video signals in addition to audio signals. In the case of CAT-5e systems, we think that you can actually get a higher-quality video signal around the house than you can with a modulator system. That's because the process of modulating and then *demodulating* a video source (when it gets back into your remote TV) tends to diminish your picture quality. Some of these CAT-5e systems can even carry component signals and digital audio for high-quality video (even HDTV!) and *surround sound* audio in remote locations. (You need an A/V receiver and surround speakers in these remote locations to take advantage of this.)

A simpler way of getting video around the house is to use a phone line system. The Leapfrog HomeNetwork by Terk (a division of Audiovox, www.audiovox. com) is a device — or rather a pair of devices — that transmits video and/or audio signals from a source device (such as a satellite receiver or PVR) to a remote location over existing phone lines. The pair's transmitter half connects to the source unit's RF or line-level video and audio outputs and plugs into a standard phone jack. At the remote end, the receiver also plugs into a phone jack and connects to the RF or line-level audio and video inputs of the remote television or audio system. The Leapfrog also carries infrared control signals over your phone lines, so you can carry your remote with you to the room containing the receiver and do all the pausing, fast-forwarding, and channel-changing you like without running back and forth.

Interfacing with Your Telephone System

The days are gone when the telephone was simply something you had a conversation over. Indeed, your telephone system now can also be a data access point for dialup Internet access, an inbound interface to your system from afar, and even an in-home interface to your home automation system. (And you thought it was just a phone.)

At the simplest level, devices need to meet baseline requirements in order to interconnect with your telephone system. Your DSS receiver, for instance, requires a phone line interface so that the receiver can access your account database in order to track on-line movie purchases. And some of the gaming consoles enable you to compete in multiplayer networks via dialup connections (although after you try broadband, you'll never go back to dialup).

Nothing about interconnecting your home theater to your home telephone system is overtly complex. At the basic level, you simply plug any device that requires a phone connection into the nearest outlet. If you have multiple devices, they can share a single wall outlet if you use an inexpensive 2-in-1 jack adapter ($5 from Radio Shack).

If you don't have a phone outlet nearby, you can get a wireless phone jack (like RCA's RC926) for around $80 that uses the electrical lines in your house to transmit your telephone communications. You plug a standard telephone line into an adapter that plugs into the electrical outlet at your home theater. Then, in a room where there *is* an available phone outlet, you do the same, only this time you run a phone cable from the electrical outlet into the phone outlet. Shazaam! — one phone line.

Do not use a wireless phone jack with a surge protector because this may block the frequencies over which your phone line communicates; plug the unit directly into the wall.

A nice little device is the TV Messenger (www.smarthome.com, $79.99), which shows you on your TV screen who is calling during your favorite TV show so you know whether you want to get up to answer the phone. When the phone rings, the TV Messenger automatically pops up the Caller ID info on the top of the TV screen without interrupting the program. If you subscribe to phone-company voice mail, the LED blinks when messages are waiting, too. You want to use this only for your analog TV signals because you don't want to limit your higher-quality DVD and other video to composite connections (all that the device offers). The TV Messenger sits in-line to your video signal between the TV source and the receiver, connected via a simple composite video interconnect cable.

Connecting to Your Computer LAN

We talk in Chapter 2 about having a wiring closet for your Ethernet hubs and routers, in Chapter 6 about Ethernet ports on your DVRs, in Chapter 9 about gaming consoles with network interfaces, and so on. Computer networks are becoming an important part of your home theater infrastructure.

Accessing a whole-home computer network (also know as a *local area network* — LAN for short) opens up your home theater to any data point on your network. A good example is Danny's AudioReQuest CD server. It has an onboard Web server that allows access to this music from wherever he wants, in the house or over the Internet. He can synchronize his boxes in Maine and Connecticut because they are connected to the Internet. As soon as he finishes this book, he's going to extend that to synching with his car stereos, too — over wireless computer network connections. The same is true with his SnapStream PVR. He can record programs while he is away and download them from anywhere on the planet. Now he can catch up on *The Sopranos* from Kiev!

While we've not heard of anyone having this problem, it is possible that your ISP (Internet service provider) may forbid this kind of "server" connection. Most ISPs have absolutely frightening "terms of service" agreements that forbid just about everything but checking your e-mail and surfing the Web on your connection. Most of these agreements are not strictly observed, but if you start really using a lot of bandwidth, your ISP may either make you stop or make you pay for a more expensive connection.

Getting your home theater devices to communicate with your computer network is getting easier all the time thanks to newer technologies, lower costs, and equipment vendors' increased experience with the consumer market. It's getting to be almost automatic!

We talk about Ethernet networks because, frankly, you're unlikely to want another protocol on your computer network. You could use other LAN systems (like ATM), but Ethernet really rules the computing domain.

Accordingly, it's likely — very likely — that you'll connect your home theater with your computer LAN over Ethernet connections.

So, assuming this is the case, the question then becomes, "How do you interconnect with that LAN?" Well, it depends on the extent of your LAN, if it exists at all. Although we don't have space in this book to discuss all the ins and outs of computer networking, we want to offer a little guidance to help you on your way toward a whole-home computing backbone that can make use of your home theater system. Here are a few networking points to keep in mind:

> ✔ **You can carry data signals around your house in at least four major ways: CAT-5e cabling, wireless, electrical cables, and regular phone wiring and coaxial cables.** We recommend, if you can do it, that you run new CAT-5e cables through your walls to the places where you want it. If you use CAT-5e for your audio or video distribution, then you are likely building a new home or renovating your current one, and running the cable shouldn't be a problem. A wired infrastructure gives you much higher data rates, more reliability, and more flexibility for the future — and it can add to the value of your home.

✔ **Wireless options are great.** These are quickly coming down in price, and you can build a home data network just by adding a *wireless access point* to your network. (A wireless access point is a base station of a wireless network — think of it as the equivalent of a cordless phone base station.) You then bring your devices on-line by adding *PC cards* (which plug into standardized PC card slots on the device) or USB-based *dongles* (or adapters) that plug into the USB ports. Most devices follow the 54 Mbps 802.11g wireless standard, and a few use the 802.11a standard, which provides the same speed using different frequencies (which are less crowded with cordless phones and the like). Some time in the next year, you'll start seeing new wireless gear based on the forthcoming 802.11n standard, which will provide speeds in excess of 100 Mbps. (The final standard is still up in the air as we write, and may offer speeds nearly double that.)

✔ **You can transmit signals over electrical cables, too.** The trick here is to use low-cost devices that conform to the HomePlug standard — a standard networking protocol for Ethernet connections using AC power-lines. This standard allows up to 14 Mbps transmission rates (85 Mbps with the newest "Turbo" units), but speeds vary substantially based on where you plug in the devices and what is turned on at any particular time. NETGEAR (www.netgear.com) is one big vendor of HomePlug gear, with the Model XE102 wall-plugged Ethernet bridge that enables you to build a complete home network by doing nothing more than plugging devices into the electrical outlets. Pretty cool. In fact, a whole-home computer network for less than $50 a room is very cool. Want to add a room? Plug in an electrical module. Done.

The folks who create the underlying HomePlug technology have a new variant in the wings — HomePlug AV — which will provide speeds up to 200 Mbps. Check out www.homeplug.org for more information about this new standard and for product availability.

✔ **You can also use the coaxial cables and phone lines in your house to send signals from room to room.** A few networking systems use unused higher frequencies on the cable to send the data, so you can still talk on the phone or watch video at the same time. This is based on the Home Phoneline Networking Alliance (HPNA) standards. In general, the other options we mention are preferable to HPNA at this time, but new, faster versions of HPNA have been promised. Check out www.homepna.com for information about product availability.

Some new systems use coaxial (cable TV) cables to send data around the house. MoCA (Multimedia over Coax Alliance, www.mocalliance.com), for example, can provide speeds of up to 200 Mbps over these cables. Another similar technology, TVnet by Coaxsys (www.coaxsys.com), provides speeds of up to 70 Mbps. MoCA and TVnet are not products you can just go out and buy at the store, however. Instead, they are going to be built into devices, like cable set-top boxes, to allow cable companies to send TV signals between boxes in the home.

✔ **If you have a high-speed cable, DSL, or satellite Internet connection, you have your high-speed Internet modem located somewhere on your network.** It does not matter where you put the modem, from the home theater perspective, because there really is no specific reason the broadband Internet connection has to be located within your theater room. In fact, most people like to put their modem either close to their computing area or in the wiring closet, out of sight.

✔ **You need a router if you want to support multiple Ethernet devices on one network and have them interface with the Internet.** Often, the DSL/cable/satellite modem is also a router, but not always. The router has a built-in hub that enables you to interconnect multiple data lines.

✔ **If you are going to be routing video or large files over your LAN, consider getting an Ethernet *switch* instead of a hub** so that you can make sure you get all the bandwidth you need for a quality transmission. (Most routers include an Ethernet switch, but you may need an external switch with more ports if you have lots of devices on your network.)

Although many vendors will try to push you into one solution ("You need Wi-Fi." "No, you need HomePlug."), you might find that these various networks can complement each other. You know that we think a wired CAT-5e network should be the basis of your computer-LAN infrastructure (and phone network, and maybe even your audio and video network). But we also think that all the data networking technologies can be used in concert when you build a whole-home network.

Just for fun, here are a few examples:

✔ Build a wired Ethernet LAN but add a Wi-Fi access point in your living room for cordless, sofa-based Web surfing.

✔ Use Wi-Fi as the basis for your home-computer LAN, but use HomePlug or HPNA to extend your network to access points in distant locations out of reach of your primary base station (such as by the pool).

✔ Use wired Ethernet for your computers, but use a HomePlug system to connect your Xbox to the broadband Internet connection for on-line gaming.

We could keep this list going and going, but we think you get the picture. Think creatively and use wired and unwired technologies together to get your LAN wherever you need it to go.

Part V
Letting Your Home Theater Be All It Can Be

The 5th Wave   By Rich Tennant

In this part . . .

*I*n this part, we get a bit fancy. It's all about what to do after everything is put together. First, we discuss how to use the controls on your video systems (your television and your video source devices) to get the best picture possible.

We also discuss how to tweak your audio system so that you can adjust it to the dynamics of *your* home theater. Our friends in the installation business are constantly amazed at how bad good audio gear can sound if it's not set up properly. Conversely, even modestly priced gear can sound great if it's properly tweaked.

We also talk about ways you can improve your home theater's environment. If you think about it, home theater is really all about creating light and sound that you can interact with. If you keep environmental lights and sounds from interfering with your theater, you can get more enjoyment out of your gear.

Finally, we talk about the high end of home theater and how to go all out in pursuit of a home theater experience. Even if you have budget limitations, you can get a preview of the future of home theater.

Chapter 19

Tweaking Your A/V System

*G*etting your A/V system hooked up can be a bit of a challenge, but it's rewarding to have all that "on your hands and knees" plug-fest work behind you. You have to take one more step, however, before you sit back and really enjoy your home theater. You need to spend some time tweaking your system — adjusting the video display and getting your surround sound set up properly.

In this chapter, we discuss ways to calibrate your system. This may seem like overkill to some folks, but it is critical. Joel Silver, the president of the Imaging Science Foundation — these folks know a thing or two about setting up home theaters! — tells us that over 90 percent of home theater displays are set up incorrectly. With a few tools, you can be part of the small percentage of home theater owners who are getting the most out of what they've paid for.

Calibrating Your Video

We've said it before — and we'll say it again, because it's important — most displays come from the factory improperly calibrated. The brightness and color are set at unnatural levels in order to make the displays stand out on the showroom floor (in a brightly lit store). At these settings, if you put them in a darkened home theater, the picture looks awful.

If you have a direct-view or projection CRT (cathode ray tube) or a plasma display, you have an additional reason to calibrate your video: The overly bright settings that most of these units come with can reduce the lifespan of your display! Even if your display is not brand new or not all that fancy, a calibration can breathe new life into your picture quality.

On your average display, you (as a nontechnician) can make five adjustments. A few sets let you adjust more, and service techs with the proper manuals and codes to get into the service menus of the display can adjust just about anything. But an average person (like you or us) can adjust the following controls:

- ✔ **Contrast (white level):** Don't confuse this with *contrast ratio,* which we discuss earlier in the book. (It's the ratio between the brightest and darkest images a display can create, if you didn't get to that part of the book yet.) In terms of display adjustments, your contrast control adjusts the *white level,* or degree of whiteness your screen displays. You see, in video displays, whites and blacks are measured on a scale called IRE (Institute of Radio Engineers) units, which are represented as a percentage: 0 percent is black; 100 percent is white. You can actually drive your TV beyond 100 percent if your contrast is improperly set. If you do this, white portions of your picture tend to bleed over into the darker portions surrounding them.

- ✔ **Brightness (black level):** Now to throw in a counterintuitive statement: The brightness control on your display actually adjusts the *black level* that you see on the screen. Weird, huh? If the black level is set incorrectly, you can't discern the difference between darker images on your screen.

- ✔ **Sharpness:** The sharpness control adjusts the *fine detail* of the picture — its ability to display minute details on the screen. If the sharpness is set too low, you have a fuzzy picture; if it's set too high, your picture appears *edgy,* often with blobs around the edges of objects instead of clearly defined lines.

- ✔ **Color:** Along with tint (which we discuss next), color is one of the two controls that let you set the balance of the colors (finally, a name that says what it means!) on your display. If your color setting is too low, images begin to appear as black and white. If it's too high, images take on a reddish tinge (for example, Nicole Kidman's face will turn as red as her hair).

- ✔ **Tint (hue):** On most TVs, this control is labeled *tint,* but a few are more technically correct and call it *hue.* The tint control adjusts your display's color within a range between red and green — your job will be to find the perfect balance between them.

Almost every display we know of has an on-screen display that shows the status of these settings. Typically, you'll find a horizontal bar running across your screen, with either a moving vertical hash mark that shows your current setting, or the entire bar moves left or right as you increase or decrease these settings. Some displays also have a numeric display (usually running from 0 to 100) that shows your current setting.

We like the numeric displays because writing down a number is much easier (if you want to re-create a setting in the future) than trying to remember exactly how far across the screen a particular bar was.

Using a calibration disc

The best way to adjust your video is to use a DVD *home theater calibration disc*. We consider these discs (which cost about $50) to be an absolutely essential investment in your home theater. Unless you've had a professional calibrate your system (or you've spent so much on everything else that you can't afford the disc), we think you simply must get one of these discs. (And no, no one is paying us to say that.)

The most common home theater calibration discs are the following:

✔ **Avia: Guide to Home Theater:** Available from Ovation Multimedia (www.ovationmultimedia.com), this disc contains a ton of great background material about home theater. It explains a lot of the same stuff we talk about here in *Home Theater For Dummies*. It also contains a series of easy-to-follow on-screen test patterns and signals that let you correctly adjust all the settings we discuss in the preceding section. It also gives you test tones to help calibrate your surround sound audio systems (which we discuss in a moment). This disc runs $49.95 directly from Ovation.

We suspect most folks will find it to be overkill, but Ovation also produces a professional-quality variant of its test disc, the Avia PRO. This $400 set consists of seven DVDs and an elaborate user manual for the ultimate in calibration.

✔ **Digital Video Essentials:** Found on-line at www.videoessentials.com, this is the definitive calibration disc. One really cool thing about Video Essentials is the inclusion of video footage that you can watch to see the results of your adjustments with actual video, instead of just on a test pattern. Digital Video Essentials lists for $24.95 and is widely available on-line.

The folks at Joe Kane Productions (who created Digital Video Essentials) also have a six-disc professional set called *Digital Video Essentials Professional,* which retails for $350 and includes some high-definition calibrations (using the Windows Media system for high-definition 720p and 1080i signals). Again, like the Avia PRO, this is probably overkill for most folks (you can probably have a pro calibrate your display for less money), but we wanted to let you know this was out there.

✔ *Sound & Vision* **Home Theater Tune-up:** This one is also produced by Ovation Software, but in conjunction with *Sound & Vision* magazine (one of our favorites). In addition to general display calibration, this disc includes tests that demonstrate aspect ratios and let you test your S-Video and component video outputs on your DVD player (to see which works better in your system). You can find the disc (priced at only $21.95) at http://shop.soundandvisionmag.com.

We like all three of these discs and would be hard pressed to recommend one. The Avia and *Sound & Vision* discs are probably the best bet for regular people (in other words, people who aren't trained video calibrators). Video Essentials is geared more for the professional. Avia is probably a bit more detailed and comprehensive, whereas the *Sound & Vision* disc is a bit easier for first-time users. Either one (any of the three, actually) gives you a better picture.

Though none are available yet, we fully expect that high-definition versions of these discs will be available in the new Blu-ray and HD-DVD formats that are hitting the market as we write. Given the relatively low price of the traditional discs we discuss above, we don't recommend that you wait for the high-def versions, but if these are available when you are building your home theater, they'll probably be worth purchasing.

When you buy one of these discs, you'll notice that a blue filter comes in the package. Don't toss it in the trash on the mistaken assumption that it's an especially pretty piece of packaging — you need this filter when adjusting some of the color and tint settings on your display. You look through the filter to block out certain light frequencies.

Using one of these discs is a fairly simple process — one we don't try to re-create here step by step because the on-screen audio and text instructions do a better job than we can in a book. Before you adjust any of these settings, get up off your comfy home theater seating and close the blinds! Ambient lighting has an immense effect on what you see on your screen (regardless of what type of display you have). So lower the blinds, close the door, and dim the lights. You want to adjust your picture in exactly the same lighting conditions that you'll have when you sit down to play movies or watch TV in your home theater. Then just follow the instructions on the DVD, step-by-step. It's easy, and it's even kind of fun.

When you're all done, you'll notice that your picture looks different. (We sure hope it does!) It's going to look darker. If you're not used to a calibrated video picture, this might be a bit disconcerting. Give yourself some time to get used to it, though, and you'll notice a more detailed picture, a picture that looks more like the movies. And isn't that what you're after in a home theater?

Some displays come from the factory either pretty well calibrated or with a picture *mode* you can select on your remote that will set your picture close to the state it would be in after you manually calibrated it. Sony displays are famous for this (Sony calls this their "Pro" mode), as are some of the high-end displays made by Loewe (www.loewe.de) and Princeton Graphics (www.princetongraphics.com). Read the reviews before you buy. Although you still may want to tweak the display a bit with a calibration disc, it's very handy to have it be 99 percent of the way there with the push of a single button (or right out of the box).

Using an optical comparator

If you want to get really fancy with your home theater calibration process, you might consider not relying on your eyeballs and instead use a tool called an *optical comparator* or a *colorimeter*. These devices are simply machines that can analyze the colors and patterns on a screen with a much higher degree of accuracy than you'll be able to do with your naked eyes.

Using an optical comparator or colorimeter can be especially useful if you are one of those folks with some degree of color blindness (which can include, depending on which study you believe, up to 1 in 12 men).

For the most part, these color-sensing devices are too expensive for the average home theater — you can buy a 50-inch high-definition plasma TV for the price of many common hardware kits. For example, Ovation Multimedia's OpticONE system, a popular hardware and software solution, retails for $2,200. Consequently, many folks turn to professional system calibrators (discussed in the upcoming section, "Hiring a professional") who can amortize this investment over a number of customers.

But there *are* solutions that are in the price range of mere mortals, like ColorVision's Datacolor SpyderTV ($249, www.colorvision.com). (The SpyderTV is so named because it has spiderlike suction-cup legs that stick to your display — ignoring the fact that it has three, not eight legs!).

To use the SpyderTV you simply stick the unit's suction cups to the front of your display and then plug the USB cable running out of the SpyderTV into your computer (Windows 2000 or XP is required, and a laptop is a heck of a lot more convenient for this task but is not required). Then place the supplied test pattern DVD in your DVD player and you're ready to start.

For flat-panel plasma and LCD displays, the SpyderTV includes a special suction-cup attachment device — you're not supposed to use the suction cups built into the three legs of the SpyderTV for these kinds of displays.

After everything is hooked up, you just need to follow the steps included in the SpyderTV software running on your PC (it comes on a separate CD with the rest of the SpyderTV gear). Have your display's remote handy and follow the on-screen steps to tweak your TV's display settings. This all takes 40 minutes or more, so have a little patience (that's one reason why the pros charge hundreds of dollars to do a calibration), but the end result should be a better and more lifelike picture.

Although we didn't have a big issue with this personally, some folks have complained that it's a bit tricky to get the SpyderTV attached to your display. You may want to consider mounting the unit on a tripod in front of your display if the suction cups don't work well for you.

Other tuning system options

If you haven't had a chance to get your hands on one of the home theater calibration discs, but you still want to improve your picture, you can do a couple of things.

One way to get a subset of the video tests on these discs is to play a movie DVD that contains the *THX Optimizer*. You find this somewhere in the disc's main menu (usually in the Special Features section). Like the discs we describe earlier, the Optimizer walks you through a series of steps to adjust your display (and your audio system). All THX-certified DVDs released since 2000 (including Pat's daughter's favorite, *The Lion King*) include the THX optimizer. You can find more detail, including instructions on THX's Web site (www.thx.com/mod/products/dvd/optimizerIntro.html). Now if he could just teach her to calibrate the plasma for him . . . ; maybe when she turns 3 she'll be able to!

You can find more detail, including instructions on THX's Web site (www.thx.com/mod/products/dvd/optimizerIntro.html).

With this program, you still need that blue filter; if you didn't get one with the DVD itself (and you probably didn't), you can get one for free from THX by filling out the order form on-line. (You do have to pay a couple of bucks for shipping and handling.)

We recommend that you at least rent one of the movies on the THX Web site so you can use the Optimizer. You can adjust your video just by eyeballing it. We recommend that, at a minimum, you turn down the brightness until the level is about ⅓ of the way across your screen, but using a test disc or the Optimizer is much, much easier and more accurate.

Getting your projector in focus

If you have a projection TV system (front or rear) and it uses cathode ray tubes (CRTs) to create its picture, getting your set calibrated is a bit more intense. In addition to all the color/hue/sharpness/brightness/contrast stuff we discuss elsewhere in this chapter, you need to *converge* these displays. Converging is the process of aligning the three separate CRTs (one each for red, green, and blue) inside these projectors so that the image projected by each CRT is exactly superimposed onto the other two. Misconvergence is obvious when you see it (the edges of images are red, green, and blue "halos" instead of a single sharp image) and is really painful to watch.

For most CRT projection systems, you need a professional to calibrate the convergence of your display. A few rear-projection models (RPTVs), from companies such as Hitachi (www.hitachi.com), are now available with automatic convergence systems. Just a few years ago (in the mid 1990s), this feature alone cost more (as an option for expensive projector systems) than an *entire* HDTV-ready RPTV with automatic convergence does today. How about that for capitalism in action? Even if you have a set with automatic convergence, you might still consider a professional calibration to get the ultimate picture from your RPTV, but the automatic convergence is *much* better than doing nothing.

One way to get your display dialed in at least somewhat close to an optimal calibration is to read the posts about your particular TV or monitor on the AVS Forum Web site (www.avsforum.com). Many models have ongoing threads for owners, and you'll often find other people's calibration advice within these forums. Remember that not every unit is going to be exactly the same. (There are always at least minor variations in manufacturing, and over time, the settings can change a bit — for example, as a projector's light bulb gets dimmer.) But you can at least find out what works for other folks and try it out as an initial setting until you do a more formal calibration.

Hiring a professional

You may decide — either right up front or after you realize that you just can't handle that remote control very well — that you want a professional to calibrate your display. Well, that's nothing to be ashamed of. In fact, if you can afford it, we highly recommend that you consider having a professional calibrate your system. They have tools (such as light meters) that you just don't have, and their calibration is more precise and ultimately better than anything you can do with a calibration DVD and your eyeballs.

Great DVDs to put your system through its paces

After your video system is calibrated and ready to go, it's time to start watching some movies. Why not enjoy the view with some real classics and with some newer movies that can really test the limits of your system's capabilities. For some reason, most home theater enthusiasts love action movies (but hey, who doesn't?) and trot out their well-worn copies of *Terminator 2* and *The Matrix*. These are indeed fun to watch in your home theater, and they can be demanding discs (*The Matrix*, in particular, seemed to overpower many early DVD players), but you also might want to check out some other films that show off your home theater in subtler ways. The ISF (yep, the same guys we mention elsewhere in this chapter) has a list of films that it recommends to its affiliated dealers as great demo discs. You can find this list on-line at `www.filmsondisc.com/ISF_Referen ce_DVD_Program.htm`. You may even be surprised to find favorites like *Muppets from Space* and *Wayne's World* — excellent!

If you have a CRT front-projection system, you really *must* have a professional set it up. You'll waste tens of thousands of dollars if you don't. In fact, if you're buying any high-end display (such as that $17,000 61-inch HDTV plasma display Pat has his eye on — don't tell his wife!), go for a professional calibration. When you start getting into this price range, you should really expect this kind of service from your home theater dealer. A professional calibration usually costs between $200 and $500, depending on what type of display you have.

If you choose to have a professional calibration done, make sure you choose someone who has been certified and trained by the Imaging Science Foundation, or ISF (we mention them earlier in the chapter, as you might recall). The ISF has trained (and continues to train) literally thousands of home theater dealers in the art of system calibration. You can find a trained calibration professional near you by searching on ISF's Web site at www. imagingscience.com.

Don't call ISF directly asking them to calibrate your system. Those folks know how to do it, but they're in the business of training others, not coming over to your house.

Adjusting Your Audio System

Just as your display needs a tune-up to look its best, your A/V receiver (or A/V controller, if you've gone with separates) needs a once-over to ensure you get the best possible sound from your home theater. You need to do the initial setup to make sure that your A/V receiver knows what kind of speakers you're using, and then you need to adjust the amplification levels for each speaker.

Get out your A/V receiver's manual before you start doing any of the stuff we recommend. Your particular receiver may have different (but similar) terminology. The manual can also help you navigate your receiver's setup menu system.

Managing bass

Your A/V receiver sends low-frequency sounds to your subwoofer through its LFE (or low frequency effects) channel. Subwoofers are very good at one thing — reproducing bass notes — and not much good at anything else. Generally speaking, you want to send only the lowest possible frequencies to the subwoofer because you want to minimize the use of the subwoofer for relatively higher frequencies.

At the same time, you must balance this requirement with the needs of your other speakers. If you have a set of small bookshelf speakers for your center, right, left, and surround speakers, and they can't reproduce bass notes very well, you're better off letting the subwoofer handle nearly all the bass.

You need to set the speaker size for each group of speakers — center, front (or main), and surrounds. So Step 1 in setting up your audio is to go into your A/V receiver's setup or configuration menu and navigate to the menu that lets you select your speaker size. You typically have a choice of Large or Small. The Small setting cuts off the low frequencies that are sent to your main speakers (the speakers other than your subwoofer) at a higher frequency than does the Large setting. In other words, the Small setting sends almost all low-frequency audio signals to the subwoofer, whereas the Large setting sends the low frequencies to *both* the subwoofer and your other speakers.

You'll probably find a setting in this menu for the subwoofer — an On or None setting that indicates the presence or absence of the subwoofer. Make sure you select On if you have a subwoofer.

You can use two criteria to select a setting for your speakers:

✔ **Frequency range of your speakers (best):** If you have access to the manufacturer's data about your speaker, find out the frequency range at which the manufacturer rates its speakers. (You may also find this information from a reviewer who has tested the speakers.) If the low end of the speaker's frequency response is rated below 40 Hz, set your receiver to the Large setting; otherwise, use the Small setting.

✔ **Woofer size (not as good):** If you don't know how low your speakers can go, you can use the size of your speaker's woofers as a rule of thumb. If the woofers are 6 inches or larger, try the Large setting; otherwise, go with the Small setting.

If you don't know either of these things (you can always take off the speaker's grill and measure the woofer), start off with the Large setting. You can always switch over to the Small setting if you notice that your main speakers aren't handling the bass very well. (In other words, they're causing audible distortions with low-frequency audio tracks.)

If you don't have a subwoofer in your system, make sure you set the front speakers to the Large setting and set the subwoofer control to Off. Even if your other speakers are small, you need to select Large here, or you'll get absolutely no bass from your system.

Setting up surrounds

After your speakers are put in the right place (see Chapter 17), turned on, and you've selected sizes, it's time to configure your surround system. You need to configure two settings, which we describe below, and then expand upon in greater detail later in this section:

✔ **Delay:** If all your speakers are the same distance from your listening position, sounds emanating from them arrive at your ears at the same time. That's a good thing because delays in the arrival of sounds can ruin your sound field. You want sounds to have delays only when the director of the movie intends it (like when a footfall echoes behind you). If speakers aren't equidistant from the listening position, your A/V receiver can compensate with its own delay settings.

✔ **Channel Balance (or level):** Set the sound level of each speaker so that you hear an equal volume from each speaker during testing. If one speaker (or set of speakers) is too loud, you experience an unbalanced sound field while listening to your system. (When you play back actual movies or music, the volume coming from each speaker depends on the volumes encoded in the source material.)

A growing number of A/V receivers have a built-in calibration tool that uses either a microphone that's built into the receiver itself or (more commonly) an accessory microphone that comes with the receiver or that you buy separately. These systems let you skip all of the steps that follow by simply invoking the auto calibration command on the receiver. A computer within the receiver sends out test tones and automatically adjusts the receiver's settings. Some people think that they can do a better job manually — with an

SPL meter, discussed in the next section, or with the audio portion of one of the video test discs discussed above — but for the average person (and by that we mean any non–audio geek!), these automated calibration systems are a lifesaver.

Setting the delay

Depending upon your A/V receiver, you'll find two ways to set the delay: You can enter either a distance or a delay time (in milliseconds). In either case, get a tape measure and measure the distance from your listening position to each group of speakers (center, front, and surround). You should have to measure only one speaker from each group, because the left and right speakers within a group should be equidistant from your listening position. If your receiver uses distance, simply enter the number of feet that you've just measured for each group of speakers.

If the receiver uses delay settings in milliseconds, things get a bit more complicated. Typically, the delay settings are measured in relation to the main (right and left) speakers, so you enter a delay for the center channel and for the surround channel (or channels in 6.1- or 7.1-channel systems). To do this, compare the distance of the group you are setting to the distance of the main speakers. If the speakers are *farther* away, you typically set the delay to 0 milliseconds (because the added distance will naturally add a delay — so you don't want to artificially increase this delay). If they are closer than the main speakers, you set the delay to 1 millisecond for each foot. For example, if your main speakers are 9 feet from your listening position, and your center channel is 7 feet away, set the delay for 2 milliseconds.

Adjusting the channel balance

Your A/V receiver will have a special Test Tone mode designed for setting your channel balance. When you enter into this mode, the receiver generates a series of tones (at an equal amplification level) to each individual speaker in your system. The tone comes out of only one speaker at a time and shifts from speaker to speaker (either automatically or when you press a button on the remote control). The goal of this test is for you to set the level of each individual speaker until you hear an equal volume from each speaker.

Even though this test tone starts off with an equal amplification level for each speaker, you may (and probably will) hear a different volume level on the first round of the test. That's because different speakers have different *sensitivities.* (We discuss sensitivity in Chapter 12; it's a measure of how loud a speaker plays with a given power input.) Even if you had five identical speakers in your home theater (with the same sensitivity), their distance from your seating position and their acoustic interactions with the room can affect the volume you hear at your listening position.

As you run through your receiver's test mode, you can adjust the volume level of each individual speaker. Most people can do a good — not great, but very good — job at this by using their ears alone. To get your channel balance really nailed down, consider purchasing an inexpensive sound-level meter (known as an SPL — sound pressure level — meter). You can get a good one for under $50 from Radio Shack (www.radioshack.com). With a meter in hand, you can get a really accurate channel balance setting. An even better approach is to mount the meter on a tripod at your seating position — that's how the pros do it.

The test tones are also a good check to make sure your speaker wires are hooked up to the right speaker terminals on the back of your receiver (or power amplifier if you're using separates). The receiver's display (or on-screen display) tells you what speaker you should be hearing each tone from. If the display says left surround and you hear a tone from your right surround, you know that you've made a mistake!

Dealing with old-fashioned stereo sources

Although most movies are designed for surround sound listening, music is generally recorded in stereo and mixed, edited, and produced for systems with two speakers. CDs, radio, cassette tapes, and LPs are all stereo recordings. In the audio-only realm, only DVD-Audio and SACD provide multichannel surround sound–ready recordings. Indeed, not all these recordings are multichannel, as many SACDs are stereo-only.

If you take a look around your home theater, you'll see that you have at least five speakers (not counting the subwoofer). What's an audiophile to do?

Using test discs

The home theater calibration discs we discuss elsewhere in this chapter — such as the Avia disc — are for more than just adjusting the video settings on your display. They also have relatively robust and elaborate audio setup sections that can supplement the test tones built into your receiver.

For example, in addition to test tones for setting channel balance, the Avia disc has a test that lets you verify the phase of each of your speakers. Just follow the instructions on the screen, and you can find out if you've accidentally wired one of your speakers with the negative and positive terminals crossed. You can even get into more advanced tests, such as checking for room interactions with your speakers (if you're working on tweaking your speakers' positioning in the room) and voice matching, which helps you decide whether certain speakers work well together.

Well, most A/V receivers let you select whether you want to listen to stereo recordings in stereo, or *direct,* mode (through the front left and right speakers) or in a surround mode (using all your speakers). Which you use is really your preference. A/V receivers can use Dolby Pro Logic II or a custom surround mode (discussed later in this chapter) to artificially create surround effects for these stereo recordings.

We prefer playing back our CDs and other stereo sources in the stereo mode. It just seems more realistic to us. If you like the surround modes, feel free to use them. It's your theater, so use it the way that makes you happiest.

Most TV shows are broadcast in stereo, and many older movies on DVD or VHS are stereo as well. For movies and TV programming in stereo (not in Dolby Digital or DTS), we like to use Dolby Pro Logic II to create surround sound.

Playing with custom surround modes

As we discuss in Chapter 11, A/V receivers and controllers use devices called *DSPs* (Digital Signal Processors) to decode surround sound signals. These DSPs are basically powerful computer chips that can do all sorts of neat manipulations of audio signals. They're designed to tweak signals, not crunch numbers like the computer chips in your PC.

Many receiver manufacturers — the majority of them, to be honest — have harnessed this computer horsepower to create *custom surround modes* (or DSP modes), which manipulate the audio signal and create artificial surround sound modes. These custom surround modes use computer-generated models to adjust the volume and delay of signals coming from the surround and center channels in order to reproduce different "venues." For example, some receivers have a mode that tries to re-create the ambience of a cathedral by reproducing the delays and echoes you'd hear in a real cathedral.

Most audiophiles despise these custom surround modes, feeling that they are artificial and just get in the way of the music. We tend to agree; but again, this is an area in which we leave you to your own devices. Feel free to play around with these modes and see what you think. We won't come to your house and turn them off if you like them.

Chapter 20

Customizing Your Home Theater Environment

In This Chapter

▶ Mounting your display

▶ Soundproofing your theater

▶ Lighting your theater just right

▶ Adding remote control capabilities

▶ Choosing your ideal theater seating

*I*n earlier chapters, when we talk about creating an atmosphere in your home theater, the context is adding equipment to your home theater. Building off the discussion in Chapter 2 about where to put your home theater, this chapter delves into more detail about how to craft a home theater environment that lets all your high-tech devices put their best foot forward.

If you are building a home from scratch or renovating an area for your home theater, you have a lot to think about. But even if you are just sprucing up your living room or that room over the garage, this chapter has a few tips for you, too.

We want to warn you in advance that some of the topics in this chapter require pretty intense construction. You need to do more research on-line and consult with your manufacturers and contractor, if you have one, to determine your exact course of action. We give you some manufacturers' Web addresses as we discuss different options, and we point out good resources as we go along.

Mounting Your (Expensive) Display (Carefully!)

One of the biggest advances in TV displays in recent years has been the depth of the units — displays are getting thinner and thinner. Instead of just plunking your new display on top of a table, consider mounting it on the wall or ceiling (such as in the case of projectors) instead.

Mounting a display can be easy if you plan and design well up front. As you will read, there's more than one way to mount a display. You should ask yourself some questions about how you intend to use your TV before you settle on a particular mounting approach:

✔ **Is viewing flexibility an important consideration?** If you want to be able to see the display from two different locations, a swing arm mount is great — you can merely swing the display around to face the desired room. You might do this, for example, so that you can watch your plasma TV in the family room, but then swing it out so that it can be viewed from the kitchen, too. It's great for watching cooking shows!

✔ **Where do you want to put the display in the room?** Plan for your cabling in advance. Are you mounting this on a brick wall or in front of a window? In these instances, a ceiling mount may be better because it will be easier to run your cables invisibly.

If you are interested in a better understanding of how to prepare your home for all your digital home wiring needs, check out our *Smart Homes For Dummies* (Wiley), which deals with whole-home networking of all types.

✔ **Are you planning on mounting your display over a fireplace?** It can get hot over a fireplace in use, and this heat can damage your display. A lot of TVs don't have a cooling fan — they use convection for cooling and have to be five inches from the wall. If you are short on space and cooling is a concern, look for a TV with a fan. If there is a lot of heat coming up from the fireplace, you will really need a mantel to deflect the heat away from your TV.

✔ **How do you want to use your display?** Will you want to view this while lying on the floor sometimes and on the couch at other times? You might want a swing mount with a high degree of pitch so that you can change the angle as you desire. Do you want to press a button and have the display automatically appear? Look for pop-up and ceiling automated products for this purpose — often used in places like apartments in the city, where you might have limited space.

If you intend to use a swing mount and have chosen to buy third-party (that is, non-display-driven) speakers, you will want to make sure you can purchase an add-on accessory to mount your center speaker onto the display itself, rather than bolting that particular speaker to a wall. Doing so ensures that your center speaker swings along with the TV . . . thus avoiding that embarrassing situation in which lips move in one place but the corresponding dialogue comes from another — yech!

✔ **Is this room subject to different lighting during different times of the day?** Pitch wall mounts — ones that can shift a display up and down — are good for rooms that have glare during certain times of the day.

✔ **Is this a permanent installation or something you might change as newer TV display models come out?** Many homes trade up TVs every few years and swap TV sets from room to room in a hand-me-down fashion. Automated lift mounts are pretty permanent installations in most instances.

✔ **How does this have to look?** Is decor an issue? If you need this to be really flush with the wall with all your cables well hidden, then you might want to go with a swing arm (as opposed to a static) mount because a swing arm allows you to use a recessed area in the wall. You can connect the mount to the wall and then pull out the mount and connect all the cables and display. When you are done, you can push the mount back against the wall, and you have a fashionable flush installation. You may not be able to do this with a static mount because it's harder to hide all the connected cables. Also, you can design your mounting so that you can go with artwork that slides over the display or opt for a decorative trim to the display. You can even buy a certain material to cover your display that acts like a mirror when the display is off but is transparent when the display is on. Pretty "James Bond" if you ask us!

✔ **Do you care about specific orientations for your display?** With some mounts, you can rotate your display into a vertical position. If you are into photography, the display can go into portrait mode, for instance, for those vertically oriented pictures. Or, you might want to view the display horizontally but store it vertically, if space is a consideration.

Understanding your mounting options

You'll run into three basic types of mounts:

✔ **Flat-panel mounts:** These are designed predominantly for plasma displays and LCDs. You will find versions for ceiling, wall, and pole mounts (for floor-based mounting). Flat-panel mounts can be static, pitch, and swing mounts. Static mounts don't move. Pitch mounts pivot the display up and down. Swing mounts articulate up and down and side-to-side.

✔ **Projector mounts:** Projector mounts are generally based around one design, but they tend to come with a lot of accessories that let you use the mount on a ceiling or wall, deal with a drop ceiling, and so on.

✔ **Automated solutions:** For superslick installations, projector ceiling lifts and pop-up plasma lifts hide your gear when not in use. You can also automate swing arms so that, with the press of a button, your TV swings into a preprogrammed position.

If you're thinking about an automated solution, there's a whole different level of expertise typically required in order to manage the environmental, electrical, and other design elements of a successful implementation. These are generally not do-it-yourself projects. If you're looking for help mounting a display, we recommend that you check with your home theater dealer, look on the mount manufacturer's Web site, or look for installers in the "homeowners" section on the CEDIA (Custom Electronic Design and Installation Association) Web site at www.cedia.ne.

What to look for in a mount

When looking for a mount, consider these attributes of a manufacturer and its products:

- ✔ **Design/ease of installation:** Look for mounts with a lot of open space within their structures so you have a lot of room to do everything else you need to do when mounting a display. Check for a wall plate with minimal surface area so that you have more flexibility in where your cable and electrical outlets are located. There's nothing worse than finding that your electrical outlet is hidden by a big piece of unnecessary metal. Also, look for "hands-free" wall mount installations. The best designs allow one person to install them — for example, Chief Manufacturing's flat-panel mounts (www.chief.com) allow you to pound a nail in the wall and temporarily mount the whole unit on that one nail, leaving your hands free for leveling and final bolting. Some swing arms can be heavy — they can weigh up to 50 pounds — so again you will want to be able to pre-install the top two lag bolts and then slide the mount over those bolts — leaving the remaining bolts easier to install. Less-installer-friendly units don't have such slide-on options — all the bolt holes are encircled with metal so you have to screw the bolt in while holding the mount to the wall. (As an installer, you make the mistake of installing a mount out-of-level only once.)

- ✔ **Ease of use:** Ease of adjustment after installation is important. You should be able to adjust the tilt of a mount with a push of your fingertip. When you move a display, it should stay there without having to tighten knobs. Truly, this is the test of a high-quality mount.

- ✔ **Weight capacity:** Make sure the mount is rated not only for your display, but also for any speakers, decorative trim, and other accessories that can add weight.

We suggest that you look for mounts that are UL (Underwriters Laboratories) listed. These are tested at several times their rated weight capacity, so you're less likely to have a failure should your annoying in-law lean up against the mount during your annual holiday party.

✔ **Range of motion (tilt, swivel, extension, and so on):** Make sure that the mount not only fits in your space, but also provides the range of motion desired when the size of the mounted display is taken into account. We've seen instances in which someone bought a mount with the expectation of a 45-degree angle, only to find that, because of the size of the display and the limited extension from the wall, the full 45 degrees could not be achieved.

✔ **Integrated cable management:** You will want to hide your cables. Spend time understanding how your wiring will be run. This is especially true for ceiling mounts in which the cabling may go through the center of the pipe. More than one installer has been tripped up trying to thread a wide DVI or HDMI connector through a too-thin mount-extension column for a projector. If you have to run cables outside of your installation, for whatever reason, check for snap-on covers that help hide the cables even when run outside the mount columns.

Be careful of ceiling mounts that have a flange at the top — make sure you understand how you will route the cables out of that flange if you are, say, mounting this to concrete. There are instances in which cabling run through the center of a mount cannot "get out" of the column due to the nature of the mounting surface itself.

✔ **Quick detach/attach capability:** If you ever have to remove your display — to change the filters or lamps in a projector, for instance — you want a mount that was designed to maintain all the mechanical settings of the mount itself. You don't want to have to reset and reconfigure your gear each time you put it back.

✔ **Integrated lateral shift capability:** While awfully techie sounding, *lateral shift* is merely the ability to install a mount off center, when taking into account the spacing of the studs in your walls. After all, it would be just dumb luck if the spacing of the studs happened to perfectly coincide with where you wanted to center your display. A high-quality mount will allow you to displace your mount at least 4 inches to the left or right with 16-inch or 24-inch centered studs. An installed display should be able to be positioned vertically as well — quality mounts allow for at least 3 inches of vertical shift.

✔ **Aesthetics:** Look for mounts that look good to you. Check for multiple colors to choose from. Low-profile mounts are important, and details count, like covers for lag bolts on the wall.

✔ **Quality:** While it's hard to judge quality as an amateur, obvious indications, like being UL-approved, are a good sign that a manufacturer cares about its quality image.

✔ **Don't go cheap on your mount:** A good mount will last you many TV displays. Consider the future when making your purchase . . . nickle-and-diming here will only hurt you later.

Tips for installing your mount

So you have your mount picked out and you're ready to install. Here are some tips to make sure you have as successful an installation as possible:

✔ **Pick the right fasteners for the job.** There are specific anchors for specific types of wood. We won't make you writhe through stories of homeowners who tried to mount a 50-inch plasma with drywall screws. Most mounting instructions start with the assumption of wood stud installations, but there are specialty kits with most mounts for concrete anchors, drywall anchors, metal studs, and so on. Don't go cheap here; your homeowner's insurance probably has a big deductible, and you don't want to have to use it. A good rule to plan around: Your anchors need to hold five times the weight of what you are putting on the mount. Most manufacturers test their products with ⁵⁄₁₆-inch lag bolts (some use ⅜-inch) — a 2½-inch-long lag bolt is generally acknowledged to be acceptable for large mounts. The main goal is to hit the center of your stud with the bolt. To be sure you do, drill pilot holes to find the width of the stud so you can determine its exact center.

✔ **Range of motion/clearance requirements.** On most mounts, the display is lowered onto the mount. This means you need to have a little more clearance above the mount to make sure you can slide the display into place. Generally, this ranges from 4 inches to ½ an inch of extra space, depending on the manufacturer. So if you have a really tight space, think about this in advance. If you are installing an electric lift for a plasma display or LCD, know that these lifts are generally wide open to the elements in its hidden state — so if you lift this into an attic that has no moisture controls, the plasma will be exposed when not lowered into the house. (That's bad, in case you needed us to tell you that.) Projector lifts, on the other hand, tend to be enclosed in a box that has a plenum rating (meaning they're safe for installation in air flow areas — they have special fireproof coatings) and can go in a false ceiling.

✔ **Properly gauge your wall structure to make sure it can hold the weight.** Having a top-of-the-line mount that is secured to a wall studded with 2-x-2-inch wall studs won't get you far with a 60-inch display. The bigger the display, the more you may need to create a special mounting structure to support the mount — and you'll probably want to call in the cavalry (that is, a professional).

✔ **Triple-check your measurements (and then ask your spouse to recheck them for you).** Use the actual screen and mount when taking measurements, and where possible, confirm your measurements by holding the equipment in the space itself. Having good lateral and vertical shift will help, but that can cover up only the most minor of mistakes.

✔ **Consider hiring a professional installer.** This is one area you don't want to mess up. There's no honor in a broken 36-inch LCD screen. The more precise the installation needs to be, the more likely it is you will need to hire a professional to help.

Adding that extra touch

Some available accessories for your mounted display can really add to its attractiveness in your house (that is, if black matte finish doesn't turn you on as much as it does Pat). For instance, you can get old-style picture frames that make a display look more like a painting on the wall than a TV.

Many home theater sites carry "masking" systems that will also hide your screen altogether. For instance, BEI Audio/Visual Products (www.beionline.com) has something called the BEI Motorized Artwork System that is designed for raising and lowering a framed canvas artwork to conceal or reveal a plasma display. Just tap a button and the canvas slides away and the NCAA basketball tournament game comes on. The system offers more than 300 reproductions of works by the Great Masters — Monet, Manet, Millet . . . you have a broad selection of the most popular works of art. (Danny's partial to Caillebotte's "Nude on a Couch" but is pretty sure his wife won't agree.) You pick from a range of more than a dozen classic wooden frames to match your decor. A BEI system will cost you around $2,500.

(Curiously, BEI has the option of shipping the unit with bulletproof glass. We've heard of hating a picture, but that's a little extreme. However, if you really need to protect that plasma, this product's for you!)

Of course, no picture-framed display would be complete without digital art. Get a Roku Labs HD Photobridge (www.rokulabs.com, $399) to push high-definition pictures to your display. (We discuss this product more in Chapter 22.) Or, if you have your PC connected to the screen, check out GalleryPlayer Media Networks (www.galleryplayer.com). GalleryPlayer is a digital home gallery service that delivers museum-quality art and photography to any high-definition display, transforming it into a digital canvas. The application is free, and you can display hundreds of free images, as well as browse premium (i.e. "for-pay") services containing individual pictures and collections that will turn your screen into an art gallery. Images cost less than $1 each, so check it out.

Soundproofing and Improving Acoustics

No matter how good your system, if you put it in an environment that is not geared toward good sound quality, even the best audio system will sound horrible. The room's construction, furnishings, and window and wall treatments have a massive impact on the quality of sound from your home theater.

Many of the rooms chosen for home theaters are substantially less than optimal from a sound perspective. Your biggest enemy is vibration. Just about everything — the walls, the ductwork, suspended light fixtures, the drop ceiling — can vibrate. When a subwoofer produces its strong low-frequency acoustic energy, that sound wave travels through the room, hitting walls and ceiling surfaces. It's absorbed by the walls, which vibrate in reaction to this energy. This vibration then is conducted through any solid surface that it's in contact with, including studs, joists, and flooring. From there, it travels up through the framing of the house, and you end up with a shaking house, making a special noise of its own. That's where you need sound planning (pun intended).

You want to try to control two major types of sound distortions:

✔ Intrusive sounds from outside your home theater (and, to be fair, sounds from inside the home theater that seep into the house and keep Mom and Dad awake until the end of the midnight movie)

✔ Sound reflections and refractions from the audio system itself

If you are building a new home from scratch or renovating, you have the opportunity to address this at the architectural level. You essentially want to create a room within a room so that you can isolate and control the impact of the sound system's signals on the room itself. Seek to isolate your inside walls, ceilings, and floors from the rest of the house as much as possible. The following list gives you some ideas on how best to go about this task:

✔ **Place studs appropriately, double your drywall, and insulate for sound.** You want to avoid having the studs of two adjacent walls touching each other. By keeping studs from touching, you cut off a primary means for sound to travel between the room and the house (in both directions). You can also dull vibrations by adding a second layer of drywall.

To further dampen any sounds, apply insulation inside the wall cavity. (If this is a concrete basement, you need to consider a vapor barrier as well to keep moisture out of your home theater.)

✔ **Apply soundproofing between studs and drywall.** Consider adding a layer of soundproofing material between the studs and drywall. This serves not only to suppress sounds going back and forth, but also as a vibration trap between the drywall and the studs themselves — further reducing unintended effects from your sound system. For instance, Acoustiblok (www.acoustiblok.com) sells a very effective sound barrier that comes in rolls like tarpaper.

When applying soundproofing layers, keep it somewhat limp between the studs so it can absorb the acoustic energy more efficiently. Also, soundproofing materials are usually pretty heavy, so be sure to buy some prime steaks and beer before you ask your neighbors to help!

✔ **Apply soundproofing to the floor.** Think about a *floating* floor, which is a multilayered floor designed to isolate your home theater from the rest of the house. For example, the topmost floating layer might consist of tongue-and-groove chipboard bonded to a layer of plasterboard. That in turn would be laid on a spongy layer made of some sort of mineral fiber. You could then glue the spongy layer to the existing floor or even mount the whole thing on its own joists.

✔ **Apply a soundproofing system to the finished drywall.** Adding specialized sound control panels to the walls can help control unwanted reflected sounds. When placed at your speakers' first reflection points (typically, the sidewall boundaries and rear wall behind the main listening position), sound treatment panels reduce your reflected sound. (This reflected sound could cause a blurring of the sound image and lack of intelligibility.) Sound treatments also reduce the overall sound volume in the room, enhancing low-level dialogue and environmental effects delivered over today's high-quality audio systems.

A good way to find your speakers' first reflection point is to sit in your listening position and have one of your home theater–loving buddies move a mirror along the walls. When a speaker becomes visible in the mirror (from your perspective in your comfy theater seating), you've found the first reflection point.

Who you gonna call?

The following companies offer products that can be used when soundproofing your walls:

✔ **Kinetics Noise Control** (www.kinetics noise.com): Kinetics Noise Control offers a Home Theater Absorption Kit that contains special decorative panels. The midwall absorptive panels take care of sound reverberation, and the triangular corner panels are specifically engineered to absorb low-frequency bass sound that tends to gather in corners. This company also makes special spring mounts for suspending your ceiling (so it doesn't rattle) and other special items for dampening other sounds in your room.

✔ **Acoustic Sciences** (www.acoustic sciences.com): Acoustic Sciences has a neat product called the Acoustical Soffit, which is a very discreet acoustic treatment that runs around the ceiling borders of your room. This architectural acoustic component is designed to control low-end bass responses while also serving as an internal raceway to hide wiring, HVAC, and lighting. Pretty neat idea.

✔ **Acoustic Innovations** (www.acoustic innovations.com): When it comes to in-room soundproofing treatments, there are many different approaches, and often your taste in decorations drives your selection. For instance, Acoustic Innovations has really nice solid hardwood frames in mahogany, cherry, walnut, and oak stains for its Maestro line of panels that can reduce unwanted sound reflections.

✔ **Additional resources:** Check out other offerings from companies such as Auralex (www.auralex.com) and Owens Corning (www.owenscorning.com).

Our friend Jim Millay decided to make his own acoustical treatments. He got some stiff insulation — like you'd put in your house — and wrapped it with professional-looking fabric — and voila, instant inexpensive panels. We can't really compare these with the professionally manufactured ones just discussed, but if you are on a budget, consider Jim's approach. Of course, he'll want a contribution for his idea. . . .

The cost of the materials for soundproofing a home theater fluctuates, depending on what you decide to do. You can spend a few hundred dollars or upwards of $35,000. Over time, you'll probably at least add some of these interior sound treatments to deal with the sound in the room.

Remember that your cheapest first line of sound defense is simply securing everything that is around the room and listening for things that add noise. Subwoofers can definitely shake things up; if that problem rears its ugly head, get some inexpensive isolation pads for the subwoofer's feet. Projectors can make a ton of noise, too; consider a special mounting for the projector that contains its noise, but remember not to block the fan and airflow because it puts off a lot of heat, too.

In Chapter 2, we discuss having a central wiring hub and a media hub for your electronics. People often put these all in a place where they can show them off, but with that approach comes heat and noise (from cooling fans) that you must deal with. If you can put all the power amplifiers outside the room, there is less heat and noise to dissipate, which is something to think about in your plan.

Dealing with Home Theater Lighting

Lighting plays a crucial role in setting the right atmosphere for your home theater. A bright light in the wrong place or the wrong glare from an open window can be just as annoying as someone's cellphone going off in the middle of a show.

Most home theater planners agree that the video on your display looks best when the room lights are off (or significantly dimmed), the doors are closed, and the shades are drawn. This is where creative use of dimmers, motorized drapes, window treatments, and a lighting control system can become pivotal pieces of your home theater environs.

Wall-mounted dimmer switches allow you to control the intensity of an individual light or series of connected lights. In most instances, this is a simple and cheap way to change the ambience, and you can do it with $5 and a trip to Home Depot.

If you want to have real fun, think about moving to a complete lighting control system. For as little as $300, you can get into systems designed specifically for controlling your lights within one room (your home theater). From either a wall-mounted keypad, a remote control, or both, you can turn on/off, brighten, dim, or otherwise control each light fixture in the room.

If you choose a sophisticated lighting control system (we talk about a few in this section), you can actually program the system to do some pretty elaborate lighting tricks. For example, you might set up a Preshow mode that has lights on all over the room, maybe accentuating your bar area or the couches, if you have them. You could press a Preshow button on your lighting controls to activate that mode. Then you might have a Viewing mode that would dim the sconces, cut the overhead lights, initially highlight the front of the home theater, then fade, open the curtains in front of your home theater, and start the show. (These different lighting modes are known as *scenes.*) Way cool.

With not too much more effort, you can use remote controls, like the ones we talk about in Chapter 15, and integrate your electronics further. So in Preshow mode, you can control the music, and in Viewing mode, you can control the projector or display. With a good system, the macros you can set up are limitless. (*Macros* are those stored programs in your remote that let you perform multiple commands with a single button push, allowing you to create new modes for whatever mood.)

There are new construction and retrofit solutions for lighting control, depending on whether you are building from scratch or making a system fit into your existing space with existing wiring. Systems can communicate via wireline signaling (using existing AC power lines) or wirelessly. You can get single-room systems from players such as Leviton (www.leviton.com), Lightolier Controls (www.lolcontrols.com), LiteTouch (www.lite touch.com), Lutron (www.lutron.com), Powerline Control Systems (www.pcslighting.com), SmartHome (www.smarthome.com), Vantage (www.vantageinc.com), and X10 (the company — www.X10.com).

Lutron's $1,800 Home Theater Package is also designed for existing rooms where rewiring isn't practical. This package includes four dimmers, a table-top master control, and an infrared receiver so that users can control lights from their favorite universal or learning IR transmitter. Lutron also has a higher-end system that sports RadioRA, a wireless, whole-home lighting control system that uses radio frequency technology instead of AC power lines — most lighting systems use the X10 protocol and your home's power lines — for signal communication.

X10, INSTEON, Z-Wave, ZigBee, and more

In the not-too-distant past, if you wanted a whole-home lighting system, you had to install a really expensive package from a brand-name lighting retailer. Now, many of these same retailers are adopting new industry approaches that use your home wiring and wireless technologies to provide low-cost lighting that everyone can afford.

You'll run across X10 in many instances. X10 is the granddaddy protocol for controlling (turning on and off and dimming) electrical devices, such as lights and appliances, through your home's electrical lines. It has been around for years, establishing itself to such an extent that it is now an open standard — meaning that other companies are free to sell devices that use this protocol as well. All standards-compatible products display an X10-compatible logo on their packaging or on the product itself. When you see this logo, you know that the product works with other X10 products regardless of the manufacturer.

As you explore the world of X10, you'll find a bunch of different tools in the X10 toolbox, but the two that ended up being most applicable to home theaters are their wall outlet modules and dimmer switches. *X10 modules* are devices that receive and translate X10 signals to control individual lights, appliances, or other electrical devices. An X10 wall module is a small, box-shaped device that's no bigger than the AC plug-in transformers that power many home appliances, such as telephones and answering machines.

Setting up an X10 module is pretty easy. The module has a standard electrical plug on the back and a place to plug in your lamp or other device on the front or bottom. First, turn the device "on" (for example, turn on the light switch), and then the X10 module turns the device off and on and dims as appropriate. *X10 dimmer switches* replace your normal switch and are likewise controlled via the X10 signals over your electrical lines, or manually by you at the switch.

X10 doesn't require specific network architecture other than your existing electrical system to work in a home. X10 sends its control signals from the controller over your power lines to every outlet in the house. The controller can have remote control or PC interfaces. Figure 20-1 shows a limited X10 network.

Figure 20-1:
Plugging into an X10 network.

X10 (the company) has many cheap, easy-to-install, X10-protocol-driven lighting controls. Its $19.99 UltimateREMOTE Home Control Kit entry-level package includes a radio remote control, a transceiver control module (which takes radio frequency commands from X10 remote controls and converts them to X10 signals carried over household wiring), and a lamp module. You can get extra lamp modules, dimmer switches, and other additional lighting controls for around $10–$30 each, as well as other automated home controls for heating, remote monitoring, and other applications. X10.com is a great site with lots of reasonably priced products for lots of applications (just learn to ignore the pop-up ads!).

The successors to X10

But X10 is old, almost older than Pat and Danny (but not *that* old). It has had its share of problems, and at least three new initiatives — each backed by their share of industry powerhouse names — are vying for your previously X10-bound, home-automation budget.

- ✔ **INSTEON** (www.insteon.net)**:** Backed by the founders of SmartHome. com (one of our favorite sites), INSTEON is the next generation of X10 — it's an integrated dual-mesh network that combines wireless radio frequency (RF) with the home's existing electrical wiring for communications. (By the way, in case your head just spun around, *integrated dual mesh* means that INSTEON can use both RF and powerline signalling at the same time, in an integrated way.) Homeowners with existing X10 networks can migrate to an INSTEON network without having to discard all their existing X10 devices.

- ✔ **ZigBee** (www.zigbee.org)**:** ZigBee uses only RF transmission instead of X10's powerline transmission protocols to create a home wireless network for home automation. We discuss Control4, a whole-home networking company that uses ZigBee, in Chapter 21.

- ✔ **Z-Wave** (www.z-wavealliance.org)**:** Z-Wave also focuses just on RF, using a mesh network that hops from location to location in your home — making it easy to extend the network throughout even a large home.

These are all just different approaches to the same problem. Each offers similar modules: plug-in dimmers, plug-in on/off switches, wire-in dimmers with the standard "paddle" design, wire-in dimmers with a keypad, wire-in on/off switches, and so on.

In choosing from among the X10 successors, here are some thoughts:

- ✔ **You're smart to buy an X10 successor rather than X10 proper.** We recommend you look at these new technologies over X10 unless you've already made a commitment to X10.

✔ **Be mindful of X10 compatibility.** If you have X10 already installed, we recommend you still look at INSTEON because it is compatible with X10.

✔ **All of these successors work.** These represent the next generation of home automation and as such provide the best performance for your money. Each of these new approaches is sound and has its pros and cons.

✔ **All of these successors are mesh.** Each of these wireless technologies uses some form of a mesh network, meaning each device in the network can communicate with each other device and retransmit a signal if it can't confirm a signal was received.

✔ **All of these successors can be programmed and controlled through multiple access points.** How multiple are we talking here? How about computers, Web browsers, mobile phones, remotes, and wall switches, for starters?

✔ **The number of supported devices should not matter.** Z-Wave's addressing scheme allows for only 256 devices. INSTEON and ZigBee have addressing schemes that allow many thousands of devices to be added to a network. Some pundits will argue that that matters. We would be surprised if you need more than 50 addresses in your home, so we think this is not an issue.

✔ **Wireless frequencies could be a concern, but it's too early to tell.** INSTEON and Z-Wave use the 900 MHz frequency spectrum to transmit their wireless signals in the United States; ZigBee primarily uses the 2.4 GHz frequency spectrum, which is also used by Wi-Fi and other wireless technologies. If you have a lot of 802.11-based systems in your house, you could conceivably run into issues with a ZigBee system. However, ZigBee uses all 16 channels in the 2.4 GHz band, and if a channel gets too noisy, the network moves to a clear channel, so it was designed to deal with this. It's not enough for us to get too worried about it in our own implementations.

In the end, it's likely to come down to the cost for you to install a particular set of capabilities in your home — price out each solution and see what works best for you. Some of these will likely have a package — like a home theater lighting package — that makes it easy to accomplish what you want. Such packages are easier to install the first time, and you can grow off of these as your needs change.

A great resource for ideas about lighting control systems — and your home theater in general — is *Electronic House* magazine (www.electronichouse. com). It's inexpensive, available on newsstands, and has helpful hints about how to approach your projects from lots of different angles (including lots of home theater–specific articles).

Hidden advantages of lighting control systems

Although having a lighting control system for your home theater makes sense, expanding it to other parts of your home makes even more sense. In addition to setting the mood in your home theater, a lighting control system

✔ **Saves money on electricity bills:** Want to turn off all your lights at night and enter Sleeping mode? One button can do that, no matter the condition (on/off) of the lights at that time.

✔ **Adds security:** Automatically illuminating dark halls or that creepy space by the garage at night not only adds to peace of mind, but also reduces the likelihood of problems.

✔ **Supports your lifestyle:** Whether it's really making sure your kids' lights are out at 9:30 or automatically turning on your lights when you drive in the garage, a lighting control system can help support the way you use your home.

If you want to find out more about extending your lighting control system to the rest of your house, check out *Smart Homes For Dummies* (Wiley), which we also wrote.

Controlling Your Home Theater Environment Remotely

Many lighting control systems can interface with or drive whole-home automation capabilities. Although whole-home automation is beyond the scope of this book (Dare we say it? Why not? Read our *Smart Homes For Dummies* book for a whole-home approach), you can get whole-room automation with many systems.

Many of the better remote controls we discuss in Chapter 15 support home-automation commands. And some manufacturers offer complementary products that work off the same remotes. For instance, Lutron's Sivoia (www.lutron.com/sivoia) motorized shade and drapery system is integrated with the firm's GRAFIK Eye, RadioRA, and HomeWorks lighting and home control systems. Each new control offers Open, Close, Raise, and Lower buttons, along with three programmable, preset stop locations for shades or draperies. With this, you can control the dimming of the lights and opening of the drapes, just like in a real theater.

Closing the drapes and shades without leaving the couch

Motorized shade/drape kits are simple to install and can add a professional touch to your home theater. You can get electronic drapery kits that open and close on your command. If you have ever installed a drapery rod, a kit is basically the same thing with a motor.

For instance, the Makita Motorized Drape System (www.smarthome.com) is a self-contained system for your home theater drapes. You can get a single drape system or a double drape. You screw in the tracks, mount the drapes, and plug it in. You can customize the length merely by cutting the tracking. Pretty simple.

You can also get motorized window-treatment hardware from manufacturers such as BTX (www.btxinc.com), Hunter Douglas (www.hunter douglas.com), Lutron (www.lutron.com/sivoia), and Somfy (www. somfysystems.com).

Check to see if these systems can link to your home automation system as well. Somfy has announced, at the time of this writing, that its products will support INSTEON. Because the Somfy automated shades use radio signals for control, it makes sense to link them to your INSTEON network for remote control using a switch or tabletop controller — you can even use computer software to schedule the shades to open and close automatically at a certain time of day.

Starry, starry night . . .

Fiber optics can add a really neat effect to any home theater. Here are some ideas, suggested by Acoustic Innovations (www.acoustic innovations.com):

- **Starlight fiber optic ceilings:** To make your ceiling look like a nighttime sky, you can have fiber-optic ceiling panels applied to your existing ceiling. The panels not only make your ceiling more fun, but offer acoustical correction as well. However, you might find yourself spreading out a blanket on your home theater floor to watch the ceiling!

- **Infinite starfield panels:** What a better accompaniment to your Pink Floyd *Dark Side of the Moon* midnight laser show than an infinite starfield in your home theater. These are made of multiple polycarbonate mirrors and fiber optic lighting and create an illusion of infinite depth. (Not suggested for theater ceilings.)

- **Fiber-optic carpeting:** This carpet is filled with tiny points of light (50 fiber-optic points per square foot, to be precise).

- **Fiber-optic curtains:** These classic, velvety curtains can twinkle, too. Très chic.

All illuminators come complete with a remote locatable dimmer, speed control for twinkle, and an on/off switch. You even get to choose between a twinkle or color change wheel. Decisions, decisions.

Turning up the heat from the comfort of your recliner

Automation isn't just lights and drapes. You can monitor and control temperature settings as well. Don't forget that you need to maintain the temperature for all those electronic components per manufacturer specs — usually above 55 degrees Fahrenheit at a minimum. If your theater is located in a part of the house where you might have to warm it up or cool it off in advance, then consider integrating the heating system in your home theater room into your controller system, too.

Going Hollywood all the way

For those of you who want to really go all the way with the theater theme, you can buy all sorts of add-ons to create that atmosphere:

✔ **Personalized home theater intro:** Open each showing with your own customized one-minute video, just like in the theaters. (Your DVD player must be able to play DVD-R for this to work.) For $160 or so for a customized DVD from www.htmarket.com, you can personalize one of five home theater intros, from an awards night theme to a classic popcorn theme. How fun is that?!

✔ **Specialty rugs:** You can get rugs festooned with stars, film reels, popcorn, and so on. The cost is about $50 per square yard on average (but there's a huge range). HT Market (www.htmarket.com) has these rugs.

✔ **Posts and ropes:** If you wanted that velour rope and stainless steel post look, you've got it. Expect to spend around $120–$300 a post and $80–$100 a rope. Maybe there is some poetic justice about making your boss wait in line at your home theater! Pat's going to buy a set of these the next time Danny is in town. Check out www.homecinemaaccessories.com if you're interested in picking up some posts and ropes for yourself.

✔ **Popcorn machines:** Complete with the swing down popping bucket, these $300–$900 machines give you freshly popped popcorn and that movie theater smell. Check out www.popcornpopper.com for some cool models.

✔ **Wall sconces:** You can get cool theater lighting that will give you that interior decorated look on a budget (about $200–$250 apiece). You don't need to go anywhere special for these — you can hit your local hardware store or go to Lowes or Home Depot.

✔ **Film posters:** Decorate the outside of your theater with current and past movie posters, just like you see while waiting in line to get your tickets. These run about $10 to $20 for current films, in their usual 27-x-40-inch formats. Check out www.allposters.com for new ones or find vintage posters at places like www.moviemarket.com.

✔ **Sound Edgelits:** Add some of these tabletop back-lit signs to let your viewers know which sound systems you have in your theater. These $225 signs sport Dolby Digital, THX, DTS, and other surround sound logos.

You can find these and more at places like www.hometheaterdecor.com and www.htmarket.com.

Again, without getting waist deep in detail, you can get X10-, ZigBee-, Z-Wave-, and INSTEON-controlled heating and air conditioning modules that interface with your environmental controls to

✔ **Make sure they stay within a specified temperature range**

✔ **Allow you remote control in case you want to prep your theater**

Many of the firms mentioned for lighting control systems also have similar systems for heating and air cooling. These systems are usually tack-on modules to their other systems and can cost as little as $30 to $50. A decent bidirectional home automation thermostat will probably run you $200. Check out www.smarthome.com, www.automatedoutlet.com, and www.X10.com for some good options. Again, whole-home options cost considerably more because you start getting into multiple zones and probably several interface formats. But for your home theater, the ability to preset your environmental controls from remote locations won't cost much.

Getting Comfy

Finally, *getting comfortable* in your home theater means different things to different people. To Danny's wife, it probably means having about 20 large pillows from Pier One Imports lying around the floor. To Pat's wife, it would mean having theater seats wide enough for Opie the beagle to sit next to her (with some beagle-proof fabric covering them).

Lucky for you, you have many options for home theater seating comfort: chairs, couches, and lounges; seating that's motorized or manual; some with storage and control compartments; some with speakers built-in . . . the list goes on.

You're probably looking at around $300 and up per seat for specialty theater seating, and seats can quickly get into the $2,000–$3,000 range if you start piling on the extras. You can really sink money into your seats.

Some things to keep in mind, no matter what you buy:

✔ **Sound implications:** You'll set up your sound system so that no matter where you sit in your theater, you hopefully have a similar (breathtaking) aural experience. Three couches in a U-shaped configuration may sound right for you, but make sure that your speaker configuration is designed to handle it. You may need some additional speakers or different capability to support weird configurations. Seating configuration and speaker configuration simply go hand-in-hand.

✔ **Visual implications:** Although high-backed theater chairs may look good in the showroom, they can block your rear surround sound speakers. If you want multiple rows, these high-backed seats may necessitate a tiered floor (so back-row viewers see the screen, not the back of a chair).

✔ **Food:** The "You can't take food into the living room" rule does not go over well with a viewing population trained to eat popcorn while they watch the movies. So you need to consider how you will handle food. You may want built-in trays or drink holders, or nothing. Maybe you need tables between chairs instead. All we ask is that you think about how you'll handle food when you are buying the furniture and rugs. No sense setting yourself up for yelling at the kids later.

You need to think about seating more than some other aspects of your home theater because many people are used to viewing movies in bed, on couches, on the floor, and so on. You really need to think through how you define *comfortable* and then design toward that.

Cuddlebags (www.cuddlebag.com, $250–$600) has some really neat theater beanbag-style pillows — they're comfortable, washable, and malleable, too. They come as big as 8 feet wide. Wow, that's a lot of cuddling!

Chapter 21

Moving Up to the High End

....

....

*O*ne somewhat vaguely defined concept that we talk about throughout *Home Theater For Dummies* is the idea that you can move up to the high end when you're buying components and setting up a home theater. Everyone has his or her own definition of *high end,* but for us, it means equipment that is designed to offer the ultimate reproduction of music and movies.

In this chapter, we quit talking about high end in the abstract and get real concrete by introducing you to some really awesome high-end systems. (Watch out for nosebleeds here.) The systems' designers are so single-minded in their pursuit of musical and video fidelity that they've created their own proprietary systems that they feel do a better job than standard mix-and-match components. When we say a system is *proprietary,* we mean that it is designed to work best (or in some cases only) with other components from the same vendor. So if you buy part of your home theater from one of these vendors, you'll probably end up buying all of it from them — at least on the audio side. These systems usually work with any display. When you buy a proprietary system, you are in effect taking a bet on this company's ability to do things better than the industry in general does — and on its ability to stay in business and support you in the future.

Later in this chapter, we also talk about some of the *video processing* systems that let your top-of-the-line display really look as good as (or better than) the movies you see in the theater.

Introducing High-End Home Theater

In the introduction to this chapter, we start to define what we think high-end theater is. Our definition of *high end* starts and ends with the philosophy of the designers and engineers who create the product (which can be speakers, a display, an A/V controller or power amplifier, or even an A/V receiver, though high-end systems usually go with separates).

Anybody designing a piece of consumer electronics equipment has to balance a lot of different (and often conflicting) requirements: price, aesthetics, size, performance, interoperability with other gear, and so on. High-end gear skews this very delicate balance toward the performance side of the equation, and as a result, the high-end components can be much more expensive, big, proprietary, and even ugly.

A few years back, there was a bit of a geographic divide (or at least, a perceived divide) between high-end and mass-market A/V components. High-end vendors were located in the United States, Canada, and Europe, while big consumer electronics companies based in Asia were focused on high-volume, middle-market products. We're not convinced that this perception was ever correct, but we're sure that it's not true today. Although many high-end manufacturers are indeed based in the traditional places, you can find some really awesome (and expensive) gear coming from those big Asian consumer electronics companies. Just because a company sells a ton of $299 A/V receivers doesn't mean that it can't build a great $3,000 receiver. So throw any perceptions of brand bias out the door because you may be surprised by who's got some really fine high-end products these days.

Separating Your Amps

Within the audio realm of the home theater domain, the most common step for manufacturers moving up to higher-quality products is to move from the all-in-one A/V receiver into separates. We talk a little bit about separates in Chapter 11, but in this chapter, we get a bit more detailed.

Basically, separate components take the many functions of an A/V receiver and divide them among several separate components. Doing this has two major benefits: greater flexibility and better performance.

A/V receivers are really pretty darned good these days, and there is such a thing as a high-end A/V receiver. These receivers (from companies such as Denon, Yamaha, and Marantz, to name just a few) compete performance-wise with most separates systems in their price range.

The functions of an A/V receiver are usually doled out to the following components:

✔ **A/V controller:** This device handles all the surround sound decoding and digital-to-analog conversions. It also switches audio and video (from source devices to the amplifiers or display) and performs the *preamplifier* functions (from adjusting the power level of audio signals going to the amplifiers, to adjust the listening volume). A few A/V controllers include a built-in radio tuner, making them essentially A/V receivers without built-in power amplifiers.

Depending on who's talking, you might hear these devices referred to as *surround sound processors, home theater preamps,* or something else entirely. If it decodes the surround sound signals and switches between audio and video sources, it's an A/V controller.

✔ **Power amplifier:** These devices boost the power of analog audio signals coming out of the controller in order to drive the speakers and create sound. As we just mentioned, you don't control volume with the power amplifier (the A/V controller does that). Basically, a power amplifier is a big box with an on/off switch, speaker terminals, and one or more RCA jack audio inputs on the back for connecting to the A/V controller. Most home theater power amplifiers are *multichannel* amplifiers, meaning they have five, seven, or more built-in amplifiers for powering all your surround sound speakers. Some systems are designed around *mono* power amplifiers, in which *each* channel in the system has its own amplifier. (You can also find two- and three-channel amplifiers to mix and match into a five- or more channel system.)

✔ **Radio tuner:** We discuss these in Chapter 5. Just remember that the majority of A/V controllers don't have a built-in tuner, so if you want to listen to the radio, you need to buy a separate tuner. If you have digital cable or a DSS satellite dish, you might get around this requirement if you can receive radio stations through these systems (and if you like the channel line-ups they offer).

Connecting a separates system is really only minimally different from the process of hooking up a home theater that's based on an A/V receiver. Just as you do with an A/V receiver, you want to route all your source components through the A/V controller. All your analog audio, digital audio, and video connections connect directly from the source device to the A/V controller. (The only exception to this rule is this: If you don't have enough of the right kind of video inputs on your A/V controller — specifically if your controller doesn't have component video switching — you might connect the video cables from some of your components directly to the display.)

Your powered (active) subwoofer connects directly to the A/V controller, just as it connects to your A/V receiver. The rest of your speakers, however, are connected differently. You use an audio interconnect cable (the standard RCA plug cables we discuss in Chapter 16) for each channel of your 5.1-, 6.1-, or 7.1-surround sound system and route this signal from a set of Power Amplifier Out connections on the back of your controller to the appropriate Preamp In connections on the back of your power amplifier(s).

Moving into Integrated Systems

One way that many high-end vendors create their high-performance systems is to create their own integrated ways of doing home theater. Some of these systems use proprietary connection systems (their own special cables) to link components, whereas others use standard connectors and cables but have components that are specially designed to work together.

These systems are basically the steroid-enhanced siblings of the inexpensive home-theater-in-a-box systems we discuss in Chapter 2. You buy a complete system from a single manufacturer, rather than picking and choosing between components from different vendors. It's a high-end, soup-to-nuts approach; the power amplifiers, A/V controllers, DVD and CD players, and speakers — everything but the display itself, in most cases — come as one integrated package from one company.

In the sections that follow, we talk about some of the leading integrated systems. (Just keep in mind that these aren't the only manufacturers who build these kinds of systems, just a sampling.)

NHT Xd System

NHT (Now Hear This, www.nhthifi.com) has long been one of the preeminent loudspeaker manufacturers in the United States (Pat's pair of their tiny little SubZero models have graced his home office for over ten years). They've recently moved beyond the traditional loudspeaker and into a new integrated high-end home theater system called the NHT Xd (www.nhtxd.com).

The NHT Xd is a DSP (Digital Signal Processor) based system that includes special satellite speakers, bass units (essentially subwoofers), and the secret sauce — the XdA amplifier/DSP unit.

Essentially, the Xd system is a "closed" environment that "knows" the exact properties of the XdS satellite speakers and the XdW bass units connected to the system and then uses the digital signal processing and digital amplification built into the XdA unit to provide exceptional sound. With these characteristics in mind, the XdA electronically modifies the sound coming out of your source devices and tailors it to sound better (closer to the original sound) when it comes out of the speakers. How it all works is rather complex (and no doubt a trade secret for NHT).

This is a really neat trick that allows the relatively small Xd system to sound like it should be taking up half of your room and be installed only by piano movers.

You still need to add your own source devices and surround sound decoder into the Xd system, but you won't need any other amplification. You make only three simple one-time settings: tell the Xd system how many bass units you are using, tell how many satellites/where they are located, and set the volume control for the bass. Otherwise, it's just set it and forget it.

You can configure the Xd system in different ways, depending upon your home theater requirements — NHT recommends a 6.2 system, with six satellites and two bass units, but you can mix and match. The basic component setup consists of two satellites, one bass unit, and one XdA DSP/amplifier unit (which can support two satellites and up to two bass units) and retails for about $6,000 (including stands for the satellites and all the wires and cables you need to hook things up).

Meridian

Meridian (www.meridian-audio.com) offers some of the coolest, highest-end A/V equipment available anywhere. One Meridian feature that we think really reflects the future of A/V gear is the computer-like construction. Meridian systems are incredibly modular and upgradeable. So if your current Meridian processor, for example, doesn't support a new surround sound format, you can simply have your dealer pop in a new card.

Meridian's products are known for being some of the finest in terms of dealing with digital audio signals (no surprise given Meridian's expertise in the field), and Meridian does a couple of things differently than most other A/V component vendors:

  ✔ **Smart Link:** Meridian has an all-digital connection called Smart Link for carrying DVD-Audio signals to the controller. In Meridian's own words (and we believe what they're saying), Smart Link allows "the full resolution of multichannel audio from DVD-A recordings [to] be losslessly transferred in the digital domain from player to surround controller to loudspeaker." That's a mouthful, but it means that digital audio signals remain digital until the very final link in the audio chain — the speakers. Meridian can do this because of Smart Link, and also because of the item we discuss next.

✔ **DSP loudspeakers:** Meridian builds active loudspeaker systems designed to connect and integrate with its lineup of CD/DVD players and A/V controllers. Like all active speakers, these have built-in power amplifiers, so you don't need a separate amp. The difference comes with the DSP that gives them their name. This digital signal processor allows Meridian to send fully digital audio signals to the speakers. So the digital chain is broken only when the speakers themselves convert this signal to analog internally. You benefit from a clean, interference-resistant digital connection. Additionally, the DSP speakers do all the things that normal loudspeakers do (such as *crossovers* that send different frequencies to different drivers within the speaker) entirely in the digital domain. There's even a separate amplifier within the DSP speakers for each individual driver.

All this modularity, flexibility, and digital audio goodness doesn't come cheap. Meridian's flagship speakers, the DSP8000, cost $40,000 a *pair.* They're not for the faint of heart or the shallow-walleted. But the sound is simply awesome.

We understand that most folks can't afford (or won't spend the money on) $20,000-a-piece loudspeakers. (We can't either, to be honest, at least not without second mortgages and angry wives.) But we're telling you about this product because these kinds of systems give you a feel for what's possible in home theater. And the technologies featured in these systems will eventually, in the words of Ronald Reagan, "trickle down" to more affordable gear. We certainly can't wait for DSP-based active loudspeakers and modular, upgradeable components to hit the Crutchfield catalog instead of the super-expensive boutique audio stores.

Exploring High-End Video Systems

Audio isn't the only part of home theater that fits into the high-end category. If you've read earlier parts of the book (particularly the discussions of front-projection display systems in Chapter 14), you already know that high-end video systems (such as the $30,000 three-chip DLP projectors we keep mentioning) are out there on the market, waiting to be gobbled up by well-to-do home theater enthusiasts. If you want to go high-end with front projection, look for units from Faroudja (www.faroudja.com) or Runco (www.runco.com).

In this section, we talk about a group of high-end devices called *video processors* that complement these displays (particularly projection systems) in many home theaters.

Improving resolution

If you go for a front- or rear-projection system or the biggest plasma display, you get a really big picture in a home theater. The problem is, the picture is so big that you begin to see the line structure of analog NTSC television broadcasts (and other low-resolution sources, such as VHS VCR tapes). These sources just don't have sufficient resolution, and you end up in a situation in which a picture that looks okay on a 20-inch TV in the bedroom looks like a disaster on your fancy projection TV. Simply put, the 250 horizontal lines that make up a VHS picture will be so far apart on a big-screen display that you can see them (and the black lines between them) without sticking your face up next to the screen. To say the least, this is annoying.

To get around this, many high-end projectors (and other displays as well) use a device known as a *line doubler.* A line doubler, in its simplest form, takes the two fields that make up a frame in an interlaced video system and combines them. (We discuss frames and fields in Chapter 4 if you're not sure what we're talking about here.) These newly reconstructed frames are then sent to the display twice in a row, until the next pair of images comes along ($\frac{1}{30}$ of a second after the first). For example, with NTSC broadcast TV signals, the 480 interlaced scan lines of the broadcast come out of the line doubler (and head into your display) as 480 progressive-scan lines. This makes for a much smoother image and helps hide those visible scan lines because twice as many are displayed at a time.

To take advantage of a line doubler, your display must be able to handle progressive-scan video. Look for displays with scan rates of 31.5 kHz or higher. (We discuss scan rates in Chapter 13.) Most HDTV-ready or progressive scan displays already have an internal line doubler built in. As you start moving into really high-end home theater installations, many experts like to bypass these by using a top-of-the-line external line doubler (or more likely, one of the devices we discuss in the next section).

Investigating top-of-the-line video processors

Video processors go beyond simple line doubling. You can find processors that *quadruple* the number of lines on your display, and increasingly you can purchase a processor that *scales* a video source to a specific (and often custom) fixed resolution suitable for displays like plasma, LCD, and DLP, which have a specific number of pixels on-screen.

Going quad

Some video processors do more than just double the lines of resolution. For example, *line quadruplers* (as the name implies) quadruple the number of scan lines being sent to the display. These systems don't wait for four fields to come in and then repeat them four times (which is what you might think they do, given how line doublers work). Instead, line quadruplers do some math and *interpolate* what might come between a pair of lines. (Because there's no actual picture data for the new extra lines, the quadrupler uses various mathematical models to guess what might be there.) For NTSC analog video signals, a quadrupler gives an output of 960 progressive-scan lines. (In other words, it doubles the 480i output to 480p, and then doubles that again to 960p.)

If you are using a CRT display with a line quadrupler, you need a display that can handle a scan rate four times as fast as the standard NTSC scan rate (which is about 15.7 kHz). So your display needs to be able to handle a 63 kHz scan rate.

Line quadruplers are pretty rare these days simply because most folks have begun using digital displays (like DLP projectors or plasma flat panels), which have fixed resolutions. If you want to enhance the video quality for these types of displays, you use one of the *scalers* we are about to discuss.

Scaling the video heights

The most advanced video processors available (usually called *image scalers*) can convert an incoming video signal to a customized resolution — a resolution that is most suitable for a particular projector or other display. In other words, these particular video processors don't do a simple doubling or quadrupling of a signal. For example, if you were using a 1080p DLP projection system, the scaler would convert an incoming video signal to a resolution of 1920 x 1080 pixels, with progressive scan.

Instead of a scan rate or a number of lines of resolution, fixed-pixel displays need a video signal that contains a certain number of horizontal and vertical pixels. For example, if you have a DLP-based projection system using Texas Instruments HD-2 chip (which has a resolution of 1280 x 720 pixels), you want a scaler that can output a 1280 x 720 video signal.

All the fixed-pixel displays on the market have their own internal scalers that can perform this image scaling. Many home theater enthusiasts (at least those who are spending $10,000 or more on a display) bypass these internal scalers and use an external image scaler that they feel does a better job of interpolating and creating video signals.

Most image scalers also contain circuitry to perform *3:2 pulldown,* the process of removing artifacts found in video when a 24-frame-per-second video is converted to a 30-frame-per-second video. (We discuss this in detail in Chapter 4.) This feature is also found in many DVD players and a number of displays, but standalone image scalers often have superior systems for this process.

The following models are a couple of the most popular image scalers:

- **Silicon Optix OptiScale:** Silicon Optix (`www.siliconoptix.com`) manufactures several well-respected scalers. A model that can fit into the budgets of those slightly below "tycoon" status is the OptiScale. This model, which retails for $1,995, can accept DVI, VGA, component, S-Video, and composite video inputs and can scale standard-definition video to high definition, as well as de-interlace 1080i high-definition video into 1080p. A feature we especially like is on the output side: The OptiScale offers a 1366 x 768 resolution output, which matches most high-definition plasma displays' resolutions.

- **DVDO iScan VP30:** DVDO (`www.dvdo.com`) is one of the original big names in the imager scaler business, and its iScan VP30 is a neat unit that can play several roles in a home theater. For $1,999, the unit combines a high-quality scaler with an HDMI switch — accepting up to four HDMI inputs from different video source components in your home theater (a big deal because very few TVs have more than two HDMI inputs, and even fewer receivers have any HDMI switching at all — so the VP30 can come in useful if you're trying to connect an HDMI set-top box, a DVD player, and a PS3 all at the same time!). The VP30 can scale any input resolution up to HDTV resolutions, including 1080p, and also offers a *Precision AV LipSync* function that ensures that your digital audio and video always stay synchronized (so you don't end up thinking you're watching a poorly dubbed Kung Fu movie due to audio/video timing issues).

Relating scaled images and HDTV

You may have noticed that some video processors can output video at resolutions that would qualify as HDTV resolutions (720p or higher). So the question may have entered your mind, "What's the relationship between scaled images and HDTV?" Well, to begin with, a scaled image (no matter how high the resolution and how good the system that created it) is not high definition. After a lower-resolution video signal is run through a high-quality scaler, the signal can look great — spectacular even. But no interpolation system (which is what all scalers are, in essence) can put missing information back into a video signal. Scalers can come close, but they can't match the real thing.

Having said that, we hasten to add that scalers make great companions to HDTVs and HDTV-ready displays. For this reason, the majority of HDTV displays on the market already have some sort of built-in internal scaler, which *upconverts* lower-resolution video sources to an HDTV resolution. External image scalers can often improve upon these internal systems and make everything you watch on your HDTV look better.

Using High-End Controls

One of the most common things folks add to a home theater is a high-end control system for providing local and remote control of your audio and video masterpiece. You can get a complete system that provides this control, and such systems are most often focused on whole-home control.

Crestron

Crestron (www.crestron.com) is a well-known company in this space. Crestron doesn't make DVD players, A/V receivers, or projection displays, but their products (along with those of a company called AMX, www.amx.com, which offers a similar line-up of products) can be found in many high-end home theaters. Crestron offers a whole lot more than the remote controls we mention in Chapter 15. In a nutshell, Crestron builds whole-home control systems that use LCD touchpads to control just about any electrically operated device in a home. A Crestron system can raise and lower your drapes, dim your lights, adjust your HVAC (heating, ventilation, and air conditioning) system, *and* control all the devices in your home theater. And this list is by no means exhaustive. There's really not much you can't do with a complete Crestron system.

Specifically for home theater, Crestron makes several models of home theater control systems that incorporate wired or wireless touch pads and centralized controllers (not A/V controllers, despite the name). These pads and controllers interface with the IR or RS-232 ports on your A/V gear. Crestron's computer-like devices have enough intelligence that you can easily program them to perform complex *macros* (or sequences of control actions). So with only a single tap of a virtual button, you can set into motion all the things you might do manually when turning on your home theater's systems and getting ready to watch a movie.

Crestron sells literally hundreds of components designed to control a home theater (and a home!), and we won't even try to run through them all here. This isn't off-the-shelf, DIY-type stuff. You need to go through a Crestron dealer (many high-end home theater installers also install Crestron) to have a system designed for, and installed in, your home theater. All this automated goodness doesn't come cheap. The typical Crestron installation is over $50,000, and that *doesn't* count the home theater components themselves.

Control 4

A new competitor to Crestron, Control4 (www.control4.com) has made a big splash in 2006 with a wide range of components that do a lot of the same things that Crestron's systems do but at a significantly lower price.

Control4 offers products that fill all sorts of roles in an automated home, ranging from controllers that can dim your lights, lower the drapes, and adjust your heating or air conditioning to touch pad systems that let you send commands to your home theater gear. Control4 even offers audio distribution systems that can store digital audio and send it wirelessly throughout the home.

Control4 keeps the price down (and their gear is significantly cheaper than Crestron's) by leveraging standardized components and technologies (like Ethernet and Wi-Fi wireless networking). So Control4 gear doesn't contain a bunch of custom-built electronics, but instead uses some of the same components as PCs — stuff that is built in the tens or hundreds of millions for very low prices.

Among the most interesting parts of the Control4 lineup (from a home theater perspective) are the audio distribution systems. The Media Controller ($1,495) contains an 80GB hard drive for storing digital music, a CD player for importing new music, and Ethernet and Wi-Fi outputs for distributing the music around your home. You can mix this with the company's $1,995 touchscreen controller and use its big 10.5-inch LCD screen to control your music or anything else in the home connected to one of Control4's systems.

Part VI
The Part of Tens

In this part . . .

Top-ten lists abound here! Look in this part of the book for our top-ten lists on some key home theater topics. We start with ways to accessorize your home theater with fun add-ons, like a theater-style popcorn popper without the $6 per bag price tag!

Then, find out where to go for more information — those extra-special places where you can track down more ideas for your home theater experience.

Are you having fun yet? We are!

Chapter 22

Ten (or So) Accessories for Your Home Theater

Depending on where you put your home theater, you can envision adding all sorts of extras to flesh out your home operation. But in our minds, there are some things you just gotta have — well, stuff you might really *want* to have if you're going for the ultimate home theater. We list a lot of them here so that you have a checklist next time you're on-line or at that home theater store.

Wireless Headphones

Ever want to use the home theater when your spouse, significant other, or roommate is asleep, working, or performing brain surgery in the other room? Ever get told to *"Turn it down!"* in no uncertain terms? Well, maybe you need that marriage/friendship-saving device, the wireless headphone.

You can find some really cool models of headphones out there. Some cancel out ambient noise (so the kids can scream and smash things and you won't hear a thing), others use some special digital signal processing to re-create 5.1-channel Dolby Digital surround sound. Some fit in your ear canals, and some totally cover your ear with a huge "can." Whatever you like, you can find it in the headphone world.

We love wireless headphones because they enable you to get more popcorn or let the dog out without catching a long cord on something and wreaking havoc. So wireless headsets, which use radio waves to connect to a base station plugged into the home theater receiver (like a cordless phone uses radio waves to connect to the phone base station plugged into a phone jack), are the way to go for us.

For really serious listening (what the high-end audio types call *critical listening*), you might not want to use cordless headphones, which probably don't have quite the ultimate fidelity of corded models. But for more casual use, we find that many cordless models sound great.

One of the cooler wireless headsets we've seen comes from Sennheiser (www.sennheiserusa.com). The RS 130 wireless headphone, which has a list price of $169.95 (and can be found for about $20 cheaper many places) is a good entry point into the world of wireless headsets. It even includes a switchable SRS surround sound function so you can simulate the surround sound effects of your home theater's speakers with just the two speakers built into the phones. (See Chapter 12 for more about headphones and surround sound.)

Dolby has a capability called Dolby Headphone (www.dolby.com/dolbyheadphone) that can take up to five channels of audio from any source, feed it to your normal two-channel headphones, and make it sound like it's coming from that many speakers in a real listening room. The difference relative to stereo headphones is amazing. Look for the Dolby Headphone logo on your receiver.

Power Conditioner

Close your eyes and think about your electrical power lines. No, really. Imagine a current flowing (or alternating) from Homer Simpson's nuclear power plant, over the high voltage lines of Springfield, across hill and dale, and finally ending up in a transformer on a pole outside your home. Think about all the other junk attached to that electrical power grid. Even within your home, tons of different electrical devices are connected to your power lines. All this stuff adds its own little bit of degradation to the nice, clean, pretty, sine-wavy alternating current coming out of those turbogenerators at the power plant. End result: power at your home theater's outlets that may be of an incorrect voltage or that may be full of electrical noise that keeps all your A/V components from being their best.

At a bare minimum, you need (absolutely need) some surge protection in your home theater. But even with surge protection, you still may have issues. For example, if your voltage drops (not an uncommon occurrence), it may actually lower the output of your amplifier. You can also run into ground issues that can either cause hums in your audio or create annoying lines in your video display. So you might want to consider investing in a power conditioner that improves and stabilizes your AC power. For example, Monster Cable has some really cool (and cool looking) Home Theater Power Centers that provide surge protection, voltage stabilization, and noise filtering. The more expensive ones even have a cool digital voltmeter readout on the front. Check them out at www.monstercable.com/power.

Shake It Up, Baby! (With Transducers)

If you are like us (and we feel that you are if you've read most of this book), then you like to get totally into what you're watching. After all, a home theater is supposed to help suspend disbelief.

With audio transducers from companies like Clark Synthesis (www. clarksynthesis.com), you can get one giant, T. Rex–step closer to the ultimate goal of suspending disbelief! You'll see these called many things — *bass shakers, tactile transducers,* or as one vendor calls them, *butt kickers.* They add an element that goes well beyond the sensation of a subwoofer, one that helps change your whole theater into a sensaround environment. (Remember *Earthquake* in the theaters?) The units are screwed onto the bottom of your furniture or into the frames of your floorboards. Transducers operate a bit like a subwoofer — vibrating in time with low frequency sounds — but instead of moving air (and therefore creating sounds), they actually transmit vibrations into solid objects (like the floor) for bass that you can *feel* as well as hear.

These transducers are friendlier to the rest of the house than cranking up massive subwoofers that can seem to shake the whole neighborhood. Because the low end of the sound is effectively isolated to a more specific area, namely the couch or chairs, transducers virtually eliminate any bleeding of this sound into adjoining rooms or connected housing units.

Transducers are also great for houses that are built on concrete slabs. Unlike wood subfloors, concrete slabs don't conduct bass particularly well.

The sky is the limit with transducers. You can get low-budget ones (such as Aura Bass Shakers for under $100, www.aurasound.com) that do a fairly good job. If you want more power and precision, check out the Clark Synthesis models, which can run from $100 to $300 depending on the model (www.smarthome.com), or the Buttkicker from The Guitammer Company,

Inc. (www.guitammer.com). The difference is astounding and noticeable. One thing to note: Some products support frequencies up to 200 Hz, and some go even higher (up to 800 Hz). We prefer keeping it low, say between 5 Hz and 200 Hz; otherwise, you find there is a constant background rumble that gets nauseating after a while. Keep the effect directed and precise — you'll like it better. To control the frequency sent to your transducer, consider an equalizer like Audio Source EQ, which runs about $120.

Consider using more than one; try, say, three across the bottom of your couch. The middle transducer would acquire its signal from the LFE/sub-woofer out of the processor-receiver and the two side ones would derive their signals from the left and right front channels, respectively. With this setup, you can get a better sense of the action in three dimensions. If you are watching *U571,* for instance, when a depth charge goes off to the right of the submarine, you get a sensation from the right channel, and when the lower part of the compression from the bomb and water splash enters into the soundtrack, you feel the subchannel and right channel together.

If you mount transducers directly to your furniture, you can get rubberized molded mounts for your chair or couch legs that isolate the noise and vibration to your furniture.

If you install more than one of these transducers, you probably would do well to power each unit with its own amp. Read the manufacturer's recommendations closely. For some of the cheaper models, powering them with anything over a 20-watt amplifier is probably not a good idea. Some of the fancier models call for an amplifier of at least 100 watts. You can find transducers that come bundled with an amplifier (active transducers); consider getting one of these if you have questions. In any case, the amp should have its own volume control so that you can tune the effect relative to the audio level. The hi-fi quality of the amp is not critical, so you can use relatively inexpensive amplifiers.

You can get shaker units that attach to the floorboards of your house and can shake the whole room. There are pros and cons to this. On the pro side, you don't have to worry about being on a particular piece of furniture in order to get the effect. On the other hand, you are shaking the foundation of your house (never really a good thing), and the vibrations can bleed into other areas of your house. So, before you experiment with your foundation, think about which surrounding rooms will be affected.

Motion Simulators

If moving with a movie is really your thing, and you've got a fairly open budget, then check out the Odyssee motion simulators from D-BOX (www.d-box.com). Unlike bass shakers, which provide only vibration or "shaking" in response to the audio track and are in reality merely transducers that vibrate rather than move air, Odyssee is a sophisticated motion-simulation system that lifts seating and occupants on an X-Y-Z axis (pitch, roll, and yaw) at up to 2Gs (think F-14 at full throttle) of acceleration.

Odyssee provides dramatic motion that is precisely synchronized with on-screen action, which draws in viewers even more by allowing them to accurately experience the accelerations, turns, and jumps that they could previously only imagine. When a car rounds a corner in a 007 chase scene, turn with it. If the *Top Gun* jet fighter suddenly moves into a climb, climb with it.

Just about everyone who's tried this system loves it, but the price tag will set you back. An entry-level system runs $15,000 and up.

Back in January of 2004, D-BOX launched a 2nd-generation motion simulator. Sold with its own armchair, this new product uses a simpler, more affordable technology without compromising the whole effect. The basic model sells for around $5,000 per chair.

The experience is possible thanks to a D-BOX DVD with controller codes that actually maps motion to movies. You can see a listing of supported movies at www.d-box.com/en/codes/index.html. Movies not on this list don't have the controller codes and therefore cannot provide the motion simulation experience.

Turn It Up! Turn It Down! Turn It Up Again! Argh!

Sometimes, you just want everything at a quiet but intelligible level (like when everyone else is sleeping). To help you in this endeavor, many A/V receivers (and some TVs) have a *compression* circuit built into the digital signal processor that keeps the louds from being too loud and the quiets from being too quiet (this is often called *night mode*).

If you're using older equipment that doesn't have this feature, you need a *leveler* (also called a *levelizer* or a *stabilizer*). This device automatically adjusts your volume to a reasonable level (even as the source material gets louder or quieter). If the source volume increases, a leveler will attenuate the signal down; if the source signal decreases, it will adjust the signal up.

To use a leveler, you generally adjust the volume to where you want it, and the leveler keeps the volume at that level. An audio leveler connects between any line-level stereo or mono audio source and an amplifier (with RCA output/input jacks) or between your TV or VCR outputs and the inputs to your stereo tuner. Levelers range in price from $70 to $300 (you can check out various units at www.smarthome.com).

No more having to constantly juggle that remote (at least not for changing the volume). Keep in mind, however, that these devices are really not for serious movie watching, when you *want* to have all the loud parts loud and the quiet parts quiet. They are instead intended for nighttime viewing, when you just don't want to wake up the whole family *and* still want to hear the quiet parts.

Be sure to check the types of audio input/output jacks supported by the system you buy. You don't want to have digital audio connections everywhere in your system and then buy an audio leveler that takes it down to a lower common denominator with analog connections.

Riding Your Bike on TV

We talk about the power of true immersion with a great home theater — that ability to suck you right into the display so you think you're truly there. For years, the health industry has been trying to make exercise gear that can combine the power of digital technologies with the raw metal exercise equipment to create an experience that people would pay extra for — to lose those extra pounds and stay in shape.

You've probably at some time seen high-end exercise gear at a workout center that sported the ability to view your competition as you row, row, row your rowing machine. Or, to be able to visually take in the countryside in a virtual environment as you ride your exercise bike. But it's never been quite realistic enough to really be convincing.

A couple of firms have tried to take this to a higher level. The company that owns the ProForm, Reebok, NordicTrack, Image, and HealthRider exercise gear product lines added Internet networking to these product lines and launched a Web presence at www.iFIT.com to coordinate your Internet-based workouts. Any iFIT-enabled exercise device can be remotely controlled via your in-home LAN or broadband Internet connection.

If you have a treadmill, for instance, there are three types of iFIT.com workouts:

- **Basic workouts,** which control the speed and incline of your treadmill.
- **Music workouts,** which stream the device controls for your treadmill through your computer to your device, accompanied by your choice of music or the voice of a virtual personal trainer to get you going and keep you going.
- **Scenic workouts,** which create a virtual landscape by streaming photos and video clips to your computer screen along with the music, the trainer's voice, and device control signals.

Pretty neat, huh?!

Intel's Digital Health Group thinks it has the ability to take this to a much higher level, however. In early 2006, Intel demonstrated high-definition video clocked to your pace, so you could truly roam the countryside. We watched professional bike riders cruise through the Tour de France and the French countryside, with the screen matching the pace of the device and truly providing an out-of-country experience. With high definition, you can almost forget you are working out.

Anything still missing from the experience? Well, you can't steer your bike and go down different roads — that would be nice. And there needs to be a fan attachment of sorts that really truly mimics the pleasure of cruising down a big hill with the wind in your face. That's the best part.

But it's light years better than other Internet or media-enabled gear out there and really opens up the idea of being able to experience the world from the comfort of your home theater (and lose weight at the same time). By the time you read this, some of Intel's technologies will have hit the market through its software partners.

Putting Your Face on the TV

For more than 40 years — since AT&T (then Bell Telephone) demonstrated the first "Picture Phone" at the 1964 New York World's Fair — the telecommunications industry has been trying to get people to video conference. Whether it's shyness from being seen on a screen to a discomfort with the quality of the picture, video conferencing has been limited to select business populations — the mass consumer market has not caught on.

But recently, with the boom in Web cams and camcorders that connect to PCs, not to mention newfangled cellphones that can stream video from an onboard camera, people are finally coming around to sending live video of themselves.

Adding video conferencing to your TV set so the kids can conference with Grandma and Grandpa is easier than ever before. Companies like D-Link (www.dlink.com) have launched products specifically designed for adding video conferencing to your TV set. D-Link has its DVC-1000 i2eye VideoPhone ($200), which is designed to allow video conferencing without an intermediary computer. You just plug one cord of the DVC-1000 into a standard telephone, plug another cord into a television via RCA composite connections, connect the DVC-1000 to your broadband Internet connection using a standard Ethernet network cable, and you are ready to conduct real-time video conferencing.

You cannot use a telephone plugged into the i2eye VideoPhone to place regular phone calls because the phone would not be connected to a standard phone line. Only VideoPhone calls over the Internet can be made with a telephone connected to the DVC-1000.

The DVC-1000 can send and receive video at up to 30 frames per second. The remote control that comes with the DVC-1000 allows you to easily answer an incoming videophone call or initiate a new one. Or, you can use the attached telephone to initiate calls if you are more comfortable with that interface.

The DVC-1000 has a port for an external microphone, too, if you'd rather talk into a headset or a mic.

D-Link also has a DVC-1100 version ($225), which has wireless broadband access instead of a wired Ethernet connection. It also sells the DVC-2000 ($350), which includes a built-in, 5-inch, color LCD screen, in case you don't want to use the TV display as your screen.

Putting Fish in Your TV

What do you do with that HDTV when you're not watching TV? How about putting an aquarium on the screen? Roku Labs (www.rokulabs.com) is one of our favorite vendors, and if you don't have Roku somewhere in your house, well, you're just not enjoying your home theater for all it's worth.

Roku's PhotoBridge HD Digital Media Player ($400) is simply stunning. You pop in your digital camera's memory card or browse the files stored on your computer via your home network (Ethernet or Wi-Fi), and voilà, your images are displayed in pixel-perfect detail on your HDTV. You can also play digital video and digital music from the media player as well. All navigation is via an on-screen interface and Roku's remote control.

But what really rocks us is Roku's PhotoBridge HD Gallery Collection, which turns your HDTV into a brilliant work of art. You can choose from a lot of different image collections to create that particular atmosphere to which you aspire. Picasso, Monet, Leonardo da Vinci, Gauguin, Renoir . . . your pick. Or maybe outer space images of far-off galaxies are what you like. Or mountains. Or a poppy field. Danny loves his Aquarium Art Pack, which displays a lifelike saltwater aquarium right in his living room. Watch tranquil fish swim across your big screen while the water plants sway back and forth. Now that's how we want to see a puffer fish!

Roku has other awesome, award-winning product designs, like its SoundBridge music streaming devices or SoundBridge Radio. You should check them out — we talk a bit more about them in Chapter 10.

The PhotoBridge is expected to be upgraded to a new model in 2006, so look on Roku's site for more details about what the latest product offers.

Improving Your Game Console Connection

If you read Chapter 16, you had a chance to check out our discussion of interconnect cables — the short run cables that hook A/V components together. Hopefully, we convinced you of the importance of the hierarchy of these cables and of using the best cable you can in all situations. (In the video world, component is best, S-video is a close second, composite video lags way behind, and RF coax connections are back on the bench trying to get the coach to let them in the game.)

When it comes to game consoles, however, we do find that many people just use whatever cable came in the box. As Jeremy Piven says in that movie masterpiece *PCU*, "Don't be that guy." (If you missed *PCU*, the whole line is: "You're wearing the shirt of the band you're going to see? Don't be that guy.") If you stick with the simple, composite video cable that comes in the box with the console, you strangle the gorgeous (and possibly high-def) picture your system is capable of putting out. Use an S-Video cable or, if your TV can handle it, a set of component video cables. (We recommend going with the component video cables for your gaming console, simply because this gives you the capability to play progressive scan and even HDTV-quality games on your TV. And let your games give your eyeballs a treat.)

Turning Down the Lights Automatically

An excellent way to improve your picture is to minimize the light that comes from anywhere but your video screen — in other words, to minimize the ambient lighting by turning off light bulbs and closing drapes. You could get up to turn off the lights and pull down the shades. A little exercise (and that really is a little!) never hurts anyone. But how cool would it be to press a button — a single button — and have the lights dim, the motorized drapes lower, and the A/V system power up? Pretty cool, we think.

Sound kinda like *The Jetsons*? It's really not. Home automation isn't rocket science. For just a few hundred dollars, you can put together a simple X-10 system that dims the lights (theater-style, even) and activates the drape motors. You can find lots of packages at www.smarthome.com. Automation systems are also a task that a good dealer can help out with. The superstore isn't going to do this for you, but if you find a good home theater dealer/installer, chances are good that automation packages are part of what the folks there do.

This is too big a topic to cover in one section of one chapter. Home automation is a really cool addition to your whole home. We like this stuff so much, we wrote a book about it (*Smart Homes For Dummies,* Wiley), and you can find out how all this automation stuff works there.

Stick This on Your DVD!

If you have a personal video recorder in your home theater — or you have a lot of MP3s, digital photos, or home videos — chances are you're going to burn these to CD or DVD at some point — possibly for Mom and Dad for their birthdays. That's great — burning CDs and DVDs is something that's easy to do.

But after you've crafted a movie from all your camcorder footage and painstakingly matched it to your favorite musical score — and managed to get it onto a DVD for playing on any DVD player on the planet — there's something sinful about taking a black marker and scribbling on the disc.

Well, lucky for you, a few companies have put together very easy-to-use labeling kits that help you design and print self-adhesive labels that stick to your DVDs and CDs. (So next time you're in a bar, you can tell that good-looking person next to you, "I own my own CD label.")

Check out products from Fellowes and Avery — both are good and come with software to help you create the label images. The kits also contain paper that you stick in your laser or inkjet printer, and out come beautiful color labels worthy of an award. Figure on spending $15–$30 for a kit that comes with about 100 sheets of label sticker blanks. You can also buy spine labels and blank plastic packaging for a truly impressive custom DVD package.

For a few more bucks, you can consider upgrading to a printer that can print directly onto the discs themselves. Epson (www.epson.com), Canon (www.canon.com), and others make inkjet printers that let you feed "printable" DVDs and CDs (like TDK's *PrintOn* blank discs) right into the printer itself. We think that this is the best-looking labeling system for the discs themselves — though you may still want some of the other labeling products described earlier for your CD/DVD storage cases, booklets, and the like.

Coming soon to a set-top box near you may be the ability to burn a disc *and* print a silkscreen-quality label on the disc, all inside the set-top box. That's right, set-top boxes from your cable, satellite, and telephone providers soon will be outfitted with the ability to not only burn a movie or other content to a DVD, but also to print that movie's label by using HP's LightScribe technology (already available on some PCs). So not only can you order a movie on demand whenever you want, but you could also buy the movie, burn it to a DVD, and then print the label on the disc — without having to go to any old video store. Now that's useful — and legal, because when you "buy" the movie, you are actually buying the rights to create your own DVD copy of the movie.

Disc-O!

Although they're not as sexy as fish on your TV or tush-rattling transducers, there are some disc accessories that you simply must have in your high-def cabinet.

First and foremost are disc cleaning and repair kits. You can find these for $10 at Radio Shack, Crutchfield.com, or just about any electronics store. These kits include a disc-spinning device and a solution to polish the plastic CD/DVD to get rid of scratches (we *hate* those), smudges, and other generally unwelcomed surface anomalies on your discs. Just pop your disc into the unit, give it a spin, and voilà! — clean disc. SmartHome.com sells a really nice battery-powered unit for around $40.

There are disc cleaning kits and disc repair kits — cleaning kits do not necessarily repair scratches. Be sure you get a cleaning and repair kit in one.

You may also want to get a lens cleaner kit, which will clean your DVD/CD player's laser eye to make sure your discs are read as clearly as possible. Again, this is as easy as sticking the cleaning disc into your DVD or CD player and "playing" the disc. These also are inexpensive — around $15.

An optical head should not need cleaning very often, unless your room is really dusty. (In which case, you should get an air filter!) Often, merely blowing your lens area with canned compressed air is the easiest and safest way to deal with such problems. You can get compressed air at any office or computer supply store. However, many people like the simplicity of using a lens cleaner kit, which is fine, too.

Do not attempt to use a lens cleaner kit designed for CD/DVD players on your notebook or laptop computer DVD drives. The locked spindle in most computer drives would cause the brush to push against the optical head with too much force. That could knock the head off its alignment track, damaging the drive permanently.

Finally, believe it or not, there are special cleaning solutions for your expensive displays too. The problem with using regular window cleaning spray is that it will run down the screen and get into your display — that's not good because these displays don't like moisture. And even if you are smart enough to spray the rag and not the display before swiping, regular window spray can streak (very annoying) and regular paper towels and rags can also scratch your screen.

Some displays have special anti-reflective coatings that can be damaged by cleaners that contain ammonia, alcohol, or some other substances. Read the manual for your display before you try cleaning it!

So leave it to the folks at high-end accessories maker Monster Cable (www.monstercable.com) to come up with the Monster ScreenClean product ($20). There's no dripping — Monster ScreenClean's drip-free cleaning solution stays where you spray it until you wipe it off. It cleans without leaving annoying streaks, and the kit sports a scratch-free microfiber cloth that polishes screens with crystal clarity and color. You can use this for your camera lenses and other glass-outfitted gear, too.

So spend the few extra dollars to really take care of all the expensive gear.

Chapter 23

Ten Great Sources for More Information

*W*e can in no way cover the entire home theater industry in one book. So we're leaving a few nuggets for other publications to cover. It's only fair.

Here's a listing of the publications that we read regularly (and therefore recommend unabashedly) and that you should get your hands on as part of your home theater project. Most publications allow you to purchase back issues of their magazines, so you can have a library at your fingertips in about a week. You know what they say: You can never be too rich or read too much about home theater before you become too poor.

Because this is the 21st century, we include some "virtual" items in our home theater library — Web sites, in other words. Keep in mind that the Web sites we mention here have just a *ton* of information on-line, but you might have to try different search keywords to find exactly what you're looking for. Topics vary substantially from site to site. All sites are free unless otherwise noted.

Home Theater Magazine

Phone: 800-264-9872 or 850-682-7644
Web site: www.hometheatermag.com

Home Theater Magazine is one of the main sources for information about home theater. It is a very high-end publication and will certainly expose you to a range of systems, from budget items to those on the finer side of home theater. Don't be surprised when you see $30,000 projectors reviewed, for instance. Don't let that scare you, however, because every issue has something to offer, no matter what budget constraints you're dealing with. And you can always find out about the leading trends in the industry, which is important because there's nothing like buying yesterday's technology on sale and thinking you got a great deal. (How *about* that sale on Betamax VCRs, huh?) The accompanying Web site offers archives of prior articles. An annual subscription costs $12.97 for 12 issues — quite a deal.

The same folks also publish a dynamite *Home Theater Buyer's Guide Annual Directory,* which lists more than 5,000 source devices, controllers, speakers, home-theater-in-a-box packages, video displays, and all sorts of accessories. The buyer's guide is broken into three sections — audio component products, video component products, and speaker products — for $3.95 a section or all three for $9.95. They are delivered in .pdf form to your e-mail.

Ultimate AV

Web site: www.guidetohometheater.com

Ultimate AV focuses on the high-end sector of the home theater market. It used to be a nice glossy magazine called *Stereophile Guide to Home Theater,* but is now a fully Web-based publication called *Ultimate AV.* The guide's cadre of industry experts is dedicated to providing in-depth gear reviews on everything from projectors to line conditioners to DVD players to HD tuners. Instructional how-to columns on fine-tuning your system, special features, and software reviews help you get the most out of your system. But it's the reviews we crave here.

Stereophile

Phone: 800-666-3746 or 850-682-7644
Web site: www.stereophile.com

Stereophile is devoted to the high end of the market, concentrating on the better audio equipment and recordings available. Again, that does not mean there is nothing for the budget-minded — it's found in the feature stories and advice columns on topics like placement of speakers for maximum effect. If you are going to buy some new audio gear, check out the reviews here. You can also check out the AV Marketplace for what's for sale — you tend to find dealers dumping demo models here for fairly decent prices. An annual subscription runs $12.97.

Top on-line HDTV buying guide centers

Many sites are getting into the HDTV game by offering on-line areas devoted just to getting an HDTV. While certainly not as complete or as friendly as our *HDTV For Dummies* book (Wiley), they do help you find info fast if on-line researching is for you. Here's a sampling of sites focused on HDTV articles, reviews, and buying tips all in one place:

✔ **Cnet HDTV World:** `www.cnet.com/4520-7874_1-5102926-1.html?tag=cnetfd.dir`

✔ **ExtremeTech's HDTV Buying Guide:** `www.extremetech.com/article2/0,1558,1736620,00.asp`

✔ **PC Magazine's Essential HDTV Buying Guide:** `www.pcmag.com/article2/0,1895,1630224,00.asp`

✔ **Ziff Davis's HDTV Web Buyer's Guide:** `www.webbuyersguide.com/sub/hdtv`

✔ **Sound & Vision Magazine HDTV Buyer's Guide:** `www.soundandvisionmag.com/custom/default.aspx?cid=14`

✔ **Consumer Reports's TV Decision Guide (Subscription required):** `www.consumerreports.org/cro/electronics-computers/tvs.htm`

✔ **INHD - HDTV Buyer's Guide:** `www.inhd.com/buyersGuide/index.jsp`

✔ **Amazon.com's HDTV Buying Guide:** `www.amazon.com/exec/obidos/tg/feature/-/372297/002-9198507-1808064`

And if you want to get an idea of who has the best coverage in terms of reviews, in a "turn the table on the reviewer's" approach, Consumersearch.com reviews the most recent HDTV articles and reviews of HDTVs at `www.consumersearch.com/www/electronics/hdtv/reviews.html`. What a neat idea!

Sound & Vision

Phone: 800-876-9011 or 212-767-6000
Web site: `www.soundandvisionmag.com`

Another respected home theater publication that captures the essence of home theater and its various components is *Sound & Vision*. This publication regularly has helpful articles in layman's non-techie language about how to set up your speakers, tune your system, and so on. The buyer's guides are ample and feature checklists. All in all, this is a very friendly publication for the beginner, with meat for the more advanced home theater enthusiast as well.

The accompanying Web site contains archived issue content, and its S&V Forums are a great place to ask questions. The editors moderate the forums, which are heavily trafficked. You can even listen to Sound & Vision Radio streamed via RadioAmerica.org.

A one-year subscription to the printed publication costs $10.

Electronic House

Phone: 800-375-8015 or 508-663-1500
Web site: www.electronichouse.com

Electronic House is one of our favorite publications because you can read a lot of very easy-to-understand articles about all aspects of an electronic home, including the home theater domain. It is written for the consumer who enjoys technology.

Although only a portion of each issue deals with home theater topics, *Electronic House* provides a coverage of the key issues of the systems a home theater comprises, including audio, video, remote controls, speakers, wiring, lighting, and other home theater components. Each issue also devotes time to neat new things on the market — most within the budget of any family — such as new remote controls, cool new consumer devices, and accessories for your entertainment system. *Electronic House* also offers an *Electronic House Planning Guide,* which walks you through all sorts of issues you're likely to encounter when upgrading your home for the 21st century.

We think that, after you start reading this magazine, you'll want to expand your interests beyond home theater to the whole home at large. (Then you'll want to buy our *Smart Homes For Dummies* book, too!) A one-year subscription to *Electronic House* is $19.95.

Crutchfield

Phone: 800-955-9009 or 434-817-1000
Web site: www.crutchfield.com

This is the perennial catalog that sits by the toilet for constant perusing while in the, er, office. *Crutchfield* offers a free catalog of all sorts of A/V and home theater gear, and it's great for just getting ideas about what's out there. Its companion Web site is laid out very simply and offers a Home Theater and A/V Info Center. For instance, you can find some great photos of the various connectors at `www.crutchfieldadvisor.com/learningcenter/home/connections_gallery.html`. (This URL might change, so look around for their Home A/V Connections Photo Gallery if you can't find it.) Overall, we pick up our *Crutchfield* when we want to know, "Does anybody have something that will. . . ."

CNET.com

Web site: `www.cnet.com`

CNET.com is a simple-to-use, free Web site where you can do apples-to-apples comparisons of home theater and electronic equipment. You can count on seeing pictures of what you are buying, videos of an editor playing with it, editor ratings of the equipment, user ratings of the gear, reviews of most devices, and a listing of the places on the Web where you can buy it all — with the actual pricing along with it. It's a one-stop resource for evaluating your future home electronics purchases. What we especially like is the ability to compare, side-by-side, different devices, so we can see who has which features. Overall, a solid stop on your Web research trip.

Home Theater Forum

Web site: `www.hometheaterforum.com`

Home Theater Forum is a massive Internet messaging site where people interested in home theater gather to discuss their issues and solutions. You can find areas for discussion of home theater basics, construction, DIY solutions, sources, displays, and so on. You really should check it out, if for no other reason than to see that lots of other people just like you are also trying to figure out what's going on in home theater.

The HT Construction, Interiors, and Automation forum is a great place to find out issues other DIYers have had with putting in their home theaters, and tips and tricks for avoiding problems. When we last checked, there was a great thread about how to find old theater seats that you could renovate and put in your home theater. Fun!

Home Theater Talk

Web site: www.hometheatertalk.com

Home Theater Talk is another great site. This site is run by none other than the technical editor for the first edition of this book, Mike Knapp, who was an admin on the Home Theater Forum for several years before striking out on his own. Home Theater Talk isn't as big as Home Theater Forum, but it has a nice, friendly atmosphere — it's the "neighborhood pub" of on-line home theater sites. There are lots of handy DIY features posted by readers and others; one person had just bought a set of Aura Bass Shaker tactile transducers and showed how to put them in and his results — "I am somewhat pleased with the results. Allow me to qualify that. I WILL NOT use these for music EVER! But in all honesty, they aren't designed for music anyway."

AV Science

Web site: www.avsforum.com

Similar to Home Theater Forum, AV Science's AVSForum.com is an on-line community of technical enthusiasts who indeed wallow in the minutest details of a home theater installation. But think of it this way: It's a collection of the-guy-next-door-who-knows-how-to-install-A/V-gear's pearls of wisdom — a proverbial hothouse of information and opinions that you can tap into to help solve your problems.

The site is organized in folders according to interests. If you want information on how to fine-tune your TiVo, there's a whole group devoted to that, for instance. There are also places where people are selling their old gear. As the techies buy the latest gear, they sell off their leading-edge stuff from a few years back — at great prices. The manufacturers themselves monitor this site for feedback from customers about what they want in their next versions. It has that much to offer.

If you're considering buying a specific piece of gear for your home theater, check the appropriate forum folder and see if there's an owner's thread. We find that these discussions (where folks who actually have that equipment discuss their experiences and issues they've encountered) are the best part of AVS Forum. For example, when Pat was considering buying his Vizio P50HDM plasma, he spent a ton of time on this forum and was able to find out about some issues with the initial versions of this TV and was also able to figure out that the unit he was buying had already had the "fix" performed as a running change on the factory assembly line.

eBay

Web site: www.ebay.com

Although eBay started out as a place where people could sell everything in their attics, it has really matured into a place where all sorts of equipment is bought and sold. Companies sell excess gear here. Old home theater gear is available in the listings. Even new stuff is being sold on-line. You never know what you are going to find here, and it is a "let the buyer beware" type of environment. You, indeed, get what you pay for. Nonetheless, you can get a good handle for street prices for used gear here, and we've known people who have grown their home theater by trading up equipment through eBay, spending a fraction of what they would have if they had bought new components in the stores.

Other Sources

Almost any major retail store chain where you might purchase home theater equipment has a Web site. These sites often contain information centers about home theater and are a good stop before going to meet the geeks at the store. For instance, Circuit City has a starter section on the basics of home theater. Sears has its Buying Guides.

In addition to these information boutiques, here are some other sites for you to sample:

Magazines:

- *Home Theater Builder* (www.hometheaterbuilder.com)
- *Audio Video Interiors* (www.audiovideointeriors.com)
- *Widescreen Review* (www.widescreenreview.com)
- *The Perfect Vision* (www.theperfectvision.com)

Web Sites:

- Remote Central (www.remotecentral.com)
- PC Gamer (www.pcgamer.com)
- Video Help (www.videohelp.com)
- Game Spot (www.gamespot.com)

Organizations:

- ✔ CEDIA (www.cedia.net)
- ✔ Consumer Electronics Association (www.ce.org)

Industry:

- ✔ Dolby (www.dolby.com)
- ✔ DTS (www.dtsonline.com)
- ✔ THX (www.thx.com)

Index

• *B* •

• E •

• T •

• X •

• Z •

BUSINESS, CAREERS & PERSONAL FINANCE

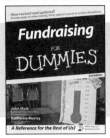

0-7645-9847-3

0-7645-2431-3

Also available:
- Business Plans Kit For Dummies
  0-7645-9794-9
- Economics For Dummies
  0-7645-5726-2
- Grant Writing For Dummies
  0-7645-8416-2
- Home Buying For Dummies
  0-7645-5331-3
- Managing For Dummies
  0-7645-1771-6
- Marketing For Dummies
  0-7645-5600-2

- Personal Finance For Dummies
  0-7645-2590-5*
- Resumes For Dummies
  0-7645-5471-9
- Selling For Dummies
  0-7645-5363-1
- Six Sigma For Dummies
  0-7645-6798-5
- Small Business Kit For Dummies
  0-7645-5984-2
- Starting an eBay Business For Dummies
  0-7645-6924-4
- Your Dream Career For Dummies
  0-7645-9795-7

HOME & BUSINESS COMPUTER BASICS

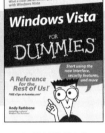

0-470-05432-8

0-471-75421-8

Also available:
- Cleaning Windows Vista For Dummies
  0-471-78293-9
- Excel 2007 For Dummies
  0-470-03737-7
- Mac OS X Tiger For Dummies
  0-7645-7675-5
- MacBook For Dummies
  0-470-04859-X
- Macs For Dummies
  0-470-04849-2
- Office 2007 For Dummies
  0-470-00923-3

- Outlook 2007 For Dummies
  0-470-03830-6
- PCs For Dummies
  0-7645-8958-X
- Salesforce.com For Dummies
  0-470-04893-X
- Upgrading & Fixing Laptops For Dummies
  0-7645-8959-8
- Word 2007 For Dummies
  0-470-03658-3
- Quicken 2007 For Dummies
  0-470-04600-7

FOOD, HOME, GARDEN, HOBBIES, MUSIC & PETS

0-7645-8404-9

0-7645-9904-6

Also available:
- Candy Making For Dummies
  0-7645-9734-5
- Card Games For Dummies
  0-7645-9910-0
- Crocheting For Dummies
  0-7645-4151-X
- Dog Training For Dummies
  0-7645-8418-9
- Healthy Carb Cookbook For Dummies
  0-7645-8476-6
- Home Maintenance For Dummies
  0-7645-5215-5

- Horses For Dummies
  0-7645-9797-3
- Jewelry Making & Beading For Dummies
  0-7645-2571-9
- Orchids For Dummies
  0-7645-6759-4
- Puppies For Dummies
  0-7645-5255-4
- Rock Guitar For Dummies
  0-7645-5356-9
- Sewing For Dummies
  0-7645-6847-7
- Singing For Dummies
  0-7645-2475-5

INTERNET & DIGITAL MEDIA

0-470-04529-9

0-470-04894-8

Also available:
- Blogging For Dummies
  0-471-77084-1
- Digital Photography For Dummies
  0-7645-9802-3
- Digital Photography All-in-One Desk Reference For Dummies
  0-470-03743-1
- Digital SLR Cameras and Photography For Dummies
  0-7645-9803-1
- eBay Business All-in-One Desk Reference For Dummies
  0-7645-8438-3
- HDTV For Dummies
  0-470-09673-X

- Home Entertainment PCs For Dummies
  0-470-05523-5
- MySpace For Dummies
  0-470-09529-6
- Search Engine Optimization For Dummies
  0-471-97998-8
- Skype For Dummies
  0-470-04891-3
- The Internet For Dummies
  0-7645-8996-2
- Wiring Your Digital Home For Dummies
  0-471-91830-X

* Separate Canadian edition also available
† Separate U.K. edition also available

Available wherever books are sold. For more information or to order direct: U.S. customers visit www.dummies.com or call 1-877-762-2974.
U.K. customers visit www.wileyeurope.com or call 0800 243407. Canadian customers visit www.wiley.ca or call 1-800-567-4797.

SPORTS, FITNESS, PARENTING, RELIGION & SPIRITUALITY

0-471-76871-5

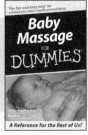

0-7645-7841-3

Also available:
- Catholicism For Dummies
  0-7645-5391-7
- Exercise Balls For Dummies
  0-7645-5623-1
- Fitness For Dummies
  0-7645-7851-0
- Football For Dummies
  0-7645-3936-1
- Judaism For Dummies
  0-7645-5299-6
- Potty Training For Dummies
  0-7645-5417-4
- Buddhism For Dummies
  0-7645-5359-3

- Pregnancy For Dummies
  0-7645-4483-7 †
- Ten Minute Tone-Ups For Dummies
  0-7645-7207-5
- NASCAR For Dummies
  0-7645-7681-X
- Religion For Dummies
  0-7645-5264-3
- Soccer For Dummies
  0-7645-5229-5
- Women in the Bible For Dummies
  0-7645-8475-8

TRAVEL

0-7645-7749-2

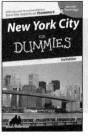

0-7645-6945-7

Also available:
- Alaska For Dummies
  0-7645-7746-8
- Cruise Vacations For Dummies
  0-7645-6941-4
- England For Dummies
  0-7645-4276-1
- Europe For Dummies
  0-7645-7529-5
- Germany For Dummies
  0-7645-7823-5
- Hawaii For Dummies
  0-7645-7402-7

- Italy For Dummies
  0-7645-7386-1
- Las Vegas For Dummies
  0-7645-7382-9
- London For Dummies
  0-7645-4277-X
- Paris For Dummies
  0-7645-7630-5
- RV Vacations For Dummies
  0-7645-4442-X
- Walt Disney World & Orlando
  For Dummies
  0-7645-9660-8

GRAPHICS, DESIGN & WEB DEVELOPMENT

0-7645-8815-X

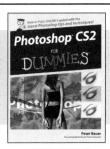

0-7645-9571-7

Also available:
- 3D Game Animation For Dummies
  0-7645-8789-7
- AutoCAD 2006 For Dummies
  0-7645-8925-3
- Building a Web Site For Dummies
  0-7645-7144-3
- Creating Web Pages For Dummies
  0-470-08030-2
- Creating Web Pages All-in-One Desk
  Reference For Dummies
  0-7645-4345-8
- Dreamweaver 8 For Dummies
  0-7645-9649-7

- InDesign CS2 For Dummies
  0-7645-9572-5
- Macromedia Flash 8 For Dummies
  0-7645-9691-8
- Photoshop CS2 and Digital
  Photography For Dummies
  0-7645-9580-6
- Photoshop Elements 4 For Dummies
  0-471-77483-9
- Syndicating Web Sites with RSS Feeds
  For Dummies
  0-7645-8848-6
- Yahoo! SiteBuilder For Dummies
  0-7645-9800-7

NETWORKING, SECURITY, PROGRAMMING & DATABASES

0-7645-7728-X

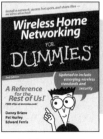

0-471-74940-0

Also available:
- Access 2007 For Dummies
  0-470-04612-0
- ASP.NET 2 For Dummies
  0-7645-7907-X
- C# 2005 For Dummies
  0-7645-9704-3
- Hacking For Dummies
  0-470-05235-X
- Hacking Wireless Networks
  For Dummies
  0-7645-9730-2
- Java For Dummies
  0-470-08716-1

- Microsoft SQL Server 2005 For Dummies
  0-7645-7755-7
- Networking All-in-One Desk Reference
  For Dummies
  0-7645-9939-9
- Preventing Identity Theft For Dummies
  0-7645-7336-5
- Telecom For Dummies
  0-471-77085-X
- Visual Studio 2005 All-in-One Desk
  Reference For Dummies
  0-7645-9775-2
- XML For Dummies
  0-7645-8845-1